24

China's Republican Revolution

Harvard East Asian Series 81
The East Asian Research Center at Harvard University administers research projects designed to further scholarly understanding of China, Japan, Korea, Vietnam, Inner Asia, and adjacent areas.

China's Republican Revolution
The Case of Kwangtung, 1895–1913

Edward J. M. Rhoads

Harvard University Press, Cambridge, Massachusetts, 1975

Preparation of this volume has been aided by a grant from the Ford Foundation.
Library of Congress Catalog Card Number 74-84090
ISBN 0-674-11980-0
Printed in the United States of America ·

To
my father
HOWARD G. RHOADS

and
to the memory of
my mother
CHI-KIT NGAN RHOADS

ACKNOWLEDGMENTS

Like countless others before me, my greatest debt is to John King Fairbank, under whom this study began as a doctoral dissertation. He has overseen every stage of its subsequent progress down to its present publication. I am also indebted to Kwang-Ching Liu, who similarly guided this work at its beginning.

I have benefited greatly from many friends and colleagues, from their conversations and critiques. Edward Friedman and Marianne Bastid deserve special mention because they both influenced the study at its inception. Marianne Bastid also kindly furnished me with copies of the French consular dispatches from Kwangtung. Those who read and criticized the final drafts of the manuscript include William Braisted, Joseph Esherick, Philip Kuhn, Ezra Vogel, and Ernest Young. I thank them for their suggestions and corrections. The errors that remain are, of course, my responsibility.

This work would not have been possible without the active cooperation of numerous libraries—and librarians—around the world. I am particularly grateful to the Institute of Modern History, Academia Sinica, Taipei, the University of Hong Kong and the Supreme Court Library, Hong Kong, the Public Record Office, London, the Library of Congress and the National Archives, Washington, the University of Texas at Austin, and, especially, Eugene Wu and the Harvard-Yenching Library, Harvard University.

Finally, my thanks to Carol Foyt LeStourgeon, for typing the original thesis, to Bill Hazlep, for drawing the maps, to Howard G. Rhoads, for suggesting many stylistic improvements, to Evelyn Bohn Kain, for being cheerful and optimistic, and especially to Suzanne Kain Rhoads, not only for the frequent retyping of the manuscript but also for her constant encouragement.

Contents

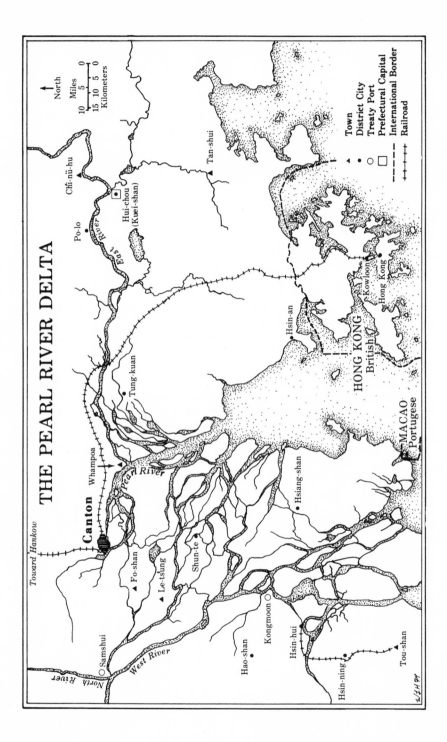

THE PEARL RIVER DELTA

North

Miles
0   5   10
0   5   10   15
Kilometers

Town ▴ •
District City ●
Treaty Port ○
Prefectural Capital □
International Border
Railroad

Toward Hankow

North River

West River

Samshui ○

Fo-shan ▴

Le-tsung ▴

Canton

Whampoa ◄

Pearl River

Hao-shan •

Kongmoon ○

Shun-te ▴

Hsin-hui •

Hsin-ning •

Tou-shan ▴

Tung-kuan •

Hsiang-shan •

MACAO
Portugese

East River

Po-lo •

Hui-chou
(Kuei-shan) □

Chi-nü-hu

Tan-shui ▴

Hsin-an •

HONG KONG
British

Kowloon
Hong Kong

L.H.M

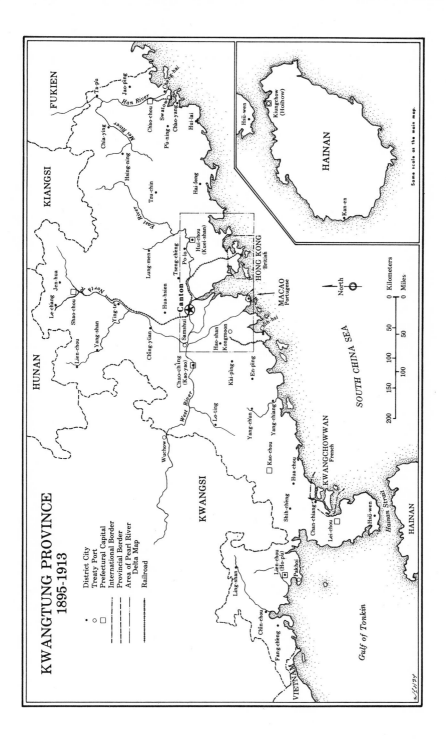

KWANGTUNG PROVINCE
1895-1913

- District City
○ Treaty Port
□ Prefectural Capital
--- International Border
---- Provincial Border
— Area of Pearl River
— Delta Map
++++ Railroad

FUKIEN

KIANGSI

HUNAN

KWANGSI

VIETNAM

Ta-pu
Jao-ping
Han River
Chia-ying
Chao-chou
Swatow
Chieh-hai
Mei River
Pu-ning
Chao-yang
Hsing-ning
Hui-lai
Tzu-chin
Hai-feng

Le-chang Jen-hua
Shao-chou
North R.
Ying-te
Yang-shan
Lien-chou
Chʻing-yüan
Hua-hsien
Lung-men
Tseng-cheng
Po-lo
Hui-chou
(Kuei-shan)

Canton
Samshui
Chao-chʻing
(Kao-yao)
Hao-shan
Kongmoon
Kai-ping
En-ping
Shih-hai

HONG KONG
British

MACAO
Portugese

Lo-ting
Yang-chun
Yang-chiang
Wuchow
Kao-chou

Hua-chou
Shih-cheng
KWANGCHOWWAN
French
Chan-chiang
Lei-chou
Hsii-wen

Ling-shan
Lien-chou
(Ho-piu)
Pakhoi
Chin-chou
Fang-cheng

Gulf of Tonkin

SOUTH CHINA SEA

Hainan Strait

HAINAN

North

0   50   100   150   200 Kilometers
0   50   100   Miles

HAINAN

Hsii-wen
Kiungchow
(Hoihow)

Kan-en

Same scale as the main map.

China's Republican Revolution

Note on Romanization

With few exceptions, all Chinese words in this book are romanized according to their Mandarin pronunciation and the Wade-Giles system. One special convention was observed for place names in Kwangtung. All foreign enclaves and treaty ports are given in the old postal spellings in order to draw attention to their special status; all other places are transcribed according to Wade-Giles. Thus, Hoihow rather than Hai-k'ou, but Fo-shan (which was not a treaty port) rather than the usual Fatshan; similarly, Samshui for the treaty port, but San-shui for the surrounding district. Names of organizations, newspapers, books, and the like have all been translated into English; where applicable they conform to the suggested translations in Mary Clabaugh Wright, ed., *China in Revolution.*

Introduction

"Revolutions," we are told, "must be studied in the context of the social systems in which they occur." [1] Until recently, studies of the Chinese republican revolution have generally ignored this common sense advice. Instead they have been focused almost exclusively on the activities of the revolutionaries to the neglect of all other contemporary social groups and movements. As a result, the history of the revolution has become synonymous with the history of Sun Yat-sen and the Revolutionary Alliance. [2] This study of the revolution utilizes the "contextual" approach as synthesized from a number of recent theoretical works on the revolutionary process. The approach and its general application to the 1911 Revolution may be summarized as follows.

What is, first of all, a revolution? It is, according to a widely accepted definition, change that, first, is effected by violence and, second, is directed at the restructuring of a government or society. Revolution thus differs from other forms of social violence, ranging from banditry to rebellion, insofar as it is intended to bring about a new government or society. At the same time, it differs from reform because it is carried out by violence. Nonviolent social change, no matter how extensive or radical, is, by definition, reformist and nonrevolutionary. [3]

The basic precondition of revolution, according to Chalmers Johnson, is a "disequilibrated social system," that is, a system in which the society's "values" no longer harmonize with its "environment" because of either internal or external pressures. Unless this disharmony exists, "a society is immune from revolution." Until the end of the nineteenth century, China was so immune insofar as foreign pressures were concerned. Even though China had been opened to foreign trade and evangelism, its social system had been able to maintain its equilibrium by means of what Johnson calls "homeostatic changes," such as the reforms of the T'ung-chih Restoration and the self-strengthening movement. It was the Sino-Japanese war of 1894–95 and the subsequent imperialist pressures that produced a critical dissynchronization between China's values and her environment. Those pressures, which impinged upon both her values and her environment, were so sudden, so intense, and so unprecedented that they exceeded the "homeostatic capacity" of the system for self-maintenance. The war, by producing a disequilibrium, thus set the revolutionary process in motion in China.[4]

In a disequilibrated society, "alternative value structures" that attempt to reestablish a harmony with the environment are produced.[5] Thus, according to Crane Brinton, the English, American, French, and Russian revolutions all took place against "a background of political and moral discussion which in these societies seems particularly intense." Brinton's conclusion from this was "no ideas, no revolution." [6] In China too, the decade and a half preceding the revolution was a period of intense political and moral discussion, as new ideas (new "values")—constitutionalism, republicanism, social Darwinism, anarchism, socialism, nationalism, and the like—flooded into the country.

It is, however, "up to the vested leadership of a system to develop policies which will result in resynchronization," Johnson insists; "whether resynchronization or revolution occurs depends, *ceteris paribus*, on the abilities of these leaders." The rulers may refuse to adjust to the changes by carrying on "business as usual" or becoming "intransigent," in which case they perpetuate a situation in which a revolution is more than likely. Or they may make the necessary "conservative changes" and "co-opt the protesters," in which case they may produce a new equilibrium and avoid a revolution.[7]

As an example of elite mismanagement causing a revolution, Johnson cites the government of China after the Boxer Rebellion of 1900: "Led by the uneducated and, even according to the system's values, incompetent Empress Dowager, it promised reforms which it had no intention of realizing, created a revolutionary group by sending thousands of students abroad, and otherwise pursued policies of business as usual." [8] As we shall see, this was far from the case. The rulers did resort initially to a policy of intransigence during the Boxer Rebellion, which led predictably to a revolutionary situation. Only a quick realization of its folly saved the dynasty then. Thereafter, the dynastic rulers pursued a program of conservative change, making what Harry Eckstein aptly calls "adjustive concessions." [9] Thus, in China too as in all four of Brinton's societies, "Nothing can be more erroneous than the picture of the old regime as an unregenerate tyranny, sweeping to its end in a climax of despotic indifference to the clamor of its abused subjects." [10]

The Ch'ing tried to reproduce a social equilibrium by making adjustments to both values and environment. It jettisoned many of the Confucian ideas and adopted new, foreign ones, most notably by abandoning the traditional educational *cum* civil service system, encouraging study abroad, and inaugurating constitutional government. Also, but with less success, it worked to modify the environment by relieving the imperialist pressures upon China through the rights recovery movement. Contrary to Johnson's charge of insincerity, the post-Boxer reforms were a serious and, in the short run, successful attempt to forestall a revolution. The revolutionary threat did, in fact, wane.

If the rulers seek resynchronization, why may a revolution occur nevertheless? For one thing, the attempts to restore equilibrium produce new problems for the rulers. As Eckstein points out, there are limits to their adjustive concessions. "These cannot be indefinitely increased, for, in the end, they would be tantamount to surrender." Moreover, Lawrence Stone observes, "measures designed to restore equilibrium in fact upset equilibrium." For example, one by-product of the rulers' concessions in Brinton's four countries was "an intensity of action on the part of pressure groups, an action more and more directed as time goes on toward the radical alteration of existing government." [11] Similarly, the post-Boxer reforms in China produced a proliferation of popular associations and pressure groups that greatly altered the traditional relationship between the rulers and the ruled. In an unprecedented fashion the people began to demand for themselves a more active role in the government of their country.

What may occur at this point, unless the rulers are extraordinarily careful, is a revolution of rising expectations. According to James C. Davies, as restated and generalized by Stone, "The recipe for revolution is . . . the creation of new expectations by economic improvement and some social and political reforms, followed by economic recession, governmental reaction, and aristocratic resurgence, which widen the gap between expectations and reality." [12] This is approximately what happened in China in 1911. Confronted by the growing political demands of the newly organized pressure groups, the Ch'ing leaders, who since the death of Empress Dowager Tz'u-hsi were "divided and inept" like Brinton's other doomed rulers,[13] became intransigent. The result was, in Brinton's memorable phrase, the "desertion of the intellectuals" (along with other members of the elite) and a loss of the ruler's authority, as demonstrated by the nonrevolutionary rebellion in Szechwan in September 1911 over the Hu-kuang railroad loan. This is what may be called a "revolutionary situation."

Even in such a critical situation a revolution is not inevitable, as the case of China in 1900 suggests. A precipitant is still required, or what Johnson calls an "accelerator," a single, unique event "exposing the inability of the elite to maintain its monopoly of force." This, everyone agrees, is "the final cause of a revolution." [14] In the French Revolution, it was, of course, the taking of the Bastille, which according to Brinton, was "an involved and confusing process, at least as much the result of the weakness of the royal governor . . . as of the strength of the besiegers." The very same characterization may be made of the Wuchang New Army mutiny that precipitated the Chinese revolution.[15]

A revolution, however, does not necessarily end with the coming to power of the revolutionaries.[16] The new incumbents must now deal with the possibility of a counterrevolution, which may come from disaffected revolutionaries, partisans of the old regime, or hostile foreign countries. To remain in power the revolutionaries must overcome this counterrevolutionary threat. Otherwise they will fall victim to it. The Chinese republican revolution, of course, suffered the latter fate.

According to all these theorists of revolution, it is the incumbents rather than the insurgents who are most decisive in determining whether there is a revolution or not. Elite estrangement rather than insurgent conspiracy, or put another way, a revolutionary situation rather than a revolutionary party, is the more important precondition of a revolution. This explains the Taoistic paradox of the Revolutionary Alliance in China: when the Alliance was strong and active, during 1905–07, it failed; when it was weak and divided, in 1911, it succeeded. The weakness of the Revolutionary Alliance became painfully apparent during the post-revolutionary struggle when it lost out so easily to the power-minded militarists.

Such a comprehensive analysis of the Chinese republican revolution has yet to be written. The aim of this study is considerably more modest. It is to take some of the theoretical ideas regarding the revolutionary process and apply them to the single province of Kwangtung. Although the revolution was a national event, it is possible to restrict the study geographically in this fashion without too much distortion of the total historical reality. This is so because the Ch'ing administrative system allowed considerable autonomy to the provinces. Also, when the revolution broke out, it took the form of individual provinces seceding from the central empire. Furthermore, in the first couple of years of the Republic the provinces, particularly those in south China, were virtually independent of the center. However, it remains to be determined to what extent the experiences of Kwangtung during this revolutionary era were typical of China's other provinces. This study should therefore be compared with similar case studies of the 1911 Revolution in other provinces.[17] (It might, incidentally, also be compared with two previous studies of Kwangtung at other revolutionary times, the Taiping period and the Communist period.) [18] A provincial case study such as this is especially useful for tracing the process of elite estrangement, one of the critical ingredients of a revolution. But by its very nature it reveals little about the incumbents in Peking, whose actions brought about the estrangement in the first place. Our understanding of the revolution will thus remain imperfect until it has also been examined from the perspective of the Manchu court.

Finally, there are some built-in biases to this study. Despite an effort to cover the entire province, the study stresses Canton at the expense of other regions like Swatow. But Canton is undeniably the center of the province. It also stresses political and social developments at the expense of economic developments. But at this time economic changes did not keep pace with political and social ones.[19] Last, it stresses the city at the expense of the countryside, and the urban elite, both gentry and merchants, at the expense of the rural masses, the peasants. But despite extensive and perhaps worsening rural misery, the peasantry were at most rebellious without being revolutionary. In short, the biases of the study are those of the revolution it analyzes: socio-political rather than economic, urban rather than rural, and "bourgeois" rather than peasant.

1

On the Eve of Change

The significant *non*-event in nineteenth-century Chinese society was its unresponsiveness to the modern West. This was, surprisingly, as true of Kwangtung as the rest of the country. Of the twenty-six provinces of China Kwangtung has had the longest association with the West. Because of its situation on the southeast coast, it was where the Portuguese mariners landed when they "discovered" China for the Europeans in 1514. Canton, its chief port and city, was where the Western maritime nations conducted most of their trade with China during the following three centuries. When Canton lost its trade monopoly in 1842 as a consequence of the First Opium War and the opening of other ports to direct foreign trade, its decline was more than offset by the rapid rise of Hong Kong as a British colony. Kwangtung continued to be a prime area of Western activity. The Western presence in its many guises, traders, missionaries, gunboats, was established in most parts of the province. And yet in 1894, fifty years after the "opening" of China and more than three hundred and fifty years after the arrival of the Portuguese off its coast, the West had scarcely changed Kwangtung politically and socially. Leaving aside the abortive innovations of the Taiping Rebellion, the few changes that had occurred were tentative and superficial. On the eve of the Sino-Japanese war, Kwangtung was still basically a "traditional" society. Among the traditions intact then was that of popular noninvolvement in the political process.

The Geographical Setting

Kwangtung is a large and populous province of China bordering on the South China Sea. It covers about 85,000 square miles of territory and has a population today of approximately forty million people; its population at the turn of the century was an estimated thirty million. In both area and population it is only slightly smaller than Great Britain. Set off by mountains and sea, it constitutes by itself a more or less distinct geographical unit. The Nan-ling (Southern Range) runs along the northern edge of the province and forms the watershed between the Yangtze valley of central China and the West River valley of south China. Other mountains, running athwart the West River, separate the upper West River basin in the neighboring province of Kwangsi from the lower West River drainage in Kwangtung.[1]

The overwhelming majority of the people of Kwangtung are engaged in agriculture. Rice is the primary crop. Some industrial crops, like mulberry trees for silk culture, sugar cane, tea, and tobacco, are also grown, and fishing is important along the lengthy coastline. Practically the whole province is hilly, so that no more than 15 to 20 percent of the land is cultivated. Most of the arable land is concentrated in the West River and Han River deltas and in numerous narrow alluvial river valleys. In these areas the population pressure and, correspondingly, the economic pressure are intense. In the West River delta, for example, an average of three thousand people are squeezed into one square mile of land. As a result, individual landholdings, in the years before the collectivization of agriculture, were generally very small, about two thirds of an acre for a family of middle peasants.[2] Fortunately, the climate in Kwangtung is subtropical and the growing season lasts the year round. Rainfall is also plentiful and dependable. Double cropping is usual, and in many areas triple cropping is possible. Even in former days when China was called the "land of famine," severe food shortages were almost unknown in the province.[3]

Because of the mountainous terrain, the numerous waterways in the province have provided the most convenient means of internal communication. The major road in Kwangtung, before the road building program of the present century, was the imperial highway along the North River up through the Mei-ling pass to Kiangsi and ultimately to Peking. Otherwise, according to an account of the province in the 1920's, "Few roads are necessary. Those that do exist are merely narrow pathways between rice fields, paved with slabs of stone . . . Few vehicles of any sort are seen." [4] Instead, travel has usually been by boat. While large ocean-going ships can sail up the West River only to Whampoa (Huang-p'u), twelve miles below Canton, junks and river steamers can go as far as Wuchow, just above the Kwangsi border. Smaller vessels with shallower draught can reach practically every part of the province, particularly in the summer months when the water is high. Inland and coastal shipping is so prevalent that it has produced its own occupational caste of boat people or Tanka (*Tan-chia*), numbering more than 300,000, who spend their whole life aboard their boats. They were until recently an "oppressed and pariah people without social status." In the Ch'ing period, they were included in the small category of mean people who were prohibited from taking the all-important civil service examinations. [5]

The mountains and rivers divide Kwangtung into three major regions and a number of subregions. The major regions are Central Kwangtung, East Kwangtung, and West Kwangtung, each defined by a drainage system. Central Kwangtung is drained by the West River and its two important tributaries, the North and East rivers. The West River originates in the Yunnan plateau far to the west, enters Kwangtung just below Wuchow, two hundred miles from the sea, flows eastward to Samshui (San-shui), where it meets the North River, originating in the Nan-ling, and together they fan out through a large and intricate delta to the South China Sea. The East River, originating in Kiangsi and flowing down through northeastern Kwangtung, is, strictly speaking, separate from the West River, but it reaches the sea through the same delta.

The Pearl River delta, which is the more usual name for the delta, is a hill-studded plain cut up by a maze of channels, creeks, and canals; it is the heartland of Central Kwangtung and of the entire province. Measuring seventy miles from north to south and fifty from east to west, it is the largest extent of relatively level land in Kwangtung. This subregion is farmed intensively, and its agriculture is highly commercialized. It is the chief rice growing area, and an important producer of silk, which was one of the major items of Canton's foreign trade down through the First World War. It is also the most highly urbanized area in the province and at the same time the area with the most densely settled rural population. [6] About one third of the population of Kwangtung is concentrated into this relatively small area.

Its major city is, of course, Canton, with a population of perhaps 600,000 at the turn of the century, 1,599,000 in 1953 (according to the census taken then), and about three million today. Located on the north bank of the Pearl River, the main channel in the delta, Canton (which the Chinese today prefer to call Kwangchow) has been a center of commerce and shipping for over fifteen hundred years. Just as it was the center of Western trade in the early Ch'ing, so it had been for the Arab trade in the T'ang. It was also the hub of the domestic trading network that spanned the entire West River basin. Besides its commercial functions, Canton was also the center of governmental administration for both Kwangtung and Kwangsi. Next to Canton, the most important city in the delta is Fo-shan (Fatshan), twelve miles to the southwest, a manufacturing center of 123,000 in 1953. Other large cities in the delta are Kongmoon (Chiang-men), in Hsin-hui district, with a population in 1953 of 85,000, and Shih-ch'i, seat of Hsiang-shan (now Chung-shan) district, with a population of 93,000. In addition, the two territorial cessions, Hong Kong and Macao, both lie on the edge of this subregion.

Central Kwangtung also includes the areas to the west, north, and northeast of the Pearl River delta. The subregion to the west, the West River valley, borders on Kwangsi and is traversed by the West River before it reaches Samshui. It is not nearly so urbanized or economically developed as the delta. Its major city is Chao-ch'ing (also named Kao-yao), a spacious but sparsely populated city that in the Ming period had served as the capital of the province. The subregion to the north is the drainage area of the North River. Its largest city is Shao-chou (also Shao-kuan and Ch'ü-chiang), a major transportation center on the old imperial highway and now the Canton–Hankow railroad; it had a population of 82,000 in 1953. Its population at the turn of the century, before the building of the railroad, was considerably less; the entire North River valley was then, along with Hainan, the least developed and urbanized area in the province. About 41,000 aboriginal Yao tribesmen live in the mountains adjoining Hunan and Kwangsi. Finally, the subregion to the northeast, bordering on Kiangsi, is the drainage area of the East River. Its major city is Hui-chou (Waichow), a city of less than 60,000; its level of development was roughly the same as the West River valley.

East Kwangtung, the second of the three major regions, is defined by the drainage of the Han River and its tributary, the Mei River. This region, which is an extension of the maritime hill lands of Chekiang and Fukien, is separated from the East River valley of Central Kwangtung by a spur of mountains that juts out from the Nan-ling and runs down to the sea near the small city of Hai-feng. It is divided by the Lien-hua shan (Lotus Flower Mountains) into two subregions: the Han River delta and coastal lowlands and the interior Mei River valley. The Han River lowlands, especially the six hundred square miles of the fertile alluvial delta, is very densely populated and highly urbanized; next to the Pearl River delta, it is the most developed area in the province. Along with rice growing, the production of sugar is an important part of the local economy. Its largest cities are Ch'ao-chou (now Ch'ao-an), at the head of the delta, and Swatow (Shan-t'ou), the port for the region; their population in 1953 was 101,000 and 280,000 respectively. The Mei River valley, because of its interior location and mountainous terrain, is only moderately well developed and not very urbanized. Its center is the small city of Chia-ying (now Mei-hsien).

West Kwangtung is characterized by no single river system; instead, all its rivers are short and run directly to the sea. A belt of mountains, the Yün-wu shan (Misty Mountains), divides it from the West River drainage system of Central Kwangtung. It consists of two subregions: the coastal lowland and Hainan island, which is separated from the Lei-chou (often Luichow) peninsula on the mainland by a ten-mile-wide channel. Because of its infertile soils and its isolation from the rest of the province, the whole region has until recently been quite underdeveloped. The coastal lowland has three fairly important cities now: Chan-chiang (also Hsi-ying; known under the French as Fort Bayard), at the head of the Lei-chou peninsula, with a population of 166,000 in 1953; Pakhoi (Pei-hai), on the Gulf of Tonkin, with a population of 80,000; and the fast-growing city of Kao-chou (also Mao-ming). (Under the Communists the western half of this area, including Pakhoi, has off and on been separated from Kwangtung, to which it has traditionally belonged, and attached to Kwangsi in order to give the latter province an outlet to the sea.) The major city of Hainan island is the port of Hoihow (Hai-k'ou), with a population of 135,000 in 1953. About 360,000 aboriginal Li people live in the mountains of southern Hainan. In addition to Hainan, there are several small groups of islands and coral reefs lying in the South China Sea between the Philippines and Vietnam that belong to Kwangtung. They are generally uninhabited but are frequently visited by Chinese fishermen.

There is perhaps a fourth "region" of Kwangtung, its overseas extension embracing the seven million natives of the province living in Southeast Asia, Japan, and the Americas. They come from practically every coastal district of Kwangtung stretching from Swatow to Hainan island. But perhaps the most notable center of emigration in the province was the area in Central Kwangtung on the edge of the Pearl River delta that includes Hsiang-shan and the "Four Districts" (Ssu-i) of Hsin-ning (now T'ai-shan), Hsin-hui, K'ai-p'ing and En-p'ing, which provided the vast majority of the emigrants to the United States in the late nineteenth century. The remittances of the overseas Chinese were often indispensable to these emigrant districts. In one community near Swatow in the mid-1930's, such remittances accounted for at least 75 percent of the average family income at every income level.[7] Moreover, the overseas Chinese seldom lived abroad permanently. They were usually sojourners who left their home only long enough to improve their family's livelihood. When they returned to Kwangtung from abroad, they were important agents of social and cultural change.

Ethnolinguistically, Kwangtung is a complicated province. Apart from the Yao tribesmen along the Hunan and Kwangsi border, the Li tribesmen in southern Hainan, and the Tanka boat people scattered along the inland and coastal waterways, there are three major ethnolinguistic groups living in the province, Punti, Hakka, and Hoklo. Each speaks a dialect of Chinese that is unintelligible to the other two groups. Each has its own cultural traits too. Hakka women, for example, did not use to bind their feet as did Punti and Hoklo women.[8] In the 1930's, it was estimated that the Puntis numbered twenty-five million, the Hakkas four million, and the Hoklos three million.[9]

Each of the three groups is more or less regionally defined to form what amounts to a language province.[10] The Puntis (Pen-ti, or "natives"), the original settlers of the land, are concentrated throughout the fertile lowlands of the Pearl River delta and the West and North river valleys of Central Kwangtung. They are also found in much of the rest of the province, particularly in the cities and towns, because trade is generally in their hands.[11] The Hoklos (Fu-lao) entered Kwangtung from southern Fukien, whose speech their dialect closely resembles. Some settled in the nearby Han River lowlands and are known as Teochius (from the Hoklo pronunciation of Ch'ao-chou). Others migrated to the Lei-chou peninsula and Hainan island in West Kwangtung; known as Hainanese, they speak a slightly different version of the Hoklo dialect from Teochiu. The Hakkas (K'o-chia, "guests") were the last to arrive, entering from Fukien and Kiangsi in the thirteenth century. Since the

Puntis and Teochius had occupied all the lowlands, they were forced to settle in the less desirable hill country of northern Kwangtung. They are found primarily in the Mei River and the upper East River valleys. As a result of later migrations out of this heartland, Hakkas are also found in scattered communities in many other parts of the province.[12]

Contention and at times outright warfare have characterized relations among the three groups. One of the causes has been the contempt of the Puntis toward both Hoklos and Hakkas, whom they consider not as Han Chinese at all but as uncultured aborigines.[13] Another has been the aggressiveness of the Hakkas. Born to adversity, the Hakkas developed a reputation for hard work, frugality, and studiousness.[14] This assertiveness, especially when applied to the stiff competition for land, generated much resentment among their neighbors. The rivalry between the Hakkas and the Puntis has been particularly bitter. For thirteen years (1854–67) amidst the general confusion of the Taiping Rebellion, they waged an intermittent but devastating communal war over the southwestern corner of the Pearl River delta, with thousands of casualties.[15] The rivalry between the Hakkas and Teochius, confined to East Kwangtung, has been only slightly less bitter. This was most apparent after the republican revolution when the two communities fought one another for political control of the Ch'ao-chou area.

In sum, the geography of Kwangtung has emphasized its distinctiveness from the rest of China and also the divisions within the province. Kwangtung is separated from the rest of the country, and particularly from the center of power in Peking, by mountains and great distances and by a formidable language barrier. Except among the educated elite, Mandarin, the North China dialect that served as the language of administration in the Ch'ing period, was not spoken at all. While every Chinese province has a sense of its own uniqueness, Kwangtung has been perhaps more self-conscious than most about it. Even today the people of Kwangtung tend to regard all northerners as outsiders. On the other hand, the province itself is by no means homogeneous. Physically and ethnolinguistically, it is divided into several distinct regions. These intraprovincial differences narrow down to two sets of rivalry. One is the rivalry between Central Kwangtung and East Kwangtung, between the Pearl River delta and the Han River delta, between Canton and Swatow, between the Puntis on one side and the Teochius and Hakkas on the other. The other rivalry, within East Kwangtung itself, is between the Teochius and the Hakkas, between

Ch'ao-chou and Chia-ying. Thus, the differences that divide Kwangtung itself have been almost as great as those that divide Kwangtung from the rest of China.

The Western Presence

In 1894 the full force of imperialism had yet to appear in China. The Western powers, led by Great Britain, were until then concerned primarily with commercial opportunities rather than territorial aggrandizement or political power. While the development of foreign trade clearly affected the Chinese economy, it had surprisingly little effect upon the broader society, perhaps because most of the foreign trade transactions within China were actually handled by the Chinese and not by the foreigners. Thus, in physical terms, the Western presence in China, fifty years after its opening to the West, was still remarkably superficial. Even in Kwangtung, which bore the brunt of European and American expansionism, it was mostly limited to two small territorial cessions and four treaty ports, where the foreigners could dwell and trade. Only the missionaries were free then to live and work in the interior of the province, but they were not yet very intrusive either.

The centers of Western population in Kwangtung were the two territorial cessions, British Hong Kong and Portuguese Macao. Of the two Hong Kong was by far the more important. It consisted then of Hong Kong island and Kowloon peninsula, which Britain had obtained from China after the first and second opium wars in 1842 and 1860 respectively; it totaled 36 square miles of territory. Blessed with a deep, spacious, and protected harbor, Hong Kong developed under British rule from "a barren island with hardly a house upon it" (as it was described originally) into a great international shipping center, handling (in 1890) 55 percent of all China's imports and 37 percent of her exports. Its population in 1898 was 254,000, slightly less than half of Canton's, of whom only 15,190 were foreigners. The small colony of Europeans generally kept to itself. Through housing ordinances, certain sections of the island, including the Peak, were reserved for Westerners.[16]

Located on a tiny peninsula on the coast of Hsiang-shan district, forty miles west of Hong Kong across the Pearl River estuary, Macao has been occupied by the Portuguese since 1557. It was originally a leasehold, for which the Portuguese paid an annual ground rent of five hundred taels (ounces) of silver. It became a colony in 1849, when the Portuguese unilaterally expelled the local Chinese authorities and stopped payment of the ground rent; it was not, however, formally ceded by China to Portugal until 1887. The areas under Portuguese rule then were Macao peninsula and two small nearby islands, Taipa and Coloane, altogether 6 square miles of territory. Because of its shallow harbor, which required constant dredging, Macao never prospered in the way that Hong Kong did in the nineteenth century. Its population in 1897 was 79,000, of whom 4,000 were foreigners.[17]

In addition to Hong Kong and Macao, Westerners in Kwangtung were established in the four "treaty ports" open to foreign trade and residence. They were Canton, Swatow, Hoihow, and Pakhoi, located strategically so as to tap the trade of all three major regions of the province. Of the four, Canton was the most important and the first to be opened. Although it was opened by the Treaty of Nanking in 1842, fierce local opposition prevented the foreigners from entering the walled city itself until December 1857, when during the Second Opium War an Anglo-French expedition fought its way into the city and occupied it until October 1861. With the growth of Hong Kong and the opening of other treaty ports along the China coast, Canton no longer enjoyed a monopoly of the foreign trade. It remained, however, vitally important as the center of much of the domestic trade of south China.

The Western community in Canton centered on the small 56-acre settlement of Shameen (Sha-mien), an artificial island reclaimed from a sandbar in the Pearl River by the British and French during their four-year occupation of the city. It lies off the Western Suburbs, the bustling commercial quarter of Canton, separated from it by a hundred-foot-wide canal. Holding it on a nominal long-term lease from the Chinese government, the British and French ruled Shameen directly and maintained it as an exclusively European colony. No Chinese was allowed to own property on the island; the only Chinese living there were the servants in the various foreign homes and businesses. The Western population on Shameen alone was about 200; throughout the city, it was about 350.[18]

The second treaty port to be opened, and the second most important, was Swatow, which was opened by the Treaty of Tientsin in 1858. At the time of its opening, Swatow was "little more than a fishing village on a mud-flat." But like Hong Kong, it grew rapidly with the development of foreign trade; it eventually surpassed Ch'ao-chou, the prefectural capital, as the leading city in East Kwangtung and now rivals Canton itself. Its population at the turn of the century was about 35,000. The

number of foreign residents then was 200. Most of them lived at Kakchio (Chiao-shih), an informal settlement on a rocky promontory opposite Swatow city.[19]

Hoihow, at the northern end of Hainan island, was opened by the
same 1858 Treaty of Tientsin that opened Swatow, but Westerners did
not take up residence in the city until 1876. The treaty port of Hoihow
technically included both the port town of Hoihow and the prefectural
city of Kiungchow (Ch'iung-chou), two and a half miles inland; the
treaty port was thus also known as Kiungchow. Like Swatow, the port of
Hoihow prospered with the growth of foreign trade, until it too eclipsed
the nearby prefectural capital to become the leading city in its area. But
Hoihow did not prosper nearly to the same extent as did Swatow, partly
because its harbor was too shallow for ocean-going ships but, more important, because the area it tapped, Hainan, was poor and underdeveloped. A foreign visitor to Kiungchow city in 1882 found it to be
sparsely populated. There were then only ten or twelve Western residents scattered around the city.[20]

The last treaty port to be opened in Kwangtung before 1894 was
Pakhoi, located on the Gulf of Tonkin in the western panhandle. It
was opened by the Chefoo Convention in 1876. Like Hoihow, though it
developed as a treaty port into the premier city of its area, it never
prospered because of its poor harbor and the poverty and limitations of
its hinterland. There were few resident Westerners. In 1901, the foreign
community consisted in its entirety of the Customs Commissioner, who
was a fixture at all treaty ports, a British consul, a French vice-consul, a
French postmaster, a Catholic priest, and a German merchant.[21]

The Western traders by and large restricted their activities to the territorial cessions and the treaty ports, which in Kwangtung at this time
were all located on the coast. The missionaries, on the other hand, were
free, according to the 1860 Convention of Peking, to live and work
throughout the interior. By 1894 Christian missionaries had established
stations in about two thirds of Kwangtung's ninety-odd districts,
usually in the more populous cities and market towns situated along the
major waterways. They were particularly active in the Pearl River and
Han River deltas and also among the Hakkas along the Mei River and
the upper East River.[22] The Catholics, under the direction of the Society
of Foreign Missions of Paris, had 21 foreign and 3 Chinese priests working in the province in 1870, with about 12,000 adherents (not including those in Macao). In 1890 the number of adherents had increased to

30,500, with perhaps a corresponding increase in the number of priests.[23] The Protestants were represented by several different denominations and nationalities, including Presbyterians and Baptists from the United States, Presbyterians and Wesleyans from Britain, and the Berlin Missionary Society from Germany. In 1895 the foreign Protestant missionaries numbered about 100, and the Chinese communicants about 9,000.[24] The total missionary force, including both Catholics and Protestants, thus amounted to at most 200 foreigners, with about 40,000 Chinese adherents, which was hardly more than one tenth of 1 percent of the total population of Kwangtung.

In addition to the trader in the treaty port and the missionary in the interior, there was also a Western military presence in the form of gunboats and soldiers. These saw to it that the foreigners enjoyed the extraterritorial privileges to which they were entitled under the treaty system. For example, in 1883 German troops landed at Swatow to support the claim of a German firm to a piece of disputed land, although the land "probably in fact belonged to the firm's [Chinese] comprador." The gunboats defended also their own right to be there. In January 1869, after some villagers had stoned the gunboat *Cockchafer* while it was "exercising on the river above Swatow," a force of British sailors went ashore and nearly burnt the whole village to the ground.[25]

By 1894 there were thus close to 20,000 foreigners living in Kwangtung. Their contact with the Chinese, however, was circumscribed. The only territory they then occupied consisted of Hong Kong, Macao, and Shameen, which totaled less than 42 square miles in area and where all but about 400 of the 20,000 lived. Outside the two territorial cessions and the four treaty ports, only the few and isolated missionaries had penetrated into the interior of the province.

Response to the West

With the intrusion of the West, particularly after 1860, China began slowly to modernize. On the one hand, the foreigners in China brought with them their own way of life. On the other, leading Chinese officials initiated the "self-strengthening" movement. Kwangtung was a center for both types of activity. However, before 1894 the impact of these efforts was quite limited. In particular, the gentry elite clung tenaciously to their traditional ways. Only a few individuals responded favorably to the innovations, but they were generally without influence.

Through Hong Kong and through the missionaries, the Westerners introduced many innovations into Kwangtung. In Hong Kong, they established many new forms of financial and industrial enterprise, such as shipyards (for example, the Hong Kong and Whampoa Dock Co., 1863), banks (the Hongkong and Shanghai Banking Corporation, 1864), the telegraph (1870), sugar refineries (China Sugar Refining Co., 1876), cement works (Green Island Cement Co., 1889), and electric street lighting (1890).[26] Also they created new social and governmental institutions, like the chamber of commerce, an independent judiciary, popular representation in government, but not, it may be noted, popular elections. (The Legislative Council included several unofficial members, one of them a Chinese since 1880, but they were all appointed by the governor and not popularly elected. Chinese representation on the council was increased to two in 1896.)

More important, the Westerners reproduced their own kind of education. The missionaries established a large number of schools in Kwangtung. For example, the American Northern Presbyterians, perhaps the most active Protestant group in the province, operated in the mid-1890's fourteen primary day schools, one secondary boarding school and one training class, with a total of 490 pupils.[27] Since these schools were intended to instruct converts in Christian doctrines and to train Christian workers, the language of instruction was usually Chinese. Some of them, however, also offered instruction in English, as did the Canton Christian College, which the American Presbyterian missionary Andrew Happer founded in 1888 as the apex of the missionary school system in south China. In its second year of operation the college had 65 students. But because of Happer's ill health it was forced to close down in its third year and did not reopen until 1894. Despite this shaky start, the college later developed into the well-known Lingnan University.[28] Meanwhile, in Hong Kong in 1898, 23 out of a total of 115 schools gave an education generally in English. The most prominent of these were the Anglo-Chinese secondary schools, notably Queen's College (formerly the Central School).[29]

The foreigners also initiated the practice and teaching of modern Western medicine. Among the Protestant missionaries, medicine was as important a component of their work as education. At almost every mission station, they established a dispensary offering out-patient care; in the larger cities, like Hong Kong, Canton, Swatow, and Fo-shan, they maintained hospitals. It was as an outgrowth from the work of the hospitals that modern Western medical education began in Kwangtung.

Thus, in 1866 the Canton Missionary Hospital, under Dr. John G. Kerr, began offering medical courses. Then in 1887 was founded the Hong Kong College of Medicine for Chinese, attached to the Alice Memorial Hospital. Unlike the school in Canton, the Hong Kong College of Medicine was "an organized medical school whose courses led to a recognized diploma." [30]

Finally, the foreigners were pioneers in education for women. In Hong Kong, for example, 32 percent of the pupils attending school in 1890 were girls. So were half of the 346 pupils in the schools operated by the English Presbyterians in the Swatow area in 1896. The Canton Hospital Medical School also accepted women students. [31]

Apart from the Westerners, the provincial authorities, in the generation following the Second Opium War, attempted a number of innovations of their own that were characteristic of the self-strengthening movement. The movement aimed to strengthen China's defenses by borrowing the superior technology of the West while preserving intact the rest of her traditional culture. The single most influential official in Kwangtung's self-strengthening was Chang Chih-tung, who was governor-general at Canton from 1884 to 1889. [32]

One of the first self-strengthening innovations was the creation of the Translators' College (T'ung-wen kuan) to train interpreters to assist the officials in their dealings with the foreigners. One of the three colleges in the country was established in Canton in 1864. Staffed by Western instructors, it offered a three-year course in English, mathematics, and Chinese; it had 20 students. The college in Canton, however, turned out poorly. Enrollment was restricted to the Manchu and Chinese bannermen from the Canton garrison, while the school itself was under the control of the garrison commander, the Tartar-general. The college eventually degenerated into little more than a source of patronage and stipends for the bannerman. [33]

The heart of self-strengthening, however, was military modernization. In Kwangtung this consisted principally of an arsenal in Canton, founded in 1874, a shipyard at Whampoa, acquired from a British firm in 1876, and a naval and military academy, also at Whampoa. [34] The academy began in 1881 as a naval school attached to the Whampoa shipyard. Known as the School of Solid Learning (Shih-hsüeh kuan), it was modeled after the Foochow Shipyard School and offered a five-year training course for naval engineers and deck officers. It opened with 50 students. In 1887 the school was reorganized by Chang Chih-tung. He shortened the course work from five to three years, expanded the curriculum to include military training as well as naval, and gave the school a new name, the Naval and Military Officers' Academy (Shui-lu shih hsüeh-t'ang). English instructors were hired for the two naval divisions; German ones for the military division. The academy, however, had considerable difficulty in getting students to attend. Unable to attract them locally, it was forced to rely on transfers from the Foochow Shipyard School and on recruits from as far away as Tientsin. Even then it failed to get enough. In 1891, only 25 students were enrolled. With the school losing money steadily, Governor Kang-i, a leading conservative official, closed it down completely in 1894.[35] Also at Whampoa was a Torpedo School, founded in 1886 by Chang Chih-tung, with a German naval officer as instructor. It evidently survived the retrenchment of the early 1890's.[36]

Another innovation of the period was the telegraph. In 1884 lines were strung up between Canton and Shanghai and between Canton and Hong Kong. Later, the system was extended to all parts of the province. By the end of 1908 there were 1,200 miles of telegraph lines in Kwangtung. A telegraph school in Canton, established in 1887 by Chang Chih-tung, trained operators for the system.[37]

Besides the establishment of a modern mint in Canton in 1889, also by Chang Chih-tung,[38] such were the self-strengthening reforms inaugurated in Kwangtung by the provincial authorities. In addition, Kwangtung was involved in one other important project of the time, the Chinese Educational Mission of 1872–81, sponsored by the Chihli governor-general, Li Hung-chang. Of the 120 boys who were sent to the United States for technical studies, over 70 percent came from Kwangtung, many of them from the emigrant community of Hsiang-shan. This was because the head of the mission, Yung Wing (Jung Hung), was himself a native of Hsiang-shan. When the mission was abruptly terminated in 1881, however, only one of the students, Chan T'ien-yu (Tien Yow Jeme), a graduate of Yale in civil engineering and later a famous railroad builder, came back to work in Kwangtung, where for a couple of years he taught engineering at the Naval and Military Officers' Academy. Many of the other returned students found employment in Li Hung-chang's personal secretariat in Tientsin.[39]

The self-strengthening movement clearly was a significant departure from the traditional order, but equally clearly it had a very limited effect in Kwangtung. The range of the reforms was narrow, with defense as the almost exclusive concern. The reforms were few in number; the successful ones were fewer still. Geographically the reforms were very localized. Every project, with the exception of the telegraph, was located in or near Canton; the rest of the province was hardly affected. Finally, most of the reforms were in one way or another the work of Chang Chih-tung; his predecessors and successors did little to promote the movement.

Neither the Westerners' innovations nor the government's self-strengthening projects produced a favorable response from the gentry elite of Kwangtung. They were actively hostile toward the missionaries, whose intrusion into their midst they particularly resented. In retaliation, they fomented numerous attacks against the missionaries and their property throughout the province.[40] Toward self-strengthening, the gentry's attitude was less one of hostility than of disinterest, as the failure of the Naval and Military Officers' Academy to attract students locally would suggest. One reason for their disinterest was complacence. Even after China's defeat in the war with France in 1885, part of which took place on the Kwangtung–Vietnam border, the overwhelming majority of the gentry remained unconcerned about either China's weakness or the threat from the West. They saw no need to change. As Liang Ch'i-ch'ao later remarked of the Hsüeh-hai t'ang, one of Canton's most distinguished academies, which he entered in 1885, "One might not know there was anything in the universe but commentaries and fine style."[41] Another, probably more nearly basic, reason for the gentry's lack of interest in reform was the unwillingness of the government to make it worth their while to study the West, since it made no provision for Western learning in the civil service examinations.

One of the few gentry members in Kwangtung to see the need for reform at this time was K'ang Yu-wei. In 1879, when he was only twenty-one years old, K'ang visited Hong Kong and came away greatly impressed with "the elegance of the buildings of the foreigners, the cleanliness of the streets, the efficiency of their police." He then realized, he later recalled, "that we must not look upon them as barbarians, as our older and more conservative people have done."[42] (Hong Kong had a similar effect on the young Sun Yat-sen, as he contrasted it with his native district. "Hsiang-shan and Hong Kong are only fifty miles apart. How is it that they are so different? The foreigners in seventy or eighty years have developed this from a desolate island, while China, with her four thousand years of civilization, has nothing like it.")[43] Spurred by China's defeat in 1885, K'ang then began the study of West-

ern matters that was eventually to lead him to a wholly new interpretation of Confucianism. In 1891, he founded a school in Canton, known
as the Thatched Hut among Ten Thousand Trees (Wan-mu ts'ao-t'ang),
where he stressed not only the traditional classical curriculum but also
"current events," "barbarian [that is, foreign] affairs," and even physical
culture.[44] By 1894 K'ang Yu-wei had gathered about himself a small
coterie of disciples, including Liang Ch'i-ch'ao, but he had yet to make
an impact upon the wider society. Indeed, he was at that time only a
recent provincial graduate; he did not achieve the degree of metropolitan
graduate until 1895.

Apart from K'ang Yu-wei and his small group of gentry reformers,
those who were concerned with Western affairs and reforms were almost
all Westernized Chinese. They were the products of the hybrid culture
of Hong Kong and the treaty ports, of whom Yung Wing was both the
pioneer and the paradigm. They were almost always educated in Western schools, including missionary schools. They usually dressed and
lived according to Western fashions. They were often professed Christians. They sometimes married Western women. Since they lacked the
classical education that qualified them for the regular civil service, they
either found employment in the personal secretariat of a reform-minded
official like Li Hung-chang or else worked for the foreigners, as in the
Imperial Maritime Customs, the foreign shipping companies, and the
Hong Kong government.[45] Two of these Westernized Chinese reformers
from Kwangtung were Ho Kai (Ho Ch'i) and Cheng Kuan-ying. Ho, a
British-educated barrister-at-law in Hong Kong, and Cheng, a former
comprador and a member of Li Hung-chang's secretariat, both saw even
more clearly than did K'ang Yu-wei the need for a much more far-
reaching transformation of Chinese society. Writing separately, they
both called not only for military and economic reforms but also for political reforms, including the establishment of a Western-type parliamentary system in China. But their views carried little weight, precisely
because of their nongentry background.[46]

Thus, the innovations of the self-strengthening period made an impression only upon the Westernized Chinese, but they were beyond the
pale. They did not count. Among the regular gentry, with few exceptions, the innovations were ignored. As a result, on the eve of the Sino-
Japanese war, the traditional way of life and the traditional values in
China were still essentially intact.

Tradition of Political Passivity

In traditional China, the political process was the exclusive and carefully guarded monopoly of the state. The officials alone were to play a formal role in government. Everyone else was barred from direct involvement in the political process. Voluntary associations of most sorts were discouraged. The expression of public opinion was restricted. This condition of popular political passivity lasted down through the self-strengthening period, with only one major departure from the traditional order, the development of the daily press.[47]

Under the centralized bureaucratic system of the Ch'ing, local government was a direct extension of the central government in Peking. Kwangtung, for example, was ruled at the top by the governor-general of Kwangtung and Kwangsi, assisted by the governor of Kwangtung, with Canton as the seat of administration. Below them were two layers of supervisory officials, the taotai (or circuit intendant) and the prefect. At the bottom, the province was divided into ninety-three independent departments (*chih-li chou*), independent subprefectures (*chih-li t'ing*), ordinary departments (*chou*), and most commonly, districts (*hsien*), each ruled by a magistrate (or in the case of the independent subprefecture, a subprefect).[48] Every one of these officials, from the governor-general down to the district magistrate, was an appointee of the central government, to which he was responsible. He was not responsible to the local community, and by the rule of avoidance, he was not allowed to be a native of the province to which he was assigned. The system, in short, was one of "government by officials" (*kuan-chih*) rather than "self-government" (*tzu-chih*). Where self-government existed, as in the villages, it did so only at the sufferance of the officials.

The bureaucratic elite who staffed the local as well as the central administration were drawn from the ranks of the scholar-gentry, the landed, literate, and leisured class composed primarily of those who had attained at least the degree of senior licentiate (*kung-sheng*) in the civil service examinations. But for most members of the gentry office holding was infrequent and brief. When not holding office, they retired to their native provinces, where, as the local elite, they played a critical though informal role as advisers to the local officials, their different degree statuses generally determining their sphere of activities. The lower gentry, composed of the senior licentiates as well as scholar-commoners like the licentiates (*sheng-yüan*), were seldom influential beyond their home district, while the upper gentry, composed of the provincial and metropolitan graduates (*chü-jen* and *chin-shih* respectively), mingled easily with the provincial officials.[49]

The court, however, jealously guarded its monopoly of political power; it restrained all forms of associational activity that might encroach upon it. It was, for obvious reasons, most watchful of the scholar-gentry. All scholars were expressly forbidden by successive imperial decrees from organizing factions or associations.[50] It was unavoidable, of course, that the gentry would develop customary associations among themselves in the course of their work as the local elite. Such associations remained strictly informal until the time of the opium wars and the Taiping Rebellion, when they were formalized in the local defense associations (*t'uan*).[51] However, these gentry-led organizations, which frequently assumed policing and tax-collecting powers, were really an adjunct of local administration rather than gentry associations. The ban on self-government and the law of avoidance had been breached to some extent, but the ban on voluntary associations still stood. K'ang Yu-wei discovered this in 1883 when he formed a society in his native Nan-hai district to campaign against the practice of footbinding among women. "When people in the district voiced the fear that the very word 'association' (*hui*) might be a violation of the prohibitions (of the government against popular organizations), many of the members gradually drifted away." [52] About the only type of association which the gentry could safely organize was the literary society.

The court was less concerned about other social groups forming associations so long as they were not politically motivated. In the rest of society, the merchants were the best organized. They had their guilds (*hang*), which were organized according to a common service, craft, or product, and their *hui-kuan,* organized according to a common place of origin. For example, in Canton at the turn of the century, there were about one hundred guilds and twenty-five *hui-kuan*.[53] Characteristically, the guilds and *hui-kuan* were primarily economic, secondarily social, and not at all political in nature. Their economic function was clear-cut: "mutual protection (by controlling the conditions of trade, nominally in the interests of all) and resistance to official demands in excess of what custom allowed." In the economic sphere, through the use of the boycott, they were quite powerful. In 1881 the Swatow Guild (Wan-nien-feng, lit., "prosperity for ten thousand years"), which was strictly speaking a combination of six district *hui-kuan* rather than a guild, paralyzed the external trade of East Kwangtung for two weeks in a dispute with the Commissioner of Customs.[54]

The guilds and *hui-kuan* were active in the social sphere as well. They looked after the welfare of their own members, particularly those in need. In Canton, the guilds also supported about ten "charitable halls" (*shan-t'ang*) to help others. These charitable halls were a recent development; the first one, the Ai-yü Charitable Hall, was founded only in 1871, prompted in part by the work of the foreign medical missionaries. They performed a variety of services. The Ai-yü Charitable Hall provided free out-patient care to the indigent sick, financial support for destitute widows, and free coffins for the elderly poor; it also supported several free primary schools for the children of the poor. Charitable halls similar to those in Canton existed in Hong Kong and Macao as well. In Hong Kong, the Tung Wah Hospital (Tung-hua i-yüan), founded in 1870, and the Po Leung Kuk (Pao-liang chü), a refuge for girls founded in 1878, were (and still are) very influential organizations; their directors constituted the colony's Chinese elite. In Canton too, the directors of the various charitable halls were probably the merchant elite of the city.[55]

However, despite their economic and social importance, the guilds and *hui-kuan* were politically impotent and assiduously refrained from political activity. The reason was a lack of independent authority. The government allowed the guilds and *hui-kuan* to control their trade and to regulate their own affairs in return for their assuming the responsibility for collecting the taxes levied on their trade, but it never granted them official recognition. Unlike their medieval European counterparts, the authority that they exercised, which was considerable, was not a formal delegation from the officials. Therefore, in order not to jeopardize their economic privileges, which they held so insecurely, the guilds and *hui-kuan* minded their own business and avoided political involvement.[56] Not only did they as a group keep to themselves, each guild also kept to itself.

Because of the government's attitude, the only popular associations that were politically motivated were necessarily secret. In Kwangtung, the most common of these secret societies (*hui-tang*) were collectively known as the Triad Society. The declared aim of the society was to overthrow the alien Ch'ing and restore the native Ming dynasty, and on a number of occasions in the nineteenth century it did rebel against the government. Nevertheless, the society was probably a good deal less of a political organization than it appeared. In particular, its anti-Manchu stance seems to have been largely ritualistic. As the republican revolutionaries were to discover repeatedly, few of its members were very conscious of their anti-Manchu heritage. Thus, fifty years after the overthrow of the Manchus, the Triad Society in Hong Kong was still using the anti-Ch'ing pro-Ming formulas to initiate its members.[57]

Stripped of its rituals and its secretiveness, the Triad Society, in fact, resembled the mutual aid societies so characteristic of traditional Chinese society. Its regulations stressed the obligations of its members to help one another and to provide for one another's families.[58] It was probably this promise of mutual aid rather than its call for the expulsion of the Manchus that attracted its many supporters. For, by all accounts, the society was omnipresent in Kwangtung. The countryside reportedly was honeycombed with Triad lodges, which because they were bound to one another by little more than a common ritual, were all but impossible for the officials to eradicate. Whether as byproduct or as cause, they contributed to the general turbulence that by the late nineteenth century was endemic in every part of the province.

Just as the formation of voluntary associations was discouraged, so the expression of public opinion was restricted. Consider, for example, the press. In traditional China, the prevailing form of "newspapers" was the official gazettes, which were published regularly both in Peking and in provincial capitals like Canton. They were published privately but contained only government notices. They circulated primarily among the bureaucratic elite and were of little interest to the rest of the population. Another form of newspaper, the newsprint (*hsin-wen chih*), had greater popular appeal, in part because they were written in a simple style and often carried illustrations. These however appeared only irregularly to publicise extraordinary events. In neither case did the newspapers voice political criticism, because, as with the merchants' guilds, "the press had all the advantages and disadvantages of freedom. There were no arbitrary monopolies in printing, no prior censorship, no tax, no license or even registration. Conversely, there was no positive guarantee of free press or speech." The traditional press thus reflected and reinforced the popular indifference to public affairs that the regime tried so hard to inculcate.[59]

The opening of China to Western influence in the nineteenth century did little to change this tradition of political passivity. The self-strengthening movement was characteristically a reform from above that neither required nor produced any popular involvement from below. The one departure from tradition during these years was the development of a modern press. This helped to create a public opinion where it had scarcely existed before.

Modern Chinese newspapers developed not out of the traditional gazettes and newsprints but rather out of the Western-language press that had been founded in the foreign enclaves along the China coast.[60] In 1894 three major daily English-language newspapers were being published in Hong Kong: the *China Mail* (founded in 1845), the *Daily Press* (1857), and the *Telegraph* (1881). The first Chinese-language newspapers in the colony were either spin-offs from these papers or were pioneered by Westernized Chinese. Thus, the *Sino-Foreign News* (*Chung-wai hsin-pao*) first appeared in 1857 as an insert in the *Daily Press;* the *Chinese Mail* (*Hua-tzu jih-pao*) was founded in 1872 with the help of the *China Mail;* while the *Universal Circulating Herald* (*Hsün-huan jih-pao*) was established in 1873 by two Westernized Chinese, Huang Sheng and Wang T'ao. All three of these papers were still being published at the turn of the century. In addition, at least one other daily paper, the *Kwangtung News* (*Yüeh pao*), was published in Hong Kong during this period. Founded in 1885 or 1886 by a comprador, it may not have survived into the new century.[61]

At least three daily newspapers were founded in Canton as well. The first was the *Kwang News* (*Kuang pao*), founded in 1886 by Kuang Ch'i-chao, a returned student who had studied in the United States. Supported at first by Governor-General Chang Chih-tung, it irritated his successor, Li Han-chang, and was suppressed in 1891. It then transferred ownership to a British subject and resumed publication on the foreign settlement of Shameen under a new name, the *Sino-Western Daily News* (*Chung-hsi jih-pao*). The other newspapers publishing in the early 1890's were the *Ling-nan Daily News* (*Ling-nan jih-pao*) and the *Chinese Daily News* (*Chung-hua jih-pao*). They regularly carried local and national news, official announcements and memorials, translations from the Western-language papers, as well as commercial news and advertisements. Their attitude was generally reformist. They included articles criticizing traditional shortcomings, such as the hiring of substitutes to take the civil service examinations, or explaining new developments, such as the uses of electricity. Like the traditional newsprints, they avoided direct criticism of the officials lest they be suppressed. Their daily circulation was about 5,000 copies each.[62] Hong Kong and Canton were the only two cities in the province where daily newspapers had been founded by

1894. However, these six or more papers evidently circulated through the whole province.

The founding of daily newspapers in Hong Kong and Canton indicated a stirring of interest in public affairs among the people in the two cities. But as of 1894 this interest was not accompanied by any additional involvement in the political process. (The refusal of the Chinese cargo boatmen in Hong Kong to work on French ships in September 1884, during the Sino-French war, was apparently an exception.) [63] To this extent Kwangtung society still conformed to the traditional mold. It was the shock of defeat in 1894–95 which was to break the mold and to inaugurate the long and difficult search for a new set of relationships between the people and the government.

2

The Postwar Period,
1895–1900

The defeat by Japan in the war of 1894–95 was one of the decisive events of modern Chinese history. It demonstrated the shortcomings of military "self-strengthening." It triggered the Scramble for Concessions among the foreign powers that almost destroyed China. And it shocked a number of Chinese out of their past indifference and forced them to re-evaluate their former policies and programs and to seek new ones. In a hectic half decade, self-strengthening gave way in rapid succession to radical reform, reaction, and revolution.

Kwangtung was not directly involved in the war with Japan, which took place far to the north. Its major contribution to the war effort was the dispatch of its small fleet, part of which was mauled by the Japanese navy.[1] The province, however, shared in varying degree the different consequences of the defeat.

The Menace of Imperialism

Japan's victory inaugurated the age of imperialism in China. In the postwar years the foreign powers were, simply, far more rapacious than they had ever been. Acting both separately, as in the Scramble for Concessions in 1897–98, and jointly, as in the allied expedition against the Boxers in 1900, the powers in these few years practically tore China apart in their haste to extract one concession after another from her.

Fresh from the partition of Africa, they seemed ready to do the same to China. To foreign and Chinese observers alike, the breakup of China was only a matter of time.

The postwar imperialism took many forms. In the first place, the foreigners greatly expanded their rights and privileges under the treaty system. By the 1895 Treaty of Shimonoseki, Japan acquired for them the right not only to trade and reside at the treaty ports but also to engage in manufacturing. In Kwangtung, the effect of this concession was slight, since foreign enterprises had already been well established in Hong Kong. But elsewhere it obviously handicapped those Chinese industries and handicrafts which were in competition with the foreigners. In 1896 Japan reasserted the right of foreign traders to be free of the likin (or inland transit taxes) after payment of a small commutation tax. This too gave the foreigners a decided advantage over their Chinese competitors, who were still subject to those taxes. It also cut deeply into the revenue collected from the likin, on which the provincial authorities, including Kwangtung's, had been very dependent since the days of the Taiping Rebellion.[2] A year later Britain gained the opening of additional treaty ports, including two in Kwangtung. These were Samshui, at the head of the Pearl River delta, and Kongmoon, on its western edge. Finally, in 1898 Britain secured the opening of all of China's inland waterways to foreign steamers, thus abrogating one of the crucial attributes of a sovereign nation.[3] In Kwangtung, one side effect of the opening of the West River to direct trade by foreign ships was to put many of the coolie-propelled stern-wheelers out of business and force the Chinese to adopt steam-powered launches too.[4]

Second, the postwar years saw a remarkable increase in missionary activity, epitomized in the motto of the American Student Volunteers for Foreign Missions, "The evangelization of the world in this generation." In Kwangtung, new missionary societies entered the field, while established ones expanded their operations. Almost universally they found the people less hostile than before, perhaps because China's defeat in the war with Japan had weakened the hold of the traditional cultural values upon the populace. They were able to make many more conversions. For example, the Berlin Missionary Society, which worked among the Hakkas in northeastern and eastern Kwangtung, had averaged only 50 baptisms a year from 1882 to 1894, but between 1895 and 1900 inclusive, the average number of baptisms rose sharply to 251.[5]

Third, and most menacing, the foreign powers went far beyond the commercial expansionism of earlier decades and began seizing territory. Beginning with the German occupation of Kiaochow Bay in Shantung in November 1897, they vied with one another in acquiring "leased territories" and "spheres of interest." In Kwangtung, the French, working from Vietnam, competed vigorously with the British, entrenched in Hong Kong. In April 1898 they secured a 99-year lease on Kwangchowwan, 325 square miles of territory on the east coast of the Lei-chou peninsula, which they wanted to develop into a naval and coaling station.[6] In June the British kept pace with their rivals by obtaining a similar 99-year lease on 356 square miles of territory (known as the New Territories) adjoining Hong Kong. The quantitative difference between the earlier expansionism and the postwar imperialism is obvious: the New Territories, amounting to three fifths of Hsin-an (now Pao-an) district and with a population of 100,000, enlarged the British holding at Hong Kong almost tenfold.[7]

In April 1898, when France acquired Kwangchowwan, she also secured an "assurance" from the Tsungli Yamen, the Ch'ing foreign ministry, that "China will not cede to any power all or part of the provinces bordering on Tongking," that is, Kwangtung, Kwangsi, and Yunnan. While technically the French sphere of interest included all of Kwangtung, in practice it took in only West Kwangtung. Within her sphere France was accorded preferential economic rights. Thus, she acquired the authority to build a railroad from her leasehold at Kwangchowwan across the Lei-chou peninsula to the Gulf of Tonkin. She also had preferential rights to a railroad linking the treaty port of Pakhoi with the projected line in Kwangsi from Nanning to Lung-chou near the Indochina border. She had special mining rights too in the three mainland prefectures of West Kwangtung. French influence was particularly strong in the two treaty ports of the region, Pakhoi and Hoihow, where French schools and dispensaries were established; in Pakhoi the postmaster in the newly created Imperial Post Office was a Frenchman.[8]

France was the only power to have a *formal* sphere of interest in Kwangtung. Other powers, however, had what amounted to informal spheres elsewhere in the province. Great Britain, because of Hong Kong, was unquestionably the dominant power throughout the West River basin. It was to prevent the British from acquiring a stranglehold over Central Kwangtung that the Ch'ing government in April 1898 awarded the concession for the Canton–Hankow railroad to the United States instead. Britain then obtained a promise of preferential consideration if and when a railroad from Canton to Hong Kong was built.[9] Japan, from her formal sphere of interest in Fukien, extended her influence into the Teochiu-speaking area of East Kwangtung that is contiguous to and has strong ethnolinguistic affinities with Fukien, while Germany, because of the work of its missionaries among the Hakkas, was quite influential in the East River and Mei River areas in northeastern Kwangtung.

Finally, twice during this brief period, once at the beginning and again at the end, the powers imposed outrageously heavy war indemnities upon a prostrate China. The indemnity to Japan for the war of 1894–95 amounted to 230 million Kuping taels (about US$ 166 million), to pay which China borrowed heavily abroad. The Boxer indemnity, divided among the eight powers that participated in the allied intervention of 1900, was even more burdensome, 450 million Haikwan taels (about US$ 334 million). Annual payments for these two indemnities alone totaled close to 40 million taels, or about 43 percent of Peking's annual revenue. They forced China to go chronically into debt.[10]

By the turn of the century, the foreign presence in Kwangtung was no longer confined to a few coastal ports, as it had been just five years earlier. It was practically all-pervasive. No one could escape it. The threat of foreign intervention hung over almost every decision and every act, from the holding of a "pagan" celebration that might irritate a resident foreign missionary to the carrying out of a revolution that might upset distant foreign ministries. The possibility of partition, the ultimate form of intervention, was uppermost in the minds of most concerned Chinese. The following editorial in a Canton newspaper in late 1899 reveals the apprehensive mood of the times. Observing the activities of the Russians in Manchuria, the British in the Yangtze valley, the Germans at Kiaochow, the French at Kwangchowwan and the Japanese in Fukien, the paper concluded that "the attitude of all foreigners towards China is guided by one principle; they unite their energies and combine their forces, in order to gratify their one ambition which is partition, and rob us of our country." The only hope was for China to come to her senses and bestir herself. "If she exerts herself to her full ability, she will then be able to foil the strategies of her enemies, if she will but exert herself to any extent, she can ward off, for a time at least, the actual partition." [11]

There was, however, aside from the Boxers, little organized opposition to the foreign encroachments. In Kwangtung, some of the villagers in Kwangchowwan resisted the French takeover sporadically during

1898–99. Similarly, the villagers in the New Territories, organized in local defense forces, resisted the British takeover in April 1899. In both instances, the opposition was confined to the affected area; there was no support from other parts of the province.[12]

Postwar Reforms and Reaction

The Sino-Japanese war had the same effect upon the Confucian scholar-gentry that the Sino-French war ten years earlier had had upon the Westernized Chinese: it made many of them realize the inadequacies of self-strengthening and the need for much more far-reaching reforms if China were to survive in the jungle of nations. As the war ended, a number of gentry members, both in and out of office, agitated openly and in an unprecedented manner for radical changes in some of China's basic institutions. Their suggestions, reminiscent of Ho Kai's and Cheng Kuan-ying's, included the abolition of the formalistic "eight-legged" essay from the civil service examinations and the incorporation of new, modern subjects, like foreign languages and the sciences, into the examinations; the establishment of a country-wide system of schools of Western learning; the active promotion of commercial and industrial development; and most daringly, the encouragement of greater popular participation in the political process and the gradual transformation of the Ch'ing autocracy into a constitutional monarchy similar to Meiji Japan.[13]

Unlike the self-strengthening movement, the postwar reform movement included not only reforms from above but also reforms from below, as members of the local gentry elite organized "study societies" (*hsüeh-hui*) and published newspapers and journals to discuss and publicize their ideas. In the moment of national crisis and uncertainty, they thus managed to breach the dynasty's long-standing ban on gentry associations. The movement flourished in 1897–98 in Hunan province under the auspices of its governor and in the summer of 1898 in the capital itself, where it had the support of the young idealistic emperor. It reached its climax on August 2, 1898, when "in an action without precedent in the history of the dynasty" the Kuang-hsü Emperor gave permission to all his subjects, not just officials, to communicate with the throne, thus opening the way to the politicization of the whole populace.[14] But with no power behind him, the emperor was unable to enforce his numerous reform edicts. On September 21, the entire movement, in the provinces as well as in the capital, came to an abrupt halt, as Empress Dowager

Tz'u-hsi executed a palace coup, imprisoned the emperor, and resumed her regency.

Natives of Kwangtung were extraordinarily active in the reform movement. The writings of K'ang Yu-wei, portraying Confucius as a reformer, provided the ideological justification for the movement. K'ang himself and his students from the Thatched Hut among Ten Thousand Trees, including Liang Ch'i-ch'ao, Ou Chü-chia and Hsü Ch'in, took a leading role in the various activities of the movement. They founded the Self-Strengthening Society (Ch'iang hsüeh hui) in Peking and Shanghai in 1895–96 and the Society to Preserve the Nation (Pao-kuo hui) in Peking in 1898, the two most important study societies of the period. (Twenty-seven of the 186 listed members of the Society to Preserve the Nation were natives of Kwangtung; most were probably provincial graduates in Peking in 1898 to take the triennial metropolitan examinations.) [15] Also they published the *China Progress* (*Shih-wu pao*) in Shanghai, the most influential journal of the reform movement, and taught at the School of Current Affairs (Shih-wu hsüeh-t'ang) at Changsha, the center of the movement in Hunan. Finally, they advised the emperor during the "hundred days of reform" in 1898.

In Kwangtung itself, however, there were only a few reforms from below and practically none from above. Before they were summoned to more promising fields elsewhere, K'ang Yu-wei and his followers inaugurated three reform projects in the Canton–Macao area. In 1895 K'ang renewed his attack on the custom of footbinding among women and founded the Anti-Footbinding Society (Pu-ch'an-tsu hui) in Canton. It rapidly developed into a nationwide organization, with its headquarters moved to Shanghai. This was quite a change from 1883, when a similar effort had been frustrated by popular fears that it violated the dynasty's ban on associations. [16] In February 1897, with the financial assistance of Ho Sui-t'ien, a sympathetic merchant, K'ang founded the *China Reformer* (*Chih-hsin pao*) in Macao, which appeared every ten days. Like other reformist journals of the time, it contained a mixture of political commentaries and translations from the Western and Japanese press. The first issue, typically, warned of German and French designs on China. [17] Those associated with the *China Reformer* also founded a school in Macao. [18]

Other reform organizations formed in Kwangtung at this time, evidently by people who were not affiliated with K'ang Yu-wei, included four study societies, three or four private schools, and a journal. The journal was the *Chinese Students' Review* (*Ling-hsüeh pao*), published in Canton every ten days during 1897–98. It carried translations of German, English, and Japanese articles on politics and on the arts. One of the schools was the Shih-min School (Shih-min hsüeh-t'ang), founded in Canton in the spring of 1898. Its aim, as stated in the prospectus, was to train men in subjects that would be "useful" in helping China overcome her recent "humiliations" at the hands of the imperialists, a succinct expression of the nationalism and reformism of the gentry members and merchants who took part in the postwar reforms.[19]

Unlike Hunan, the reform movement in Kwangtung did not have the support of the provincial officials. They showed no interest in K'ang Yu-wei while he was in Canton. (In contrast, the governor of Kwangsi, Shih Nien-tsu, invited him to Kweilin for several months in early 1897 to discuss his ideas.)[20] They instituted few reforms of their own. They evidently established a bureau for commercial affairs (*shang-wu chü*) in Canton to help promote commercial and industrial development in the province.[21] They expanded the curriculum of the Translators' College at Canton; in response to the changed international situation, they added Russian, Japanese, and French to its original offering of English. They added a "hall of Western studies" to the Kuang-ya Academy (Kuang-ya shu-yüan) in Canton in 1898. Lastly, the provincial director of education in 1898 incorporated modern subjects into the civil service examinations and gave them equal attention as classical subjects. Thus, at the prefectural examination at Canton the essay topics included the opening of railroads and the strategic importance of Kiaochow Bay.[22]

Despite the deluge of imperial decrees, the officials initiated no other reforms in Kwangtung. They established no new schools of Western learning. They did not reopen the Whampoa Naval and Military Officers' Academy, which had been closed down several years earlier in an economy move. They sent no students abroad. They did not modernize the provincial army, whose soldiers in 1899 were "undrilled and undisciplined, and many of them unarmed."[23] The man most responsible for the paucity of reforms in Kwangtung was T'an Chung-lin, governor-general at Canton from 1895 to 1899 (and incidentally, father of T'an Yen-k'ai, later a leading constitutionalist reformer in Hunan). In August 1898 Governor-General T'an was explicitly rebuked by the emperor for not carrying out his edicts. He was reportedly on the point of being dismissed from his post when, fortunately for him, the Empress Dowager staged her coup d'etat.[24]

The contrasting experience of Hunan and Kwangtung suggests that the attitude of the provincial officials was a crucial element in the success or failure of the postwar reforms. But equally important was the attitude of the local gentry. In Hunan, the reforms flourished only so long as the gentry supported them and withered as soon as the gentry withdrew their support. In Kwangtung, apart from K'ang Yu-wei and his group of followers, who in any case were usually active elsewhere in China, the gentry were generally indifferent to the reforms. Indeed, according to Liang Ch'i-ch'ao, merchants, not scholars, were the predominant group in the Kwangtung reform associations.[25] Despite the shock of defeat in 1894–95, most members of the scholar-gentry in the postwar years were not yet convinced that such drastic measures as K'ang Yu-wei advocated were absolutely necessary to China's survival. Many were still committed to the traditional views of Confucianism and abhorred K'ang's reinterpretations. To them, as it has been said of the gentry of Hunan, "the primary threat to China lay not with the West, but with Confucian revisionists."[26] It was to take the additional shock of 1900 finally to shake them loose from their lingering commitment to the traditional orthodoxy.

A period of reaction followed the Empress Dowager's coup d'etat. Practically all the emperor's reform decrees were countermanded, and many of the reform projects were dismantled. The ban on popular associations was reimposed, with the result that probably all the study societies in Kwangtung were closed down. Schools of Western learning that already existed, like the Shih-min School in Canton, were allowed to remain, but no new ones were founded. The *China Reformer* continued to appear because it was established in Macao, outside Chinese jurisdiction, but the *Chinese Students' Review* in Canton evidently ceased publication. The prefectural examination given at Ch'ao-chou after the coup, in contrast to the one given earlier at Canton, included the eight-legged essay once more and made the "new learning" optional rather than required. Canton also experienced a brief reign of terror, as the government hunted down friends and relatives of K'ang Yu-wei and confiscated their property. Many reformers fled to Macao for personal safety. A few leaders joined K'ang Yu-wei in exile in Japan.[27]

Nevertheless, it was during the reaction that the merchants of Canton banded together and formed the very important Seventy-two Guilds. The occasion was the visit to Canton in 1899 of the Grand Secretary Kang-i, a former governor of Kwangtung who was soon to be a leading supporter of the Boxers at court. On a tour of the southern provinces to raise funds for the imperial treasury, Kang-i asked that Kwangtung produce an additional 1.2 million taels in revenue by reorganizing the collection of the likin. Following custom, he placed the responsibility for collecting the desired increase upon the guilds of Canton. Accordingly the guilds, headed by the silk, tea, timber, and banking guilds, combined to form a "merchants-guaranteed likin bureau" to supervise the new collection system.

The guilds, however, soon found that it was impossible to realize the increased revenue that Kang-i had demanded. After five months, they abandoned the effort, with presumably the merchant "guarantors" making up the difference between the amount collected and the amount promised. The likin collection reverted to the officials. But the cooperation among the guilds that Kang-i's extortion had called into being did not end. It continued and became formalized as the Seventy-two Guilds (Ch'i-shih-erh hang). (There were actually more than seventy-two guilds in the association; "seventy-two" is a generic designation.) It marked a major effort by the merchants of Canton to overcome the barriers that traditionally had separated guild from guild and to develop a comprehensive city-wide association of merchants.[28] A similar coordinating body known as the Nine Charitable Halls (Chiu shan-t'ang) also developed among the merchant-controlled charitable halls of Canton. Meanwhile, in Hong Kong, leading Chinese merchants, headed by compradors like Robert Ho Tung and Feng Hua-ch'uan, founded the Chinese Chamber of Commerce (Hua-shang kung-chü) during this same half decade.[29]

The reaction led ultimately to the court's embrace of the Boxers in 1900 and its declaration of war on June 21 against the nations whose troops were then advancing on Peking. The Boxer Rebellion, however, was localized in north China; the declaration of war was ignored in south China. Consequently, Kwangtung was little troubled by these events. About fifteen chapels in the province were destroyed. Over one hundred Chinese Christian families were driven from their homes; "for months it was not safe for them to meet for public worship," but no one was killed.[30]

In the short run, of course, the postwar reform movement in Kwangtung had been almost uniformly unsuccessful. Moreover, even at its height, it was geographically restricted, with Canton and Macao as the twin centers of activities while the rest of the province was almost completely unaffected. Nevertheless, the movement, if only momentarily, had challenged the dynasty's monopoly of the political process. For the first time in the Ch'ing period, the scholars and merchants had organized in public associations, published their views, and openly agitated on political issues, in the earnest belief that reforms of an unprecedented nature were needed to deal with the unprecedented crisis confronting China. Despite the obvious setbacks, the net effect of the reform movement was a slight increase in the level of public awareness as measured by the growth of the press. Between 1895 and 1900, the number of daily newspapers in Canton rose by one, from three to four, though in 1898 it may have been as high as five or six. In Hong Kong, the three major established dailies, the *Chinese Mail,* the *Universal Circulating Herald,* and the *Sino-Foreign News,* were still being published, as well as perhaps two or three new ones.[31] However, the rest of the province still lacked their own newspapers.

Revolutionary Efforts

The inability of the Ch'ing government to cope with its many problems, in particular the paramount threat of partition by the foreign powers, produced the first serious challenge to the regime since the Taiping Rebellion. As a result of the successive humiliations in 1895 and 1900, erstwhile reformers among both the Westernized Chinese and the scholar-gentry despaired of the possibility of peaceful change and turned to revolution. Kwangtung was a center of revolutionary activities in both these years.

While Japan's defeat of China in 1894–95 galvanized many members of the scholar-gentry to initiate radical reforms, its effect upon the Westernized Chinese was more far-reaching. Many of these Westernized Chinese, like Ho Kai, had already been committed to radical reforms before the war. The war, to them, proved the futility of mere reformism and the necessity for more drastic measures. The reaction of Wu T'ingfang, who was Ho Kai's brother-in-law and a member of Li Hungchang's secretariat, typified their frustrations. In July 1895 Wu complained openly to the British consul in Tientsin that there was no longer any hope that China could reform herself and called on the foreign powers to "unite and force China to reform." When reminded that foreign intervention would lead to China's extinction as an independent nation, Wu replied in utter despair, "I do not care. Anything is better than this. I would rather see China a second India than that she should go on as she is, disgraced, powerless and with no hope of amendment." [32]

It was in such a mood that a group of Westernized Chinese in Hong Kong joined the Society to Restore China's Prosperity (Hsing-Chung hui) for the explicit purpose of overthrowing the Ch'ing regime. The society had been founded by Sun Yat-sen in November 1894 among the overseas Chinese in Honolulu, Hawaii. The Hong Kong branch of the society was formed in February 1895, after Sun's return to China, with about a dozen members. Others in the branch, besides Sun, were Yang Ch'ü-yün, Hsieh Tsan-t'ai (Tse Tsan Tai), Cheng Shih-liang, Ch'en Shao-pai, Lu Hao-tung, and Huang Yung-shang. All were young; at age 35, Yang Ch'ü-yün was the oldest of the group. All had received a Western education, usually in a missionary school or in one of the Anglo-Chinese colleges in Hong Kong. All were engaged in modern, Western lines of work. All were Christians. Except perhaps for Ch'en Shao-pai, who came from a lower gentry family but himself had studied at Canton Christian College and the Hong Kong College of Medicine, none was a part of the Confucian gentry-dominated mainstream of Chinese society. All, in short, were Westernized Chinese in the mold of Ho Kai. [33]

Indeed, like Ho, several of them had espoused political reformism before the war of 1894–95. Thus, Yang Ch'ü-yün and Hsieh Tsan-t'ai were leading members of the Fu-jen Literary Society (Fu-jen wen-she) an informal political study group formed in Hong Kong in 1892. Sun Yat-sen himself had been a reformist before the war. Early in 1894 he and his boyhood friend Lu Hao-tung had gone north to Tientsin to present a reformist petition to Governor-General Li Hung-chang. Only after his failure to secure an interview with Li did Sun turn to revolution. Almost certainly what motivated the others to join him in making revolution was the frustration and anxiety voiced by Wu T'ing-fang on the occasion of China's defeat. Even Ho Kai approved of the switch from reformism to revolution, though he personally did not become a member of the society, nor, it should be added, did Wu T'ing-fang. [34]

Publicly, the Society to Restore China's Prosperity resembled the score or more of reformist study societies that were organized in different parts of the country in the wake of the Sino-Japanese war. The preamble of the society's regulations thus spoke of the imminent threat of partition and deplored China's debility: "China has become increasingly weak. . . . Now powerful neighbors encircle us, glaring like tigers and

staring like falcons . . . We have already seen the result of earlier prece-
dents—to be dismembered . . . Our descendants may become the
slaves of other races! China can only be restored by assembling men of
determination." Its published aim was to achieve the traditional "wealth
and power" by means of such reforms as founding of newspapers, establishment of schools, and promotion of industry. The real aims of the
society, however, were expressed in the secret oath that each member
was required to swear: "Expel the barbarians [that is, the Machus],
revive China, and establish a republic." [35]

Once it was formed, the society in Hong Kong set to work making
preparations for a revolt in Canton.[36] Its strategy was to launch a coordinated armed attack on the provincial capital from several directions with
the hope of capturing various governmental offices and killing the officials. Since the society had no more than fifty enrolled members in the
Hong Kong–Canton area, the actual fighting was left to members of
secret societies and bandit gangs hired for the purpose (at a price of ten
dollars a month a head).[37] The society itself was to provide the overall
direction. It was responsible for recruiting the fighters, buying arms,
raising money, and getting foreign support. Huang Yung-shang personally contributed HK$8,000 to the society to pay for the men and the
arms, while Ho Kai, working behind the scene, used his influence to get
the backing of the foreign community in Hong Kong. The leading
English-language dailies, the *China Mail* and the *Telegraph,* whose editors had learned of the plot from Ho Kai, voiced their support and took
pains to explain to their readers that the revolutionaries, unlike the
Manchus, were not hostile to foreigners. Thus, as early as March 12,
Thomas Reid of the *China Mail,* in the condescending tone typical of
the foreign treaty-port press, wrote, "What they desire . . . although it
seems impossible to realize any such feelings amongst a body of China-
men, is a constitutional upheaval, to rid their country of the iniquitous
system of misrule which has shut out China from Western influences,
Western trade, and Western civilization." [38]

Several months later preparations were well enough along to set the
uprising for October 26, the day of the Ch'ung-yang grave-sweeping festival, when a large-scale movement of men into Canton would be least
likely to arouse official suspicion. Responsibility for the revolt was divided between Sun Yat-sen in Canton and Yang Ch'ü-yün in Hong
Kong. The final plans called for Yang to dispatch his group of hired
fighters on the twenty-fifth aboard the evening ferry to Canton. The

ferry would arrive the next morning in time for Yang's men to rendez-vous with the group of fighters whom Sun had recruited in Canton. The two groups would then enter the city and attack the government offices together.

Unfortunately, Yang Ch'ü-yün was unable to keep to the schedule. In the early morning of October 26, when Sun Yat-sen had already rounded up his men in Canton, Yang notified Sun that his group would arrive from Hong Kong two days late! Sun hurriedly decided not to risk the delay and possible discovery. He disbanded his own men and wired Yang to postpone sending the Hong Kong contingent indefinitely. However, perhaps because it was a weekend, the telegram did not reach Yang until after he had already sent the four hundred fighters. In the meantime, Hong Kong officials had discovered the conspiracy and no-tified the Canton government. As a result, when the ferry arrived at Canton on the morning of the twenty-eighth, Yang's men were greeted at dockside by the local authorities. In the ensuing confusion, most of the men escaped, but about fifty were arrested. The plot had been foiled without a single shot having been fired.

As the officials hunted down the conspirators in Canton, Sun Yat-sen eluded arrest and escaped to Hong Kong. His friend Lu Hao-tung, how-ever, was caught as he was destroying the society's membership list. Because he was a Christian, the American Presbyterian mission in Can-ton, through the American consulate, interceded on his behalf and vouched for his character.[39] But Lu was defiant in captivity. He succes-sively denounced the Manchus for their corruption and despotism, the Ch'ing officials for their greed and ineptness, and the foreigners for their plots against China. On November 7, 1895, ten days after his arrest, Lu Hao-tung was beheaded and became the revolution's first martyr.

The suppression of the 1895 plot broke up the Society to Restore China's Prosperity in Hong Kong. Most of its leaders were banished from the colony for varying periods of years. Sun Yat-sen, Cheng Shih-liang, and Ch'en Shao-pai all fled to Japan, while Yang Ch'ü-yün went to Southeast Asia. When Huang Yung-shang died two years later, the only leading member of the society left in Hong Kong was Hsieh Tsan-t'ai. During the years of the scholar-gentry's radical reform movement, 1895–98, the revolutionary society was virtually nonexistent in Hong Kong.

A new revolutionary opportunity, however, began to develop late in 1898. The Empress Dowager's termination of the postwar reform move-

ment plunged many politically concerned Chinese into deep despair.
Speaking for what they themselves called the "Anglicized Chinese" of
Hong Kong, the Legislative Councillors Ho Kai and Wei Yuk (Wei Yü)
in January 1899 deplored China's weakness in terms that were almost
identical to Wu T'ing-fang's in 1895: "We would prefer to see China
partitioned at once, and good government introduced by the dividing
Powers. National death is preferable to national dishonor, corruption,
and degeneration." [40] The gentry reformers were no less frustrated by
the court's reactionary policies than the Westernized Chinese. Both
groups, working separately, attempted a revolution in 1900, while the
court was preoccupied with the Boxer Rebellion and the allied intervention.

As the political situation within China deteriorated once more in the
autumn of 1899, Sun Yat-sen reactivated his revolutionary organization
in Hong Kong. Mindful of the emphasis that the gentry reformers had
placed on journalism, he sent Ch'en Shao-pai back to Hong Kong to
found a newspaper that would serve as the organ of his movement. In
January 1900 the *China Daily News* (*Chung-kuo jih-pao*) began publication. According to its "program" that appeared in an early issue, China
was in "an utterly corrupt condition." The paper put the entire blame
on the Manchus and demanded a "complete change." It called specifically for the preservation of China's territorial integrity and the establishment of a "Constitutional government which would place the leg-
islation of the country entirely in the hands of the people." It appealed
for British support in carrying out these changes. [41]

The Boxer Rebellion and the subsequent foreign intervention completed the revival of Sun Yat-sen's revolutionary movement in
Kwangtung. It developed in a strangely roundabout way. [42] As the
Boxers took control of the area around Peking in the spring of 1900 and
Empress Dowager Tz'u-hsi threw her support behind their antiforeign
activities, the gentry and merchants of Canton were fearful that the
foreign powers would intervene militarily in south China as they were
beginning to do in north China. To prevent an extension of the rebellion
into their region and so forestall further intervention, they proposed to
their governor-general, Li Hung-chang, that he declare Kwangtung and
Kwangsi independent of the court. With the court apparently on the
verge of extinction, the once powerful Li, who had replaced T'an Chung-
lin in January 1900, may have harbored imperial ambitions for himself,
for he expressed an interest in the proposal. The gentry and merchants

next got in touch with Sun Yat-sen, evidently on the assumption that if there were to be any disturbance in the region he would be the cause of it, since Sun had become a revolutionary of international renown after the celebrated kidnapping attempt in London. Acccordingly, the metropolitan graduate Liu Hsüeh-hsün, who was both an adviser to the governor-general and a fellow townsman and acquaintance of Sun Yat-sen, wrote to Sun in Japan, inviting him to come to Canton to discuss the scheme.

Upon receipt of this unexpected communication from Liu Hsüeh-hsün, Sun left Japan immediately and arrived in Hong Kong on June 17. He did not, however, go to Canton. Fearing a trap, he sent Miyazaki Torazō and two other Japanese friends to negotiate with Liu, while he himself sailed on to Singapore to await their report. The negotiations at first were inconclusive. Li Hung-chang refused to commit himself to an irrevocable course, especially since the court had once again turned to him for help in reaching a settlement with the foreign powers. In the end, after a month of procrastination, he ignored the pleas of the Canton gentry and merchants and accepted the summons from court. He left Canton on July 17. But before leaving, Li had joined with the Wuchang and Nanking governors-general in refusing to recognize the validity of the court's June twenty-first declaration of war on the powers. He had thus removed the threat of foreign intervention in his two provinces and so calmed the fears of the local gentry and merchants without the drastic recourse to outright independence.

Sun Yat-sen returned to Hong Kong from Singapore just as Li Hung-chang was leaving for the north. As prospects of an independent Kwangtung and Kwangsi under Li vanished, Sun turned to plans for a new attempt at a revolutionary uprising in Kwangtung. On July 17 Sun, who was still barred from landing at Hong Kong, met aboard his ship with other members of the Society to Restore China's Prosperity to develop strategy. Attending the meeting were old associates like Yang Ch'ü-yün, Hsieh Tsan-t'ai, Ch'en Shao-pai, Cheng Shih-liang, Teng Yin-nan, and two new recruits, Li Chi-t'ang and Shih Chien-ju. Afterwards Sun sailed back to Japan to arrange for supplies.

The strategy for the revolt was similar to the 1895 plot.[43] It called for several uprisings in the lower East River area of Kwangtung intended to draw government troops away from Canton, followed by a concentrated assault upon the capital city. As before, the society would arrange for and lead the uprisings, while bandits and secret society members were to do the actual fighting. Because he was a native of the East River area and a member of the Triad Society, Cheng Shih-liang was put in charge of the initial risings, while Teng Yin-nan, one of Sun Yat-sen's original followers in Honolulu, was responsible for the operations in Canton. The new recruit Li Chi-t'ang, son of a wealthy Hong Kong merchant, contributed HK$20,000 to finance the effort. Ho Kai came forward once more to appeal for British support for the revolution. As in 1895, most of the leaders of the revolt were Westernized Chinese. Thus, nearly half of the 33 members of the Society to Restore China's Prosperity newly enrolled in 1900 in Hong Kong and Canton are definitely identifiable as Christians.[44]

Soon after the strategy sessions with Sun, Cheng Shih-liang began recruiting a band of fighters in his native Kuei-shan (now Hui-yang) district. His base was at San-chou-t'ien, five miles from the coast and less than ten miles from the British-held New Territories, thus easily accessible to outside help. It was an area notorious for pirates, salt smugglers, and other outlaws. By the end of the summer, Cheng had assembled a force of six hundred men, mostly members of the Triad Society, ready to rise up at any time. All they lacked was adequate arms and ammunition, which Sun was expecting to get from his Japanese friends. They also held back to give Teng Yin-nan time to make his preparations at Canton.[45]

As Cheng's men waited with growing impatience for Sun and Teng, they were forced into a premature uprising. Their activities at San-chou-t'ien had aroused the suspicions of nearby officials, who closed in upon them for a check. On October 6, without instruction from Cheng Shih-liang, who was in Hong Kong awaiting word from Sun, the rebels struck back at the intruders and routed them. Following their initial victory, the rebels proceeded north toward Hui-chou city, the prefectural capital, perhaps with the intention of making their way to Canton. During the next ten days, they won most of the skirmishes with the government troops, capturing much needed arms and attracting adherents. The populace generally received them well. When they arrived on October 12 at Shang-yang-wei, the people welcomed them warmly; five or six hundred of the villagers left to go with them the next day. When they ambushed a government force and captured the assistant district magistrate on the fifteenth at P'ing-t'an, a few miles from Hui-chou city, over a thousand men from nearby villages joined in the ambush.[46]

Meanwhile, Sun Yat-sen had scrapped the original plans for the revolt. At almost the same moment that the San-chou-t'ien rebels began the uprising, Sun received word from his friends that the Japanese colonial government on Taiwan, which was looking for an excuse to establish a foothold in Amoy, would be willing to arm his rebels if they could make their way to that Fukienese city. He immediately advised Cheng Shih-liang in Hong Kong to disregard Canton, at least for the while, and to head for Fukien. When Cheng reached his men with Sun's directive, they had already fought their way to the outskirts of Hui-chou city.

On October 17 the rebels, now grown to about ten thousand men, moved away from Hui-chou and head up a tributary of the East River toward Hai-feng and ultimately Amoy. As they moved eastward, they scored several more victories over the government troops. But on the twentieth a battalion of government soldiers under the command of Captain Wu Hsiang-ta caught up with the rebel force and defeated it. Three days later, Cheng Shih-liang received a further message from Sun Yat-sen in Taiwan with the unhappy news that he could expect no aid from the Japanese at Amoy after all. Realizing the futility of further fighting, Cheng ordered his men to disband and make their separate way home. The revolt had lasted two and a half weeks.

In Canton, the premature uprising in Hui-chou had caught Teng Yin-nan unawares. Originally he had intended to lead an armed assault upon the capital city, but with the revolt already underway there was no time to complete the elaborate preparations. At most there was time enough to create a diversion and relieve the military pressure on the Hui-chou rebels. Shih Chien-ju, who came from an upper scholar-gentry family but who himself attended Canton Christian College, volunteered to assassinate the provincial governor, Te-shou.[47] (Te-shou was a Manchu, but he was picked as the target for no other reason than because he was the highest ranking official in Canton following the departure of Governor-General Li Hung-chang in July.) When Teng and Shih had smuggled the necessary dynamite from Hong Kong into Canton and prepared it, the Hui-chou revolt was already coming to an end. Shih Chien-ju nevertheless went ahead with his plans. On October 28 he succeeded in exploding a crude bomb along one wall of the governor's official compound. Six people were killed and several others were wounded, but Te-shou himself was unharmed. Unable to flee at once because the foreign-staffed Maritime Customs did not allow the Hong

Kong ferries to operate on Sundays,[48] Shih was spotted in Canton the next day and arrested. Teng, however, escaped. Once more, as in the case of Lu Hao-tung in 1895, the American consulate intervened at the request of the Presbyterian mission to try to save the life of the accused revolutionary.[49] It was once again unavailing. On November 9 Shih Chien-ju was beheaded.

The crisis of confidence in 1899–1900, on which the Society to Restore China's Prosperity had capitalized with such striking success in Kwangtung, produced another revolutionary organization, the Society to Protect the Emperor (Pao-huang hui), which K'ang Yu-wei founded in July 1899 among the overseas Chinese in British Columbia, Canada.[50] Like Sun Yat-sen's society, K'ang's society was composed primarily of frustrated reformers, but they were typically gentry members with a classical Confucian education rather than Westernized Chinese. The leaders of the society were essentially the same men who had initiated and led the postwar reform movement. When their movement was cut short in September 1898 and they had been forced to flee China, they turned to revolution. The aims of their society were less sweeping than those of the Society to Restore China's Prosperity. They did not call for the overthrow of the dynastic regime and the establishment of a republic. They aimed only to topple the government of the usurping Empress Dowager, to restore to power the captive emperor, and to resume the postwar radical reforms leading ultimately to a constitutional monarchy. During the court's reactionary tack in 1899 and 1900, the achievement of even such a moderate program required a revolution. As Liang Ch'i-ch'ao declared during these years, the aims of the society were "emperor-protection in name, revolution in fact." [51]

The Society to Protect the Emperor, like the postwar reform movement from which it sprang, included many natives of Kwangtung but was only tangentially active in Kwangtung. It maintained a branch office in Macao, though its headquarters were in Japan. The Macao branch of the society was headed by Ho Sui-t'ien, the wealthy merchant who two years earlier had founded the *China Reformer* as the organ of the reform movement in Kwangtung. Members of the society in Macao founded two schools and continued to publish the *China Reformer*.[52]

The society's main revolutionary effort, the T'ang Ts'ai-ch'ang revolt, occurred a couple of months before Sun Yat-sen's Hui-chou uprising. With the revolt supposed to take place along the Yangtze valley, there were few preparations in Kwangtung. In Chia-ying, in East

Kwangtung, the rebels were in contact with Hsieh I-ch'iao, a young Hakka from a wealthy family with overseas connections. Hsieh was to use his influence to form a local defense force which would support the revolt once it broke out. Nothing, however, came of this, since T'ang Ts'ai-ch'ang's revolt was crushed before it got very far.[53]

Probably the major contribution of the Society to Protect the Emperor to the revolutionary movement in Kwangtung was its publication of the *New Kwangtung* (*Hsin Kuang-tung*), by Ou Chü-chia. A native of Kuei-shan district, Ou was a student and follower of K'ang Yu-wei. During the postwar reform movement, he had taught at the School of Current Affairs in Hunan. After the Empress Dowager's coup, he had fled with K'ang to Japan, where he assisted Liang Ch'i-ch'ao with the publication of the *China Discussion* (*Ch'ing-i pao*). In 1900 he went to San Francisco and edited a Chinese-language newspaper there. It was in the San Francisco paper that the *New Kwangtung* first appeared, probably in 1901, as a series of articles; in 1902 it was reprinted as a pamphlet by Liang Ch'i-ch'ao's press in Yokohama.[54] It was only one of numerous revolutionary tracts published at this time. The ideas that it expressed were by no means original or unique. It was, however, addressed directly at the natives of Kwangtung and spoke of conditions in their province.[55]

The starting point for Ou Chü-chia, as for others, was the imminent partition of China. In Kwangtung itself, the foreigners had successively seized Hong Kong and Macao, Kwangchowwan and the New Territories. Yet, Ou lamented, the people of Kwangtung, particularly the wealthy merchants, had shown no concern. When residents of Kwang-chowwan and the New Territories resisted the foreign takeover in 1899, the rich people, thinking to ingratiate themselves with the new rulers, had stood aside and given the resisters no help. They had shown no awareness that their future as individuals was inextricably bound up with the future of their nation. They ignored the fate of the Jews: though they were the wealthiest people on earth, the Jews were hounded wherever they went precisely because they had no homeland of their own.

The ultimate responsibility for the plight of the Chinese, however, lay not with themselves but with their Manchu rulers. Because the Manchus were foreigners in China, they had no qualms about sacrificing the interests of their Chinese subjects in order to preserve their own position as rulers. They preferred to turn China over to their foreign "friends" than to see the Chinese take the land back for themselves. Moreover, the

Manchus had deliberately kept the Chinese people passive and docile. They had made government the private preserve of the court rather than the public responsibility of all the citizens. This was why the Chinese people had been incapable of defending themselves against the foreign imperialists.

Therefore, the Manchu court must be overthrown and China become autonomous. The court itself, Ou insisted, had broken the bonds that tied it to its subjects. As a nation-state China was equivalent to a large joint-stock company. The four hundred million citizens, in whom the sovereignty of China resided, were the shareholders; the Manchu court was only the management. When the management of a company failed to look after the interests of its shareholders, or worse yet, when it betrayed their interests, ought the shareholders remain silent and do nothing? Ought they not replace the management?

But how could the Ch'ing be overthrown, particularly when the court by its policies had ensured that the Chinese people were politically apathetic and lacking in national consciousness? In the first place, Ou proposed to offset the underdeveloped sense of nationalism by appealing to the long-standing resentment in Kwangtung toward external control. Kwangtung, he insisted, belonged to the people of Kwangtung. Kwangtung ought therefore to be autonomous (*tzu-li*). (Provincial autonomy seems to have been an idea that was in the air at this time. The Canton gentry and merchants had urged it upon Li Hung-chang in 1900; similarly, Liang Ch'i-ch'ao had recommended it to the governor of Hunan in 1897.) [56] Once Kwangtung or any other province had seceded from the Ch'ing empire and declared itself autonomous, the other provinces would necessarily follow suit. In this way, the Ch'ing could be overthrown. Afterwards, the secessionist provinces could come together to reconstitute the Chinese nation as a confederation along the lines of the United States of America.

In addition, Ou proposed a massive educational effort to overcome the political passivity of the people. It included the establishment of newspapers and private schools, preferably in the relative freedom of Hong Kong. These would instill in the people the ideal of provincial autonomy and prepare the way for Kwangtung's secession. He also proposed that the revolutionaries ally themselves with the secret societies, like the Triads. He recognized that the Triads' anti-Manchu pro-Ming stance was essentially ritualistic, but he thought that it was possible to "reawaken" them to their anti-Manchu heritage.

Finally, was a struggle for national independence at all possible within a colonial or semi-colonial situation? If there were a revolution in China, would not the foreign powers intervene to protect their interests? This was the key question. All that Ou could offer in reply was the hope that if domestic order were maintained during the revolution and if the foreign powers were not provoked, then intervention might be avoided.

K'ang Yu-wei's Society to Protect the Emperor and Sun Yat-sen's Society to Restore China's Prosperity were alike in at least three important respects. Both were revolutionary organizations, founded for the purpose of overthrowing either the Empress Dowager's government or else the whole dynastic regime. Both were composed primarily of frustrated reformers who took to revolution as a last resort. And both were composed largely of natives of Kwangtung.

Beyond these similarities, however, the two organizations were quite different. Each drew its leading personnel from a different segment of society. Sun's followers were mainly Westernized, foreign-educated Chinese; K'ang's were traditional classically educated gentry members. Sun's followers were usually Christians; K'ang's were Confucians. K'ang himself had nothing but disdain for Sun's following. Thus, the Great Harmony School (Ta-t'ung hsüeh-hsiao) in Yokohama, run by his disciple Hsü Ch'in, required its pupils to kneel before the portrait of Confucius and pointedly excluded Christians.[57] K'ang's contemptuous attitude toward Sun Yat-sen spoiled a promising effort in 1899 to work out a united front between the two groups against the Ch'ing.[58]

Moreover, the two societies differed over the question of priorities. Both agreed that China's two enemies were the aggressive foreign powers and the reactionary Ch'ing court. But which of the two was the greater foe? For Sun's group it unquestionably was the Manchu court. In order to "expel the barbarians," they actively sought the assistance of the foreigners, British colonials in Hong Kong in 1895 and 1900 and Japanese adventurers as well in 1900, even at the cost of sacrificing a certain amount of Chinese sovereignty. For K'ang's group, on the other hand, the greater threat was the external threat, the threat of foreign intervention and partition. It is significant that nowhere in the *New Kwangtung* did Ou Chü-chia speak of foreign assistance as a means to China's salvation. The Chinese themselves had to make their own revolution.

3

Early Years of the Post-Boxer Decade

In 1900 China and her Manchu rulers relived the crisis of 1860. The capital was in the hands of the foreigners; the court was in exile; and the southern provinces were out of control. As before, the only hope of salvation for the dynasty was a complete change of policy in order to ward off further foreign encroachments and to recapture the loyalty of its subjects. The result in the 1860's was the T'ung-chih Restoration. The result in the 1900's was the post-Boxer reform movement. Its achievements have been obscured by the republican revolution, but in the course of a decade the movement produced a fundamental transformation of Chinese society.[1]

During its first years, from 1901 to the middle of 1905, both the intentions and the accomplishments of the reform program were rather limited. Its consequences, however, were far reaching. One was a marked increase in popular involvement in governmental affairs. Another was a deflation of the revolutionary threat and a new lease on life for the Manchus. Yet another, perhaps tangential, consequence was an abatement of imperialist pressures on China.

Inauguration of the Post-Boxer Reforms

As Empress Dowager Tz'u-hsi and the Manchu court languished in exile at Sian, it was obvious to them that their recent reactionary policies were bankrupt. In the grips of a revolutionary situation, they had to change, and change quickly, if they were to survive. So in 1901 the Empress Dowager, through the emperor whom she still held captive, issued a host of decrees promising radical reforms in a wide variety of fields. In a remarkable turnabout, she revived many ideas of the postwar gentry reformers whom she had driven from power in 1898. Accordingly, the schools and the civil service examination system were reorganized. The army was modernized. Chambers of commerce were introduced.

In Kwangtung, the reform movement benefited greatly from the leadership of its two governors-general, T'ao Mo (February 1901 to September 1902) and Ts'en Ch'un-hsüan (April 1903 to September 1906), both of whom were, in contrast to T'an Chung-lin in 1898, reformers. Of the two, Ts'en was particularly active. A native of Kwangsi, his appointment as governor-general was a rare exception to the rule of avoidance: evidently he was regarded as the official best qualified to deal with the long-smouldering secret society rebellion in his home province. Despite earlier associations with two of K'ang Yu-wei's reformist organizations, Ts'en was nevertheless a protégé of the Empress Dowager, to whom he owed his rapid rise to power after the Boxer Rebellion.[2]

Educational reform was the most urgent task facing the post-Boxer government. There was growing agreement that China's weakness in the world stemmed from a shortage of men trained in the modern Western learning. Therefore the court began at once to establish schools to teach the new subjects. The difficulty was how to relate the new learning to the civil service recruitment system, for in China education had always been oriented toward a career in government. The court at first hoped to be able simply to incorporate the new learning into the civil service examinations alongside the traditional subjects, but it found out eventually that this was not feasible. In the end, it was forced to disestablish Confucianism and to support the Western learning exclusively.

The court's educational reforms went through three phases. In the first phase, the court in August and September 1901 ordered the creation of a country-wide hierarchy of Japanese-style schools (hsüeh-t'ang) teaching modern as well as classical subjects. It directed local officials to convert old-style academies (shu-yüan) into new schools. Academies located in the provincial capitals were to become universities (ta hsüeh-t'ang); those in prefectural seats, middle schools (chung hsüeh-t'ang); and those in departmental and district cities, primary schools (hsiao hsüeh-

t'ang). It also approved the sending of students abroad for study. Finally, it incorporated current affairs and Western subjects into the civil service examinations. These were all ideas resurrected from the 1898 reform movement. Their effect was to reduce but by no means eliminate the Confucian content in the examinations. Confucian learning was still essential for entry into the civil service; Western learning was only an adjunct to it. Nevertheless, the monopoly that the Confucian classics had enjoyed in the educational system for about a thousand years had been abolished.[3]

In Kwangtung, under the auspices of Governor-General T'ao Mo, new schools were founded in compliance with the imperial regulations. In Canton the Kuang-ya Academy was converted in June 1902 into Kwangtung University, offering a variety of modern subjects, such as English, mathematics, physics, agriculture and mining, map drawing, and physical drills, as well as such traditional subjects as the classics, history, government, and geography. It had 150 to 200 students drawn from Kwangtung and Kwangsi.[4] Also in Canton, the Yüeh-hua Academy was converted into the Kuang-chou Prefectural Middle School. It opened in April 1903 with 120 students. It is unclear whether the officially prescribed middle schools were established in the other prefectural capitals. In Swatow, however, a group of Hakka scholar-gentry members on their own initiative organized the T'ung-wen School in 1901, a middle school utilizing "new European methods" of teaching.[5] At the district level, apparently few primary schools were founded. Even in Nan-hai district, which included the western half of Canton city, only one modern school was organized in 1902, and three in 1903.[6] The educational reforms were clearly off to a slow start, especially at the local level.

There were two reasons for the hesitant beginning. One was a lack of personnel qualified to teach the new subjects. The demand far exceeded the supply. As one English-language paper commented sardonically, "Almost anyone with a smattering of English and a little acquaintance with Western books can get a rich man to pay him a good salary and fit up a school." [7] As a short-term solution to the problem, Governor-General T'ao in 1902 sent a group of about twenty students to the Kōbun Institute (Kōbun gakuin) in Tokyo for an accelerated six-month course in teachers' education. They were the first large group of Kwangtung students to go to Japan to study, as only a few private scholars had gone previously.[8] Some members of the provincial gentry also helped alleviate the teacher shortage. Two metropolitan graduates, Ting Jen-chang and Wu Tao-jung, founded the Chiao-chung Normal School in Canton in 1902. But since only three middle schools—the Shih-min School in Canton, founded in 1898, the Swatow T'ung-wen School and the Canton Prefectural Middle School—were turning out graduates at this time, the Chiao-chung Normal School discovered that qualified students were in almost as short supply as qualified teachers.[9] The other and more important reason for the slow progress in educational reform was the court's ambiguous support for the new learning.

In the second phase, the court in January 1904, after prodding by some of its officials, issued a set of detailed "regulations for the schools." The new regulations slightly modified the organization of the school system. They provided for the establishment of primary schools in all departmental and district cities, middle schools in prefectural seats, "higher schools" (kao-teng hsüeh-t'ang) rather than universities in the provincial capitals, and an imperial university in the national capital. They also provided for a variety of "specialized schools" (chuan-men hsüeh-t'ang), like vocational, normal, and professional schools, which were equivalent to higher schools. More important, the court at this time drastically revised the relationship between the new learning and civil service recruitment. Instead of simply adding modern subjects onto the Confucian-based examinations, it made the new schools a separate and independent part of the examination system. Thus, students who passed the school examinations were to be awarded the same degrees as the classically educated scholars who passed the traditional examinations. Specifically, graduates of the "higher primary schools" (kao-teng hsiao hsüeh-t'ang) were to be given the degree of licentiate; graduates of middle schools, senior licentiate; graduates of the higher schools, provincial graduate; finally, graduates of the Imperial University, metropolitan graduate. Similar provisions applied to graduates of schools and universities abroad, but not missionary institutions within China. While the court had not completely abandoned its support of the traditional learning, it now accorded the new learning equal official recognition.[10]

In Kwangtung, the Commission for Educational Affairs (Hsüeh-wu ch'u), which Governor-General Ts'en Ch'un-hsüan created late in 1903,[11] had to overcome two obstacles in responding to the new imperial decrees in support of the modern schools. One was inertia and inexperience on the part of the local officials and gentry. It therefore directed each district magistrate to set up an office of educational affairs (hsüeh-wu kung-so), to be staffed by members of the local elite, to take charge of establishing and administering the new schools within his jurisdiction. In addition, it organized in August 1904 a four-month "training course for school officials" and urged each district to send one to three gentry members who were "qualified to administer schools" to attend the course in Canton. About 160 gentry members enrolled in the course, which included practical training at an attached primary school. Graduates of the course were expected to return to their native district and supervise the opening of new schools.[12]

The other obstacle was the continuing shortage of teachers. The Commission for Educational Affairs, also in August 1904, established in Canton a normal institute with a six-month course to train primary school teachers in the new subjects; the course had 60 students. Early in 1905 it followed up the work of the institute with a larger, more rigorous training program lasting about a year and a half; it had 240 students. The Canton Prefectural Middle School also organized a one-year course in 1904 to educate primary school teachers who would work in the outlying districts of Kuang-chou prefecture.[13] To prepare teachers for the middle and higher schools, the commission encouraged students to go to Japan for the advanced training then unavailable in China. Early in 1904, the Kwangtung government sent 56 young men of gentry background to Tokyo for two years of study in law and administration.[14] This was the second group of government scholars to go to Japan. Others continued to go as private students. By 1905 the number of Chinese students in Japan had increased from only about a hundred in 1900 to about eight thousand. At least several hundred were from Kwangtung, many of them preparing for teaching careers.[15]

As a result of these intensive efforts to train school administrators and teachers, the opening of modern schools during 1904 and early 1905 increased significantly in terms both of number and of geographical spread. In Nan-hai district, for example, where four new schools were established during 1902 and 1903, seven more primary schools were opened in 1904 and another nine in 1905. In P'an-yü district, in which the other half of Canton city is located, four primary schools were founded in 1904; eleven in 1905. In Shun-te, the wealthy and populous silk-producing district in the Pearl River delta, the first two new-style primary schools were established in 1904; three more opened in 1905. During 1904 and 1905, the first modern schools appeared in K'ai-p'ing, Ch'ih-hsi, Lo-ting, and Lung-men also.[16]

However, despite the acceleration, progress was still slow. Many districts in Kwangtung still had not opened a modern school by 1905, while most districts with a modern school probably had but one. Moreover, practically no new middle or higher school seems to have been founded during these years. Meanwhile, in conformity with the court's reorganization of the school system, Kwangtung University was downgraded and renamed as the Kwangtung Higher School.[17] The lack of qualified personnel continued to hold back the pace of educational reforms. The various short-term courses in teacher training had barely begun to produce their graduates. The court's lingering attachment to the traditional examinations also created doubts among both the old literati and the new students about its commitment to the modern schools.[18] To ensure the success of the schools the court was, in a later third phase, forced to do away with the old examination system completely.

One immediate consequence of the educational reforms was to make it possible for youths of gentry background who were interested in Western learning to pursue their interests without necessarily alienating themselves, as Ch'en Shao-pai and Shih Chien-ju had, from the mainstream of Chinese life. They checked the growth of the Westernized Chinese as a significant, if marginal, group in Chinese society. At the same time, they produced a new and increasingly important group, the "new gentry," degree-holders with a modern education.

In addition to the reorganization of the school system, the benefits of education were extended to two previously disadvantaged groups in Kwangtung. One group was the Tanka or boat people. In 1904 the River Police Inspector (Ho-po-ssu) at Canton directed the local boat people to establish their own primary school to prepare them for higher schooling. By so doing he hoped that "in the future they would be able to erase their classification as 'boat people' and achieve equality with the rest of the population."[19]

The other group was women. Early in this period women in Canton founded at least two schools for themselves, the Yü-hsien Girls' School and the Kwangtung Girls' School. The organizers were Chang Chu-chün and Tu Ch'ing-ch'ih respectively, both among China's pioneer feminists. Chang Chu-chün was especially outspoken and was known as "the female Liang Ch'i-ch'ao," though as a missionary-educated medical doctor she was more accurately the feminine counterpart of a Westernized Chinese like Ho Kai.[20] Later, in 1904, Governor-General Ts'en Ch'un-hsüan ordered the Commission for Educational Affairs to consider extending public education to women. He noted that this was done in "civilized nations." The commission tentatively approved the suggestion, but no school was established right away.[21] These were the beginnings of women's education in Kwangtung outside the missionary schools.

Military modernization was hardly any less urgent than educational reforms. Whereas the self-strengthening movement had concentrated on such technological innovations as shipyards and arsenals, the post-Boxer reforms in the military sphere went beyond that to institutional innovation. In August and September 1901, at the same time that it issued its first educational decrees, the court called for an extensive reorganization of the army. Specifically, it abolished the antiquated system of military examinations and replaced it with a nationwide system of military academies. It also created new military formations to replace the traditional armies. As with the educational reforms, the model for the military reforms was Japan.[22]

In Kwangtung, after the abolition of the military examinations, two modern military academies were organized in accordance with the court's decree. In 1902 Governor-General T'ao Mo founded the Military Preparatory School (Wu-pei hsüeh-t'ang) at Whampoa, probably at the site of the defunct Naval and Military Officers' Academy. The school graduated its first class, from an accelerated two-year course, in October 1904. Of its 110 graduates, the 20 best were sent to Japan for further study, some to the Army Officers' School (Rikugun shikan gakkō). Other graduates were sent to train with the government troops fighting the Kwangsi rebellion. The school's regular course was five years. Early in 1905 it had about 180 students.[23]

In 1904 Governor-General Ts'en Ch'un-hsüan founded a second school, the Military Officers' School (Chiang-pien hsüeh-t'ang) in Canton. It offered a two-year course to update the training of existing officers and noncommissioned officers. When the British military attaché saw the school at the beginning of 1906, it had 180 students, 60 in infantry and 40 each in engineering, artillery, and transport. The staff included four Japanese instructors, one for each branch, and five Japanese-trained Chinese officers.[24] In addition to the two military schools, the naval school that had been at Whampoa originally as a part of the Naval and Military Officers' Academy evidently was revived during this period. It had about 60 students in 1904. The naval installation at Whampoa also included a torpedo school.[25]

The reorganization of the army, the second aspect of the military reforms, began with Governor-General Ts'en in 1904. The armies then in existence were the Manchu and Chinese bannermen, the Army of the Green Standard, and the braves. In spite of the reforms attempted during the self-strengthening period, most of these armies were still poorly armed, poorly trained, and poorly led; according to foreign observers, they were generally useless. The bannermen, descendants of the force that conquered China for the Ch'ing dynasty in the seventeenth century, were garrisoned within the walls of Canton city in their own separate neighborhood known as the Tartar Quarter. They numbered about 50,000, of whom two thirds were Han Chinese and one third Manchu. Since they were dependent on government allowances and were prohibited from engaging in other remunerative occupations, most of them lived in near poverty. The bannermen fighting force, composed of adult males, numbered somewhere between 7,500 and 15,000 men. Commanded by the Tartar-general, their principal function was to guard the gates and walls of the capital city. In 1906 many were still armed with antique gingals that required two men to fire.[26]

The Army of the Green Standard (Lü-ying), originally the Chinese auxiliary of the conquering bannermen, was not concentrated in one spot, as the bannermen were, but was scattered in small units across the province. There were 104 companies (tui) of the army in Kwangtung, but because of repeated slashes in their quota strength after the Taiping Rebellion, each company had hardly more than a hundred men. They were under the command of the provincial commander-in-chief in Hui-chou city and seven brigade-generals stationed in different parts of the province. According to the British military attaché in 1907, these troops were "absolutely untrained and often armed with tridents." They were generally used as a local constabulary against bandits in their districts.[27]

The braves (yung) were developed in the course of the Taiping Rebellion in order to make up for the ineffectiveness of the banners and the Army of the Green Standard. As the ranks of the Army of the Green Standard were successively pruned in the interests of economy in the last part of the nineteenth century, the more capable among the demobilized soldiers were recruited for the braves. The braves soon became the principal military force in Kwangtung. Their table of organization is unclear, but they were stationed across the province.

In September 1901 the court had called for a further weeding out of the Army of the Green Standard and for the creation of a new, Western-style standing army (*ch'ang-pei chün*) and a supporting reserve force (*hsü-pei chün*). Evidently in accordance with this decree, Governor-General Ts'en Ch'un-hsüan proposed in the spring of 1904 that the Army of the Green Standard in Kwangtung be completely disbanded by July 1904 and that with the savings thus achieved the existing braves be reorganized as the projected standing army and reserves. The central government, however, was apprehensive lest the immediate demobilization of the Army of the Green Standard increase the endemic banditry within the province or strengthen the rebellion in neighboring Kwangsi. Ts'en's proposal was denied. In the end he had to be content with a 70 percent demobilization beginning in October 1905.[28]

Meanwhile, Ts'en had gone ahead with reorganizing the braves into the standing army. The new army consisted of 83 battalions (*ying*), totaling about 24,000 men. They were divided into five detachments covering the whole province, with at least one company stationed in each district city and important market town. They functioned primarily as a local constabulary, much like the Army of the Green Standard which they were intended to replace.[29]

As for the Kwangtung fleet, little or nothing was done to modernize it in this period. It continued to be primarily a river patrol force. But even against the river pirates, it was relatively ineffective, as both Chinese and foreign traders frequently had reason to complain.

Apart from the educational and military reforms, the court also sanctioned the formation of chambers of commerce (*shang-hui*). Spokesmen for merchant interests, like Cheng Kuan-ying, had long pressed for greater cooperation among the merchants than was possible within the existing framework of guilds and *hui-kuan*. The provincial bureaus for commercial affairs created during the 1898 reforms did not represent the merchants, while representative merchant associations like the Seventy-two Guilds of Canton lacked official standing. In 1902 Sheng Hsüan-huai, who was then the imperial commissioner for negotiating commercial treaties, impressed upon the court the important economic role that chambers of commerce played in the West and in Japan. As a result, the court in January 1904 issued an edict officially approving the formation of such private merchants' associations in the provincial capitals and important commercial cities.[30] In Kwangtung the merchants of Canton began in the middle of 1904 to hold discussions among themselves and with the provincial officials, but they did not complete their arrangements for the formation of the Kwangtung Chamber of Commerce until a year later, in July 1905.[31]

Several other official reforms were inaugurated during these years. In December 1902 the court ordered each province to organize a police force on the Japanese model. In Kwangtung a Central Police Bureau (Hsün-ching tsung-chü) was established in Canton in January 1903 and the police began to patrol the city the following March. Local police offices were organized in some of the outlying districts of the province too.[32] Reviving another recommendation of the 1898 reformers, the court abolished a number of sinecures and redundant positions in order to reduce costs and simplify administration. Among the posts abolished in 1904 and 1905 were the superintendency of the Canton Customs (Yüeh hai-kuan chien-tu), otherwise known as the Hoppo, and the governorship of Kwangtung, both of whose duties were entrusted to the Canton governor-general.[33] Finally, the Imperial Post Office, the adjunct to the foreign-staffed Maritime Customs that was created in 1896, began to extend its services outward from the treaty ports to the hinterland.[34]

The era also witnessed the introduction of electric power and steam locomotion in Kwangtung. In 1903 electric lighting and a telephone system were installed in Canton.[35] In 1904 the American China Development Company, owner of the Canton–Hankow railroad concession, completed a 32-mile branch line from Canton to Samshui by way of Foshan in the populous Pearl River delta.[36] In the same year, a Chinese company headed by Chang Yü-nan, a wealthy overseas Hakka businessman, began work on a 24-mile line between Ch'ao-chou and Swatow, with Japanese technical and financial assistance.[37]

In sum, the initial post-Boxer reforms were limited achievements. Though they far exceeded the narrow limitations of the self-strengthening movement, they fell short of the constitutional monarchy that the postwar gentry reformers had proposed. But unlike the 1898 reforms, these were in fact implemented. Moreover, they were only a beginning.

Imperialism and Nationalism

Contrary to widespread expectations in 1900, China escaped dismemberment. Partly because of the court's sharp change of policy and partly because of rivalry among the powers, China was not carved up. Nevertheless, as a cumulative consequence of earlier encroachments, the foreign presence in China was more pervasive than ever. Moreover, the threat of partition, while no longer imminent, had by no means disappeared. In response to the continuing menace of imperialism, a sense of nationalism developed among both the ruler and the ruled in China. Nationalism in turn encouraged greater popular involvement in domestic politics.

During the early years of the post-Boxer decade, the foreign threat to China remained acute. It was especially so in Manchuria, where Russian troops sent to quell the Boxer Rebellion stayed on in virtual occupation of the region until they were defeated by Japan in the war of 1904–05. Elsewhere in China, the powers enjoyed the fruits of the treaty system and their recent Scramble for Concessions.

In Kwangtung, except for the grant in 1902 to a Portuguese syndicate of the right to build a railroad from Macao to Fo-shan to link up with the American-owned Canton–Samshui line (which was never taken up),[38] the foreign powers acquired no new concessions. Even so, they were more entrenched in the province than ever before. Commercially, through the three territorial cessions, the six treaty ports, the right of inland navigation, and the railroad and mining concessions, the entire province lay open to foreign exploitation. Militarily, the foreigners were out in force. In October 1901, following the Boxer troubles, twenty-nine warships from six different nations, Britain, France, the United States, Portugal, Germany, and Holland, were stationed in Kwangtung waters: twenty-one at Hong Kong, four at Canton, two on the West River, and two at Swatow.[39] Indicative of the expansion of imperialist activities in the province at this time, new foreign post offices were established, in competition with the recently organized Chinese Imperial Post. Until 1900 only the British had maintained their own postal service in Kwangtung, with stations at Hong Kong, Canton, Swatow, and Hoihow. But between 1900 and 1906 the French, Germans, and Japanese each established their own service. All had an office in Canton; in addition, the French had offices at Kwangchowwan, Hoihow, and Pakhoi, within their sphere of interest in West Kwangtung, while the Germans and Japanese had offices at Swatow to collect mail from East Kwangtung where both were influential.[40] Similarly, the foreign population at Canton jumped from about 300 or 350 in 1899 to 1,200 in 1905.[41]

Aroused by the martyrdom of hundreds of Christians during the Boxer Rebellion and encouraged by the new reformist climate of opinion in China, the missionaries too expanded their activities. They now had "a greater opportunity to imprint their message upon its people than they had had in all the centuries of their presence in the Empire." In Kwangtung new denominations of different nationalities, including the United Brethren in Christ and Seventh Day Adventists from the United States and Presbyterians from Canada and New Zealand, began work, while established ones sent additional workers. For example, the American Presbyterians sent 18 new missionaries during 1901–05, a larger number than in any previous five-year period. Moroever, receptivity to the foreign teachings continued to grow. Thus at the Berlin Mission among the Hakkas, the annual number of baptisms, which had risen from an average of 50 during 1882–94 to 251 during 1895–1900, rose sharply again during 1901–05 to 977. Similarly, in the "Four Districts" of Hsin-hui, Hsin-ning, K'ai-p'ing, and En-p'ing on the edge of the Pearl River delta, the American Presbyterians opened 13 new churches during 1901–05, which more than doubled the number of churches they had founded in all of the preceding twenty years. Catholic missionary activities increased as well. In 1905 the Society of Foreign Missions of Paris, working with a staff of 69 foreign and 15 Chinese priests, reported a total of 54,000 adherents in Kwangtung (exclusive of Hong Kong and Macao), which almost doubled the 30,500 adherents reported for 1890.[42] In addition to the Christian missionaries, Buddhist missionaries from Japan also began to proselytize in the Canton and Swatow areas.[43]

Finally, the foreigners made their presence felt no less painfully, if indirectly, through the war indemnities, which in Kwangtung amounted to 720,000 taels a year. Payment of the indemnities necessitated higher taxes throughout the province. Levied mostly on consumer goods in daily use, such as salt, tobacco, and wine, these taxes aroused much opposition and an occasional riot.[44]

Confronted by the overwhelming presence of the foreign powers, the Ch'ing court no longer tried, as it had in earlier decades, to ignore them or, alternately, to eject them by force. Instead, it adopted a policy of nationalism similar to that advocated by the gentry reformers in the late 1890's. Its central concern now was to defend China's "sovereignty" as it was understood in the modern West, to resist further encroachments upon her rights as a nation and to recover the rights previously lost through neglect or weakness.[45] Thus, the court reduced foreign interference in China's new educational system when it refused to accord official recognition to the missionary schools in the country and disqualified their graduates for the civil service degrees.[46] It also encouraged the recovery through diplomatic means of the railroad and mining concessions granted under duress in the Scramble for Concessions. Its greatest success here was the redemption of the Canton–Hankow railroad concession in 1905.[47] Similarly, the court in 1904 refused to renew the Chinese Exclusion Treaty with the United States, which denied Chinese laborers the right of entry into America; it sought, though without success, to negotiate a less discriminatory treaty.

The court's new sense of nationalism motivated some of its reforms. The chambers of commerce were in part devised, as the court's edict of 1904 made clear, to resist the West's economic aggression against China. Specifically, by promoting greater cooperation among Chinese merchants, the chambers might reverse the decline in China's traditional exports, tea and silk. At the same time, by encouraging the domestic production of goods that were in daily use, they would reduce China's dependence upon imports and thus minimize the foreign influence over the Chinese economy.[48] The new schools, including the military schools, were intended to provide China with the modern expertise necessary to challenge the West and Japan on their own grounds, while the new standing army would provide the national defense that China so obviously lacked.

Spurred by imperialism from without and by radical reforms from above, the people too became nationalistic; in the process, they were also politicized. The reform movement of the late 1890's had involved primarily members of the scholar-gentry. The emerging nationalist movement after 1900 began to involve merchants and students as well. This was most apparent in Shanghai and among the Chinese students in Japan. In Shanghai, in the spring of 1903, the gentry, merchants, and students organized two mass demonstrations to protest infringements of China's sovereignty. One was occasioned by rumors of an agreement in which the governor of Kwangsi allegedly promised railroad and mining concessions to the French in Indochina in return for financial and military help in putting down the rebellion in Kwangsi. The other was caused by the retention of Russian troops in Manchuria beyond the scheduled date of withdrawal. These were the first demonstrations of nationalism in China to involve a broad spectrum of people.[49] The growing number of Chinese students in Japan also displayed a strong sense of nationalism. They published a number of journals and other writings with nationalist themes, one of which was Ou Chü-chia's *New Kwangtung*. They organized demonstrations too. In the spring of 1901, a handful of Kwangtung students in Tokyo joined with several hundred overseas Chinese in Yokohama to form the Kwangtung Independence Association (Kuang-tung tu-li hsieh-hui) to oppose the rumored cession of Kwangtung to the French. In 1903 another group of Chinese students in Tokyo formed a student volunteer army and offered to go and expel the Russians from Manchuria.[50]

In Kwangtung the nationalist movement developed more slowly. During the Manchurian crisis in the spring of 1903, which aroused such emotion in Shanghai and Tokyo, a group of gentry members met in Canton on May 18 and dispatched a telegram to Peking promising help to force Russia out of Manchuria.[51] Late in 1904 the gentry of Canton, joined by some merchants, played a slightly more active role in the redemption of the Canton–Hankow railroad concession. The concession had been let out to the American China Development Company with a proviso prohibiting its American owners from transferring their rights to citizens of any other nation. When the owners of the company defied the prohibition and sold over half of their shares to a group of Belgians, the Wuchang governor-general Chang Chih-tung initiated a campaign to have the company's concession canceled for violation of contract. Encouraged by the officials, several hundred gentry members and merchants in Canton, led by two provincial graduates Liang Ch'ing-kuei and Li Kuo-lien, met a number of times in October 1904 to debate the question. They criticized the Americans for transferring the company to Belgian control and accused the Peking government heatedly of "indifference in the matter" and of "relinquishing its authority and partitioning the country without the slightest emotion of any kind." They proposed to raise the necessary funds to buy back the concession by means of a special lottery and savings bond. However, when the concession was finally redeemed in September 1905 for a sum of US$6,750,000, it was largely financed by a loan from the Hong Kong government contracted by Chang Chih-tung.[52]

Moreover, in the campaign to redeem the Canton–Hankow railroad concession, it was the officials, particularly Chang Chih-tung, who played the leading role, while the gentry and merchants were only the supporting cast. (This was also the case in Shantung, where the initial efforts to curb the German sphere of interest were almost exclusively the work of the provincial officials.)[53] When the comprador Ho Ts'ai-yen was shoved into Shameen Creek by a group of American sailors and drowned in September 1904, the popular reaction was similarly reserved. The Canton newspapers complained about the U.S. government's hesitation to go along with the findings of a Sino-American court of inquiry and pay the victim's family a small indemnity: "Whenever foreigners have been killed, a tremendous ado is made . . . Indeed even parcels of China have been sliced off. But now when a lot of drunken American sailors deliberately drown a Chinese gentleman, little is made of it." The papers deplored China's weakness and inability to "secure the rights she is entitled to." But there was no other organized response to the incident.[54] Furthermore, what there was of a nationalist movement was limited to Canton; the rest of the province was not yet affected by it.

Nevertheless, popular interest in public affairs increased significantly during these years, as measured by the development of the press. In Canton the number of daily newspapers doubled from four in 1902 to eight in 1905. The most influential ones were the *Cultural Daily News* (*An-ya jih-pao*), the *Canton Daily News* (*Yang-ch'eng jih-pao*), and the *Ling-hai Daily News* (*Ling-hai jih-pao*); their circulation in 1906 was between 3,000 and 4,000 copies each.[55] Equally important, newspapers were being published in other parts of the province. In Swatow the *East Kwangtung Daily News* (*Ling-tung jih-pao*), evidently the port's first, was founded sometime during 1902–04; its circulation in 1906 was 1,500 copies. In Kiungchow, on Hainan island, the taotai published a daily government gazette from January 1902 to August 1903; its circulation was 3,000 copies. In Pakhoi the Kieler Mission published a weekly paper, the *East-West News* (*Tung-hsi hsin-wen*), which was affiliated with one of the Chinese-language newspapers in Hong Kong and reproduced its leading articles. It lasted from March 1903 to March 1906, with a peak circulation of 1,800 copies. In Fo-shan, a weekly miscellany was being published early in 1905. Of course, in addition to the newspapers published in Kwangtung, the Hong Kong papers continued to circulate in the province.[56] Moreover, to make the newspapers readily available and also to foster the habit of newspaper reading, public reading rooms were established by public-spirited individuals and organizations. By the end of the decade, they were a common feature of many cities and towns in the province.[57]

Finally, a women's movement emerged in Kwangtung during these years. In addition to the two girls' schools founded by Chang Chu-chün and Tu Ch'ing-ch'ih, a group of twenty women in Canton, including Tu, set up in 1904 a book and newspaper reading room for the use of their own sex.[58] Perhaps the best indicator of the growing emancipation of China's women from their traditional bondage was the rapid progress of the anti-footbinding movement. A custom which went back a thousand years to the Sung period, footbinding had come under increasing criticism toward the end of the nineteenth century from Chinese reformers and foreign missionaries as a barbaric practice. K'ang Yu-wei's Anti-Footbinding Society had been a prominent feature of the postwar reform movement. In 1902 the court, picking up yet another idea from the gentry reformers, issued an edict condemning footbinding. (Since Manchu women did not bind their feet, this was perhaps an easy decision. The Manchu court had a much more difficult time later on deciding what to do about one of its own customs, the wearing of the queue.) As a result of the edict and the preceding agitation, the number of women with unbound, natural feet rose sharply among those born in the 1900–04 period, at least according to statistics gathered in Ting Hsien, Chihli. Specifically, 18.5 percent of the women born between 1900 and 1904 had natural feet, as against only 5.7 percent of those born during the previous decade and a mere 0.8 percent of those born before 1890; these were women who ordinarily would have had their feet bound between 1903 and 1907. There are no such statistics for the women of Kwangtung, but their experience was probably comparable.[59]

Thus, by the middle of 1905, the people of Kwangtung of both sexes had begun to stir from their traditional social and political passivity. Across the province there was a growing interest in public affairs, while in Canton, among the gentry, merchants, and students, there was beginning to be a more active involvement in those affairs. But like the reforms of the period, it was only a start.

The Revolutionary Movement

From its peak of activity in 1900 the revolutionary movement slowly subsided. Previously, the movement had drawn much of its support from reformers who in the dark days of 1895 and 1900 had doubted that the Ch'ing regime could be changed without the use of violence. In desperation they had espoused revolution. Now, as the Ch'ing turned its back on its reactionary past and began to demonstrate a willingness to reform itself, they no longer saw revolution as the only answer to China's ills. Many of them, including both scholar-gentry members and Westernized Chinese, drifted back into the reformist fold. Thus, the revolutionary movement in Kwangtung throughout these years was relatively subdued. After their remarkable outburst in 1900, Sun Yat-sen's followers settled down to less violent activities, with an emphasis on newspaper work and propaganda. They took no part in either of the two revolutionary attempts within the province during this period. However, just as the old revolutionary threat began to ebb, a new one appeared on the horizon.

As in the aftermath of the 1895 attempt, the revolutionary organization that Sun Yat-sen had built up in Hong Kong for the Canton–Huichou revolt in 1900 practically disintegrated afterwards. Yang Ch'ü-yün, next to Sun in importance in the Society to Restore China's Prosperity, was murdered in the colony in January 1901 by agents of the Kwangtung government. Cheng Shih-liang, organizer of the Hui-chou uprising, died several months later under mysterious circumstances. Most of the other leaders were in exile. Sun himself was in Japan, where he was relatively inactive.[60] Of Sun's associates who remained in Hong Kong, the most active was Ch'en Shao-pai, editor of the *China Daily News*. In the spring of 1901 he was joined by Cheng Kuan-i (also known as Cheng Kuan-kung), who had come from Japan at Sun's request to help with the editing of the paper. From 1901 to 1905 the twin centers of Sun's revolutionary movement in Hong Kong were Ch'en Shao-pai and Cheng Kuan-i; the major activity was their newspaper work.[61]

During the time that Ch'en and Cheng worked together on the *China Daily News* in 1901, the paper hit hard at corruption in the Kwangtung government and was widely read for its political exposés. When the reform-minded T'ao Mo was governor-general in Canton, his office alone subscribed to 200 copies of the paper. Because of Cheng Kuan-i's radical ideas and his flamboyant personality—he styled himself the "Chinese Moses"—the *China Daily News* also won a wide following among the youth of Hong Kong and Canton. But Cheng was a hard man to get along with. After less than a year's collaboration, he and Ch'en parted company. Thereafter, each went his separate way, although both remained personally loyal to Sun Yat-sen.[62]

After their split, Ch'en Shao-pai continued to edit the *China Daily News*. But the paper was in frequent financial trouble. Its emphasis on political news was not popular with the merchants, while Cheng's departure from the paper cost it its following among the young. In the end, the paper was dependent on the generosity and concern of Li Chi-t'ang, the merchant who had helped to finance the Canton–Hui-chou revolt, to make good its deficits. Cheng Kuan-i, after leaving the *China Daily News*, founded his own newspaper. In the winter of 1903–04, with the financial support of a group of Chinese Christians in Hong Kong, he established the *Commonweal* (*Shih-chieh kung-i pao*). But after less than a year, he resigned from this paper as well, in protest against editorial restraints by his backers. In the spring of 1905, he founded the *Kwangtung Daily News* (*Kuang-tung jih-pao*).[63] However, both Ch'en Shao-pai and Cheng Kuan-i were of course prevented by British press regulations from openly preaching revolution. It is doubtful that if the *China Daily News* had sounded particularly revolutionary at this time, T'ao Mo and Ts'en Ch'un-hsüan would have subscribed to it so liberally and allowed it to circulate freely within Kwangtung.

While Sun's lieutenants concentrated on newspaper work, other revolutionaries not so closely associated with him tried a more direct approach. Between 1901 and 1905, there were two revolutionary attempts in Kwangtung, one in Canton and one in Ch'ao-chou. Both were abortive.

The attempt at Canton, planned for January 1903, originated with Hsieh Tsan-t'ai, one of the founding members of the Society to Restore China's Prosperity in Hong Kong. He began to plot the revolt in 1901, perhaps as a means of avenging the murder of his friend Yang Ch'ü-yün by the Canton authorities. Through his family's Triad connections, Hsieh became acquainted with Hung Ch'üan-fu, a putative nephew of the Taiping leader Hung Hsiu-ch'üan and himself a veteran of the mid-century rebellion, who agreed to recruit a force of secret society members large enough to seize Canton. The financial support for the revolt came once again from the merchant Li Chi-t'ang. Although Li apparently gave his promise of support as early as September 1901, Hung Ch'üan-fu unaccountably took more than a year to complete his preparations.[64]

The revolt was finally scheduled for the early morning of January 29, 1903, New Year's Day, when every official in Canton would be in attendance at the Emperor's Temple (Wan-shou kung) to offer good wishes to the emperor and the Empress Dowager in the coming year. Hsieh and Hung planned to wipe out all the officials present with one swift bombardment of the temple. There would also be simultaneous uprisings outside the city, presumably by secret society mercenaries, who would secure the capital for the revolutionaries. The aims of the revolt, according to Hsieh's English-language memoir, were to overthrow the Ch'ing and establish a "Commonwealth Government under a 'Protector.' " The Chinese-language proclamations prepared for the revolt, however, stated the aims differently. They announced the creation of the "Great Ming Heavenly Kingdom" (Ta-Ming shun-t'ien kuo), a name that evoked the anti-Manchu associations of both the Ming dynasty and the Heavenly Kingdom of the Taipings.[65] Unfortunately for the conspirators, on January 25, four days before the scheduled uprising, officials in Hong Kong and Canton discovered their activities, raided their headquarters in both cities, and foiled their plot.[66]

This revolutionary attempt in 1903 followed closely the basic formula that Sun Yat-sen had used in 1895 and 1900.[67] It was led by Westernized Chinese. Aside from Hsieh Tsan-t'ai, one of Hung Ch'üan-fu's principal assistants, Li chih-sheng, was an associate of the Berlin Mission in Canton; moreover, Hsieh's choice as the Cromwellian "Protector" was Yung Wing, the pioneer Westernized Chinese. The revolt depended upon secret society mercenaries, recruited by the Triad leader Hung Ch'üan-fu, to do the actual fighting. It aimed at a putsch in Canton supported by uprisings in the countryside outside the city. It counted on the support of the foreign treaty-port press. Once more the editors of the Hong Kong *Daily Press* and the *China Mail* offered to cooperate, as did apparently G. E. Morrison, the China correspondent of the London *Times*. Finally, the revolt ended again with foreign consular intervention on behalf of the arrested rebels. In this case, the German consulate offered protection for the converts of the Berlin Mission and the comprador of a German firm.[68] All that was different in 1903 from 1895 and 1900 was the absence of Sun Yat-sen. Both Sun and his Hong Kong agent, Ch'en Shao-pai, were aware of Hsieh's plot, but they took no part in it.[69]

The other revolutionary attempt in Kwangtung during this period occurred in Ch'ao-chou, in East Kwangtung, in 1905; it was the first outside the Canton–Hong Kong–Macao triangle. It was planned and organized by Hsü Hsüeh-ch'iu, the son of a wealthy Teochiu merchant in Singapore. While in Singapore, Hsü had been converted to the anti-Ch'ing cause by an itinerant Fukienese revolutionary. In the autumn of 1904 he returned to China with the intention of starting a revolution in his native Ch'ao-chou. Capitalizing upon his membership in the local elite, formalized by the official rank of taotai that he had purchased, Hsü secured permission from the local officials to form a self-defense force of four hundred men. He also recruited several hundred secret society members, whom he arranged to assign to the construction gangs working on the Ch'ao-chou–Swatow railroad. These two groups were to be the main fighting force in the uprising. However, sometime before the scheduled outbreak, which had been tentatively set for April 19, 1905, the local officials learned of the plot and put a stop to it. They arrested some of the conspirators but allowed Hsü to escape because of his standing in the community. Hsü returned to Singapore to raise new funds and to plot again. He was later to link up with Sun Yat-sen.[70]

While some in Kwangtung struggled to keep the revolutionary movement alive, many drifted away. The most serious defection involved the entire Society to Protect the Emperor, which abandoned the way of revolutionary violence after its one attempt at it in 1900. As the Ch'ing began to implement its reforms, which were nearly identical to the program that K'ang Yu-wei and other gentry reformers had advocated in the late 1890's, the society gradually shifted its stance from opposition to conditional support. As before, it agitated for the establishment of a constitutional monarchy in China, but now it saw the possibility of this change coming about without resort to violence.[71] In Kwangtung its major activity, after the demise of the *China Reformer* in Macao sometime before the end of 1901, was the publication of the *Commercial News* (*Shang pao*) in Hong Kong beginning early in 1904. Edited by Hsü Ch'in and Wu Hsien-tzu, its daily circulation in 1905 was 5,000 copies.[72]

Others left the revolutionary movement individually, including some who had been associated with Sun Yat-sen since the beginning of his revolutionary career. After the failure of the 1903 uprising, Hsieh Tsant'ai devoted his time to the publication of the *South China Morning Post,* the English-language daily newspaper in Hong Kong which he helped found. He played no further part in the movement.[73] Teng Yin-nan, who had taken part in the 1895 and 1900 attempts, and Li Chi-t'ang, who had dissipated most of his inherited wealth in support of the 1900 and 1903 revolts and the *China Daily News,* each retired to a farm in Hong Kong. Although both later joined the Revolutionary Alliance, neither was very active in the movement after 1903.[74] Ho Kai, who was never formally a member of the Society to Revive China's Prosperity, apparently stopped lending his support to revolutionary activities just about this time too.

In the meantime, while Sun Yat-sen's group disintegrated organizationally and K'ang Yu-wei's lapsed back into reformism, a new group of revolutionaries was emerging from among the growing number of radical, nationalist youths attending the new modern schools within China or studying in Japan. Like the two older groups, they were impelled to revolution because they despaired of reform, but more so than the others they were concerned about the ability of the Ch'ing to meet the on-going foreign threat to China and dubious about its reforms in view of their hesitant and limited beginnings. In terms of social background and ideology, they stood close to the scholar-gentry of the Society to Protect the Emperor during its brief revolutionary phase, but they had refused to go along with their intellectual mentor Liang Ch'i-ch'ao when he returned to the reformist camp in 1903. They had little in common with Sun's group of Westernized Chinese and conditional nationalists. Many of them had been politicized and radicalized during the 1903 Manchurian controversy. Their centers of activity were Shanghai and Tokyo, which were also the centers of the anti-Russian agitation. They were not active in Kwangtung, where radicalism and nationalism had not developed very extensively. The student revolutionaries, however, suffered from disorganization and lack of leadership. They were as yet no serious threat to the Ch'ing.[75]

4

Middle Years of the Post-Boxer Decade, I: Reform

The middle years of the post-Boxer decade, from mid-1905 to the end of 1907 or the beginning of 1908, were the years of China's breakthrough into the modern age. In September 1905 the court abolished the traditional civil service examinations; it thereby eliminated one of the central institutions of Confucian China and knocked out the ideological underpinning of the old society. A year later it proclaimed its adherence to the principles of constitutionalism; in so doing, it promised an early end to the old autocratic system and conceded to the people a considerably enlarged role in the political process. These two actions together spelled the end of the old society and the emergence of the new.

The shape of the future politics was already apparent in these years. When the post-Boxer reforms were inaugurated in 1901, they had come almost entirely as reforms from above. However, one of the consequences of these initial reforms was to increase popular involvement in public affairs, as the anti-Russian agitation in Shanghai in 1903 had intimated. The trend became unmistakable in the nationwide anti-American boycott in 1905–06. Increasingly, the court found that it could no longer act without taking into account organized political pressures from below. The reforms that it newly decreed in this period, the anti-opium campaign and the constitutional program, were in a small but significant way initiated from below.

Imperialism created no new problems for China during these years, though it remained an all-pervasive threat to China's integrity. Where possible, the court pursued its rights recovery campaign, but it was limited by its weaknesses in what it was able to accomplish. Meanwhile, popular nationalism developed into an independent movement of its own. The victory of Japan over Russia in 1904–05, hailed by nationalists all over Asia, gave additional impetus to those who argued that domestic reform was ultimately China's best defense against foreign pressures.

In Kwangtung the old and the new reforms were put into effect by its three governors-general of the period, Ts'en Ch'un-hsüan (to September 1906), Chou Fu (November 1906 to July 1907), and Chang Jen-chün (September 1907 to July 1909), all of them reformers.[1] During these years, the people of Kwangtung, particularly the urban elite, became involved in the political process to an unprecedented extent.

Progress of the Established Reforms

By mid-1905, the court had established the main outline of its program for the modern schools, the new army, and the chambers of commerce. In the case of the schools and the army, it subsequently made some significant changes, but these were modifications of existing policy, not new departures. By mid-1905 also, although the reforms had been enunciated, they had scarcely been implemented with thoroughness. It was during these middle years of the post-Boxer decade that, in Kwangtung, the modern schools were founded in any large number, the new army took shape, and the chambers of commerce were established.

In education, the court's regulations of 1904 had specified the creation of a hierarchy of new, Japanese-style schools, ranging from primary schools in all district cities to the Imperial University in Peking. These regulations also had provided for the incorporation of the modern schools into the civil service recruitment system, thus enabling the graduates of the schools to acquire the coveted civil service degrees. But they had not done away entirely with the traditional Confucian-based examinations, which were allowed to coexist with the schools. This cautiousness on the part of the court was grounds for persisting doubts about its ultimate intentions regarding the traditional examinations and the new schools. Therefore, the court on September 2, 1905, decreed the immediate and complete discontinuance of the traditional examinations. Beginning in 1906 civil service degrees were to be awarded only to students who had passed their school examinations. The schools thus acquired the monopoly on the access to office and power that the traditional examinations had previously enjoyed.[2] As a result there was a rapid expansion of the new school system after 1905.

In Kwangtung the provincial authorities continued in various ways to prod the local officials and gentry to overcome their conservatism and inertia and found new schools. Governor-General Ts'en Ch'un-hsüan, in the second half of 1905, directed each district in the province to send several members of the local elite to Japan to study the educational system there. Shun-te and Yang-chiang accordingly each sent six men, while K'ai-p'ing and Kao-yao each sent one.[3] At about the same time, the provincial Commission for Educational Affairs dispatched a number of officials to various districts, especially those in the interior of the province, to supervise the starting of new schools and to ensure that the government funds previously allotted to the old-style academies were being diverted as required to the use of the new schools.[4] As a result of such efforts, by 1907 sixty-one districts, or two thirds of the districts in the province, had established an office for the encouragement of education (ch'üan-hsüeh so). Formerly called the office of educational affairs, this was the official body responsible for setting up schools and supervising their operation in each district.[5]

After 1905 the new schools proliferated. In Kwangtung progress was especially noteworthy at the level of the higher schools and the primary schools. Four special-purpose colleges were founded in Canton in 1906 and 1907 to complement the work of the previously established Kwangtung Higher School. The largest and most important was the Kwangtung College of Law and Administration (Fa-cheng hsüeh-t'ang), offering a two-year program in law, administration, and finance for students interested in a career in government. Its teaching staff came from the group of 56 youths that the provincial government sent to Japan for two years of study in 1904. The college had 804 students in 1907. The other higher-level schools were the Kwangtung–Kwangsi College of Languages (Fang-yen hsüeh-t'ang), formed out of the Translators' College of the self-strengthening period, which offered courses in English, German, French, and Japanese and prepared students to serve as translators or to go abroad for study or to teach in middle schools; the Kwangtung–Kwangsi Normal School (Shih-fan hsüeh-t'ang), reorganized in March 1908 as the Higher Normal School (Yu-chi shih-fan hsüeh-t'ang), which trained teachers for lower normal schools (*ch'u-chi shih-fan hsüeh-t'ang*) and middle schools; and finally, the Kwangtung–Kwangsi Higher Industrial School (Kao-teng kung-yeh hsüeh-t'ang), which taught such subjects as machinery and industrial chemistry.[6]

Relatively few middle schools were founded, although they were obligatory in prefectural seats. One was formed in Kao-yao, the capital of Chao-ch'ing prefecture, in 1905. In Canton two were established in 1907, one in the Nan-hai half of the city and one in the P'an-yü half; they were in addition to the Prefectural Middle School and the Shih-min School previously established. By 1907 there were altogether 25 middle schools across the province, with 2,600 students.[7]

The vast majority of the modern schools founded during 1906–07 were primary schools. In districts where new schools already existed, many more were started. In Nan-hai, which had about 20 primary schools at the end of 1905, 28 more were established in 1906 alone, and another 18 in 1907. In Shun-te, which had 5 primary schools at the end of 1905, 13 more were set up in 1906 and 8 in 1907. In most districts where no modern schools had been established, they were founded for the first time. In Hsü-wen, on the Lei-chou peninsula, an old charitable school was converted in 1906 into the district's first higher primary school. In Le-ch'ang, in the North River valley, an academy was similarly converted into a higher primary school. The first new schools were established at this time in Ch'ing-yüan, Jen-hua, and Kan-en also. By 1907 there were 1,441 primary schools in the province, with 65,986 pupils. There were probably few districts without at least the obligatory one primary school.[8]

The major obstacle to faster progress continued to be the teacher shortage. Many districts were required to operate their own short-term normal schools in order to meet their own demand. In 1907 there were 44 normal schools in Kwangtung, with 3,400 students.[9] Many students also went abroad for advanced schooling. In 1906–07, the total number of Chinese students in Japan, both private and government scholars, rose to between 8,000 and 15,000, the peak figure for the post-Boxer decade. A good number of those must have been from Kwangtung.[10]

Finally, public education for women, only recently initiated, progressed slowly. In 1907 there were a mere six girls' schools in Kwangtung, with a total of 391 students, all of them probably located in Canton. One was the Canton Women's Normal School, which opened in early 1907. It had 67 students in 1910. Attached to the Normal School was a girls' primary school, with 297 pupils in 1910.[11]

As the new schools were founded across the province, they encountered surprisingly little resistance from the scholar-gentry. The Confucian ideology no longer stood in the way of reform. As recently as the late 1890's, it had been the touchstone for both the reformers and their conservative opposition. K'ang Yu-wei had justified his radical reforms in Confucian terms; his opponents had denounced them as an unacceptable distortion of Confucian teachings. But after 1900 and especially after 1905 and the abolition of the Confucian-based examinations, Confucianism quickly lost its relevance. Like Hunan, Kwangtung "had entered a new era in which conflicting interpretations of Confucian doctrine would never again have serious political significance." [12]

Once the jealous defender of Confucian values, the scholar-gentry accepted the abolition of the traditional examinations and the creation of the modern schools with little difficulty. Indeed, for reasons for self-interest most gentry members welcomed the new schools. As they realized, the abolition of the examinations had not done away with the gentry elite but had simply subjected it to a different set of qualifications, to produce the novel subtype, the "new gentry." It is only with the 1911 Revolution, when all connection was severed between civil service and the schools, that the scholar-gentry as a distinct social group disappeared. Until then gentry status was dependent upon the modern schools. The gentry, therefore, had good reason to ensure the success of the schools. This is reflected in the fact that the overwhelming majority of the new schools in Kwangtung were of the "public" (*kung-li*) type, founded mostly by the gentry, rather than the "government" (*kuan-li*) type, founded by the officials.

Furthermore, the new schools offered the gentry new opportunities to extend and formalize their authority at the expense of the local officials. The officials generally limited themselves to encouraging the gentry to set up the schools, imposing a set of guidelines and trying to maintain minimum standards. Otherwise the gentry were in charge. Education, of course, had been traditionally one of the prime functions of the scholar-gentry, but hitherto the function had been an informal one. Under the post-Boxer reforms, the gentry's role in education came to be formalized in two bodies: the office of educational affairs (later, the office for the encouragement of education), the gentry-staffed official body charged with the administration of the new school system, and the unofficial education association (*chiao-yü hui*), whose purpose was to help popularize the schools.[13]

Finally, the main beneficiaries of the new schools were the gentry themselves. The post-Boxer educational reforms did not represent an enlargement of educational opportunities for the people. The almost 76,000 students enrolled in the Kwangtung schools in 1907, according to statistics published by the Ministry of Education in Peking, constituted less than three tenths of 1 percent of the total population of the province.[14] It is probable that, because of the expenses and the complexities of the modern schools in contrast to the old tutorial system, the number of students may actually have declined after the implementation of the reforms. Thus, only a very small group of people benefited from the new education, most of whom undoubtedly came from gentry families.

The resistance to the schools after 1905 came not from the gentry, who on the whole were satisfied, but from groups and individuals who had been displaced by them or who bore their ultimate costs. Some gentry members opposed the schools. Those who were too young to have succeeded in the traditional system but too old to adjust to the new system faced an uncertain future. Some also objected, in the words of one foreign correspondent, to "the cost of the education in itself, the result of the absurdly high salaries paid to half-trained teachers, and the expenses to which the parents are put to provide books, and uniforms." [15] Buddhist monks too opposed the schools, because many monasteries and temples along with their property were confiscated by the officials and used for the schools. (Some monasteries and temples, including at least one in Canton, avoided confiscation by affiliating themselves with temples in Japan and thus gaining the same type of extraterritorial protection accorded to Christian churches.) [16] Finally, the peasants and urban poor objected to the new schools because of the additional expense, which was passed on to them in the form of higher taxes and higher rents, in return for which they received few or no benefits.

There were many instances during these years of the peasants and urban poor being stirred up by displaced gentry members and dispossessed monks to attack the new schools and harass the pupils, much as in former years they had attacked Christian chapels and converts. For example, in June 1906, at a town near Canton, a member of the local gentry led an attack on a modern school one month after it opened. In self-defense the teachers and pupils barricaded themselves inside the school. But as they left to go home that evening, the angry crowd pounced on them, threw them into a fish pond, and thrashed them. Similarly, in July 1907 in a town near Hong Kong, where a temple had been converted into a school, "the priests stirred up the people and told them that the wrath of the idols would assuredly fall upon them if these things were allowed to go unchecked. Thereupon the people gathered, drove out the masters and workers, collected all the furniture of the school, and burnt it. The next day they returned and tore off some of the tiling, and attempted to burn the roof of the building." [17]

The peasants also rebelled against the taxes that were levied to finance the new schools. In May 1907 the sugar cane growers in Ch'in-chou, in the western panhandle, resisted the imposition of just such a levy. They went to the prefect to plead that the tax be reduced or withdrawn, pointing out that a typhoon had destroyed a good part of their crop the previous September. The prefect refused. When the growers continued their agitation, he had the leaders arrested. Their aroused followers then proceeded en masse to Ch'in-chou city and forcibly released the prisoners. While in the city, they also wrecked the school and looted the grain dealers' shops. The officials finally called out the local braves, but the tax-resisters overwhelmed the braves. The disturbance rapidly developed into an open rebellion. Sun Yat-sen and the revolutionaries were later to try to capitalize upon it. [18]

In the military field the court's 1901 decrees had ordered the establishment of modern military schools and the formation of a Western-style standing army in every province. The standing army, however, retained many of the shortcomings of the traditional armies, including a highly decentralized organization. Consequently, in January 1905 the court called for the immediate creation of a completely new military force, a nationwide Army (Lu-chün), also known as the New Army (Hsin-chün), and redesignated the standing army as the Reserve Forces (Hsün-fang tui). While the Reserve Forces were dispersed and charged with maintaining internal order and quelling rebellions, the New Army was to be concentrated in strategic centers and concerned with external defense. Altogether thirty-six divisions (*chen*) of the New Army were to be created by 1913. At the same time, the court also reorganized the military schools into a nationwide hierarchy, consisting of military primary schools in every province, four military middle schools, an officers' school and a general staff college. [19]

In Kwangtung in response to the court's decrees the two existing military schools, the Military Preparatory School at Whampoa and the Military Officers' School at Canton, were reorganized, and a couple of new ones were started. In June 1905 Governor-General Ts'en Ch'un-hsüan established the statutory military primary school at Whampoa; it had 80 pupils. At the same time he tried to redesignate the existing Military Preparatory School as a military middle school, but as Kwangtung was not one of the four provinces slated to have such a school this was disallowed. Subsequently, in late 1906, Governor-General Chou Fu transferred the Military Preparatory School from Whampoa to Canton and merged it with the Military Officers' School there to form the Short-term Officers' School (Lu-chün su-ch'eng hsüeh-t'ang). Renamed in 1909 as the Course of Military Instruction (Chiang-wu t'ang), the school offered a one-year program to update the training of senior army officers. There was another course of military instruction at Hu-men, established in 1907 or 1908. In the meantime the newly founded Military Primary School continued to operate at Whampoa. (Its facilities were later utilized by the famous Whampoa Academy.) These three schools provided many of the officers for the Kwangtung New Army.[20]

In the nationwide New Army, decreed in January 1905, Kwangtung's scheduled contribution was two divisions; it fell far short of that target. Helped financially by the 70 percent demobilization of the Army of the Green Standard that the court had previously sanctioned, Governor-General Ts'en Ch'un-hsüan began at once, with the assistance of Japanese advisers, to build toward the first of the two divisions. He took the best of his standing army and infused them with new recruits from Anhwei and northern Kwangtung to form by early 1906 two regiments (*piao*) of infantry, totaling about 6,000 men. He later added to them two battalions (*ying*) of artillery and one each of engineers and transport, which produced a "mixed brigade" (*hun-ch'eng hsieh*), or about half a division. He was training a third infantry regiment when he left Canton. An American military attaché, visiting one of their barracks near Canton in the spring of 1906, found "about two thousand fairly good looking modern-type soldiers, quartered in really good, clean, sanitary barracks."[21]

Ts'en, however, had sacrificed quality for quantity. When his successor Chou Fu arrived, he found the Kwangtung New Army in terrible shape. Because of transfers, dismissals, and illness among the extraprovincial troops unaccustomed to Canton's subtropical climate, the army was severely understrength. It had also been poorly trained. Consequently, Chou inaugurated a policy of retrenchment and consolidation. He immediately merged the three infantry regiments into two, and he called for the training of additional junior officers. Still dissatisfied after a military review at the beginning of 1907, he reduced the infantry another third by cutting the two regiments back from three to two battalions each. The Ch'in-chou anti-tax uprising later in the year set the New Army back even further, as several units were permanently detached and sent to West Kwangtung to quell the rebellion. At the end of 1907 the army was left with only three or four infantry battalions and two batteries of artillery.[22]

The creation of the New Army, although far from complete, marked the emergence of a radically different view of the military profession. Traditionally, soldiers were a despised group. Usually forced into service by economic considerations, they behaved accordingly; they plundered and pillaged wherever they went, living off the land. Such behavior was characteristic of the Reserve Forces and other old-style armies. The New Army was altogether different. It was an elite group and was highly regarded by the people. Recruiting regulations in Kwangtung specified that only volunteers were wanted; they must also be healthy and literate and come from reputable families. Moreover, unlike the Reserve Forces, many of whose soldiers were from outside the province, the Kwangtung New Army was composed largely of natives of the province. Local ties thus reinforced the social ties to enhance the reputation and popularity of the New Army.[23]

In contrast to the army, little was done to modernize the Kwangtung navy. At the end of 1907 it apparently consisted of two transports, nineteen gunboats, and eight torpedo boats. It was still a riverine and coastal force; it had no ocean-going vessels.[24]

Regarding chambers of commerce, the court had called for their establishment in all provincial capitals and commercial centers in January 1904, but none was established in Kwangtung until the middle of 1905. In July 1905, after more than a year of discussion between the local merchants and the officials, the Kwangtung General Chamber of Commerce (Shang-wu tsung-hui) was founded in Canton. A month later, the first branch chamber was organized in Swatow. According to statistics published by the Ministry of Agriculture, Industry, and Commerce in Peking, five more branches were established in 1906 and another ten in 1907. These were located in all but the most underdeveloped parts of the province, such as the North and East river valleys and Hainan island. In the spring of 1907, in recognition of its trade prosperity and its economic independence of Canton, the Swatow branch was raised to the status of a general chamber too.[25]

The significant feature about the chamber of commerce was that it was a commercial association that was explicitly sanctioned by the government. Unlike the provincial bureau for commercial affairs set up during the postwar reform movement, it was not an official organization but a merchant association. But at the same time, unlike the Seventy-two Guilds, it was registered with the Peking government and derived its authority from the government. As the regulations of the Canton General Chamber clearly state, the chamber of commerce was to be the recognized spokesman for the merchants and entrepreneurs. It was to act as the middleman in dealings between the guilds and the government, a bridge across the gulf that traditionally had divided merchants and officials. It was to break down the parochialism of the traditional guild system, to tear down the barriers that separated guild from guild and to encourage greater cooperation among all merchants not only within a city but also across the entire province. It was to promote the growth of commerce and industry by, among other things, publishing a commercial daily newspaper, the *Chamber of Commerce News* (*Tsung shang-hui pao*), and opening a products exhibition hall. Finally, it was to assist the Chinese merchant in his life-or-death struggle with economic imperialism by improving his competitive position vis-à-vis the foreign trader and by resisting further foreign encroachments upon the Chinese economy.[26]

The chamber of commerce was superimposed upon the existing merchant associations without displacing any of them. In Canton the General Chamber of Commerce did not do away with the Seventy-two Guilds, despite apparently overlapping functions. Each, for example, published its own daily newspaper, the *Chamber of Commerce News* and the *Seventy-two Guilds' Commercial News* (*Ch'i-shih-erh hang shang-pao*).[27] In Swatow too the General Chamber of Commerce may have coexisted with the older Swatow Guild.

This suggests that the chambers of commerce, while they spoke for all merchants, did not necessarily represent all merchants equally. If their leadership is any indication, the chambers were more representative of the socially prominent merchants, the merchant—gentry. In the seventeen chambers founded in Kwangtung during 1905–07 and registered with the Ministry of Agriculture, Industry, and Commerce, nearly all the chairmen had an official rank or civil service degree. Some had acquired it simply through purchase. Others had earned the status of licentiate, which placed them only marginally in the ranks of the gentry. But several held degrees that were not available for purchase and that conferred regular scholar-gentry status. For example, the chairmen of the Canton and the Hsing-ning chambers were provincial graduates, while the chairmen of the Hsin-ning and Shun-te chambers were senior licentiates.[28] Where it is known, the leadership of the Canton Seventy-two Guilds fell far short of such social prominence.

Moreover, the chambers of commerce may have catered more to entrepreneurs than to merchants per se. Thus, Cheng Kuan-ying, a vice-chairman of the Canton chamber, formerly had managed a number of Li Hung-chang's economic enterprises, including the China Merchants' Steam Navigation Company, while Chang Pi-shih, the second chairman of the chamber, was well known for his diversified operations stretching from plantations in the Dutch East Indies to a winery in Shantung. Similarly, the vice-chairman of the Swatow chamber, Hsiao Yung-hua, was a prime promoter of the Swatow waterworks in 1907. The Canton Seventy-two Guilds, on the other hand, seems to have been more nearly representative of the ordinary merchants.[29]

Politicization of the Urban Elite

As these initial post-Boxer reforms were implemented more and more widely during the middle years of the decade, they produced a sharp increase in the degree of political involvement among the people, especially the urban elite. In Kwangtung the gentry, merchants, and students, particularly in Canton but increasingly also in other cities, were roused from their traditional passivity. In response to the ongoing challenge of imperialism, they became especially nationalistic. Even some of the Westernized Chinese began to resent their ties to the foreigners; in 1906 in Canton they set up their own "Chinese independent Christian Church."[30] As a foreign correspondent in Swatow commented in mid-1905, "Russian aggression [in 1903] stirred Shanghai, but the fervour of the [Chang] Garden meetings found only a faint echo here. Today it is plain that events of recent years had laid the seeds of a national consciousness, and that these have been slowly maturing . . . China is no longer a congeries of independent molecules."[31]

The reforms themselves contributed directly to this upsurge of patriotism and political activism. The modern schools fostered a keen sense of nationalism and a martial spirit among the students. At several schools China's decrepitude was especially impressed upon them and they were told that it was their duty "to rouse youthful China to activity and patriotism." At another school the classroom walls were decorated with charts delineating the evolution of the modern gun and pictures depicting Japan's recent military successes. Students were often drilled in the use of dummy rifles.[32] Moreover, the gathering of hundreds of students within a single place on a daily basis, which was without precedent in traditional times except during the examinations, was a further stimulus for collective action. Late in 1906, for example, when the Ch'ao-chou taotai complained about absenteeism at the T'ung-wen School in Swatow, the students denounced him for interfering in the affairs of the middle school and even published an open letter to him in the local newspapers. A few months later, in March 1907, when one of their teachers was beaten up by an employee of the Ch'ao-chou-Swatow railroad, students at the same school telegraphed the taotai and the railroad head office for redress. Student strikes similar to the "student tides" (*hsüeh-ch'ao*) of the 1920's and 1930's were not infrequently called. These were clearly the forerunners of the May Fourth generation of student radicals and activists.[33]

The soldiers in the New Army were hardly different from the new students. The popularity of athletics and military drills and military-style uniforms among the students indicated not only a radically new attitude toward physical labor and the military life but also a spiritual kinship between themselves and the soldiers. Soldiers of the New Army, an elite army intended for defense against foreign aggression, demonstrated a strong sense of patriotism and dedication themselves. When two thousand young men from Shao-chou, in the North River valley, enlisted in the New Army in the winter of 1907–08, they put up a big banner pledging to "Regard death as home." [34]

Similarly, the organization of the chambers of commerce gave the merchants a sense of self-esteem and independence that they traditionally had lacked. Thus, the merchants of Canton in 1905 demanded the abolition of all the humiliating formalities that previously had marked their relations with the officials and the gentry.[35] Moreover, like the schools for the students, the chambers facilitated collective action by the merchants on both a city-wide and a province-wide basis. Finally, the chambers were specifically called upon to resist further foreign economic penetration into China by joint merchant action.

The press continued to reflect the growth of popular interest in public affairs. In Canton the number of daily newspapers practically doubled again, from eight in 1905 to fourteen in 1907, in addition to which several illustrated magazines were also published. The total circulation of the nine dailies and two magazines in Canton in mid-1906 was 26,500 copies. In Swatow two daily papers, an increase of one since 1905, as well as a semi-monthly journal and an illustrated tabloid were published in 1906 and 1907. Meanwhile, newspapers were being founded in at least two new cities, Hsiang-shan, in Central Kwangtung, and Ta-p'u, in East Kwangtung.[36]

The newspapers, of course, not only reflected but also fostered the growing concern with political matters. One of them in Canton, the *Citizens' Daily News* (*Kuo-min jih-pao*), was founded for the explicit purpose of "arousing the spirit of citizenship and developing the feelings of patriotism" among its readers.[37] The press became increasingly outspoken in its comments on public issues; it no longer refrained from criticizing the officials, though not without risks. In one extreme instance in July 1906, Governor-General Ts'en Ch'un-hsüan responded to press criticism by suppressing one Canton newspaper and imprisoning its editor, fining the editor of another Canton daily, and on top of this banning all but three of the Chinese-language newspapers in Hong Kong from circulating in the province.[38] Nevertheless, despite occasional official displeasure, the papers became an independent force for expressing and molding public opinion.

As a consequence of the spread of the post-Boxer reforms and the growth of the press, there was a sharp rise in direct popular participation in political affairs during these years. In Kwangtung this took shape first in the anti-American boycott and then in the Canton–Hankow railroad controversy. In the former demonstration the people and the officials together confronted a common foreign foe; in the latter they confronted each other.

The anti-American boycott of 1905–06 grew out of the Exclusion Treaty of 1894 which prohibited the immigration of Chinese laborers into the United States for a period of ten years. There were several objectionable features to the treaty and its enforcement. First, at a time when other nationalities were still freely admitted to the United States, the Chinese were the only ones to be so discriminated against. Second, American officials enforced the treaty arbitrarily and capriciously. The treaty specifically exempted Chinese merchants, teachers, students, and travelers from the ban, yet immigration officers at the ports of entry often classified Chinese who clearly belonged to these exempted groups as "laborers" and refused to allow them into the country. Moreover, corrupt consular officials in China issued many costly but worthless visas. As a result, fully one quarter of the Chinese arriving at San Francisco in 1905 were turned back. Finally, when the United States acquired Hawaii and the Philippines in 1898, it extended the immigration ban to the two territories. Both were places where large numbers of Chinese had previously emigrated.[39]

Consequently, when the Exclusion Treaty expired in 1904, the Chinese government, displaying its new nationalist temperament, refused to renew it. Instead, it sought a modest revision of the treaty that would have enlarged the category of exempted groups and secured better treatment for members of those groups. It also wanted a relaxation of the ban on Chinese immigration to Hawaii and the Philippines. It did not insist that the United States abandon its exclusion policy and admit laborers to the mainland. Nevertheless, the American government opposed any substantial modification of the treaty; it wanted a simple extension of the treaty. Negotiations on treaty renewal, which began in 1904 in Washington, quickly stalemated.

Around the beginning of April 1905, the U.S. government succeeded in transferring the talks to Peking, evidently with the hope that its newly designated minister W. W. Rockhill would achieve better results by dealing directly with the Chinese Foreign Ministry. This possibility agitated the opponents of treaty extension in China. They worried that the Peking government would be less likely or able than its envoy in Washington to stand up to the Americans. It needed backing up. Therefore, at the suggestion of some overseas Chinese, the Shanghai Chamber of Commerce met on May 10, 1905, and announced that it was organizing a boycott of American goods. It called on merchants in other cities to join the boycott. Timed to coincide with Rockhill's arrival in China, the boycott was clearly designed to impress both Peking and Washington with the strength of popular sentiment on the issue.[40]

Since most of the Chinese immigrants to the United States were natives of the province, Kwangtung responded to the boycott call with alacrity. On May 27 several hundred representatives of the charitable halls, guilds, newspapers, and schools in Canton met at the Kuang-chi Hospital to discuss steps for putting the boycott into effect. They agreed, however, with the Shanghai boycott organization to delay the actual beginning of the boycott for two months in order to allow the American government time "to make modifications" in its treaty proposals.[41]

The American response to the announced boycott, while partly conciliatory, did not satisfy the boycotters. On June 24 President Theodore Roosevelt ordered immigration officers in the United States and consular officials in China to be more scrupulous in their application of the Exclusion Treaty. But at the same time he directed Minister Rockhill and the consuls to protest vigorously to the Chinese officials any injury to American economic interests. He also refused to yield on the principle of excluding laborers.[42] Consequently, when the two-months' moratorium came to an end, the boycotters decided to go ahead as planned with their protest. The boycott was formally launched in Shanghai on July 20.

In Kwangtung the boycott was inaugurated on July 23 at a meeting of the Society to Oppose the Treaty (Chü-yüeh hui) in Canton. Within a month it had taken a strong hold of the capital city. The boycott's effectiveness depended above all else upon the merchants and their associations, for whom it was a traditional form of protest. The leaders of the Society to Oppose the Treaty included Cheng Kuan-ying and Wu Chieh-ming, vice-chairman and resident manager respectively of the newly formed Chamber of Commerce. The headquarters of the society was the Kuang-chi Hospital, one of the merchant-dominated charitable halls. Once the boycott was agreed upon, representatives of the society went around to the various guilds and shops collecting pledges from them not to contract for more American goods, especially the principal imports, flour, oil, tobacco, and cotton cloth, while the eight largest guilds dealing in American products formed a supervisory and investigatory body to ensure that the pledges were kept. Most merchants simply substituted other foreign imports for the boycotted items, replacing American oil, for example, with oil from Sumatra. However, a few merchants took advantage of the boycott to promote their own enterprise. Thus, while American tobacco was boycotted, two Hong Kong entrepreneurs, Chien Chao-nan and his younger brother Yü-chieh, founded the Kwangtung Nanyang Tobacco Company, forerunner of the famous Nanyang Brothers Tobacco Company. Women, as consumers, also contributed to the boycott's success. For the mid-autumn festival many refused to buy moon cakes made with American flour.[43]

Students in the new schools were perhaps the boycott's most avid supporters. They were particularly active in publicity work. They lectured to crowds at street corners, marketplaces and temples on why they should not buy or use American products and taught them how to recognize American labels and brand names. They also prepared and distributed handbills and posters to shops and homes. One typical poster read, in large characters, "This shop (or home) does not sell (or use) American goods." Alongside it, in smaller characters, ran the explanation: "The maltreatment of the Chinese laborer by the Americans is unprincipled. Now our citizens have joined together to oppose it. It is right that we do not sell (or use) American goods. Anyone who trades in American goods is without shame." The students, especially those at the Nan-wu and Chin-ch'ü schools in Canton, also worked on the society's bulletin, the *Oppose the Treaty News* (*Chü-yüeh pao*), which began appearing on August 21. Finally, the newspapers in Canton and Hong Kong helped to publicize and maintain interest in the boycott. They served up a steady diet of progress reports and first-hand accounts of anti-Chinese discrimination in the United States. [44]

Even though the idea that a boycott was necessary to back it up was implicitly a rebuke for its weakness or lack of resolve, the Ch'ing government tolerated the boycott at the beginning and gave it tacit support. But as the boycott took effect across central and south China, American officials increased their pressures on the government and eventually forced it to speak out against it. On August 14 Minister Rockhill broke off the treaty negotiations; two days later the Foreign Ministry in Peking telegraphed the provincial authorities urging them to hold the boycott in check. When this did not stop the boycott, Rockhill warned of the possibility of an international incident, especially in connection with the scheduled visit to China of the American Secretary of War, William Howard Taft, and the President's daughter, Alice Roosevelt, early in September. As a result, the court itself issued an edict on August 31 calling for an end to the boycott in order that the Foreign Ministry might resume negotiations with Rockhill. [45]

In Kwangtung Governor-General Ts'en Ch'un-hsüan personally sympathized with the boycott and supported it even when the central government had turned against it. He was also mindful of the tremendous interest that the boycott had aroused in Canton; it was beyond his control. When the American consul Julius Lay protested to him in mid-July about the impending boycott, Ts'en replied that there was no law in China that compelled the people to buy certain products. If they refused to buy American goods, he said, there was nothing that he could do to force them to do otherwise. A month later, when also urged by the Foreign Ministry, Ts'en agreed to issue a proclamation calling on the local boycotters to suspend, but only to suspend, their meetings and street lectures and allow the merchants to trade freely again until December, when the U.S. Congress was to reconvene. His proclamation promised that "if, when the time comes, the proposal for modifying the Treaty is not carried out [by Congress], then they may again devise retaliatory plans." The boycotters, however, did not go along completely with Ts'en's suggestion. On August 26, at their regular weekly meeting at the Kuang-chi Hospital, they refused to suspend the boycott. They agreed only to curb their public agitation in the streets.[46]

A week later Secretary Taft's visit to Canton precipitated a crisis among the boycotters. Three or four days before the visit, scheduled for September 4, a group of radical students, led by Ma Ta-ch'en and P'an Hsin-ming, plastered the Western Suburbs and other sections of Canton with a scurrilous poster warning the sedan chair porters not to deal with the visiting Americans.[47] Perhaps fearful that the zealous radicals might cause a diplomatic incident, some of the moderate leaders of the boycott society, including Wu Chieh-ming and the metropolitan graduate Chiang K'ung-yin, identified Ma and P'an as the culprits to the American consul. Pressed by Consul Lay, Governor-General Ts'en had Ma and P'an and a companion, the student Hsia Ch'ung-min, arrested secretly on September 2.[48] It was not until after the Taft visit had taken place, without incident or demonstration, that news of their arrest leaked out. The boycott society was scandalized, especially when it learned who had been responsible for the arrests. It promptly repudiated the actions of its two leaders. It censured Wu Chieh-ming and was very critical of Chiang K'ung-yin. Chiang was reviled in doggerels and posters as a "bandit gentry member" and accused of having been bribed by the Americans. The society urgently petitioned the prefectural authorities to release the three prisoners but to no avail. The three were to remain in prison for thirteen months.[49]

The boycotters, however, recovered from the shock of the arrests and the internal dissension. In other parts of China the boycott gradually died down after the promulgation of the imperial edict on August 31, but in Canton, where the edict was generally interpreted as "allowing the boycott, but warning the people to keep the peace," it persisted with no let-up except for publicity. Probably to minimize the chances of

American intervention, the boycott society on September 20 asked the newspapers in Canton and Hong Kong to cease publicizing its activities. But, as Consul Lay reported on September 28, the society continued to meet privately and to publish the *Oppose the Treaty News,* and the city was still covered with boycott posters.[50] A three-day memorial service in mid-October in honor of Feng Hsia-wei, the boycott martyr who three months earlier had committed suicide in front of the American consulate in Shanghai, attracted thousands of admirers, mostly students. It was an occasion for "fiery speeches . . . by excited orators inciting the people to persevere in the boycott." As Lay complained in a private letter to Rockhill, "trade is suffering more [now] than when the Edict was issued."[51]

The boycott had the greatest effect in Canton, but it was by no means limited to the capital city. It was a province-wide movement. In Swatow merchants and students met together in June to plan the boycott. Later, gentry members and students, both male and female, attended a memorial service for Feng Hsia-wei that was marked by "several hours of speeches on the hero and on the rise of the new China."[52] In Hong Kong an attempt by the Chinese Chamber of Commerce to organize a public boycott demonstration was frustrated by an ordinance prohibiting unauthorized meetings of a nonreligious character. Moreover, when the radical paper *Commonweal* reprinted the cartoon poster that appeared at the time of the Taft visit, two of its editors were expelled from the colony. Nevertheless, despite these difficulties, the boycott flourished in Hong Kong.[53] In Macao, where meetings and the posting of placards in connection with the boycott were also prohibited, the boycotters got around the ban by holding their rallies in Ch'ien-shan and Wan-tzu (Lappa), just beyond its borders.[54]

Boycott activities were also reported in various districts in the Pearl River delta, West River valley, and North River valley of Central Kwangtung as well as in East and West Kwangtung. At many of these places, as in Canton, merchants and students collaborated closely to make the boycott work. Merchants pledged to adhere to the boycott, while students drummed up popular support by giving street lectures and distributing handbills. Branches of the Oppose the Treaty Society were set up, as were exhibition halls displaying the products to be boycotted.[55] Even in the more remote parts of the province, people were aware of the boycott. It was "a subject of general discussion" on Hainan island, while an American visitor to a mountain-top monastery in

Tseng-ch'eng district, fifty miles east of Canton, discovered that "Even the old monks . . . wanted to talk about the exclusion treaty." [56]

In November the United States suddenly stiffened its stand against the continuing boycott in Kwangtung. Spurred by the murder of five American missionaries at Lien-chou near the Hunan border, though it was unconnected with the boycott,[57] President Roosevelt on November 15 ordered the U.S. Navy to "have as strong a naval force as possible concentrated on the Chinese shore, and as speedily as possible." Two weeks later, American gunboats and destroyers began arriving at Canton from Manila.[58] However, despite the show of force, the boycott persisted. Standard Oil Company's sales, which had fallen from an average of 90,000 cases a month before the boycott to 22,000 cases in October, fell again in November to 19,000 cases. Furthermore, according to the Canton consulate, "these present sales are simply deliveries made on orders placed with the Company before the boycott was declared. No new orders have been placed for the past five months." And, it added, "the same can be said of the flour interests in South China." [59]

Reproached again by the consulate for not stopping the boycott, Governor-General Ts'en Ch'un-hsüan replied that he had done all that he could possibly do. He had, he said, put a stop to public gatherings and to the printing of "inflammatory and threatening literature." (The *Oppose the Treaty News,* for example, had ceased publication toward the end of November.) But he still maintained that "in regard to the preference of the merchants as to which country's goods they will buy and as to what men they will deal with, that is in the power of every man to decide for himself. Assuredly authority and force cannot compel it." [60]

Exasperated by the diplomats' failure to stem the boycott, the American merchants in Canton and Hong Kong decided to negotiate directly with the boycotters, but they were no more successful. In mid-November, ignoring the objections of Consul Lay, they asked the Canton boycott society and representatives of the Hong Kong commercial guilds to specify what changes they wanted to enact in the American immigration laws before they would call off the boycott. On December 3 a group of moderate boycott leaders drafted a reply and presented it to the American businessmen for transmittal to the United States. Their reply took account of America's determination to exclude unskilled laborers and demanded only that the exempt class be enlarged to include "all Chinese skilled laborers and all kinds of employees for commercial stores" as well as the previously exempt officials, merchants, tourists, and students.[61]

This caused another crisis in the ranks of the boycotters. These terms were of course objectionable to the radicals, who refused to be satisfied with anything less than the complete abolition of the exclusion policy. Moreover, the moderates had presented their reply to the Americans without first seeking the endorsement of the boycott society in Canton. As a result, on December 17 the boycott society, including its head Cheng Kuan-ying, formally repudiated the reply as unauthorized and declared itself as still insisting "that no Exclusion Treaty will be negotiated and enforced." [62] Since the U.S. Congress did nothing to amend the Chinese exclusion laws when it reconvened in December, the boycott continued into January 1906. [63]

Soon, however, the boycott was overshadowed by the controversy between the gentry and merchants and the governor-general over control of the Canton–Hankow railway. It quickly lost its momentum thereafter. The more zealous students tried to keep it going, but without the cooperation of the merchants, they had little success. At the beginning of March Consul Lay thought that at long last the end of the agitation was in sight. [64]

The boycott never completely disbanded. On three occasions later in 1906 it showed signs of reviving. In July, when the remains of the boycott martyr Feng Hsia-wei were brought home to Canton for burial, an immense crowd, composed of "over 1000 scholars with bands and banners, merchants, gentry and representatives of every guild and profession," greeted the arrival. "Everywhere the cry was loud that the boycott must not be relaxed." Furthermore, thousands of people, mostly students, paid homage to him at his temporary resting place. [65] Similarly, on September 23, when Ma Ta-ch'en and his two young companions, P'an Hsin-ming and Hsia Ch'ung-min, were released from their thirteen months of confinement, several thousand students were on hand to welcome them. The boycott society later rewarded P'an and Hsia with scholarships for study in Japan. [66]

Finally, in December 1906, when the U.S. Congress convened again, there was a concerted effort in Canton to revive the agitation. A meeting at the Kuang-chi Hospital on December 30, attended by thousands and chaired by Ma Ta-ch'en, resolved to reactivate the boycott and to press the Chinese government "to re-open the emigration question with the American Minister." However, acting on the complaint of the new American consul, Leo Bergholz, Governor-General Chou Fu banned any further meetings. Chou, who was less sympathetic to mass movements than his predecessor Ts'en, also prohibited the newspapers from printing any boycott news. When Ma Ta-ch'en protested the ban, he was promptly rearrested and was not released until the following September. The boycott failed to materialize.[67]

During the boycott in 1905, the people of Canton had united with the provincial officials in common opposition to the discriminatory policies of the American government and, to a lesser extent, also the submissive foreign policy of the Peking government. The Canton–Hankow railroad controversy that developed in January 1906 broke up this common cause and pitted the populace against the provincial authorities themselves. This confrontation, from which the popular forces emerged victorious, marked a further development in the politicization of the urban elite in Canton.

Soon after the Canton–Hankow railroad concession was redeemed from the American China Development Company in September 1905, the Wuchang governor-general, Chang Chih-tung, instigator of the redemption, had met with representatives of Hupeh, Hunan, and Kwangtung and decided that the railroad would not be a single undertaking; instead, each of the three provinces would build that section of the road that lay within its own borders.[68] The controversy in Kwangtung between Governor-General Ts'en Ch'un-hsüan and the Canton gentry and merchants revolved around the appropriate means of financing and operating the Kwangtung section of the railway. The two upper gentry members who had represented Kwangtung at Chang Chih-tung's conference, Liang Ch'ing-kuei and Li Kuo-lien, drafted a set of regulations that provided for merchant financing and management of the road. Governor-General Ts'en, however, refused to concede all control of the railway to the merchants. Nor was he convinced, in view of their failure earlier to help redeem the concession, that the gentry and merchants could raise the necessary funds by themselves. Ts'en wanted to make the road an official undertaking and to finance its construction by official means. He proposed to levy a set of additional temporary taxes which would be earmarked for railway construction. The gentry and merchants, in turn, were fearful lest Ts'en's temporary levies become permanent ones; in any case they objected to any outside, official interference in what they considered to be a local, commercial enterprise.[69]

Early in January 1906 the gentry and merchants became openly critical of Ts'en's proposals. On January 12, at a meeting convened by the governor-general at the Wen-lan Academy to discuss his tax scheme, Li

Kuo-lien, supported by Liang Ch'ing-kuei, charged that the proposed taxes would merely go to enrich the officials. Angered by the accusation, Ts'en ordered Li arrested immediately and memorialized the throne impeaching Liang. This sparked a big protest movement in Canton. The gentry, led by two elderly retired officials, Hsü Ying-k'uei and Teng Hua-hsi, met on the fifteenth at the Ming-lun hall of the prefectural Confucian Temple (hsüeh-kung) and denounced Li's arrest as improper because of his gentry status. (The Ming-lun hall, the Hall for Understanding Human Relationships, in the government school cum Confucian Temple complex, was traditionally the place where the local scholar-gentry met for lectures and study.) The Chamber of Commerce, meeting the next day with over four thousand people in attendance, added the merchants' opposition to Ts'en's tax measures and expressed their support for Li Kuo-lien. The local press too was unanimously opposed to Ts'en. The central government was deluged with telegrams from Canton critical of the governor-general. It was this furor in mid-January that diverted public attention away from the anti-American boycott and caused it to subside.[70]

In the face of such united and adamant opposition, Governor-General Ts'en capitulated. On February 16 he freed Li Kuo-lien from prison. Furthermore, he gave up his resistance to the merchants' taking control of the newly formed Kwangtung Railway Company. He promised that henceforth the officials would only "protect and sustain" the company but would not interfere with its finances or its personnel policy.[71] Ts'en's defeat in the railway dispute ironically confirmed his assertions to the American consul during the boycott that the gentry and merchants could not be forced to go against their will.

The month-long controversy in Canton over the railway stimulated extraordinary public interest in the scheme that the gentry and merchants had put forth originally to finance the construction of the road entirely by means of a voluntary popular subscription. The new Kwangtung Railway Company, formed in February 1906, was to be capitalized at Mex. $40,000,000, with individual shares priced at $5 each in order to appeal to the general populace. In accordance with the nationalist temper of the times, only Chinese were allowed to buy shares in the company; no foreign capital was accepted. In the first flush of enthusiasm, the public quickly exhausted the entire issue of shares. In Canton, "The crowds that appealed for shares were so great that larger offices had to be secured." By summer the first call, set modestly at $1.00

for each $5.00 share, had netted the railway company the expected $8,000,000.[72]

Unfortunately, the leading shareholders of the railway company soon fell to bickering among themselves, thus exposing an interesting split between the gentry and the merchants in Canton. The leaders of the initial redemption campaign and the subsequent struggle with Ts'en for control of the railway had been gentry members, notably the two provincial graduates Liang Ch'ing-kuei and Li Kuo-lien, probably because the gentry were traditionally better suited than the merchants for direct dealings with the officials.[73] When these struggles had been won and it came to raising money for the railway, the merchants then took over. In mid-April, Liang and Li announced that their duties were terminated and handed control of the railway over to the local merchants. A week later, meeting at the Ai-yü Charitable Hall, the merchants elected a five-man board of directors to manage the road, at least four of whom, Cheng Kuan-ying, Huang Ching-t'ang, Hsü Ying-hung, and Tso Tsung-fan, were concurrently officers of the Canton Chamber of Commerce. Shareholders in Hong Kong, Shanghai, and elsewhere, however, promptly disputed the election. They complained that the Canton merchants had carried it out without first consulting them. They also insisted on a careful and independent auditing of the company's finances before they would deliver over their substantial subscriptions.[74]

At this point, at least according to the merchants, the gentry tried to reassert their control over the railway by joining the critics. A statement issued in mid-June by leading merchant shareholders in Canton charged that Li Kuo-lien had gone to Hong Kong, Shanghai, and Hankow "in order to stir up merchants there to attack the charitable institutions [or halls] by accusing them of secretly appointing directors and sub-directors" to the company. Several days later, the merchants of Canton met to denounce their critics in Hong Kong and to demand that neither the officials nor the gentry should interfere in the merchants' management of the railway. They formally resolved "that if the managing power of this line be snatched away by the gentry, the General Chamber of Commerce, the Nine Charitable Institutions, and the Seventy-two Guilds will never deliver up the shareholders' vital capital into the hands of the gentry." For, as the earlier statement put it, "the merchants dread the gentry as they do tigers."[75] This dispute, which shook public confidence, did irreparable harm to the company. Later, when the second call for payment was made, at $1.50 a share, it was not fully met. The dispute also delayed construction of the railroad. The first section, a 17-mile stretch from the Huang-sha (Wongsha) terminus in Canton northward to Chiang-ts'un, was not opened to traffic until July 1907.[76]

Other railways were completed or started in Kwangtung at this time. The 24-mile Ch'ao-chou–Swatow line, begun in 1904, was finished in 1906.[77] A year later construction began on the line from Canton to Kowloon. The concession for the 89-mile Chinese section of this line, from Canton to Shen-tsun (Shumchun) on the border of the New Territories, had been granted to a British syndicate in 1898, but it was not activated until 1905 as a quid pro quo for the British loan to Chang Chih-tung to redeem the Canton–Hankow concession from the Americans. Some of the Canton gentry and merchants protested against the British loan agreement for the line, signed in March 1907, but showed no interest themselves in financing its construction.[78] On the other hand, the Hsin-ning railroad, started in 1906, was built entirely with Chinese capital and by Chinese engineers.[79] Apart from railroads, other large-scale public works were begun in Canton, notably a waterworks, a brick and cement factory, and the bund along the waterfront.[80]

Initiation of New Reforms

During these years the court added two new programs to its post-Boxer reforms. One was aimed at the eradication of opium production and use in China; the other, at the transformation of the regime into a constitutional monarchy. Both were announced in September 1906. These two programs reinforced the already unmistakable trend toward popular involvement in public affairs. They were also a response to these growing pressures from below. In the early post-Boxer years, the reforms, with the possible exception of the chambers of commerce, had been exclusively reforms from above. Now politics was no longer a unidirectional process; it was becoming more and more a process of interaction between above and below.

The anti-opium campaign began as a popular crusade against the imported vice; it was taken up only later by the court. After a century of almost unrestricted use, the emergent public opinion in post-Boxer China began to speak out against opium, helped along by an American report in 1904 condemning its use in the Philippines. To its critics, opium smoking was not only harmful to the individual addict; it was also harmful to the nation. In a world governed by the single principle of "survival of the fittest," the Chinese were clearly headed for extinction unless they rid themselves of this debilitating habit.[81]

In Kwangtung scattered efforts were made in late 1905 and 1906 to combat the vice in Canton. In November 1905 a Christian dentist, Hu Jui-feng, founded an anti-opium society at the Wen-lan Academy, where he gave nightly lectures on the evils of opium use. He also organized street processions to attract popular attention to the problem. Three months later, members of the Kuang-chi Hospital founded a similar society, which proposed to publish a magazine to inform the public about the dangers of opium and also to set up a newspaper reading room where ex-smokers could while away their leisure time at night. Once the anti-opium campaign was begun, the students of Canton joined in with enthusiasm. In August 1906 they staged several street parades that attracted considerable attention. In one of them, an emaciated man, "his face painted black and shoulders shrugged up," rode by on horseback holding an enormous opium pipe, while bands of students followed distributing handbills. In addition to denouncing the harmful effects of opium smoking, the demonstrators called for official action against the vice.[82]

Spurred by such popular agitation as that in Canton as well as by indications from the government of British India that it would be willing to stop exporting opium if the Chinese government would take action against it domestically, the court on September 20, 1906, issued an edict ordering an end to the production and use of opium within China in ten years. Poppy farmers were to be licensed and the acreage they devoted to opium was to be cut back 10 percent a year. Opium smokers were to be licensed also and where possible they were to be weaned from their habit. The court also sanctioned the formation of anti-opium societies.[83]

In Kwangtung, where smoking was the principal problem since little opium was grown except in the eastern part of the province, the officially sponsored Anti-Opium Society (Chieh-yen hui) was founded, amidst much "clapping of hands and speechifying," in Canton on July 26, 1907. Hu Jui-feng was a leading member of the new organization, but the head of it was Ch'en Hui-p'u. One purpose of the Kwangtung Anti-Opium Society was "to register people to be cured of the opium habit and assist them by advice and medicine." Another was to publicize anti-opium information. It distributed large quantities of printed literature, including graphic woodcuts depicting opium smoking as a "national shame," and it organized street lectures and demonstrations. The society formally launched the anti-opium crusade with a huge street procession in Canton on August 9, in honor of which the officials declared a public holiday. The theme of the parade was "the features and behavior of opium smokers." One exhibit showed "a coffin with a man half concealed in it," indicating that a smoker was already half way to the grave. Another showed a man forced to sell his daughter in order to indulge his expensive vice. The society organized a second procession in Canton at the end of November.[84]

In its early stages, the anti-opium campaign was most effective in Canton, where many of its activities were concentrated. In cooperation with the Anti-Opium Society, the Canton authorities closed down numerous smoking divans. In October 1907 between one quarter and one third of the four hundred prepared opium shops in the city had been or were about to be closed. Also, officials and soldiers who continued to smoke were severely punished; at least several noncommissioned officers were executed. As a result, opium smoking quickly ceased to be a fashionable vice in the capital city. The effectiveness of the campaign in Canton is partially confirmed by the statistics in the Maritime Customs trade reports. During the ten years preceding 1906, the amount of foreign, mainly Indian, opium imported into Canton had risen steadily from 5,847 piculs in 1896 to 11,146 piculs in 1906, its peak year. In 1907 it began, modestly at first, to decline.[85]

In other parts of the province, the campaign had barely begun to take effect. In response to encouragement from the provincial Anti-Opium Society several hundred people, including the magistrate, formed a local society in Hsiang-shan in August 1907. There was some success in Ying-te too. In Swatow, however, the movement was reportedly a "farce," as the officials raided only poor divans while leaving the rich ones unmolested. The customs trade reports indicate no significant change, either upward or downward, in the amount of foreign opium imports into Swatow during these years.[86]

Despite the limited achievements in its first year, the anti-opium movement in Kwangtung and elsewhere had made enough progress to satisfy the British. In January 1908 they concluded an agreement with the Chinese government that provided for the gradual elimination of all opium imports from India into China over a ten-year period.[87] The anti-opium campaign was to become one of the most successful of the court's post-Boxer reforms.

Another, and obviously more important, product of the court's growing interaction with its subjects was the transformation of China from an autocratic to a constitutional regime. In its edict of January 8, 1901, inaugurating the whole post-Boxer reform movement, the court had declared that "the essential spirit" of the much-admired European civilization was the "sympathy and understanding [that] exists between rulers and people." It thus seemed to express a belated agreement with the ultimate objective of the gentry reformers of the late 1890's, which was to turn the Ch'ing into a constitutional monarchy. However, during the next four years, while it initiated other reforms, the court did nothing further to bring about a constitutional government, despite the urgings of many of its own officials as well as the popular press.[88]

Meiji Japan's victory over Tsarist Russia in 1904–05 prompted the Manchu court to act. The victory was widely interpreted in China as the triumph of constitutionalism over autocracy. As a Shanghai newspaper put it, "The question of the relative merits of a constitutional and an autocratic monarchy would not have been answered had there not been this war."[89] In July 1905 the court appointed a five-man commission to go abroad and determine what form of government would best suit China. The commission returned to China in August 1906 and reported in favor of a constitutional regime modeled after Japan's and Germany's. Accordingly, the court on September 1, 1906, issued an edict proclaiming its adherence to "a constitutional polity in which the supreme authority shall be vested in the crown, but all questions shall be considered by a popular assembly."[90] Having decided in favor of the principle of constitutionalism and popular representation, the court then waited another year before making up its mind about the detailed structure of the new regime.

In Kwangtung the court's 1906 decree promising a constitutional regime was an occasion for public rejoicing. In response to a telegram from the Shanghai Chamber of Commerce, both the Canton and the Swatow chambers organized city-wide celebrations on September 9. In Canton students carrying banners paraded through the streets, accompanied by bands playing foreign music. Afterwards they and the merchants met at the Chamber of Commerce to listen to orations hailing the promise of constitutional government and sing patriotic songs. Decorating the meeting hall were lanterns with the motto, "May a Constitutional Government last 10,000 years!" In Swatow the celebration was more subdued. The Chamber of Commerce invited all merchants and students to a meeting at which the imperial edict was read and explained. The audience also heard an address urging everyone to be a good citizen and recommending practice in local self-government as a preparation for constitutional rule.[91]

In the following months many communities in Kwangtung experimented with "local self-government" (ti-fang tzu-chich). As a pilot project, the provincial authorities encouraged such experimentation in Kuang-chou prefecture, in Central Kwangtung. Governor-General Chou Fu sent several expectant magistrates to the more important districts in the prefecture to confer with the local gentry. The officials suggested that the gentry publish newspapers written in simple, vernacular Chinese and open free schools so that the people may be "educated up to taking an intelligent interest in the Government of their districts." They also urged the gentry to send some of their members to Japan "to see how things are done there."[92] Elsewhere in Kwangtung, the gentry themselves took the lead in trying out self-government. In Chia-ying, in East Kwangtung, a group of gentry members and students organized a "society to investigate local public welfare," which was to meet every Sunday to discuss various matters of local interest and act as the mediator in local disputes. In P'u-ning, also in East Kwangtung, the scholars in one community founded a "self-government society" to promote education, reform local customs, and (again) mediate in interlineage disputes.[93]

In the autumn of 1907, the court finally announced the details of the future constitutional polity, especially the makeup of the popular assemblies that it had promised a year earlier. On September 28 it called for the establishment of a National Assembly, an embryonic parliament half of whose membership was to be elected. On October 19 it decreed the formation of fully elected deliberative assemblies at both the provincial and the local level. But it had yet to reveal the timetable for the creation of these representative bodies.[94]

The court's decision to provide for popular representation in government was to some extent influenced from below by the various experiments in local self-government that were carried out during the preceding year, including such advanced efforts as the Tientsin and Shanghai municipal councils as well as more tentative efforts as those in

Kwangtung.[95] More broadly, it was in response to all the organized, and often unauthorized, activities that had developed in the middle years of the post-Boxer decade. Politics was no longer the preserve of the court and its officials. In less than ten years it had become a matter of popular concern. This was apparent in the transformation of nationalism into a truly mass-based movement, the proliferation of all types of popular associations in disregard of the traditional ban on them, the growth of the press and the formation of an independent public opinion, and most obviously the political and social activism of the urban populace. Such activities were not in themselves antagonistic to the Ch'ing, but if left unregulated, as they had been for the past few years, they were a potential danger to the regime. The answer was the constitutional program. It sanctioned and even encouraged political activism on the part of the people, but within prescribed, and therefore controllable, channels. Thus, in encouraging local self-government and constitutionalism, the court was not only responding to popular pressures; it was also trying to reassert some control over its wayward subjects.[96]

5

Middle Years of the Post-Boxer Decade, II: Revolution

In 1901 the court had managed to deflate the revolutionary threat brought on by the palace coup of 1898 and the allied intervention of 1900 by means of a sharp reversal of policy and the inauguration of the post-Boxer reforms. Yet, paradoxically, those very reforms helped bring about a new upsurge of revolutionary activities in the middle years of the decade. In the summer of 1905 the Revolutionary Alliance was formed in Tokyo. In 1907 and early 1908 the Alliance organized or sponsored a series of daring revolts in central and south China, many of them in Kwangtung. However, these risings, unlike those in 1900, occurred in the absence of a revolutionary situation. They never seriously threatened the dynasty. They did not force the court to change policy, though they probably convinced it to step up the pace of its reforms.

The Revolutionary Alliance

The revival of the revolutionary movement began with the formation of the Chinese Revolutionary Alliance (Chung-kuo ko-ming t'ung-meng hui) in Tokyo in July and August 1905. It was a timely merger of Sun Yat-sen's reputation and experience as a revolutionary with the radicalism and enthusiasm of the student revolutionaries. The students, who had emerged as a separate revolutionary group during the early post-Boxer years, were disorganized and leaderless, while Sun, whose Society to Restore China's Prosperity had disintegrated following the Canton–Hui-chou revolt in 1900, was a leader without a following. The merger was made possible by a narrowing of the ideological differences between Sun and the students which previously had kept them apart. Before 1903 Sun had been at best a conditional nationalist. In his first two revolutionary attempts, he had been willing to sacrifice Chinese sovereignty in order to secure foreign assistance to drive out the Manchus. In 1903, however, he was greatly influenced by the students' writings during the anti-Russian controversy; afterwards he became more firmly committed to nationalism. At the same time, the students, frustrated by the impotence of the Ch'ing government in meeting foreign encroachments and skeptical of its intentions regarding domestic reform, had become increasingly anti-Manchu after 1903. The Alliance thus brought together within a single organization most of the existing anti-Ch'ing revolutionaries. More important, it attracted many new adherents to the revolutionary cause.[1]

The aims of the Alliance were revolutionary. Its platform, which every member swore to uphold, consisted of four planks. The first three were identical to the aims of Sun's Society to Restore China's Prosperity: expulsion of the Manchus, restoration of Chinese sovereignty, and establishment of a republic. The fourth was new and socialistic: equalization of land rights, whereby all unearned increments in land value would go to the state. In sum, the Alliance called for three kinds of revolution: a national revolution, to overthrow the ruling Manchus and expel the foreign imperialists; a political revolution, to replace the autocratic monarchy with a democratic republic; and a social-economic revolution, to introduce state socialism in order to industrialize China without the inequities of laissez-faire capitalism.[2]

The original membership of the Alliance, the 863 persons who are listed as having joined in Tokyo during 1905–06, included natives of all but one of the eighteen provinces of China Proper. The largest contingents were those from Hunan (157), Szechwan (127), Kwangtung (112), and Hupeh (106).[3] Who (apart from Sun Yat-sen) were the members from Kwangtung, who accounted for one eighth of the total membership? Unfortunately, the membership roster itself lists only the member's name, his native district, the date of his enrollment in the Alliance, and sometimes his age and his sponsors. Additional information is available for scarcely more than 30 of the 112 members. Individual biographies exist for 14 of these, among them Hu Han-min (listed as

Hu Yen-hung), Wang Ching-wei (Wang Chao-ming), Liao Chung-k'ai, Chu Chih-hsin (Chu Ta-fu), and Feng Tzu-yu, all of whom distinguished themselves in the Republican era.[4] Information on another 15 or 20 members has been pieced together from scattered sources. Obviously the following analysis of the Alliance membership from Kwangtung is based on very fragmentary evidence. However, it presumably includes at least all the most active members.

The only datum that is available for every member except one is geographical origin. Close to half of the membership, 48 out of 111, came from the Pearl River delta in Central Kwangtung. This is to be expected since the delta is the most populous area in the province. What is unexpected, however, is that an even larger number, 50, came from the Mei River valley in the interior of East Kwangtung, a much smaller and far less populous area inhabited primarily by Hakkas. The remaining 13 members were distributed through the other parts of Central and East Kwangtung: 3 in the West River valley, 1 in the North River valley, 4 in the East River valley, and 5 in the Han River lowlands. None was from West Kwangtung. The Hakkas' predominance among the Alliance members from Kwangtung may perhaps be traced to a latent tradition of anti-Manchu sentiment among them. For example, according to a British consular official traveling through Hakka territory in 1877, "The turbans worn by the natives in this part of the empire were first put on at the opening of the present dynasty, when, sullenly submitting to the Manchu power, they sought to hide the hated badge of slavery—the shaven head and plaited tail which the victorious Tartars imposed upon the conquered race."[5] The originators of the great Taiping Rebellion were, of course, also Hakkas.

Most of the founding members of the Alliance from Kwangtung were evidently young students. Among the 33 members whose age is known, the oldest was 36 and the youngest was 19. Their median age was about 24. Of the 32 for whom there exists some indication of the purpose for their stay in Japan, 27 were there to study. Many of these were government scholars. The largest single group of identifiable members from Kwangtung were 7 students who had been sent by the provincial government in 1904 for two years of advanced training at the Tokyo College of Law and Administration (Hōsei daigaku): Chu Chih-hsin, Wang Ching-wei, Chin Chang, Tu Kung-shih (listed as Tu Chih-chang), Chang Po-ch'iao (Chang Shu-nan), Ku Ying-fen, and Hu Han-min.[6]

Two other members, Jao Ching-hua (Jao Ch'i-kung) and Liu Wei-t'ao (Liu Ch'ün-li), had been sent to the Japanese Army Officers' Academy, from which they graduated in December 1906.[7] Others were private scholars, for example, Feng Tzu-yu and Liao Chung-k'ai at Waseda University, Li Wen-fan at the Tokyo College of Law and Administration, and Kao Chien-fu (Kao Lun) at the Tokyo Academy of Fine Arts. The large number of Hakkas among the Alliance members from Kwangtung thus may also be explained by their reputed concern for education: more of them joined the Alliance because perhaps more of them had gone to Japan to study.

The student revolutionaries of the Alliance belonged to the intellectual generation that bridged Confucian and post-Confucian China. Born around 1881, they were not without cultural and intellectual ties to the traditional order. Many of them had started out with a classical education. Some even had reaped the traditional rewards of education, a civil service degree. Thus, Hu Han-min (born 1879) and Wang Ching-wei (b. 1883) both had qualified as provincial graduates under the old examination system, while Ku Ying-fen (b. 1873), Tu Kung-shih (born ca. 1881) and Liu Ssu-fu (b. 1884) were all licentiates. As a result, they were not so free of the traditional culture as were the May Fourth radicals born nine or ten years later, such as Li Ta-chao (b. 1888) and Hu Shih (b. 1891).[8] On the other hand, since they did not come to intellectual maturity until after the Sino-Japanese war and the Boxer troubles, they were considerably freer of the traditional order than the postwar gentry reformers born about ten years earlier, like Ou Chü-chia (born ca. 1871) and Liang Ch'i-ch'ao (b. 1873).[9]

In terms of social background, most of the Alliance members who have been identified were from well-to-do families, as in many cases their very presence in Japan would suggest. Some, like Feng Tzu-yu, Liao Chung-k'ai, Kuo Kung-chieh, and Chu Shao-mu, came from overseas Chinese families. More were from scholar-gentry families. Wang Ching-wei, Hu Han-min, and Chu Chih-hsin all had fathers who were traditional degree holders. In any case, on the basis of their own studies in Japan, the student revolutionaries were almost all assured of a place of their own in the "new gentry." Liao Chung-k'ai, for example, formally qualified as a new-style provincial graduate in 1909 after the completion of his studies at Waseda and Chūō universities. Thus, unlike Sun Yat-sen's earlier Society to Restore China's Prosperity, whose typical member was a Westernized Chinese from the treaty ports and the foreign enclaves, the Alliance drew its membership largely from the orthodox elite of society, well within the mainstream of Chinese social life.[10]

Practically all the members were of course men. But at least one member from Kwangtung was a woman: Ho Hsiang-ning, daughter of a tea merchant in Hong Kong and wife of Liao Chung-k'ai. She had accompanied her husband to Tokyo in 1902 and was enrolled as a student in the Tokyo Girls' Art School, from which she graduated in 1911. Her enrollment in the Alliance, along with Ch'iu Chin from Chekiang, reflected the growing role that women were generally playing in public affairs in the post-Boxer era.[11]

Finally, most of the founding members of the Alliance were new to the revolutionary movement. Only two of them, Liang Mu-kuang and Feng Tzu-yu, had belonged to the Society to Restore China's Prosperity. Liang had participated in Sun Yat-sen's 1900 revolt as well as Hsieh Tsan-t'ai's 1903 abortive uprising,[12] while Feng had been active in the Japan branch of the society since 1895. Another six or seven had signed up for Sun's short-lived Revolutionary Military School (Ko-ming chün-shih hsüeh-hsiao) in Tokyo in 1903.[13] Most of the other members had not been involved either with Sun Yat-sen or with any kind of revolutionary activity prior to their enrollment in the Alliance.

Why then did they join the Alliance? Many probably joined because it seemed to them, as it had to others before, that China's regeneration was impossible so long as the Manchus remained in power. In this regard, the post-Boxer reforms themselves were responsible for turning many of the students to revolution. Having radicalized them, the reforms were neither fast enough nor extensive enough to suit the impatient youth. In 1905–06 it was still unclear just how far the Ch'ing intended to carry its reform program or how serious it was about it. The court did not promise a "constitutional polity" until September 1906; nor did it specify the form it was to take until September and October 1907. Also, student nationalists were frustrated by the Ch'ing's inability to resist foreign pressures, as was evident in the court's compliance in August 1905 with U.S. demands to curb the anti-American boycott. It is hardly surprising that two of the three radical agitators in Canton who were arrested and imprisoned in 1905 for trying to intensify the boycott, Ma Ta-ch'en and Hsia Ch'ung-min, later joined the Alliance.[14]

Some may have joined for more personal reasons, such as family ties. Among the members from Kwangtung, quite a few were relatives: Liu

Ssu-fu and Liu Yüeh-hang, Hu Han-min and Hu I-sheng (listed as Hu I), Ho T'ien-chiung and Ho T'ien-han, Ho I and Ho Pin, and finally, Hsieh Liang-mu (listed as Hsieh Yen-yü), Hsieh Yen-mei, Hsieh Yen-chih and Hsieh Yen-hui. On the other hand, common school ties may have helped to bring in the seven government scholars at the Tokyo College of Law and Administration. In addition, some joined perhaps because it was, for whatever reason, the thing to do. At the time, "there was something in the air that affected men of widely varying dispositions" and inclined them to associate with the revolutionary movement.[15]

However much revolution may have been "in the air," the Alliance attracted only a minority of the Chinese students in Japan. Even if all 863 of its members were students, they would have amounted to less than 10 percent of the ten to fifteen thousand students then in Japan. Of the 56 scholars sent by the Kwangtung government to study law and administration in Tokyo, only 7 joined the Alliance; the other 49 did not, though one of them, Yeh Hsia-sheng, was a contributor to its journal.[16] Thus, those who did join could not have been unaware of the revolutionary implications of their action.

Unlike Sun Yat-sen's Society to Restore China's Prosperity, which began to make revolution as soon as it was formed, the Alliance did little during its first year and a half to try to organize a revolutionary uprising. One exception was Huang Hsing's unsuccessful trip to Kweilin, Kwangsi, at the end of 1905 to urge the Reserve Forces commander Kuo Jen-chang to revolt.[17] Instead, the Alliance concentrated at first on raising funds, enlarging and extending the organization, and publicizing its program. During most of this time both Sun Yat-sen and Huang Hsing, the two leaders of the Alliance, traveled throughout Southeast Asia collecting money and establishing branches in the various overseas Chinese communities. Meanwhile, the Alliance headquarters in Tokyo was involved with the publication of the *People's Report* (*Min pao*), which was started in November 1905. The *People's Report* expounded the program of the Revolutionary Alliance and engaged in a lively "pen war" with Liang Ch'i-ch'ao's *New People's Miscellany* (*Hsin-min ts'ung-pao*) that lasted into early 1907.

Members from Kwangtung took a leading role in these activities. Some were appointed to principal positions in the Tokyo headquarters: Hu Han-min, Liao Chung-k'ai, Liu Wei-t'ao, Hsieh Liang-mu, and Ho T'ien-chiung in the executive department; Ho T'ien-han in the judiciary department; Wang Ching-wei, Feng Tzu-yu, Liang Mu-kuang, Chang Po-ch'iao, Chu Chih-hsin, and Hu Han-min (again) in the deliberative department.[18] Others accompanied Sun Yat-sen on his 1905–06 trip to Southeast Asia: Hsieh Liang-mu, Hu I-sheng, Li Yung-hsi, and Teng Mu-han.[19] Yet others wrote for the *People's Report,* namely Hu Han-min, Wang Ching-wei, Chu Chih-hsin, and Liao Chung-k'ai.[20]

As a result of their work with the Alliance, some of the members from Kwangtung became full-time professional revolutionaries, notably Wang Ching-wei, Hu Han-min, and Feng Tzu-yu. Most, however, continued their studies, and participated in the revolutionary movement only part of the time. When their studies were completed, they returned to China. Thus, of the seven members who were government scholars at the College of Law and Administration, only Wang and Hu remained behind in Tokyo, while the rest, including Chu Chih-hsin, returned to China in the summer of 1906 to take up teaching positions. Guiding these part-time revolutionaries was the slogan then current among the students: "While being patriotic, let no one forget his studies; and when studying, let no one forget patriotism." [21]

The Alliance in Kwangtung

Shortly after the formation of the Revolutionary Alliance in Tokyo, a branch of the organization was established in Hong Kong to serve south China. During its first year and a half, it was relatively idle. Few members were enrolled. As in Tokyo, the primary form of revolutionary activity was journalism.

In September 1905 Sun Yat-sen dispatched Feng Tzu-yu along with Feng's brother-in-law Li Tzu-ch'ung to Hong Kong to patch up the quarrel between Ch'en Shao-pai and Cheng Kuan-i and organize a branch of the Alliance in the British colony. Since Feng was on good terms with both antagonists, he managed to bring them together long enough to set up the branch. Its affairs were directed at first by the triumvirate of Ch'en Shao-pai as chairman, Cheng Kuan-i as manager, and Feng Tzu-yu as secretary. But this arrangement did not last. First, Cheng died of the plague in the summer of 1906. Then, during the following winter, after some new financial difficulties involving the *China Daily News,* Ch'en resigned as chairman of the branch and retired from further active participation in the revolutionary movement, much as Hsieh Tsan-t'ai and other former leaders of the Society to Restore

China's Prosperity had done before him. As a result Feng Tzu-yu in 1907 became the sole head of the Alliance in Hong Kong.[22]

Membership in the Hong Kong branch of the Alliance was very small during 1905–06, the years when Tokyo was the center of activities. In 1905 the branch enrolled only 18 members; in 1906 it enrolled an even smaller number.[23] Some of these were former associates of Sun Yat-sen from the defunct Society to Restore China's Prosperity: Teng Yin-nan, Li Chi-t'ang, as well as Ch'en Shao-pai and Cheng Kuan-i; but they were relatively inactive or only briefly active in the new organization. As signaled by Ch'en Shao-pai's retirement in 1906 the older generation of Westernized Chinese ceased to dominate the revolutionary movement in Hong Kong. Instead, most members, including the activists, were new recruits who were young intellectuals of the "new gentry" type in the mold of Feng Tzu-yu. Like their comrades in Tokyo, they belonged to the generation born around 1881: for example, Wang Fu (born ca. 1880), Ch'en Shu-jen (b. 1883), and Li Shu-fen (b. 1887). (In contrast, Ch'en Shao-pai had been born in 1869; Li Chi-t'ang, around 1873.) Like Feng Tzu-yu, many were newspapermen: Ch'en Shu-jen, Huang Shih-chung, Liao P'ing-tzu, and Lu Hsin.[24] However, the most important (though not the most active) new recruit to the Hong Kong Alliance was neither young nor an intellectual; he was more of a Westernized Chinese. He was Li Yü-t'ang, a fifty-five year old businessman known in the colony as the Chinese "Insurance King." His reasons for joining the Alliance may have been largely personal: Feng Tzu-yu was his son-in-law; Li Tzu-ch'ung, his son. In succeeding years, Li Yü-t'ang gave much financial assistance to the local Alliance.[25]

As reflected by the predominance of newspapermen in the organization, the almost exclusive activity of the Alliance in Hong Kong during these years was journalism. There were three revolutionary newspapers in the colony in 1906, Ch'en Shao-pai's *China Daily News,* Cheng Kuan-i's *Unique News,* and the *Commonweal.* These were the three papers that in April observed the anniversary of the death of the last Ming emperor.[26]

The *China Daily News,* originally the organ of the Society to Restore China's Prosperity, now became the organ of the Alliance. One of the most important articles setting forth the socialist ideas of the Alliance, Feng Tzu-yu's "Socialism and the Future of the Chinese Political Revolution," first appeared in the *China Daily News* in December 1905 and was later reprinted in the *People's Report* in Tokyo. The paper also debated with the *Commercial News,* the local spokesman for the Society to Protect the Emperor, much as in Tokyo the *People's Report* debated the *New People's Miscellany.* It was an article defaming K'ang Yu-wei's daughter, which resulted in a fine of HK$5,000, that bankrupted the *China Daily News* in the summer of 1906. Only the timely financial support of Li Yü-t'ang saved the paper from a forced sale. Afterwards the management of the paper was reorganized, with Feng Tzu-yu replacing Ch'en Shao-pai as editor. This change paved the way for Ch'en's retirement as head of the Alliance later in the year. Thereafter, until 1910, Feng was concurrently the head of the Alliance and the editor of the *China Daily News.*[27]

While he lived, Cheng Kuan-i continued to form a separate center of revolutionary journalism from the *China Daily News.* His *Unique News (Wei-i-ch'ü pao),* founded in the summer of 1905 as the successor to the short-lived *Kwangtung Daily News,* was edited with the help of a group of exceptionally talented writers and artists, including the novelist Huang Shih-chung and the artist Ch'en Shu-jen, both members of the Alliance. It was a more radical paper than the *China Daily News* under Ch'en Shao-pai. In December 1905, at the height of the anti-American boycott in Kwangtung, Ch'en sided with the moderate faction among the boycott leaders which was willing to settle for a liberalization of America's exclusionist immigration laws, while Cheng Kuan-i supported the radical faction which pressed for the complete abrogation of those laws. When Cheng died the following summer, his tabloid perished with him. Some of his disciples, carrying on his work, then established the *Orient Daily News (Tung-fang jih-pao),* which lasted only to the spring of 1907. Later in 1907 Huang Shih-chung founded *Youth News (Shao-nien pao),* evidently in the same journalistic tradition; it lasted about a year.[28] The *Commonweal,* which Cheng Kuan-i had originated and briefly edited, was the last of the three revolutionary papers in Hong Kong in 1906. Little is known about it, except that it was the paper that published the offending cartoon poster at the time of the Taft visit to Canton in September 1905, for which two of its editors were expelled from the colony.

In Kwangtung what little revolutionary activity there was during 1905–06 was concentrated in Canton and restricted to journalism also. The *China Daily News* and the *Unique News* both circulated relatively freely in Kwangtung until early 1906, when they were included among the Hong Kong papers barred from importation because of their criticisms of Governor-General Ts'en Ch'un-hsüan.[29] In Canton itself, according to Feng Tzu-yu's retrospective account, two of the proliferating journals were associated with the revolutionary movement. One was the *Current Events Pictorial;* the other was the *Masses*.[30]

Current Events Pictorial (Shih-shih hua-pao), a magazine founded in 1905 with a circulation of 3,000 copies, was well known for its "animus against the Government, and things old"; according to a contemporary foreign observer, "it did not hesitate to express its views with refreshing distinctness." [31] Its treatment of an incident reminiscent of the Ho Ts'ai-yen case of 1904 was perhaps representative. On September 16, 1906, a Chinese youth was dunked into Shameen Creek by a group of American sailors; fortunately, unlike Ho, the young man did not drown. A week later, in the twenty-fourth issue dated September 22, the *Current Events Pictorial* published a woodcut illustration of the episode with the following comment criticizing the indifference of the Chinese onlookers: "When I first heard about the incident, I was angry. Then I became bitter—bitter at the utter lack of humanitarian feelings and compassion in our feeble nation, our worthless race. We deserve to be carved up like fish and meat by the foreigners. How sad it is!" [32] The magazine folded later in 1906 for lack of funds. Only one of the five men listed as its editors, the artist Kao Chien-fu, was then a member of the Alliance; he was among the founding members in Tokyo. The illustration on the cover of the twenty-fourth issue was done by another member of the Alliance, Ch'en Shu-jen. However, two other editors, P'an Ta-wei and Ho Chien-shih, joined the Alliance later in 1909.[33]

Less is known about the *Masses (Ch'ün pao)*. It was founded in the winter of 1905–06 and lasted but half a year; it consisted of a single sheet. It was later reorganized as the *Twentieth-Century News (Nien shih-chi pao)* and expanded to two sheets; its daily circulation in May 1906 was about 1,000 copies. In February 1907 four unidentified persons accused of belonging to the "revolutionary party" were arrested at the office of the *Twentieth-Century News*. The paper presumably was closed down after that. None of the editors and writers with the *Masses* or its successor was a member of the Alliance at the time; two of them, Lu O-sheng (also Lu Yüeh-sheng) and Huang Hsüan-chou, joined it later in 1908.[34]

In sum, these two Canton journals were edited by men who evidently were sympathetic to the revolutionary cause even if they were not then formal members of the Alliance. However, both were obviously prevented from expressing their ideas openly. The comments of the *Current Events Pictorial* quoted above, while reminiscent of Ou Chü-chia's *New Kwangtung,* were radical but not necessarily revolutionary. In any case both journals were short-lived.

The Kwangtung Uprisings

After a year and a half of primarily journalistic work centering on Tokyo, the Revolutionary Alliance in 1907 plunged into a year of violent activity in central and south China. While groups associated with it organized the P'ing-Liu-Li uprising on the Kiangsi–Hunan border in December 1906 and the assassination of Governor En-ming in Anking, Anhwei, the following July, the Alliance itself carried out a spectacular series of revolts along the southern border of China that lasted into early 1908. Most of these took place in Kwangtung.[35]

This outburst of activity in Kwangtung came about largely because of a fortuitous conjunction of three events. One was Sun Yat-sen's expulsion from Japan in March 1907. Accompanied by Wang Ching-wei and Hu Han-min, Sun found a new sanctuary among the French in Hanoi.[36] Another was the escalation of the Ch'in-chou sugar growers' tax protest into a small-scale rebellion in the spring of 1907. The third, and most crucial, event was the response of the Canton government to the tax rebellion: it dispatched detachment commander Kuo Jen-chang and regimental commander Chao Sheng to West Kwangtung with troops to suppress the rebellion. Both men were reportedly sympathetic to the revolutionary cause. A year earlier, when Huang Hsing paid him a special visit at Kweilin to persuade him to revolt, Kuo Jen-chang had refused to take any overt action only on the plea that he was not free to act on his own.[37] In Ch'in-chou, he commanded two infantry battalions of the Reserve Forces. Kuo's colleague, Chao Sheng, was originally an officer in the Kiangsu New Army; he had been dismissed in 1906 for promoting revolution among his troops. He had come to Canton afterwards and had risen rapidly in the Kwangtung New Army to the position of regimental commander. At the same time he had enrolled in the Revolutionary Alliance in Hong Kong. In neighboring Lien-chou, Chao was in command of one battalion of infantry and one battery of artillery, both of them stripped from the New Army in order to deal with the tax revolt.[38]

Since Ch'in-chou is just across the border from Vietnam and easily accessible from Hanoi, Sun Yat-sen decided upon an elaborate scheme of coordinated revolts throughout Kwangtung, all keyed to the developments in Ch'in-chou. He would forge an alliance of revolutionaries, peasant rebels, and the Ch'ing armies to take over the panhandle area of western Kwangtung. He would also organize supporting uprisings in other parts of the province. With all of Kwangtung in the hands of the revolutionaries, the rest of the country would then follow suit. To implement these plans, Sun sent Huang Hsing back to Kuo Jen-chang in Ch'in-chou, Hu I-sheng to Chao Sheng in Lien-chou, and Kuang Ching-ch'uan to the tax rebels in Ch'in-chou as liaison agents between himself and the different groups. He also sent Teng Tzu-yü to Hui-chou and a couple other overseas Chinese to Yang-chiang to foment risings there, and he asked Hsü Hsüeh-ch'iu, who was already planning a revolt in Ch'ao-chou, to delay his attempt until preparations in Ch'in-chou and elsewhere were more advanced.[39] Later on, the revolutionaries in Hong Kong and Canton on their own added an assassination attempt in the provincial capital to Sun's master plan.

Unfortunately for Sun, his plans for a set of simultaneous uprisings began unraveling one by one almost as soon as they were decided upon. On May 12, while Sun's agent Kuang Ching-ch'uan (from the Haiphong branch of the Alliance) was still negotiating with the Ch'in-chou tax rebels, government troops led by Kuo Jen-chang and Chao Sheng attacked and captured the town of Na-ssu, a rebel stronghold, and killed the leader of the rebellion. It is unclear how this came about. It is possible that Kuo and Chao were as yet unaware of Sun's intentions with respect to the tax rebels. In any case, whatever the explanation, they pressed ahead with their attacks and eventually suppressed the tax rebellion. Thus vanished Sun's hopes for an immediate takeover of Ch'in-chou by the combined force of the peasant rebels and the government troops.[40]

On May 22 ten days after the Ch'in-chou tax protestors were defeated, Hsü Hsüeh-ch'iu's rebels rose up prematurely in Jao-p'ing district, at the other end of the province. Following the failure of his attempted revolt in Ch'ao-chou in April 1905, Hsü had gone to Singapore, where in June 1906 he met Sun Yat-sen and was persuaded to join the Alliance and to make another revolutionary attempt in East Kwangtung. Originally he had planned an armed attack by a secret society force on Ch'ao-chou city to take place on February 19, 1907, during the New Year holidays, but either because of indecision or because of bad weather it had been postponed at the last minute.[41] The attack was postponed again when Sun urged Hsü to coordinate it with the uprisings being planned in other parts of the province. Hsü accordingly went to Hong Kong to consult with Feng Tzu-yu and to await news from Sun in Hanoi.

Meanwhile, the secret society members that Hsü had recruited for the revolt grew restive. Their activities in the vicinity of Huang-kang, a walled town in Jao-p'ing on the coastal road to Fukien, aroused the suspicions of the Ch'ao-chou brigade-general, Huang Chin-fu, who sent a patrol to investigate and round up suspects. The secret society leaders on the scene, Yü Chi-ch'eng and Ch'en Yung-po, warned Hsü in Hong Kong that the situation at Huang-kang was becoming tense, but they were told to avoid a confrontation. Nevertheless, like the rebels at San-chou-t'ien waiting for Cheng Shih-liang in 1900, the rebels at Huang-kang decided on their own to attack first before they themselves were attacked. On the night of May 22, a force led by Yü and Ch'en struck at the small garrison of government troops at Huang-kang. By dawn they had captured the town.[42]

During the next two days, the rebels did not venture out of Huang-kang. Their occupation of the town was orderly. Immediately after their victory, they issued proclamations in Sun Yat-sen's name urging the local populace to remain calm and calling on the merchants to go about their business as usual; they also guaranteed protection to foreign missionaries and native converts. According to contemporary reports, the rebels did in fact maintain order and discipline. Nor were converts and foreigners molested. Meanwhile, the rebels, who were poorly armed with old-fashioned rifles and muskets, waited for aid and instructions from Hong Kong.

But the Alliance in Hong Kong did not learn of the uprising until it was already on the point of collapse. Hsü Hsüeh-ch'iu, rushing to Huang-kang, got no further than Swatow before the revolt was crushed. The only revolutionary leader to reach the rebels from the outside was Hsü's close associate, Ch'en Hung-sheng, who arrived from Swatow on May 25. On the same day, government reinforcements landed on the coast ten miles away. With Ch'en Hung-sheng in the lead, the rebels finally took the field to defend themselves. The government troops, however, were better armed than they and easily defeated them. As the rebels scattered to the hills, the Ch'ing forces recaptured Huang-kang on the twenty-seventh. The revolt had lasted five days.

After the revolt had been suppressed, Brigade-General Huang Chin-fu unleashed a reign of terror. He ordered over a hundred Triads whose names appeared on a captured membership list to be slaughtered. His reconquering troops also looted and burned freely. Their actions contrasted sharply with the orderly behavior of the revolutionary forces during their brief occupation of Huang-kang.

On June 2, a week after the Huang-kang uprising was crushed, another rebel band organized by Teng Tzu-yü rose up in Po-lo district, in the lower East River valley of Central Kwangtung.[43] A native of the area, a veteran of the 1900 Hui-chou revolt, and a secret society chieftain, Teng had joined the Alliance in Singapore in the spring of 1906. According to Sun Yat-sen's plan, he was to organize a revolt in his native region, using his secret society connections. When the Huang-kang rising broke out, Teng had barely arrived in Hong Kong from Singapore. Nevertheless, as soon as he heard about it, he sent agents among the secret society lodges in Kuei-shan, Po-lo, and Lung-men districts to try to get them to rebel. He himself remained in Hong Kong to buy arms and ammunition for the revolt. Like Hsü Hsüeh-ch'iu, he was to miss the revolt entirely.

Teng's agents in Po-lo were the most successful. They put together a secret society force that on June 2 attacked and overran the Ch'ing garrison at Ch'i-nü-hu, a market town less than ten miles north of Hui-chou city. After their initial success at Ch'i-nü-hu, the rebels, unlike their comrades at Huang-kang, kept on the move. During the next week they raided a number of other market towns along the East River and its tributary, the Kung-chuang River, in Po-lo and Kuei-shan districts. Whereas the rebels of 1900 had operated south and east of Hui-chou, those of 1907 operated north of the city. They generally avoided the more heavily defended places like district seats and did not directly threaten the prefectural capital. They thus managed to survive for about ten days to two weeks. However, when better-armed troops under the command of Brigade-General Li Chun finally arrived to reinforce the local braves, the rebels gave up the fight, particularly since there had been no supporting uprisings elsewhere in the area. They buried their weapons, disbanded and returned to their homes.

As in Huang-kang, the conduct of the rebels during their brief uprising had been exemplary. It was reported "that the rebels did not rob or plunder any of the shops, and that the villagers fired off crackers to welcome them." [44] But unlike those in Huang-kang, the rebels in Hui-chou evidently did not publicly acknowledge their association with the Revolutionary Alliance. Instead, the short proclamation which they issued was cast strictly in secret society terms. It called for "the expulsion of the barbarians and the restoration of the Ming dynasty." [45] Plans for a similar uprising in Yang-chiang, on the coast of West Kwangtung, were scuttled when the agent sent by Sun Yat-sen disappeared into the mainland with the money with which he had been entrusted. [46]

Finally, on June 11, as the Ch'i-nü-hu revolt was on the verge of collapse, Liu Ssu-fu bungled an attempted assassination of Brigade-General Li Chun in Canton. [47] The assassination had been planned as the contribution of the Alliance in Hong Kong and Canton to Sun Yat-sen's master plan for revolution. The target, Li Chun, was fast becoming the dominant military figure in Kwangtung. Moreover, since Li's Reserve Forces had been involved in the suppression of both the Huang-kang and the Ch'i-nü-hu uprisings, the revolutionaries thirsted for revenge. Liu Ssu-fu, a founding member of the Tokyo Alliance, volunteered for the mission. Assisting in the assassination attempt were Chang Ku-shan, Chang Po-ch'iao and Chu Chih-hsin, all members of the Alliance. Chang Ku-shan, formerly a normal school teacher in Chia-ying, was charged with finding a place in Canton for Liu to stay and make his preparations, while Chang Po-ch'iao and Chu Chih-hsin, both then teaching at the Kwangtung College of Law and Administration, were to keep track of Li Chun's movements. Chang and Chu discovered that Li reported to Governor-General Chou Fu regularly twice a month and that his next visit was scheduled for June 11.

Liu Ssu-fu's plan was to assassinate Li Chun as he left the governor-general's official compound. However, as Liu was assembling his bombs on the eleventh before setting out, one of them accidentally exploded, blowing off his left hand. Fortunately, Chang Ku-shan and a sympathetic doctor, Wu Han-ch'ih, succeeded in removing much of the incriminating evidence, including Liu's farewell letter vowing to "exterminate the pack of bandits," before he was arrested. As a result, and perhaps also because of his status as a licentiate, Liu was treated leniently by the police. Held on suspicion only, he was sentenced to a ten-year term in prison, which was later reduced to two years. The attempt to assassinate Li Chun was abandoned.

In one month the revolutionaries had scored two notable successes, at Huang-kang and in Hui-chou. But these successes were not exactly as Sun Yat-sen had intended them to be, largely because of the initial failure of the Ch'in-chou uprising, around which the other revolts had been planned. However, since Kuo Jen-chang and Chao Sheng were still stationed in Ch'in-chou and Lien-chou, Sun decided to make a new revolutionary attempt with their help. He sent Wang Ho-shun, a well-known bandit chief whom he had enrolled in the Alliance, to Ch'in-chou to form a new force from among the defeated tax rebels, the disaffected peasants, and the secret societies. At the same time, through Huang Hsing and Hu I-sheng, who were still attached to Kuo Jen-chang and Chao Sheng respectively, Sun secured the agreement of both men that if Wang was able to initiate a large-scale rebellion, they and their troops would join it.[48]

For about three months, Wang Ho-shun proceeded very slowly. Indeed, one group of rebels, led by the nephew of the former leader of the tax protest movement, grew tired of waiting on him and disbanded. Finally, at the beginning of September, the commanders of the two companies of Kwangsi troops defending the unwalled district city of Fang-ch'eng, west of Ch'in-chou, abruptly defected to the revolutionary side. Why they defected is not clear. A native of Kwangsi himself, Wang may have played upon their common provincial ties; or he may have bribed them. In any case, with their help, Wang Ho-shun and several hundred followers captured Fang-ch'eng without a fight on September 3.

Once Fang-ch'eng was secured, Wang and his band set out for Ch'in-chou city, expecting the support of Kuo Jen-chang. Kuo however was unimpressed by the size of Wang's following and was evasive. When Huang Hsing pressed him to open the city to the rebel force, he claimed that the resident taotai was suspicious of him and that he could not do so, at least for the time being. Giving up on Kuo, Wang then turned toward Ling-shan, northeast of Ch'in-chou. On September 9 he began a two-day siege of Ling-shan city and waited for Chao Sheng to arrive with help. Chao apparently was no more willing than Kuo to risk defeat by joining Wang's small and poorly armed group. Instead of helping them, Chao scattered the rebels and raised the siege. The defeated rebels eventually withdrew to the mountains on the border of Vietnam, while Wang Ho-shun retired to Hanoi to report to Sun Yat-sen. The revolt had lasted about ten days. Afterwards, Brigade-General Li Chun arrived to help Kuo Jen-chang with the pacification effort.

Once again, the rebels' behavior stood in sharp contrast to that of the officials. During their brief moment of success, the rebels reportedly had not looted and always paid for everything in gold. They had harmed no one in their custody. The only exception was the Fang-ch'eng magistrate Sung Ting-yüan and his entourage. Magistrate Sung had refused to cooperate with the rebels. He steadfastly denied that in serving the Ch'ing dynasty he was a "traitor to the Chinese people" or a "slave of the Manchus." On the contrary, he maintained, "The Manchus are Chinese; I too am a Chinese official." [49] Wang Ho-shun criticized these views as identical to those of the rival Society to Protect the Emperor. He ordered the magistrate and his personal secretaries executed. Sung's wife and daughters then committed suicide. It was a rare instance of "revolutionary justice" in Kwangtung. The officials, on the other hand, behaved harshly during and after the revolt. Kuo Jen-chang reportedly treated his prisoners most cruelly and aroused the people to more determined opposition.

While the Fang-ch'eng revolt was going on in West Kwangtung, Hsü Hsüeh-ch'iu was organizing another one in the east. Hsü had met with Sun Yat-sen in Hanoi in August to explain the failure of the Huangkang uprising and to ask his support for a new attempt, this time in the East River area. Sun agreed to supply him with a quantity of new arms and ammunition that his agent Kayano Chōchi had just bought in Japan. The shipment was to be smuggled ashore at Shan-wei, in Haifeng, just off the shipping lane between Japan and Hong Kong. Hsü was to make the local arrangements for receiving the shipment at Shan-wei.[50]

The smuggling attempt, which took place one month after the suppression of Wang Ho-shun's revolt, was a failure. When the *Kōun Maru*, nominally chartered to carry coal to Hong Kong, stopped off the coast at Shan-wei on the morning of October 12, no one was ready to accept its contraband cargo. She had been expected the previous night; when she failed to appear by dawn, all the lighters that Hsü Hsüeh-ch'iu had assembled to take the cargo ashore had dispersed. As Hsü hurried off to try to round them up again, the *Kōun Maru* waited offshore. After a while, a government patrol boat became suspicious of her odd behavior and went out to investigate. Alarmed and impatient, the Japanese skipper sailed off hurriedly, without waiting for Hsü's return. In Hong Kong the revolutionaries and their Japanese sympathizers considered another attempt to deliver the arms and ammunition to Hsü on the *Kōun Maru*'s homeward voyage. But even before her regular cargo of coal had been unloaded, the Japanese consul ordered her to leave port at once; he had been warned that the Ch'ing government had asked the Hong Kong authorities to seize the ship. After that, the smuggling attempt was abandoned, as were Hsü's plans for a revolt in the East River region.

In early December the leaders of the Alliance in Hanoi, principally Sun Yat-sen, Huang Hsing, and Hu Han-min, were diverted from their preoccupation with Kwangtung by the unexpected capture of Chen-nan-kuan in southwestern Kwangsi. But when that revolt collapsed after a week, their attention returned once more to Ch'in-chou. Brigade-General Li Chun had just been recalled to Canton to help deal with the British naval intervention in the West River, leaving Kuo Jen-chang in charge of military operations again. (Chao Sheng evidently was no longer in Lien-chou.) Hoping still to capitalize upon Kuo's supposed sympathy for the revolution, Sun and Huang now planned an invasion of Ch'in-chou by an expeditionary force composed of overseas Chinese and secret society members from Vietnam. The Hunanese T'an Jen-feng visited Kuo at his camp in Ch'in-chou and, by exaggerating the revolutionaries' resources, allegedly obtained a promise of cooperation, at least to the extent of supplying arms and ammunition to the expeditionary force once it arrived.[51]

The expedition itself was largely the work of Huang Hsing, because Sun Yat-sen was expelled from French Indochina in early March. On March 27, 1908, apparently unopposed by either French or Chinese border guards, Huang and a group of more than two hundred men crossed into Ch'in-chou at a point near the town of Tung-hsing. During the next two days the expeditionary force roamed freely, while its leaders tried and failed several times to establish contact with Kuo Jen-chang. On the third day, the twenty-ninth, Huang's men, perhaps accidentally, clashed with two of Kuo's battalions and defeated them. All hope of aid or cooperation from Kuo vanished when four days later, on April 2, the revolutionaries, now grown to six hundred men, routed his troops once more. Pursued by reinforced government troops and low on ammunition, the revolutionaries headed into the mountains on the Kwangsi border. Individually and in small groups, they painfully made their way back to Vietnam. Although Huang Hsing himself did not reappear in Hanoi until May 5, the revolt was effectively over by the middle of April. It had lasted a little more than two weeks. Unlike Wang Ho-shun the previous September, Huang Hsing had avoided the cities and towns and operated mainly in the countryside. For the first week or so, he and his men evidently had some success in attracting the support of the local peasantry and secret societies. Later on, when they were on the run and some of them resorted to indiscriminate plundering and killing, the popular support evaporated.

Except for the unsuccessful revolt at Ho-k'ou, Yunnan, in April and May, in the course of which Huang Hsing too was expelled from French Indochina, the invasion of Ch'in-chou was the last in the year-long series of revolutionary uprisings in south China. With Sun Yat-sen and Huang Hsing both barred from Vietnam, Kwangtung quieted down once more.

As a result of these revolts, the level of activity for the Hong Kong branch of the Revolutionary Alliance rose sharply. Before 1907, it included at most thirty or forty members and its major function was to publish the *China Daily News*. In 1907 "several hundred" new members enrolled in the branch, of whom 67 are listed by name. Moreover, the branch office, headed by Feng Tzu-yu, handled the arrangements for all the revolts in Kwangtung except those in Ch'in-chou, which were directed from Hanoi. It coped with the refugees who flocked to Hong Kong after each failure, too. Meanwhile, Feng continued to put out the *China Daily News,* which gave full coverage to the various revolutionary attempts. In the summer of 1907 the paper also sparked a big controversy in Hong Kong by reprinting and distributing the virulently anti-Manchu tract, *Heaven's Punishment (T'ien t'ao)*. The colonial government confiscated the issue immediately; later the Legislative Council passed an ordinance restricting such inflammatory publications. The *China Daily News* was obliged to tone down its subsequent attacks on the Ch'ing.[52]

In Canton, apart from the attempt to assassinate Brigade-General Li Chun, some efforts were made in 1907 to proselytize within the Ch'ing army. Led by Chang Ku-shan before he was forced to flee the city following his involvement in the Li Chun assassination attempt, a small group of revolutionaries engaged in propaganda work among the New Army and the Reserve Forces and within the two military schools, the Short-term Officers' School and the Whampoa Military Primary School. The results were quite promising. Among those who joined the Hong Kong Alliance in 1907 were more than a dozen military men, including Yao Yü-p'ing, Chang Lu-ts'un, Ko Ch'ien, T'an Fu, and Chang Wo-ch'üan.[53]

Curiously, despite its demonstrated ability to attract students into its ranks, the Alliance hardly utilized their services in the uprisings of 1907 and early 1908. Although they apparently constituted a majority of the Alliance membership in both Tokyo and Hong Kong, few students and intellectuals participated in the risings. The one exception was the attempted assassination of Li Chun, but that involved only a handful of individuals. A few more acted as liaison agents in Ch'in-chou between the various local forces and the Alliance leaders in Hanoi. Others were scheduled to take part in Hsü Hsüeh-ch'iu's February uprising in Ch'ao-chou, but the revolt itself never came off.[54] One reason for the remarkably low rate of participation by the student revolutionaries in these revolts was that they all took place near the periphery of the province. Except for the attempt on Li Chun's life, none took place in the Canton–Hong Kong area, where many of the student revolutionaries were concentrated. The closest was the Ch'i-nü-hu rising, but it occurred on the far side of Hui-chou city.

Consequently, the revolts of 1907 and early 1908 bear a striking resemblance to Sun Yat-sen's earlier revolts, where the intellectuals and the revolutionaries provided the leadership, while the secret societies and the bandit bands provided the manpower. The Huang-kang and Ch'i-nü-hu uprisings were led and executed by the secret societies, while the Fang-ch'eng rising was the work of the bandit chief Wang Ho-shun. The roster of those who joined the Alliance in 1907 in Hong Kong and Canton included quite a few secret society and bandit leaders, such as the leaders of the Huang-kang and Ch'i-nü-hu risings and also the notorious bandit chief of Central Kwangtung, Lu Lan-ch'ing.[55] Huang Hsing's expeditionary force that invaded Ch'in-chou from Vietnam was an interesting departure from the pattern of Sun's earlier revolts, because it was an attempt to organize an independent armed force rather than to depend on external forces. But the force itself was composed mostly of overseas Chinese with secret society connections; it included few student revolutionaries.

Perhaps an even more significant departure was the attempt to destroy the regime by subverting its own military forces. Much of what the revolutionaries did in 1907 and early 1908 was predicated on the belief that they could count on the cooperation of detachment commander Kuo Jen-chang and regimental commander Chao Sheng in Ch'in-chou and Lien-chou. Their approach to Kuo and Chao, however, differed fundamentally from what Chang Ku-shan was trying to do in Canton. Where Chang concentrated on building a network of supporters *within* the army, Sun Yat-sen and Huang Hsing lavished their attention on Kuo and Chao alone and ignored the rank and file. Such an approach was not unlike their relationship with the secret societies and bandit bands, where to convert or buy off the leader was enough to secure his following as well.

It worked in the case of the two company commanders at Fang-ch'eng; but it did not work in the case of Kuo Jen-chang and Chao Sheng. Chao Sheng seems to have been willing enough to go over to the revolutionaries; he had already enrolled in the Alliance. But he evidently felt that he could not act independently of Kuo, perhaps because his force was weaker than Kuo's. As a result, when Kuo did nothing, neither did Chao. Kuo's relationship with the revolutionaries was far more ambiguous. He apparently gave them reason for believing that he was sympathetic, or at least not unsympathetic, with their cause, but unlike Chao he never enrolled in the Alliance and he actually gave it very little assistance. He appears to have been, simply, an opportunist. When all the revolts had been suppressed, Kuo was promoted by the Ch'ing to be the taotai at Ch'in-chou, a post which he still held in 1911 when the revolution broke out.

Except indirectly through the secret societies and the bandits, the Alliance did practically nothing to capitalize upon the widespread and growing peasant discontent in the province. Perhaps because of the social gulf that separated them from the peasants, the revolutionary leaders, most of whom were intellectuals, were hardly cognizant of the problems of the peasantry or of their revolutionary potentialities.[56] Their program calling for the equalization of land rights was directed more towards preventing future problems that would arise with industrialization and urbanization than towards rectifying current inequities in the countryside.[57] In the only instance in Kwangtung where the Alliance tried to establish direct contact with a group of rebellious peasants, the sugar growers in Ch'in-chou, it proved to be tragically inept. Nevertheless, where it succeeded in mounting an uprising, the Alliance did not lack support from the rural populace. Moreover, in almost every revolt, its forces maintained order and refrained from molesting the people. As a result, it gained a popular reputation for good behavior. In contrast, the official forces often behaved abominably. Their harsh and vindictive measures, like the reign of terror after the Huang-kang revolt, served only to perpetuate the rural unrest.

Finally, while the revolts in south and central China in 1907 and early 1908 were undeniably a remarkable performance for the Alliance, they scarcely menaced the government, which managed to put down every one of them with relative ease. Their effect upon the Ch'ing was slight. They may have helped spur the court to clarify its constitutional program in the autumn of 1907, but they did not cause it to change direction or adopt new policies. The constitutional program, for example, had been proclaimed before the first of the revolts; indeed, it had been under active consideration even before the formation of the Alliance. Despite the rash of revolts and the defection of some radical intellectuals, the regime in 1907 once again enjoyed the confidence of most of its subjects, including most of those who were "politically relevant." The charges made against it by the Revolutionary Alliance did not gain wide acceptance because the actions of the court in the middle years of the decade generally belied those charges. The revolts occurred in the absence of a revolutionary situation, and so they failed.

6

Final Years of the Post-Boxer Decade, I: Nationalism

In the final years of the post-Boxer decade, roughly from late 1907 or early 1908 to the beginning of 1911, official reforms and social mobilization interacted upon each other at an accelerated pace. As reforms previously decreed continued to be implemented, new ones were inaugurated. Meanwhile, the court's decrees in September and October 1907 promising to create elected assemblies sparked a further heightening of the level of popular involvement in public affairs, including a particularly remarkable upsurge of mass nationalism in Kwangtung. This in turn made the constitutional program all the more necessary to bring such extra-constitutional activities under governmental control. During these years, Kwangtung was ruled by Chang Jen-chün (September 1907 to July 1909), Yüan Shu-hsün (September 1909 to October 1910), and Chang Ming-ch'i (January to November 1911).[1]

Reform and Politicization

During the last years of the decade, the reform movement, both from above and from below, flourished as never before. The death of Empress Dowager Tz'u-hsi and the Kuang-hsü Emperor on successive days in November 1908 had no immediate effect upon the court's post-Boxer program, as Tsai-feng, regent for the young Hsüan-t'ung Emperor, followed the policies that Tz'u-hsi had originated. The official reforms previously decreed were extended, while additional reforms were newly decreed. The most noteworthy of the new reforms were the constitutional reforms, of course, but there were others. At the same time, as the reforms were continued and intensified, the urban elite became ever more politicized.

In Kwangtung the old reforms were carried out with varying degrees of success. The modern schools, the chambers of commerce, and the anti-opium campaign all achieved what was expected of them. The New Army, on the other hand, still fell far short.

By the end of the decade the obstacles that heretofore had hindered the progress of the modern schools had all been overcome. With the founding of the Higher Normal School in the spring of 1908, the panoply of higher schools within the province had been completed. The modern education had triumphed over the traditional. When the School for the Preservation of Antiquity (Ts'un-ku hsüeh-t'ang), founded by imperial decree to promote Chinese classical studies in order to preserve the "national essence," opened in Canton in 1909, it managed to enroll only 80 to 120 students. (The school in Hupeh, which was the model for the rest of the country, had difficulty obtaining students too.) [2] Also, by 1909 there were fewer than ten districts in the province which had not established an office for the encouragement of education to oversee the founding and operation of modern schools.[3] Most important, by then the teacher shortage was over. This was reflected in the decline in the number of normal schools and normal school students in Kwangtung, from 44 schools and 3,400 students in 1907 to 9 schools and 1,003 students in 1909, and in the number of Chinese students in Japan, which dropped from a peak figure of eight to fifteen thousand in 1906 to three to seven thousand after 1907.[4]

Practically all the modern schools founded during these years in Kwangtung were primary schools; most were located in the outlying districts. Between 1907 and 1909, the last year for which statistics from the Ministry of Education are available, the number of primary schools in the province rose by about two hundred, from 1441 to 1628; the number of primary school pupils, by about thirteen thousand, from 65,986 to 78,727. In Kao-yao, in the West River valley, 16 modern schools were founded during 1908–11, as opposed to 15 in all the previous years. Similarly in Ling-shan, in the western panhandle, 17 were founded in 1908–11, as opposed to 4 previously. Because of their earlier start the pace was of course slower in the more progressive districts. In Shun-te, where there were already 30 schools by the end of 1907, only 4 were started during these years.[5] By the end of the decade even the most backward of districts in the province probably had met the government's minimum demands for educational reforms.

Chambers of commerce also proliferated. In 1908, the last year for which the government published these statistics, twelve branch chambers were added to the two general chambers in Canton and Swatow and the fifteen branch chambers already established by 1907. More were started in later years. By 1911 probably most of the commercially developed districts had at least one chamber of commerce. Some had more than one. K'ai-p'ing, for example, had four; Nan-hai, five; and Shun-te, eleven.[6]

The anti-opium crusade, begun unofficially in 1906 and given official support in 1907, achieved a remarkable success during the last years of the decade. Spurred by the provincial Anti-Opium Society, local societies were established in a number of districts across the province, such as K'ai-p'ing, Ch'ing-yüan, and Ying-te. They cooperated with the officials in publicizing the drive, dispensing anti-opium drugs, and licensing opium addicts. The Ying-te society, for example, organized a mass meeting at the district capital in November 1908 at which local smokers were given six months to abandon their habit. The society offered anti-opium drugs at cost to those who could afford to pay for them. Those who were financially less well off were to buy the drugs at 70 percent of cost; the poor were to get them free.[7]

With popular and official support, the anti-opium drive was by all accounts highly effective throughout the province. The British consulate in Canton admitted in January 1909 that "the Anti-Opium Regulations have been carried out with some thoroughness in Canton and the province; opium divans have been generally closed, and opium smoking, condemned by public opinion, is certainly on the decrease." In Lien-chou, in the west, and Ch'ao-chou and Swatow, in the east, where previously the anti-opium drive had lagged, foreign observers reported similar progress. These observations are confirmed by the trade statistics published by the Maritime Customs. In Canton the importation of foreign opium declined by close to two thirds, from 10,404 piculs in 1907 to 3,907 piculs in 1911. The importation of native opium also dropped after 1908; by 1911 it was practically nil. In Swatow foreign opium imports were reduced by 50 percent between 1909 and 1911, while native opium imports again fell to practically nothing by 1911. In Pakhoi, the statistics told a similar story.[8]

Was the success of the anti-opium campaign due to the agreement concluded in January 1908 and renewed in 1911 between Britain and the Ch'ing by which Britain reduced her export of Indian opium to China by 10 percent a year for ten years? The agreement was certainly responsible for the complete elimination of opium imports in 1917, despite the internal chaos after the revolution. However, during the first few years of the agreement, before the onset of the post-revolutionary troubles, it may actually have hindered rather than helped the Chinese anti-opium efforts. Without the agreement, which also *limited* the reduction of opium imports to no more than 10 percent a year, the opium habit might have been eradicated sooner than 1917. Thus, the import of native opium, which was not restricted by the agreement, was, in Kwangtung at least, curtailed much sooner and more sharply than the foreign imports.[9]

Unlike the schools, the chambers of commerce, and the anti-opium campaign, the New Army reforms in Kwangtung made little progress. At the beginning of 1908, after several units had been permanently detached to deal with the uprisings in Ch'in-chou and Lien-chou, the Kwangtung New Army consisted essentially of only three battalions of infantry. Two years later it had been rebuilt up to a "mixed brigade" and a training battalion, totaling 6,000 men. This was equivalent to about half a division, far from the two divisions projected for the province. Then came the New Army mutiny in Canton in February 1910. Suspected of having been infiltrated by revolutionaries, three of the six regular infantry battalions and all four of the noninfantry battalions were disbanded. As a result, the Kwangtung New Army limped into 1911 with once again only three regular infantry battalions and the training battalion. It was regarded as one of the weakest army units in the country.[10]

Meanwhile, various public works were finished. In Canton the waterworks and the brick and cement works, both begun in 1906, were completed at the end of 1908. By 1910 the waterworks was supplying piped water to more than 11,000 houses in the city. The brick factory also worked satisfactorily. The cement works, however, ran into technical trouble at the end of 1909 and suspended production during most of 1910. It was reorganized and resumed operation at the end of 1910.

Also in Canton the wide and spacious bund, two miles long, was completed along the waterfront in 1909, turning the mudflats into a paved roadway.[11] In Swatow, an electric light plant was erected during 1909–10, and about four thousand lamps were installed.[12]

The several railroad projects made varying progress during these years. The Canton–Kowloon railroad, 111 miles long, was completed and put into service on October 4, 1911. On the other hand, the Kwangtung section of the Canton–Hankow line added only 21 miles of tracks to the 45 that were open to traffic at the beginning of 1908. This slow progress was attributable in part to the difficult terrain of northern Kwangtung and in part to inadequate financing and dissension among the shareholders.[13] Elsewhere in Central Kwangtung, the Hsin-ning railroad, begun in 1906 and built exclusively with Chinese capital and by Chinese engineers, was completed in June 1909. It then ran from the coastal hamlet of Tou-shan through Hsin-ning city to Kung-i, a model town built by émigrés returned from America. The road was later extended from Kung-i to the treaty port of Kongmoon in 1913. The entire road was 67 miles long. (The line no longer exists. It was dismantled during the Second World War and never rebuilt.)[14]

Apart from the constitutional reforms, the reforms newly decreed during these years included agricultural associations, a new court system, and prison reform. The agricultural associations (*nung-hui*) were the rural counterpart of the chambers of commerce. They were formed in accordance with an October 1907 decree by the Ministry of Agriculture, Industry, and Commerce and were intended to strengthen China's economy by fostering agricultural development. In Kwangtung the General Agricultural Association (Nung-wu tsung-hui) was organized in Canton probably in 1908, which was when an agricultural and forestry experimental station was started under the direction of an American-trained agronomist. Attached to it in 1910 was a training course in agricultural techniques, with 80 students. Local branch associations were set up in other cities, such as Tseng-ch'eng, Le-ch'ang, Shih-ch'eng, and Fo-shan. Some of them, like the Tseng-ch'eng association, operated experimental stations of their own.[15] It is perhaps symptomatic of the general neglect of agriculture at this time that development of the agricultural associations lagged so far behind that of the chambers of commerce.

The new court system, approved by the throne in November 1906, provided for a Western-style judiciary that, unlike the traditional Chinese judiciary, was separate from and independent of government administration. It was to consist of a hierarchy of national, provincial, prefectural, and district courts (*shen-p'an t'ing*), to be created between 1909 and 1913. In Kwangtung the provincial court was established in Canton in 1910. Also established in Canton, probably in 1910, were the Kuang-chou prefectural court and the P'an-yü district court. Similar courts may have been created in other prefectures and districts; one, for example, was set up in Pakhoi in July 1911. It is unclear how well the new courts worked. The Canton prefectural court was criticized in 1911 as too closely dependent upon the provincial police taotai. This court system was intended as a first step toward the eventual abolition of extraterritoriality.[16]

Prison reform was another innovation encouraged by the Ministry of Justice. In Kwangtung the Nan-hai and P'an-yü magistrates in 1907 joined to operate a six-month course in Canton to train prison reformers. "Model prisons" were set up in at least Nan-hai and Hsiang-shan. According to one news report, the Nan-hai prison, built evidently in 1908, resembled "in every respect a foreign prison in point of cleanliness, ventilation, etc."[17] Because of the onset of the revolution in 1911, however, few of the official reforms decreed in the last years of the decade had a chance to become firmly established.

Concurrent with the reforms from above were numerous reforms from below. In earlier years of the decade, the traditional ban on popular associations had been breached, but relatively few societies had been founded; moreover, they usually were either official or quasi-official bodies, such as the chambers of commerce, the anti-opium societies and the education associations, or temporary ad hoc bodies, like the Society to Oppose the Treaty that organized the anti-American boycott. In the wake of the court's promise of eventual self-rule late in 1907, many more associations of a private and permanent nature were formed. In Canton newspaper publishers founded the Newspaper Association (Pao-chieh kung-hui) in March 1908 to promote the "right of speech."[18] Engineering mechanics, for whom Canton was renowned, organized in 1909 the Society for the Study of Machines (Chi-ch'i yen-chiu kung-hui), which was China's first labor union. (In May 1911 the society hosted a meeting attended by "labourers of various occupation" to consider the formation of a city-wide "Canton Labourers Union," but such a union evidently was not formed prior to the revolution.)[19] At the same time, Chinese doctors practicing Western medicine formed a Red Cross Society (Ch'ih shih-tzu hui).[20]

Other organizations founded in Canton in this period include an Athletic Association, to popularize sports in the city's schools; a Confucian Society, evidently to promote Confucianism as the national religion of China; a society to reform marriage customs, such as by reducing dowries and wedding costs; and a society for European clothes, composed of fashion-minded school youths. The Chinese in Hong Kong also formed "numerous clubs and societies," among which were labor unions seeking to "browbeat their foreign employers" about hours and conditions of work and rate of pay. The Chinese-language papers in the colony had their own Newspaper Association. The situation was a far cry from the organizational passivity about which Ou Chü-chia had complained less than ten years before.[21]

Moreover, such associations were organized not only locally but increasingly on a province-wide and even nationwide basis. In Kwangtung early in 1911 the various district-wide education associations, composed of officials and gentry members interested in promoting the new schools, came together in Canton to form the Provincial Education Association (Chiao-yü tsung-hui). It may have grown out of the Association of Educational Circles (Ch'üan-sheng hsüeh-chieh kung-hui), a province-wide group founded in Canton in 1905. Shortly thereafter, in May 1911, a nationwide Federation of Provincial Education Associations (Ko-sheng chiao-yü tsung-hui lien-ho hui) was formed in Shanghai. The Kwangtung association was not present at the founding meeting, but it undoubtedly was a member of the organization.[22] A little earlier, in September 1910, a nationwide association of newspaper publishers, the Chinese Society for the Promotion of Newspapers (Chung-kuo pao-kuan chü-chin hui), was founded also in Shanghai. Newspapers in Kwangtung which belonged to it included the *National Affairs Daily* (*Kuo-shih pao*) of Canton, the *China New Journal* (*Chung-hua hsin pao*) of Swatow, and the *Commercial News* of Hong Kong.[23] There was also an attempt in 1910 to link up the various newly organized provincial agricultural associations into a National Federation of Agricultural Associations (Ch'üan-kuo nung-wu lien-ho hui). However, a similar attempt earlier in 1907 to form a national association of chambers of commerce was frustrated by the central government.[24]

Newspapers continued to proliferate. In Kwangtung the number of dailies in Swatow increased from two in 1907 to four in 1911, with the most noteworthy addition being the *China New Journal,* which was founded in the summer of 1908 by a group of Hakka businessmen and gentry members.[25] Newspapers also appeared in Ch'ao-chou and Hai-feng, in East Kwangtung, and in Shun-te, Hsin-ning, and Huang-ts'un, near Kongmoon, in Central Kwangtung.[26] Only in Canton did the press suffer a setback, as the number of dailies dropped from fourteen in 1907 to nine in 1908 and 1909. This may have been because of the central government's new press law promulgated in March 1908, which tried to restrict political commentary to within officially approved channels. In 1910 the number of Canton dailies rose again, but only to eleven.[27]

The women's rights movement too prospered. The number of girls' schools and women students, while still small in comparison to men, increased significantly. According to figures published by the Ministry of Education in Peking, the number of girls attending schools in Kwangtung doubled from 391 in 1907 to 715 in 1909. Women continued to play a growing role in public affairs. In the summer of 1908, after serious flooding on the West River, hundreds of schoolgirls, hitherto secluded from male society, participated openly in the relief effort in Canton. The movement against footbinding continued apace. Referring once more to statistics gathered at Ting Hsien, Chihli, 40.3 percent of the girls born during 1905–09, who ordinarily would have started binding their feet during 1908–12, had natural, unbound feet. This was more than twice as many as those born during the previous half-decade. There were also the first stirrings of a movement against arranged marriages, with the formation in Canton of a "Société de l'amour libre." [28]

Finally, there was a great upsurge of mass nationalism during these years.

The West River Patrol Agitation

The partition of China by the foreign powers had been a constant source of anxiety for the Chinese since the Scramble for Concessions and the allied expedition to put down the Boxer Rebellion. With the inauguration of the post-Boxer reforms such worries had receded a bit, but they came to the fore again in the summer and autumn of 1907 as a result of a series of agreements among France, Japan, Russia, and Britain regarding their rival claims in China and the rest of Asia. This four-power entente threatened to eliminate the "international jealousies and suspicions [that] had for decades been the best allies of China and had formed the basis, almost, of China's precarious existence, certainly of her foreign policy. Now a polarization had taken place on the basis of politi-

cal understandings which reduced rival groups to two [France–Japan–
Russia–Britain vs. the United States and Germany], each of which, the
Chinese were convinced, had divided the spoils among its members." As
a group of students warned a large audience in Canton in December
1907, "The quadruple alliance meant that the partition of China was
impending." [29] There was no partition, of course, but the powers'
united stance toward China, reflected for example in the four-nation
Consortium of Banks formed in 1910, continued through the rest of the
decade.

The response was a resurgence of nationalism. While there was no nationwide single-issue movement like the anti-American boycott of 1905,
there were many localized demonstrations focusing on a wide range of issues, such as the anti-British boycott in Kiukiang, Kiangsi, in 1909 in
retaliation for the killing of a Chinese by a British policeman and the
protests in Yunnan in 1910 against plans by an Anglo-French syndicate
to open mines.[30] The nationalist movement was particularly intense in
Kwangtung, where a series of protest demonstrations directed successively against the British, the Japanese, and the Portuguese lasted from
the end of 1907 to the end of 1909. The main organizer of these protests
was the Canton Merchants' Self-Government Society, the most active of
the popular associations founded in Kwangtung at this time.

A British naval intervention on the West River at the end of 1907
provoked the first of the nationalist protests in Kwangtung and occasioned the formation of the Self-Government Society. The intervention
was intended ostensibly to protect British shipping from the piracy that
had been endemic on the river since at least the middle of the nineteenth
century. It was prompted by an attack on the British steamer *Sainam* a
year and a half earlier, in which a British missionary had been killed and
for which the Chinese government had repeatedly denied responsibility.
Exasperated by the unchecked piracies, the British authorities in October or November 1907 recommended to the Ch'ing government that the
foreign-directed Maritime Customs take over the patrolling of the river
from the transparently ineffective Kwangtung navy. When the Chinese
rejected their recommendation, the British decided to make the patrol
themselves. Forcing their unwanted "assistance" upon the Ch'ing, they
began their patrol of the West River on December 3.[31]

As a matter of fact, conditions on the West River were not quite so
perilous to foreign shipping as the British implied. Few of the launches
and steamers registered as foreign-owned actually belonged to foreigners.

Most of them belonged to Chinese who had taken out the foreign registration in order to avoid the delays and the "squeeze" that Chinese-registered launches customarily experienced at the successive likin stations on the river. This was done also to minimize the risks of piracy, since the pirates generally avoided "foreign" launches; they knew that "whenever one was pirated the whole machinery of foreign intervention was invoked by the registered owner." As a correspondent in Hong Kong acknowledged as late as November 20, 1907, "Steamers flying the British flag have not been interfered with lately." [32] The *Sainam* had been an exception in both ways: it was truly British-owned and it had been attacked.

Opposition to the foreign intervention on the West River developed very quickly in Kwangtung. It began even before the inauguration of the British patrol, when a rumor reached Canton on November 18 that the Ch'ing Foreign Ministry had acquiesced in the original British recommendation that the Maritime Customs assume responsibility for patrolling the river. Immediately and apparently spontaneously, the gentry, merchants, and students all protested their government's capitulation. The gentry, led by the retired official Teng Hua-hsi and the metropolitan graduate Chiang K'ung-yin, summoned a mass meeting for the very next day, the nineteenth, at the Ming-lun hall of the Confucian Temple; it was attended by gentry, merchants, and students alike. In addition, the merchants and students, both male and female, held their own separate meetings. The merchants, led by Huang Ching-t'ang and Ch'en Hui-p'u, met on the nineteenth at the Hua-lin Temple. On the twentieth, five hundred representatives from fifty colleges and schools in the city met at the Nan-wu School, and on the twenty-fifth, three hundred students from seven girls' schools held a meeting of their own. The different groups all objected strenuously to any foreign patrol of the river, even if it were conducted by the Maritime Customs, which was technically a part of the Ch'ing government. They made their objections known to the Foreign Ministry in a torrent of telegrams.[33]

The merchants and students did more than protest; taking advantage of the court's recent edicts promising self-rule, they organized. At a meeting on November 21, attended by three to four thousand people, the merchants founded the Canton Merchants' Self-Government Society (Yüeh-shang tzu-chih hui); its purpose, to "assist the officials" and to "safeguard the sovereign rights and privileges of the Nation." The leader of the society was Ch'en Hui-p'u, the head of the Kwangtung Anti-Opium Society and formerly an officer of the Kwangtung Railway Company; some of his critics described him also as a "bankrupt banker." Next to Ch'en Hui-p'u, the leading figures in the Self-Government Society were Lo Shao-ao, editor of the *Seventy-two Guilds' Commercial News,* and Li Chieh-ssu, apparently also a journalist. The society met regularly once a week, usually at the Hua-lin Temple, its headquarters.[34] The students formed their own organization, the Society to Recover the Nation's Rights (Kuo-ch'üan wan-chiu hui), on November 22 at a meeting at the Nan-wu School, which had been a center of student activity during the anti-American boycott too. An eleven-man directorate, headed by Shen Hsiao-tse and Ho Chien-wu, was elected to manage its affairs. Shen, in 1905, had been an editor of the allegedly pro-revolutionary Canton newspaper, the *Masses.*[35]

The inauguration of the British patrol on December 3, which the Ch'ing Foreign Ministry had been forced to sanction in spite of the opposition from Kwangtung, generated further protests. In Canton "thousands" thronged a meeting of the Self-Government Society on December 6 and passed a resolution to oppose the British intervention by "civilized [that is, nonviolent] means." The society met at least four more times during the rest of December to discuss the matter.[36] The Society to Recover the Nation's Rights also sponsored a protest meeting on December 8, which was attended by five hundred students. There was another big student meeting on the twenty-second.[37]

Outside Canton, the "Political Power Protection Association" in Kao-yao and the "Tung Chi [She] (United Society)" in Samshui also lodged protests. In Swatow, far from the scene of the patrol's operations, "a meeting of merchants and hot-headed schoolboys was convened and speeches delivered urging the people to insist upon the maintenance of the sovereign rights of China." Swatow too had a National Rights Society (Kuo-ch'üan hui). In addition, the chamber of commerce in Fo-shan, the school association (*hsüeh-hui*) and the "gentry and people" of Hui-chou (led incidentally by the former revolutionary and author of *New Kwangtung,* Ou Chü-chia), and various groups of Kwangtung natives in Shanghai, Hupeh, and Japan all sent protest telegrams to the Foreign Ministry.[38]

Behind the protests was the renewed fear of partition. As four students recently returned from Japan warned the Self-Government Society in December, "The snatching of the patrolling power [in the West River] was its foreboding." Others contended, with references to the loss of Korea, "the fate of Egypt, and the condition of affairs in Morocco," that the police power was an essential ingredient of a nation's sovereignty and that any infringement of that power was a serious loss of independence. If control of the West River were allowed to rest in foreign hands, then Kwangtung, Kwangsi, Yunnan, and Kweichow, the provinces through which it flowed, would all be lost to China. And what was to prevent the Yangtze River and the Yellow River from suffering the same misfortune? [39]

The aim of the protest movement was to get the British to withdraw their patrol. In mid-December the Self-Government Society considered but rejected a proposal to institute an anti-British boycott. Instead it took up a suggestion made originally by the merchants of Wuchow, Kwangsi, to establish a Chinese steamship line which would compete with the British and other foreign steamers operating on the West River. Modeled after the highly successful Nippon Yūsen Kaisha (Japan Mail), the proposed Kwangtung–Kwangsi Mail Steamship Company (Liang-Kuang yu-ch'uan hui-she) began with much enthusiasm. The merchants of Canton and Wuchow, the joint promoters of the project, subscribed to several hundred thousand shares, each priced at $5 to encourage investment by the common people; those at Samshui, to 60,000 shares. Chinese in the Straits Settlement and other parts of Southeast Asia subscribed another $4,000,000. But, as in the case of the Kwangtung Railway Company, the initial enthusiasm was not sustained, for the company apparently never operated any steamships. [40]

While the steamship project was foundering, the protesters also put pressure on the Chinese officials to remedy the conditions in the West River that produced the British intervention in the first place. As a speaker before the Swatow National Rights Society put it, "In today's world, there is no Right—only Might. China is weak. Our Society is founded not to mouth empty threats [against the British] but to devise a solution [to China's weakness]. In my opinion, in order to protect China we must first recognize her weaknesses . . . We must first reform our West River patrol before the foreigners will stop using it as an excuse for intervention." [41] The Self-Government Society in Canton requested specifically that the Chinese customs officials be instructed to stop discriminating against Chinese-owned launches and to give them the same treatment as foreign-owned launches and that the Kwangtung patrol be strengthened in order to cut down on the lawlessness on the river. [42]

As in the case of the anti-American boycott in 1905, the protests in Kwangtung against the British patrol were denounced by the central government but had the tacit support of the local officials. Early in the movement, the Foreign Ministry called on Governor-General Chang Jen-chün to disband the students' Society to Protect the Nation's Rights and other protesting groups.[43] Later, as the movement continued to develop, the court itself denounced such agitations not only in Kwangtung but elsewhere in the empire. On December 24 it issued an edict criticizing "those who on the pretext of constitutionalism have interfered in recent years in all matters of domestic and external governmental affairs." It reminded its subjects that the only proper forums for public debates were the popular assemblies soon to be created; it furthermore cautioned them that not everyone was entitled to speak out on public matters nor was every matter open for discussion. The next day the court issued another edict directed at the students and their growing insubordination in both school and public affairs. It reiterated the dynasty's long-standing restrictions on government school students forming alliances and associations and meddling in political affairs. It prohibited them specifically from insulting officials, contravening school directives, violating the Sacred Edicts of the dynasty, arbitrarily changing curricula, changing the style of dress (such as perhaps cutting off the queue), making demands of the state, and telegraphing government ministries in the name of the school.[44]

The directives from Peking greatly antagonized the protesters in Kwangtung. In an open letter addressed to its "brethren within and beyond the seas," issued two or three days after the court's edicts, the Self-Government Society declared heatedly, "The calamity of partition confronts us. Yet our government does nothing. It does not even strive to devise a solution. On the contrary, because the Self-Government Society has sent some blunt telegrams, it has ordered our society crushed. Why do we wait meekly for our race to be annihilated, our nation destroyed, our families killed? Why not, while we are still alive, strive for cooperation and organization? Perhaps then we may yet survive!"[45]

Governor-General Chang, the man in the middle, was by no means opposed to the popular protests. At the beginning of the movement, when a delegation from the Self-Government Society presented a petition to him stating their objections to the foreigners' patrolling the West River, he had commended them for their concern. Later, when he was directed by Peking to prohibit the protests, he simply reduced their visibility. For example, he told the students that "the policing of the river [was] no business of theirs" and that they should stay out of it, but he did not disband their Society to Recover the Nation's Rights. The public agitation subsided perceptibly after the end of December, but it did not stop.[46]

Meanwhile, the governor-general was making the reforms demanded by both the British authorities and the local protesters. He reorganized and strengthened the West River patrol by adding four new, fast gunboats to it and by recalling Li Chun from his pacification efforts in Ch'in-chou and naming him provincial naval commander-in-chief in overall charge of the patrol. He also eliminated the discriminations against Chinese-owned launches and assured them the same treatment as foreign-owned launches. Finally, he settled the long-pending British claims arising from the attack on the *Sainam*.[47]

Satisfied with these arrangements, the British terminated their patrol on January 25, 1908. From their point of view the patrol had been a success. According to a report from Wuchow in mid-March, with each foreign steamer escorted by a Chinese patrol boat, travel on the West River was now "as safe as on the Manchester Canal."[48] The protesters in Kwangtung too had reasons to be satisfied with the results of the movement. They had helped to get rid of the British patrol. Moreover, they had persuaded most Chinese steam-launch owners to revert to flying the Ch'ing flag. Thus, the number of steam launches registered with the British consulate at Canton declined from 37 in 1907 to a mere 5 in 1908; the number of other foreign-registered launches fell almost as sharply, from 50 to 18. At the same time, the number of Chinese-registered launches rose from 142 in 1907 to 245 in 1908.[49]

As soon as the claims from the *Sainam* case were settled and the British patrol withdrawn, the central government once again directed the Canton governor-general to close down the Society to Recover the Nation's Rights and presumably the various other pressure groups that had sprung up during the two months of protest.[50] But before this was done, another incident involving the infringement of Chinese sovereignty gave new life to the associations.

The "Tatsu Maru" Anti-Japanese Boycott

This incident, which produced a local boycott of Japanese goods that lasted through most of 1908, centered on the Chinese seizure of a Japanese freighter in disputed waters off Portuguese Macao. A Chinese gunboat intercepted the freighter, the *Tatsu Maru II*, on February 5, 1908, while she was anchored off the shores of Macao. Like the *Kōun Maru* only a few months earlier, the *Tatsu Maru* was ostensibly carrying coal from Japan to Hong Kong but was also engaged in running arms into Kwangtung. She was caught in the act and taken by the Chinese gunboat to Whampoa.

The Japanese and the Portuguese immediately protested the seizure of the ship. They denied for the record that the *Tatsu Maru* had been engaged in arms smuggling, though this was never in question. More important, they claimed that she had been seized in Portuguese waters and not, as the Chinese maintained, in Chinese waters; this was debatable since the exact boundary of the Portuguese holdings at Macao had never been defined. Finally, the Japanese also charged that the captain of the Chinese gunboat had insulted Japan and committed a warlike act by striking the Japanese flag after he had taken command of the ship.

In the ensuing discussions with the Ch'ing Foreign Ministry, the Japanese took an utterly uncompromising position. They refused to allow a joint investigation of the incident or to submit the dispute to arbitration by a third party. Instead, they issued an ultimatum on March 13 calling on the Ch'ing to issue a public apology for the seizure of the *Tatsu Maru* and the insult to their flag, to release the ship, to buy up (at an inflated price) the ship's cargo of arms and ammunition, to punish the captain of the gunboat who had seized the ship, and finally to pay an indemnity for damages. In return for all these concessions, the Japanese agreed privately to help halt the flow of unauthorized arms from Japan through Macao into Kwangtung.[51]

Public opinion in Canton was uniformly opposed to any capitulation to these demands. The merchants' Self-Government Society sent an urgent telegram to the Foreign Ministry pleading with it to protect China's sovereignty and not to be "cowardly." Close to two hundred members of the gentry, headed by the retired official Teng Hua-hsi, also wired the ministry to refute the Japanese account of the incident and to urge referral of the dispute to international arbitration. Governor-General Chang Jen-chün reportedly threatened to resign if the Japanese demands were accepted.[52] But the Foreign Ministry had been advised by Inspector General Robert Hart of the Maritime Customs that its case was weak. Accordingly on March 15, two days after the issuance of the ultimatum, it agreed unconditionally to Japan's terms. (Hart's action must have confirmed the doubts previously expressed in the West River patrol controversy about the customs' commitment to China's interests.)

The Foreign Ministry's surrender to Japan was roundly denounced in

Canton. On March 18, the day after the terms of the settlement were published, about twenty thousand people, many "clad in mourning robes," braved heavy rains to attend a protest meeting called by the Self-Government Society. They prepared a petition, reportedly signed by fifteen thousand people, denouncing "the unreasonableness of the Japanese and the disloyalty of the Wai Wu Pu [Foreign Ministry]." Afterwards, carrying before them a banner inscribed "Recover Our National Rights," they marched in a body to Governor-General Chang's compound to present the petition to him. Chang received a seven-man delegation headed by Ch'en Hui-p'u and explained to them that the government had had no choice, since "our nation's foreign relations are limited by our nation's strength," but he agreed to acquaint the Foreign Ministry with their opinions.[53]

On the following day, when the *Tatsu Maru* was released, a huge crowd gathered spontaneously at the office of the Self-Government Society to voice their indignation once more. They also criticized the society for not calling a meeting to devise ways of recovering from the "national humiliation" (*kuo-ch'ih*). The society accordingly called a meeting for March 20, the third in as many days. Held at the Hua-lin Temple, it was again attended by "several tens of thousands" of people. All the speakers alluded to China's perilous condition, and all put the blame on Yüan Shih-k'ai and demanded his removal from the presidency of the Foreign Ministry. The meeting designated the seventeenth day of the second month, the day that the *Tatsu Maru* was released, as "National Humiliation Commemorative Day." [54]

The March 20 meeting of the Self-Government Society also resolved to initiate an anti-Japanese boycott as a means of retaliating against Japan's arrogance and of mitigating China's humiliation. Import firms wired their agents in Japan to cancel their orders; they also stipulated that goods purchased elsewhere abroad be shipped in non-Japanese steamers. Other fims canceled their policies with Japanese insurance companies. Dock workers in Hong King refused to unload Japanese ships. National Humiliation meetings and "patriotic bonfires," in which existing stocks of Japanese goods were destroyed, were held in such places as Canton, Hsin-ning, and Fo-shan. Led by the students in a couple of girls' schools, "thousands upon thousands" of women in Canton conducted their own National Humiliation meeting, from which, incidentally, all males were barred. They urged everyone to wear a ring engraved with the words "National Humiliation" as a reminder of the incident, and they called on housewives and cooks to do without "indigestible" food products from Japan. Students and gentry members composed "hymns of national disgrace" and prepared scrolls and fans "bearing a record of what has been done" in order to popularize the reasons for the boycott.[55]

The organization of the boycott is not very clear. Obviously the Self-Government Society played a leading role. But at least two other organizations were also involved. One was the Society to Commemorate the National Humiliation (Kuo-ch'ih chi-nien hui); the other, the Rights Recovery Society, probably a holdover from the British West River patrol agitation. None of these, however, seems to have constituted the actual directorate of the boycott, which, as in the case of the anti-American boycott, may have been composed of the leading guilds engaged in the trade with Japan. Hong Kong had its own independent boycott committee.[56]

Despite numerous similarities, the anti-Japanese boycott differed from the anti-American boycott of 1905 in at least three ways. It was carried out with little of the publicity of the anti-American boycott so as not to give the Japanese an excuse for intervention. Indeed, there was, strictly speaking, no "boycott" at all, only a "movement to promote the use of Chinese goods and to develop Chinese industry."[57] Second, unlike the anti-American boycott, which had been intended to influence the making of American policy, the anti-Japanese boycott was strictly punitive. Its aim was to produce a loss in Japan's trade with China that would offset the indemnity that China had paid to Japan.[58] Finally, the anti-Japanese boycott was not the nationwide movement that the anti-American boycott had been. Despite some attempts to extend it, the boycott was confined largely to Kwangtung, particularly the Pearl River delta, and among the natives of Central Kwangtung resident elsewhere.

Within its limits the boycott was remarkably successful. As early as mid-April, leading Japanese firms in Hong Kong reported heavy losses. According to a report attributed to a Japanese correspondent in the colony, two Japanese insurance companies were each losing $20,000 a month. Moreover, Japanese "vessels can obtain scarcely any passengers or cargo." This shipping loss continued well into the summer. For example, the *Hong Kong Maru*, bound for San Francisco, picked up no Chinese passenger or cargo at Hong Kong at the end of July. In addition, "Japanese tobacco, which obtained a hold at the time of the boycott of American goods, is being ousted by the American article."[59]

In some instances, as during the anti-American boycott, the Chinese seized the opportunity presented by the boycott to develop their own enterprises. This was notably so in the case of wooden matches imported from Japan. Since they were a product for which there was no readily available foreign substitute, the Chinese began to make their own. By October at least eight large match factories had been started in Canton and Fo-shan. It was probably no coincidence that at roughly the same time the Japanese match industry in Kobe experienced a serious slump. The trade statistics indicate an almost unbroken decline in the importation of Japanese wooden matches into Canton. Though the decline began in 1907, there was a sharp drop in 1908, which was surely due to the boycott; by 1911 importation of matches from Japan was only half of what it had been in 1906. (However, it should be pointed out that this decline at Canton may have been offset to some extent by an increase in wooden matches imported into Kwangtung at Samshui.) There was no significant change in the trade statistics at either Swatow or Pakhoi, a reflection of the limited geographical extent of the boycott.[60]

The Japanese government tried without success to have the Chinese authorities put a stop to the boycott. Citing the activities of Hsü Ch'in and the *Commercial News* in Hong Kong, it warned the Ch'ing Foreign Ministry that the boycott was the work of the outlaw K'ang Yu-wei and his group.[61] But in reply to a query from the ministry in April, Governor-General Chang Jen-chün denied that there was any boycott going on in Canton. He maintained instead that the merchants in the city were only promoting the development of local industry.[62] With the governor-general's tacit support, the boycott continued into the summer.

In the late summer enthusiasm for the boycott began to wane. People in Canton resumed patronage of stores that dealt in Japanese goods, and orders from Canton for marine food products were once more received at Yokohama. The boycott leaders responded by having the guilds take action against the offending firms. For example, the guild of medicine dealers in Canton announced on October 8 that violators of the boycott would be subject to permanent expulsion. However, such actions were only partially effective in reviving the boycott. As the boycott wilted, reports appeared in the press about Japanese residents in south China ridiculing the Chinese for their lack of resolve.[63]

Frustrated by its declining effectiveness, the leaders of the boycott in Hong Kong struck back violently at those who had withdrawn their support. On the nights of November 1 and 2 they instigated a riot that for all its violence was carefully selective. According to one report, "Every godown and shop containing Japanese goods had been specially marked out." But only Chinese stores were looted; no Japanese firm was touched. The British army finally had to be called out to back up the police before the rioting stopped.[64]

The riot had been the work of the boycott committee in Hong Kong. In Canton the Self-Government Society deplored it as an "uncivilized" act and appealed to the local populace to keep quiet.[65] Nevertheless, the Japanese and the British officially blamed it on the society and pressed the Ch'ing Foreign Ministry to have it as well as the Society to Commemorate the National Humiliation suppressed. However, Chang Jen-chün insisted that Canton had been in no way responsible for the disturbance in Hong Kong. Instead, he attributed the violence to Japanese provocations and blamed the British colonial authorities for not having taken preventive measures. He defended the Self-Government Society as a responsible, reputable organization but denied any knowledge of the Society to Commemorate the National Humiliation. The latter society had in fact passed out of existence, but according to the British consul, its functions had been assumed by the Self-Government Society.[66]

The Hong Kong riot revitalized the anti-Japanese boycott briefly, as merchants, terrified by the violence, once more ceased to deal in Japanese goods.[67] A month later, however, the boycott ended almost as suddenly as it had been revived. This came about as a result of British overreaction to the riot. On December 1 the Hong Kong government, acting on a request by Japan, ordered a number of local Chinese residents expelled from the colony for alleged complicity in the disturbance. They included such active leaders of the boycott as Hsü Ch'in and Wu Hsien-tzu, editors of the *Commercial News,* who were accused of "reckless" reporting. But also expelled were Li Chieh-ssu of the Canton Self-Government Society, who was in Hong Kong collecting money for flood relief, and a number of locally prominent residents who seem to have had little or no connection with either the boycott or the riot. Not long afterwards, the Hong Kong government tacitly acknowledged that its actions had been too zealous and let the banishment orders lapse. By then, however, the boycotters had turned their attention away from the Japanese and toward the British. In January 1909 Canton's trade with Japan was nearly normal again.[68]

Nevertheless, the anti-Japanese agitation did not die out right away. A couple of new grievances kept it going for yet another year, although in a much diluted form. In the spring there was a brief excitement in

Canton caused by Japanese activities on the Pratas shoal (Tung-sha tao). An island reef in the South China Sea which fishermen from Kwangtung used as a storm shelter, the Pratas shoal was not supposed to be inhabited. Yet a ship from the Chinese Nanyang fleet found a colony of Japanese living on the islands in March 1909. Led by an entrepreneur from Taiwan named Nishizawa, the Japanese had come to these islands the previous August and were busily mining their guano deposits. They claimed that the islands were theirs by right of discovery.[69]

News of the Japanese on Pratas reached Canton at the end of March. The Self-Government Society immediately demanded that the Ch'ing government take action to protect China's fishing industry and territorial integrity. It collected various sorts of evidence, from old published accounts of travelers to the oral testimony of local fishermen, to prove that the islands were historically Chinese and to refute Nishizawa's claim of discovery. On April 11 a mass meeting of gentry, merchants, and students at the Confucian Temple in Canton added their support to the society's effort. As a result of this excitement, the boycott revived momentarily.[70] The Japanese government's response in the Pratas case, however, was more reasonable than it had been in the *Tatsu Maru* case a year earlier. When it signified its willingness to recognize China's claims to the islands, the controversy quickly died down. Subsequently Nishizawa and his group were evacuated from the islands.

In the late summer of 1909 there was another brief flurry of anti-Japanese activity in Canton. This was part of the nationwide protest against Japan's plans in southern Manchuria to improve the Mukden–Antung railway. For a while, the Canton newspapers were full of anti-Japanese articles, some of them alluding to the *Tatsu Maru* episode. On August 31 the Self-Government Society talked about a boycott. The society met again on September 27 to denounce Liang Tun-yen, Yüan Shih-k'ai's successor as president of the Foreign Ministry, as a "traitor" for selling Manchuria out. In early November several thousand copies of a placard calling for a boycott were distributed in Canton. There were some anti-Japanese stirrings in Swatow as well. However, although at least one consignment of Japanese goods was refused at Hong Kong, the boycott was never revived in full force.[71]

The "Fatshan" Controversy

An anti-British anti-Portuguese movement followed the anti-Japanese boycott. It was brought on by the controversial death of a Chinese passenger aboard the Butterfield & Swire steamer *Fatshan* on November 29,

1908. According to Chinese eyewitnesses, the passenger, who was on his way from Hong Kong to Canton, had been kicked to death by the ship's Portuguese ticket collector, named Noronha. Chinese doctors connected with the Canton Red Cross Society confirmed that the man had died from his injuries. However, at the official inquest, which was conducted at the British consulate in Canton because the death had occurred on British property, a British doctor, who had also examined the body, declared that the man had had heart trouble and that he had died a natural death. Acting Consul Harry Fox took note of the conflicting medical findings but accepted those of the British doctor. He rejected the Chinese charges of homicide and found Noronha innocent of any wrongdoing.[72]

Consul Fox's verdict outraged the Self-Government Society, the Red Cross Society, and the Newspaper Association. In a number of meetings the following week, they accused him of "racism" for brushing aside the testimony of the Chinese witnesses and doctors in order to let a European go free. As a poem in the *Canton Daily News* on December 11 complained resentfully,

> Methinks the Chinese are classed lower than ants.
> They are sent with a kick to the next world.
> A Chinese killed two missionaries in Shantung,
> So the Germans stole a port [Kiaochow] and apologies.
> Alas! Mines and railways are ceded galore.
> For two lives they take a whole province [Shantung].
> But why is Ho Tsoi Yin's case left in oblivion?

(Ho Ts'ai-yen, it may be remembered, was drowned by American sailors in Canton in September 1904. His death had aroused much bitterness at the time but nothing comparable to the *Fatshan* case.) The poem ended with the exhortation, "Stir up, brothers! Or we shall be insignificant as a handful of sand."[73]

The protesters had two objectives. One was to get Butterfield & Swire to admit responsibility for the man's death and offer compensation to his relatives. The other was to get the Portuguese consul in Canton to re-try Noronha. The campaign against Butterfield & Swire began on December 30, 1908, when the Self-Government Society, with the metropolitan graduate Chiang K'ung-yin as chairman, called for a boycott of the *Fatshan*. On January 1, when the *Fatshan* next departed Canton for Hong Kong, a noisy, menacing crowd scared away most of the prospective passengers. Governor-General Chang Jen-chün, however, con-

demned the display of violence; as a result, the society promptly disa-
vowed the boycott. On January 2 the *Honam,* sister ship to the *Fatshan,*
left Canton without incident and "with a full cargo and the usual crowd
of Chinese passengers."[74] The society then entered into negotiations
with Consul Fox regarding compensation for the dead man's family.
When these broke down, sometime in the late winter or spring, it unob-
trusively reactivated and extended its boycott of Butterfield & Swire.[75]

The boycott was quiet but effective. By the beginning of June 1909
the company was losing HK$4,000 a week, with its Hong Kong–
Manila run recording unusually big losses. Complaints by the British
consul to the Canton governor-general had no apparent effect. In desperation Butterfield & Swire bypassed Consul Fox and approached the boycotters directly, much as the American merchants had done at the height
of the anti-American boycott. On August 2 it sent its comprador, Mo
Tsao-ch'üan, to Canton to arrange for a settlement, which was announced on the fifth, at a meeting of the Self-Government Society
chaired jointly by Ch'en Hui-p'u and Lo Shao-ao. The settlement was almost a total victory for the society. In return for an end of the boycott,
Butterfield & Swire agreed to pay HK$3,200 in compensation to the
dead man's relatives, to dismiss the ticket collector Noronha from its
service, to transfer the captain of the *Fatshan,* and to post notices aboard
all its ships assuring Chinese passengers of proper treatment.[76]

As part of its settlement, Butterfield & Swire agreed to use its influence to bring Noronha to trial again. The Portuguese consul, however,
had consistently rejected all demands for a new trial. Moreover, early in
the controversy he had sharply denounced the Self-Government Society,
the Canton press, and "pseudo-patriots" in general for making a big
issue out of the incident; he had also accused the eyewitnesses to the
alleged murder aboard the *Fatshan* of having been bribed. The Self-
Government Society and the Canton Newspaper Association repeatedly
criticized his attitude. But three months after the Butterfield & Swire
settlement, Noronha, the central figure in the controversy, was dead of
tuberculosis. With his death the *Fatshan* incident itself faded away.[77]
Meanwhile, the anti-Portuguese feelings that it had generated found an
outlet in another dispute that for many months ran parallel to the
Fatshan case.

The Macao Delimitation Dispute

The other anti-Portuguese controversy in 1909 developed in response
to the summoning of a joint Sino-Portuguese commission to delimit the

boundary of Macao. When Macao was formally ceded to Portugal in 1887, specification of its boundary had been left to subsequent negotiations by a joint commission. But in the following twenty years the commission had never met, and the boundary had never been defined. During all that time, the absence of a clearly defined boundary between Portuguese Macao and China, though it had given rise to a series of minor disputes, had not attracted much attention from the people of Kwangtung except those living in Hsiang-shan, the district contiguous to Macao.[78]

The first sign of a wider concern over the uncertain boundary coincided with the West River patrol agitation at the end of 1907, when, in addition to protesting the British naval intervention, the gentry, merchants, and students in Kwangtung also denounced instances of Portuguese interference with the movement of Chinese boats across the harbor from Macao to Wan-tzu (Lappa).[79] Popular concern increased sharply following the seizure in February 1908 of the *Tatsu Maru* in the disputed waters off Macao. With the Macao boundary fast becoming an issue among the emergent Chinese nationalists, the Portuguese government in June 1908 notified the Ch'ing Foreign Ministry of its desire to settle the dispute. Subsequently, in January 1909, the two countries agreed to a joint boundary delimitation commission to meet in Hong Kong beginning in July.[80]

Shortly after the agreement on the joint commission was reached, public opinion in Kwangtung began to assert for itself a role in the upcoming negotiations. On March 8, 1909, the inhabitants of Hsiang-shan district formed the Boundary Delimitation Auxiliary Society (K'an-chieh wei-ch'ih hui), with the provincial graduate Yang Ying-lin as its head. Its declared purpose was to defend China's national sovereignty and to recover her rights to the Portuguese-occupied territory and the surrounding waters. On the same day three emissaries from Hsiang-shan notified the Self-Government Society in Canton of the formation of the new society. The choice of March 8 as the date for the founding of the Boundary Delimitation Society and the beginning of the movement was symbolic: it was the first anniversary of the *Tatsu Maru* Day of National Humiliation.[81]

Three weeks later, on March 28, a separate Boundary Delimitation Society was founded in Canton at a mass meeting of gentry members, merchants, students, and journalists at the Ming-lun hall of the Confucian Temple. According to the constitution of the society, which was drawn up by two teachers at the College of Law and Administration, Tu Kung-shih and Yeh Hsia-sheng, and two newspapermen, Ch'en Lo-sheng and Mo Jen-heng, the newly founded society became the general organization while the original Hsiang-shan society was redesignated as a branch of the Canton society. There was a similar committee in Hong Kong too. The society was open to every interested person with an introduction. It was headed by the metropolitan graduate and retired official I Hsüeh-ch'ing; the provincial graduates Yang Ying-lin and Ch'en Te-chü were vice-chairmen. Its finances were handled by Lo Kuan-shih, who evidently was a leading merchant. The general society was to meet regularly every Sunday at the Yang family temple in Canton. It vowed not to disband until the boundary dispute had been settled to its satisfaction.[82]

The aims of the movement, summed up in the constitution of the Boundary Delimitation Society, were "to collect evidence about the Macao boundary and to study and publicize the principles of international law so as to assist the Chinese negotiating commissioner."[83] According to the evidence that it and the Self-Government Society collected, the 1887 treaty ceding Macao to Portugal was no longer in effect because of repeated Portuguese violations. Alternatively, the Portuguese were entitled only to their original Ming-dynasty leasehold, which included the tiny Macao peninsula but did not include either their subsequent acquisitions, the nearby islands of Taipa and Coloane, or any of the adjacent waters.[84]

As the negotiations neared, the two societies turned to offering their unsolicited "backing" (hou-tun) to the Chinese commissioner, Kao Erh-ch'ien. As soon as Kao arrived in Canton at the end of April, the Boundary Delimitation Society presented him with its lengthy "statement of opinion."[85] Later, on the eve of the negotiation, its leaders met privately with Kao to reiterate their views regarding the boundary. They also deputized two of their gentry members to go with him as his unofficial advisers. The Self-Government Society also "assisted" Kao by threatening to use its proven weapon, the boycott, against the Portuguese if they should reject the Chinese claims to Macao.[86]

The negotiations began in Hong Kong on July 15 and deadlocked almost immediately. The Ch'ing took a position that was very close to that of the two Canton societies. While it did not go so far as to declare the 1887 treaty null and void, it insisted that the Portuguese be restricted to their Ming-dynasty holding on Macao peninsula. It refused to recognize any territory beyond this original leasehold or any of the surrounding waters as rightfully Portuguese. On the other hand, Portugal of course denied the Chinese claims to the islands of Taipa and Coloane. It also insisted on its rights to the adjacent waters. Finally, it laid claim to at least parts of three larger islands nearby, Tui-mien-shan, Ch'ang-sha-lan, and Ta Hang-ch'in, which were loosely under Chinese control. The opposing claims proved to be irreconcilable because of Chinese intransigence. The Ch'ing refused to modify any of its demands and even rejected a Portuguese suggestion that the dispute be referred to The Hague for arbitration.[87]

Meanwhile, the secrecy in which the negotiations were conducted worried the Boundary Delimitation Society. The Hsiang-shan branch complained on August 15 that the secrecy made it difficult for the people to give their "backing" to Commissioner Kao; it demanded to be kept informed about the progress of the negotiations.[88] The society was particularly apprehensive about the commissioner's personal attitude toward the talks. During his interview with the leaders of the society just before he left for Hong Kong, he had indicated a predisposition to be flexible toward the Portuguese claims. As a matter of fact, in his correspondence with the Foreign Ministry, Kao was much more willing than the ministry to accept the status quo in order to arrive at a settlement. Caught between the increasing anxiety of the Kwangtung populace and the inflexibility of the ministry, Commissioner Kao's position was not a happy one. He recommended to the ministry, without success, that the negotiations be suspended or else transferred to another city far from Canton.[89]

The arrival of Yüan Shu-hsün in Canton in early September made Kao's position even more difficult, for the new governor-general supported the demands of the Boundary Delimitation Society to be let in on the secrets of the negotiations. With the approval of the Foreign Ministry, Governor-General Yüan suggested to the commissioner that he confer privately with the leaders of the society in order to "explain" to them the complexity of the issues. Accordingly, at the end of September Kao invited twenty representatives of the society to Hong Kong and showed them the minutes of the first six of the nine negotiating sessions so far. He then outlined to them the three possible courses of action: arbitration by a third party, a "peaceful solution" through bilateral negotiation, and the use of force. While he stated his own preference for the middle course, most of his visitors opted for force as a last resort.[90]

A couple of weeks later, the Boundary Delimitation Society and other groups began to attack Commissioner Kao openly for his "capitulationism." On October 17 a meeting of the society in Canton at the Wen-lan Academy, attended by about one thousand people, denounced him for not disclosing the minutes of the most recent negotiating sessions and for failing to oppose Portugal's demands. It called for his dismissal as negotiator. The Self-Government Society in Canton and the associations for the study of self-government in Chiang-men and Hsiang-shan also criticized him for his "readiness to concede Chinese sovereignty." [91] Mercifully for Kao Erh-ch'ien, the negotiations were terminated on November 13 at the request of Portugal. They had lasted four months and had settled nothing.

Portugal's subsequent efforts in Peking to have the boundary dispute submitted to arbitration produced a new wave of anxiety in Kwangtung. After the talks were broken off in Hong Kong, the Portuguese negotiator Machado went to confer directly with the officials at the Foreign Ministry. Once again, as in the spring of 1905 with the Chinese Exclusion Treaty, there were widespread fears that the foreigners would accomplish in Peking what they had failed to do elsewhere. Consequently the ministry was bombarded with telegrams and petitions from Kwangtung pleading with it not to give in to Portugal's wishes. The ministry on December 10 publicly rejected the request for arbitration, but so long as Machado remained at Peking, the telegrams continued to pour in.[92]

After 1909, with the Macao boundary still undefined, the Boundary Delimitation Society remained vigilant. In July 1910, when Portuguese troops landed on Coloane, one of the two Portuguese-occupied islands, to clear out a bandit lair and rescue a group of kidnaped Chinese children, the society and the press condemned anew the passivity of the Canton officials. "Public opinion will not tolerate an indifferent attitude on the part of the officials," the Hong Kong affiliate of the society told Governor-General Yüan. "If Chinese are in trouble, then boats and men must be sent to protect them." [93] In 1911 the society protested Portuguese efforts to dredge Macao harbor as an infringement upon China's rights to all of the adjacent waters.[94] The boundary dispute was still unsettled at the time of the revolution and remained so for long afterwards.

One significant byproduct of the boundary controversy was the attempt to develop a new port, Hsiang-chou, as an alternative to Macao. The project was initiated by the gentry and merchants of Hsiang-shan and had the support of Governor-General Chang Jen-chün, who personally cut the first sod at Hsiang-chou on April 23, 1909. At the time, Hsiang-chou was little more than sand dunes. By the end of 1910 there were over a hundred brick or stone buildings on the site and a carriage road had been built linking it to Ch'ien-shan, the nearest large town. However, because its harbor was too shallow, Hsiang-chou never prospered as a port. It anticipated the similar efforts of a later generation of nationalists to build up Whampoa to rival Hong Kong.[95]

The Macao boundary delimitation question was the last big nationalist controversy in Kwangtung before the revolution. While there was no apparent diminution in the degree of national consciousness, the people of Kwangtung after 1909 seem to have turned their attention more toward domestic questions. Perhaps the summoning of the provincial assembly late in 1909 was responsible for this inward turn.

The Self-Government Society

What was the Canton Merchants' Self-Government Society, the organization that had a hand in all these demonstrations? It was, first of all, an unauthorized association, one of the increasingly numerous voluntary groups that were founded in the late post-Boxer years. As its name suggests, it was inspired by the court's decrees promising eventual self-government. But unlike the gentry's Association for the Study of Self-Government, it was not a part of the official program to prepare the people for constitutionalism. Formed by the merchants on their own initiative, it managed to survive because it was composed of influential men and because it had the tacit support of successive governors-general.[96] Other unauthorized groups that survived included the Boundary Delimitation Society. One of those that failed to survive was the students' Society to Recover the Nation's Rights.

The society was a merchants' political pressure group. It was open to anyone who paid its dues of a dollar a year, and one of its leading members was the metropolitan graduate Chiang K'ung-yin, despite his much criticized role in the anti-American boycott. But as its name also suggests, it was primarily a merchants' organization. Perhaps it was their answer to the gentry's Association for the Study of Self-Government, whose founding it followed by only a few days. As a merchants' organization, it was especially close to the Canton Seventy-two Guilds, and rather removed from the Chamber of Commerce. In his numerous telegrams to the Foreign Ministry, Ch'en Hui-p'u usually identified himself and his cosigners as "merchants of the Seventy-two Guilds."[97] Another leader, Lo Shao-ao, was the editor of the Guilds' newspaper, the *Seventy-two Guilds' Commercial News.* On the other hand, none of its leading members was an officer of the Chamber of Commerce and, conversely, none of the officers of the chamber (except briefly for Huang Ching-t'ang) was active in the society. The society, however, was obviously far more involved in political affairs than either the Seventy-two Guilds or the Chamber of Commerce. It, for example, lobbied repeatedly but unavailingly for official permission to create a merchants' militia in Canton.[98]

The society was a vigorous promoter of both political and economic nationalism. In addition to organizing practically every one of the nationalist demonstrations in Canton from late 1907 to late 1909, it also devoted considerable attention to encouraging the development of Chinese industry and resistance to foreign economic imperialism. Apart from joining with the merchants of Wuchow to organize the abortive Kwangtung–Kwangsi Mail Steamship Company in December 1907, the society at various times held an industrial and commercial exhibition; advised Kwangtung trunk makers to make "foreign-styled luggage cases" rather than "old-fashioned trunks" so as to "improve their trade"; encouraged the Kwong Yik Company to manufacture "portable bottles for the use of the army, instead of purchasing them from abroad"; sponsored the formation of a new "fishing company"; and talked in general about "promoting agricultural pursuits and native industries." It also endorsed the movement initiated in 1909 by the Tientsin Chamber of Commerce to form National Debt Redemption Societies whose purpose was to raise funds from among the Chinese people in order to pay off the country's foreign loans and thus "prevent [the] foreign powers from making attempts to control the finances of China."[99] In its promotion of economic nationalism, the Self-Government Society was not unlike what the Chamber of Commerce was supposed to be.

The society was also a strong supporter of constitutionalism. In January 1908 it distributed copies of basic readings in civics in order to prepare the citizenry for eventual self-rule. In March and April 1908 it joined the nationwide movement initiated in Shanghai "to ask the Government for Constitutional Government." In the summer of 1909 it helped publicize the elections to the provincial assembly. It later set up a "self-government instruction office" in Canton which gave an eight-month course on the principles of local self-government.[100] On account of its activities on behalf of the constitutional movement, the Self-Government Society is often identified with groups such as the Constitutional Preparatory Association (Yü-pei li-hsien kung-hui) in Chekiang, the Constitutional Government Preparatory Association (Hsien-cheng ch'ou-pei hui) in Hupeh, and the Constitutional Government Association (Hsien-cheng kung-hui) in Hunan; these other organizations, however, were probably gentry-dominated groups.[101]

The society supported other contemporary causes as well. It participated in the nationwide movement to elevate the veneration of Confucius into a state religion and to turn his "birthday" on the twenty-seventh of the eighth month into the Chinese equivalent of Christmas.[102] It encouraged mass education; in early 1910, it set up thirty elementary schools in Canton city and nearby Ho-nan where boys from poor families were given a free two-year education to prepare them for employment later on. And it upheld the current interest in athletics by organizing a two-day sports meet in January 1910.[103] It was, in short, a complex, multi-purpose association.

Finally, the Self-Government Society represented a far larger constituency than its own membership, as indicated for example by the hundreds and occasionally thousands of people who attended its meetings. From its founding in November 1907 until the convening of the provincial assembly in October 1909, it assumed the role of spokesman for all the people of Canton. It functioned, much as the provincial assembly later did, as the vehicle for the expression of public opinion. Though the society receded into the background after 1909, as public attention shifted to the assembly, it nevertheless remained a very influential organization. It was to play a small but pivotal role in the revolution.

The series of nationalist demonstrations that raged in Kwangtung for the two years from the end of 1907 to the end of 1909 clearly reveal the extent to which the people, spurred by the post-Boxer reforms, had become politicized. Previously, Portuguese infringements of Macao's boundary had gone unnoticed; after 1907 they became the basis for demanding the revocation of the entire cession. In 1904 and even 1906 the killing of a Chinese by a foreigner had been shrugged off resentfully in Canton; in 1909 it was a "national humiliation" requiring concerted action to right the wrong.

Such sentiments were undoubtedly strongest at Canton, but they were by no means limited to the provincial capital. Pakhoi, for example, was greatly agitated early in 1909 about the maltreatment of the Chinese in the Dutch East Indies, an issue that received relatively little attention in Canton.[104] In Swatow, the merchants and gentry, along with their compatriots in Thailand, founded a steamship company, the China-Siam Navigation Company, in 1908 to compete with the German Norddeutscher Lloyd line for the carrying trade between Swatow and Bangkok.[105] Similarly, in 1909, the Chinese shareholders in the Ch'ao-chou–Swatow Railway Company bought out the Japanese shareholders and dismissed all but two of the company's Japanese employees.[106]

The nationalist movement was essentially an urban phenomenon, with the merchants in the forefront. The gentry, who in China were essentially an "urban" group too, played a not insignificant role in the various demonstrations. Chiang K'ung-yin, for example, was active in the Self-Government Society, while I Hsüeh-ch'ing and Yang Ying-lin were leaders of the Boundary Delimitation Society. But it was the merchants and their Self-Government Society who were in charge. They were the ones, of course, who were most directly menaced by the challenge of foreign economic imperialism and who had the most to gain personally from a successful Chinese nationalist response.

Nationalism, however, was but one aspect of the broader process of politicization, a part of the general trend in the last years of the post-Boxer decade toward a liberalization of society and a transvaluation of old values. This is clearly reflected in a statement by a certain Li Ts'u-ts'ai during the *Fatshan* controversy. After lamenting China's helpless and weak condition, Li concluded that in the long run "the prosperity of a nation depends on the general intelligence of its people and this cannot be acquired without the help of education . . . It is imperative that the various old customs and traditions which have been barriers to progress during these long years should be removed. No bound-footed mother can bring out strong sons. No useful man can prosper so long as the opium vice is allowed to rule the day." [107]

The politicized activists maintained an ambivalent relationship with the Ch'ing government. They often went far beyond what the government allowed. They openly accused some of the highest government officials, such as Yüan Shih-k'ai and Liang Tun-yen, of selling out China to the foreigners. And yet they were not revolutionaries. They attacked the officials, but not the throne. They deplored and were very anxious about the government's weakness vis-à-vis the foreign powers but offered to "back it up" by mobilizing popular support behind it. As a leaflet circulated in Hong Kong in September 1909 put it, "If our country were strong and powerful, then the responsibility for resisting [the foreign pressures] lies with the government. If our country is weak, then the responsibility lies with its citizens." [108] Thus, the protesters, while at times quite critical of the government's performance, were working to assist it, not to destroy it.

Nevertheless, the court distrusted and discouraged such assistance. It tried repeatedly to restrict it to within approved channels. As it reminded its subjects in its cautionary edict of December 1907, though without immediate effect, the constitutional program was designed specifically to provide a set of proper forums for public debates. It appears, from the subsidence of the nationalist movement in Canton after 1909, that the summoning of the provincial assemblies in the autumn of 1909 did finally succeed in shifting the arena of popular political activities from the streets into the assembly hall.

7

Final Years of the
Post-Boxer Decade,
II: Constitutionalism

The most significant of the court's reforms inaugurated during the last years of the post-Boxer decade was the program to institutionalize "local self-government" (*ti-fang tzu-chih*) as previously promised in September and October 1907. It culminated in the summoning of the provincial assemblies in October 1909 and the National Assembly a year later. There were also scattered efforts to develop similar representative bodies at the local, subdistrict level. Two results flowed from the self-government program. One was to enhance the influence of the people at the expense of the officials, as when the Kwangtung assembly forced the provincial administration to outlaw licensed gambling or when the provincial assemblies together compelled the court itself to shorten the constitutional timetable by three years. The other result was to increase the power of the local elite at the expense of the massess, especially the rural masses, who on a number of occasions protested the costs to them of "self-government." Unlike the nationalist movement, which was localized in a few of the larger cities, the self-government movement affected every district in the empire and penetrated into the rural areas.[1]

Formation of the Provincial Assembly

The provincial assemblies (*tzu-i chü*) were the first and, as it turned out, the most successful product of the constitutional reforms. They were popularly elected in the summer of 1909, in the first national election ever in Chinese history and one of the very few in twentieth-century China. Although only a small minority of the people were entitled to vote in the election and those who were elected were drawn almost exclusively from the established elite, the creation of the provincial assemblies, nevertheless, was a major triumph for the people's rights movement. It capped close to fifteen years of diverse efforts, including some additional efforts even after the provincial assemblies had been promised by the court, to involve the people more actively and directly in the government of their country.

In the wake of the court's pledge in late 1907 to create representative assemblies, the officials, gentry, and merchants stepped up their activities in preparation for eventual self-rule, paying particular attention to the Japanese experience and to Yüan Shih-k'ai's municipal council in Tientsin. (Yüan, *bête noire* of the nationalists, was a hero of the constitutionalists.) In Kwangtung, the provincial authorities sent a number of expectant officials and gentry members to Tientsin and Japan to make an on the spot investigation of their self-government institutions, while the district magistrates summoned members of the local elite to meet together to study relevant documents like the Tientsin self-government regulations and to discuss their implementation.[2]

At about the same time, on November 6, 1907, the gentry in Canton formed the Kwangtung Association for the Study of Self-Government (Ti-fang tzu-chih yen-chiu she), whose purpose was "to enlighten the scholars and gentry about the principles of self-government." Founded in conformity with an earlier imperial decree, the association included many of the most prominent upper scholar-gentry members in Kwangtung, such as I Hsüeh-ch'ing (formerly a second-class secretary at the Board of Revenue), Yang Sheng (recently the Chinese minister to Germany), Lu Nai-chuang (a provincial graduate), and Teng Hua-hsi (a former governor of Kweichow). Its chairman was the provincial graduate Liang Ch'ing-kuei, who (with Li Kuo-lien) had led the gentry's opposition to the officials' attempted takeover of the Kwangtung Railway Company in 1906.[3] Some of the local elite, for example those in Chia-ying and Hsiang-shan, were similarly active in preparing the way for self-rule.[4] It was soon after the formation of the gentry's Association for the Study of Self-Government that the merchants in Canton formed their own Self-Government Society. Not long afterwards, the merchants at Swatow also "started a Bureau of Inquiry with regard to the details and methods of local government" and mapped out "a course of instruction on the lines of the Tientsin Bureau." [5]

The court, in agreeing to form a representative government, had set no specific date for its realization. The various newly formed self-government groups across the country consequently joined together to request that it hasten its decision and clarify its plans. In Kwangtung the Canton Merchants' Self-Government Society played a leading role in this nationwide lobbying campaign. In April 1908 it sent representatives to a meeting in Shanghai to discuss the effort with representatives from all the other provinces. Afterwards it circulated a petition in Kwangtung "praying for Imperial sanction for the early institution of constitutional government." It eventually gathered 150,000 signatures for the petition. [6]

In response to this well-organized campaign as well as to the nationalist demonstrations that were going on at the same time in Kwangtung and elsewhere, the court finally was forced to commit itself to a specific and detailed constitutional program. In July 1908 it issued a set of regulations for the formation of the provincial assemblies. A month later, on August 27, it announced a definite timetable for the realization of a constitutional government within nine years. Beginning with the formation of the provincial assemblies in 1909 and a National Assembly (Tzu-cheng yüan) in 1910, both of which were only deliberative bodies, the Nine-Year Plan was to culminate in 1916 with the election of a fully legislative parliament (kuo-hui) together with a responsible cabinet. [7]

The first major project under the Nine-Year Plan was the creation of the provincial assemblies. In Kwangtung Governor-General Chang Jen-chün appointed a preparatory bureau in January 1909 to take charge of organizing the assembly. In addition to seven official members, at least sixteen gentry members were appointed to the bureau. These included many members of the upper scholar-gentry, such as Teng Hua-hsi, Ting Jen-chang, Wu Tao-jung, Chiang K'ung-yin, and I Hsüeh-ch'ing. They also included some members of the merchant-gentry: Chang Pi-shih, chairman of the Canton General Chamber of Commerce, and Liang Ch'eng and Lo Kuang-t'ing, president and vice-president of the Kwangtung Railway Company. No one, however, from the Canton Merchants' Self-Government Society was on the bureau. [8]

The first task of the preparatory bureau was to compile a list of those who were eligible to vote or to stand for election. For those who were natives of the province, the minimum voting requirements were three years of teaching above the primary level or some other form of public service within the province; or graduation from a modern middle school or its equivalent; or possession of the traditional examination degree of senior licentiate; or previous service in the government at or above the seventh rank for civil posts or the fifth rank for military posts; or finally, ownership of a business or property valued at $5,000. For those who were not natives of the province, the requirements were at least ten years of residence in the province and ownership of a business or property worth $10,000. Only males 25 years of age or over were eligible to vote, and only those who were 30 years or older were eligible for election as assemblymen.[9]

These requirements restricted the franchise to the small upper class of society. In two of Kwangtung's most populous districts, Nan-hai and P'an-yü, only 11,024 and 6,041 voters respectively were registered. In the whole of the province there were altogether 141,558 registered voters, which was roughly one half of 1 percent of the total population or 2 percent of the adult male population. Of course, not all who were qualified necessarily signed up to vote. Many merchants, in particular, may not have registered because of the need to prove their financial worth, which they were probably anxious to keep secret from the government. It can be no coincidence that the Kwangtung electorate in 1909 was on the same order of magnitude as the Kwangtung gentry, which has been calculated for the late nineteenth century as numbering 110,705 members.[10] Like the modern schools, the provincial assembly elections may have altered the character of the established elite but did not significantly enlarge it.

On the basis of the provincial quota under the old examination system, the Kwangtung assembly was allotted 91 members. The preparatory bureau apportioned these among the sixteen prefectures and independent departments of the province according to a formula of one assemblyman for every 1,555 registered voters. (This was a fairly high ratio; in Shantung it was 1:1,193; in neighboring Kwangsi it was only 1:710.) Thus, Kuang-chou prefecture, which took in the Pearl River delta, was accorded 36 seats, or more than one third of the total; Ch'ao-chou and Chao-ch'ing followed with 11 and 9 seats respectively. In addition, the preparatory bureau gave 3 seats to the Manchu and Chinese bannermen in Canton, even though only 369 voters were registered in the whole garrison.[11]

The elections took place in the summer of 1909 in a two-stage indirect process. The voters in the first round nominated a number of electors, who in the second round actually chose the assemblymen. There were ten times as many electors as assemblymen to be elected. The preliminary, or popular, round was held in mid-July and in many places was spread out over three days; the electoral unit here was the district, each divided into about ten wards. The turnout for this first popular election in Chinese history was uneven but generally low. In Nan-hai, partly because of heavy rains on the third day of the election, only 4 or 5,000 out of the 11,024 registered voters went to the polls; on the other hand, in two wards of Hao-shan district, on the edge of the Pearl River delta, 940 out of the 1,634 registered voted. The average turnout seems to have been at best 50 percent. The absence of electioneering undoubtedly kept it down.[12] The second round of the elections then took place about a month later, with the prefecture or department as the electoral unit.

The elections in Yang-chiang were probably typical.[13] Yang-chiang is a district on the coast of West Kwangtung; in 1909 it and the two neighboring districts of En-p'ing and Yang-ch'un constituted an independent department, which was also known as Yang-chiang. Yang-chiang *department* as a whole had 3,297 registered voters; therefore, according to the 1:1,555 ratio, it was allotted 2 assemblymen. The 2 assemblymen were to be voted upon by 20 electors, who were divided as follows: 7 to Yang-chiang *district,* 7 to En-p'ing, and 6 to Yang-ch'un. Assuming that the electors were divided among the three districts in proportion to the number of registered voters, Yang-chiang district had roughly 1,300 registered voters.

In the first round of the elections the turnout in Yang-chiang district was quite high. Out of the estimated 1,300 registered, 991 voted. With each voter apparently nominating only one person rather than a full slate, it did not take a large number of votes to be chosen as an elector, as the results in other districts indicate. In Nan-hai the elector with the lowest number of votes had 14; in Hsin-hui, 18; in P'an-yü, 24.[14] Of the 7 electors chosen in Yang-chiang, 5 definitely belonged to the scholar-gentry: 2 of them were provincial graduates, 3 were senior licentiates. Another, an "irregular" senior licentiate (that is, a licentiate with a purchased title of senior licentiate), was a marginal member. There is no information on the background of the seventh elector. As a comparison, according to a newspaper analysis of the 69 Nan-hai electors, 48 were members of the scholar-gentry (*shen-shih*), 5 of them metropolitan graduates; 19 were merchants; and 2 were from the charitable halls.[15]

In the second round of the elections, the 7 Yang-chiang electors joined with the 7 from En-p'ing and the 6 from Yang-ch'un to choose the department's 2 assemblymen. One of the 2 chosen came from Yang-chiang district; the other, from En-p'ing. The Yang-chiang assemblyman, Liang T'ing-k'ai, is not listed among the degree holders in the district gazetteer, but he is described as having served in the Board of Revenue as a department director (*lang-chung*) during the T'ung-chih period. He thus appears to have been a retired official. Incidentally, he was not one of the electors from his district; evidently the assemblymen were not necessarily chosen from the ranks of the electors.

Inevitably, there were charges of corruption in connection with the elections. Wang Shih-hsin, whom the American consul in Canton described as a wealthy man of taotai rank but not well educated in the classics and who thus presumably was a merchant, supposedly "made strenuous efforts and spent large sums of money" to secure his election from Ho-p'u district in West Kwangtung. Similar allegations were made about another candidate, unnamed but identified in the newspapers as the son of a former vice-president of one of the Six Boards and notorious for "making mince meat of the peasants." There was also a rumor that all eleven assemblymen elected from Ch'ao-chou prefecture had resorted to bribery, paying one hundred dollars for each vote. As such cases came to light, "public feeling ran high and meetings were held to protest against these flagrant practices." Some of the newly elected assemblymen were asked to resign.[16]

Who were the 94 men elected to the Kwangtung assembly? They are listed by name and native place, but for about half of the group this is all that is known about them. The data at hand thus allow for only a partial analysis of the assembly.[17] Nevertheless, it is clear that the great majority of the assemblymen were members of the "scholar-gentry" within the broad sense of the term. A look at the degree status of 42 Kwangtung assemblymen—consisting of the 31 elected from districts for which there exists an up-to-date gazetteer and the 11 from Ch'ao-chou prefecture who were noted in a newspaper dispatch—reveals the following: 1 metropolitan graduate, 16 provincial graduates, 6 regular senior licentiates, 4 "irregular" senior licentiates, 7 licentiates, and 8 in the "others or no information" category, many of whom were probably also licentiates, since the gazetteers practically never include them on the list of degree holders.[18] Thus, 23 out of 42 (55 percent) in this limited sample of Kwangtung assemblymen were members of the regular scholar-gentry, while over half of the remainder were at least licentiates belonging to the lower fringe of the scholar-gentry. This corresponds closely with the findings from five other provincial assemblies, where the gentry accounted for 90 percent of the membership.[19] The gentry's predominance in the provincial assembly is hardly surprising. As we have seen already in the case of Yang-chiang and Nan-hai, they were predominant among the electors as well. The ultimate source of their numerical superiority was the franchise itself, since the voting requirements clearly had been tailored to the career pattern of the scholar-gentry at the expense of all other groups in society.

Specifically, in the five provincial assemblies for which detailed statistics are available, metropolitan graduates accounted for 4.5 percent of the total membership, provincial graduates 18.6 percent, senior licentiates 27.4 percent, and licentiates 39.5 percent.[20] The situation was probably much the same in Kwangtung. There were altogether three metropolitan graduates in the Kwangtung assembly: I Hsüeh-ch'ing, Ch'iu Feng-chia, and Ch'en Nien-tien. A descendant of one of the old Canton hong merchants, I Hsüeh-ch'ing was the chairman of the Macao Boundary Delimitation Society as well as a leading member of the Association for the Study of Self-Government. Ch'iu Feng-chia, a hero of the anti-Japanese resistance movement in Taiwan in 1895, was prominent in educational affairs in his native East Kwangtung, where he had lived since the collapse of the Taiwan Republic. Little is known about Ch'en Nien-tien, except that he was a recent (1903) recipient of his degree.[21] These three, however, were not the only metropolitan graduates to be elected to the assembly. Others had been elected, like Chiang K'ung-yin and Liang Ting-fen, but they had declined to serve, perhaps in order not to disqualify themselves from taking office, as office holders were barred from sitting in the assemblies.[22]

Among the provincial graduates in the Kwangtung assembly were Chao Tsung-t'an and Lo Huan-hsiung, both of whom had belonged to the Society to Protect the Nation in 1898,[23] Lin Yü, who was director of the official modern school in his native Chieh-yang,[24] and Lu Nai-chuang, who was active in the Association for the Study of Self-Government. Liang Ch'ing-kuei, the provincial graduate who was the head of that association, was another of those who declined election to the as-

sembly; incidentally, he too was a descendant of an old hong mer-
chant.[25] Senior licentiates in the assembly included Huang Ying-ch'i,
who headed the office for the encouragement of education in his native
Yang-shan, and Mo Jen-heng, who was the proprietor of the *Canton
Daily News,* one of the most influential newspapers in the province.[26]
The assembly also contained a few members of the "new gentry": Ch'en
Chiung-ming, Liu Yao-yüan, and Wu Fei, all graduates of the
Kwangtung College of Law and Administration, and Chou Chao-ling, a
graduate of the Kwangtung–Kwangsi Normal School.[27] Surprisingly,
only one assemblyman, Shen Ping-jen, had studied abroad.[28] As for the
licentiates in the assembly, although they accounted for close to half its
membership, very few are identifiable, undoubtedly because of their low
standing among the scholar-gentry. One of them, however, was Hsiao
Chih-chen, who was the chairman of the education association in Ta-
p'u.[29]

In contrast to the scholar-gentry, the merchants were a tiny minority
in the provincial assembly. In large part this was because the voting
requirements were far more restrictive for the merchants than for the
scholar-gentry and because the need for financial disclosure deterred
many who might have been qualified from registering to vote at all. As
we have seen, among the 69 electors nominated in Nan-hai district, only
19 were merchants. Furthermore, those who made it to the assembly
tended to be not ordinary merchants but rather gentry-merchants such as
Ou Tsan-sen, who was the chairman of the Canton Chamber of Commerce and a provincial graduate, Hsiao Yung-hua, the vice-chairman of
the Swatow Chamber of Commerce and a licentiate, and Liang Kuo-
hsüan, the chairman of the Chia-ying Chamber of Commerce and another licentiate. However, the assembly also included Su Ping-shu, a
rich and well-known gambling operator, and Wang Shih-hsin, who (as
noted) allegedly bought his way in.[30] Despite its activity on behalf of
the constitutionalist movement, none of the leaders of the Canton Merchants' Self-Government Society was a member of the assembly, perhaps
because it generally lacked the gentry connections that the chambers of
commerce possessed.

Finally, the Kwangtung data reveal little about the age of the provincial assemblymen. Some, like Liang T'ing-k'ai and I Hsüeh-ch'ing, who
had begun their career in the T'ung-chih period, must have been in their
sixties and seventies in 1909. Others were younger. Ch'iu Feng-chia,
born in 1864, was 45; Ch'en Chiung-ming, born in 1878, was 31,

barely above the minimum requirement of 30. The data from Szechwan indicate that the median age of its assemblymen was 41 or 42.[31] Kwangtung probably was not too different.

The Provincial Assembly in Session

The provincial assemblies across the country opened, as scheduled, on October 14, 1909. They sat for two years before they were overtaken by the revolution. Although they were only a deliberative and advisory body without any legislative power, they were nevertheless remarkably successful during the two years they were in operation in making the provincial officials pay them heed. Moreover, by joining forces they succeeded also in forcing the court to hasten the completion of its nine-year constitutional program.

The Kwangtung assembly met altogether five times during its two-year existence. It elected its officers on opening day 1909, but then recessed until November 6 to await the completion of its Western-style meeting hall in Canton. Granted an extension of its statutory forty-day term to make up for the delay, it adjourned its first regular session on December 2. An extraordinary session followed in May 1910. The assembly met for its second annual session from October 3 to November 13, 1910. Another special session followed in late March and early April 1911. The third regular session began on October 22, 1911, twelve days after the outbreak of the Wuchang uprising.

The officers of the assembly, elected at the first session to serve three-year terms, were I Hsüeh-ch'ing as president and Ch'iu Feng-chia and Lu Nai-chuang as vice-presidents. All three were leading members of the upper gentry. Assisting them in the work of the assembly between sessions were nineteen "resident assemblymen," who comprised one fifth of the total membership. In addition, there was a permanent chancery responsible for the "correspondence, accounts, and the current affairs of the Assembly." It was directed by a chief secretary, Ku Ying-fen, who was concurrently a teacher at the College of Law and Administration, and four assistant secretaries.[32]

The Kwangtung assembly concerned itself almost exclusively with domestic affairs.[33] Unlike some of the other provincial assemblies, it generally shied away from matters of foreign policy. About its only venture into foreign affairs was to voice its opposition to the Portuguese presence in Macao and to claim a right to pass on any settlement of the boundary dispute.[34]

In domestic matters, the assembly expressed itself on a variety of topics. It supported the different social and educational reforms of the period, such as the abolition of licensed gambling, the suppression of opium smoking, prison reforms, the founding of public libraries, education for women, and the establishment of schools to teach poor children how to read and write the commonly used characters. It was concerned with maintaining social order; it thus made recommendations regarding the prevention of clan fights, protection for shipping on inland waterways, and the elimination of thieves and robbers. It suggested ways for improving the conduct of local government, such as by publicizing the transactions of official business and by eliminating "squeeze" and other forms of petty corruption among the subofficials and yamen runners. And it promoted industry and commerce by encouraging forestry, clan-established industrial works, and industrial experiment stations.

Reflecting the interests of its majority element, the assembly also sought out ways to extend and formalize the gentry's role in local government. It suggested that the gentry-dominated education associations be allowed to take over the administration of school affairs from the officials and their offices for the encouragement of education. It asked that greater amounts of public funds be appropriated for school expenses, most of which had previously been met by private donations.[35] It sought official sanction for the formation of popular self-defense forces, such as gentry and merchant militias, to supplement the official forces, which were justifiably regarded as incompetent at best. It recommended the creation of gentry-staffed bureaus to receive reports of robbery from victims who were terrified of approaching the officials directly. It even offered to take the collection of the land tax out of the hands of the officials and entrust it to the various gentry-staffed "self-government societies."

These, however, were only recommendations. The assembly was not a legislature. Its role was only to advise the governor-general, who was by no means bound to accept its suggestions. In its dealings with the provincial authorities, the assembly at first was quite deferential but soon became more daring and independent. During their first regular session in the fall of 1909, according to the French consul in Canton, the assemblymen were remarkably respectful toward the governor-general. When Yüan Shu-hsün cut short their debate on the Macao boundary issue as beyond their competence, they quietly submitted to his decision. Their daily sessions were almost always conducted "in the greatest calm." [36] By their second session a year later, they had become far more assertive and defiant.

This militance developed during the intervening months when the various provincial assemblies joined together to ask the court to hasten the convocation of the parliament. According to the court's Nine-Year Plan, a National Assembly was to be established in the coming fall, but it was to be a strictly advisory body with half its membership appointed by the court and half elected by the provincial assemblies. A popularly elected, legislative parliament together with a cabinet responsible to it was not supposed to come into being until 1916, the plan's final year. The provincial assemblymen, already beginning to chaff under their own restricted authority, were impatient with the court's slow, deliberate pace. They wanted the parliament and cabinet convened at once. [37]

In late December 1909, after they had concluded their first session, fifty-one delegates from sixteen provincial assemblies met in Shanghai and formed the Federation of Provincial Assemblies (Ko-sheng tzu-i chü lien-ho hui), one of the earliest and perhaps the most influential of the various interprovincial organizations of the period. (Representing Kwangtung at the meeting were Ch'iu Feng-chia, Ch'en Chiung-ming, and one other.) [38] The conference decided to submit a formal petition to the court for the immediate summoning of parliament. Consequently, a 32-man delegation, with Shen Ping-jen as the representative from Kwangtung, went to Peking to deliver the petition directly. On January 30, 1910, the court rejected their request on the grounds that it would upset the previously announced constitutional timetable. The provincial assemblymen then decided to prepare a second petition for presentation in three or four months' time. [39]

In the meantime, the assemblymen returned home to build up grass-roots support for their movement. In Kwangtung an Association of Comrades for a Parliament (Kuo-hui t'ung-chih hui) was founded on May 15 at an enthusiastic meeting in Canton attended by about ten thousand people. It included persons who had been active in the nationalist movement as well as the constitutionalist movement. Lo Kuan-shih, a leader of the Macao Boundary Delimitation Society, was elected president of the new association. The gentry leader Chiang K'ung-yin contributed a large sum of money. Ch'en Hui-p'u, head of the Merchants' Self-Government Society, spoke, declaring that "China could not be expected to take her place any longer in the world among the civilised nations" if the court refused to heed the people's wish. At the conclusion of the meeting, thousands signed the petition demanding a fully constitutional government "at an early date." [40]

Buoyed by this groundswell of popular support, the delegation of petitioners returned to Peking in the middle of June to resubmit the request for a parliament. The court rejected it again. Disappointed but not yet without hope, the delegation met once more in Peking in mid-August to make plans for a third petition. It recommended to the various provincial assemblies, which were to reconvene for their second annual session on October 3, to throw their support behind the petition even to the extent of vowing to resign in a body should it fail for the third time. The Kwangtung assembly accordingly passed a resolution during the first week of its new session urging the throne to convene a parliament immediately. [41] The petition effort at this time also received the backing of the newly convened National Assembly and practically all the governors-general and governors, including the Canton governor-general Yüan Shu-hsün and his eventual successor Chang Ming-ch'i. [42] (Among the few who did not support the petition was Chang Jen-chün, then governor-general at Nanking, even though during his tenure at Canton he apparently had looked with favor upon such constitutionalist activities.) The court finally gave way under all this pressure. On November 4 it announced that the opening of parliament would be advanced from 1916 to 1913 and that a cabinet would be set up in 1911. While this was not all that the petitioners had hoped for, it was, nevertheless, a tremendous victory for the popular rights movement.

The petition movement and its success greatly emboldened the Kwangtung assembly as it met for its second session in October and November 1910. It was noticeably less reluctant than in the first session to confront and, if necessary, defy the provincial authorities. Moreover, it began to delve into the financial affairs of the province, despite statutory limitations on its authority in this area. During the 1909 session, the Kwangtung assemblymen had generally avoided fiscal matters; at the 1910 session, however, eight out of their twenty-six resolutions were concerned in one way or another with finances. By then they were well aware, from what they knew about the development of constitutional government in Western Europe and more recently in Meiji Japan, that there was a vital connection between control of the purse and the growth of representative institutions.

Thus, the very first matter brought before the assembly at the second session was a demand that the provincial officials furnish the body with a draft of the annual budget. Taotai Wang Ping-en, representing Governor-General Yüan, Shu-hsün, replied that the draft could not be disclosed yet "because it has not yet been memorialized to, and sanctioned by, the Throne." Supporters of the motion insisted that it was impossible for the assembly to carry on its duties without some estimate of the budget. Taotai Wang then agreed to make copies of the draft budget available in a few days. In the end the assembly declined "to consider the budget submitted by the Provincial Government because it contained only a general unitemised account of expenditures and nothing about receipts." [43]

The major clash between the assembly and the governor-general arose, however, not over the budget itself but over a related proposal to outlaw licensed gambling in the province. This controversy is a good case study of the evolution of the role of the provincial assembly. It illustrates the growing boldness of the assembly in confronting the officials and trying to force its will upon them. It also demonstrates the devices by which the assembly enlarged its role. Finally, it reveals some of the problems of financing the various post-Boxer reforms.

According to a report by Governor-General Yüan in 1909, gambling first became important as a source of government revenue in Kwangtung in 1900 when his predecessor Li Hung-chang resorted to it as a way out of some financial difficulties. There were by 1909 four principal gambling or lottery concessions, which the provincial government granted to the gambling merchants offering the highest bid. These were *wei-hsing, ts'ai-p'iao,* fantan (*fan-t'an*), and *chi-p'u shan-p'iao.* Of the four, fantan and *chi-p'u shan-p'iao* were the big revenue producers, with the former netting between 2.7 and 2.8 million taels a year and the latter, between 1.3 and 1.4 million. The other two brought in only a total of 350,000 taels. Altogether the four concessions produced about 4.4 million taels a year for the provincial treasury. They alone accounted for about 20 percent of the total revenue of the province, which was estimated for 1911 at 23.3 million taels. They and the likin were the two largest sources of revenue in Kwangtung. [44]

The proceeds from the licensing of gambling were put to a variety of uses. At the provincial level, they went to maintain the Reserve Forces, to recruit and train the New Army, as well as to support various reform projects. They also went to meet the provincial quota for the Boxer indemnity payments. The same was true at the local level. A gambling den erected on the main street of Ch'ing-yüan city in 1908 produced

$4,000 a year for the district. Of this, $2,000 was allocated to the police bureau, $500 to the office for the encouragement of education, $500 to the anti-opium society, and $1,000 to prison reforms.[45] Clearly, licensed gambling was an essential element of government financing, including the financing of reforms.

Nevertheless, there were many reformers to whom this fiscal dependence upon gambling was repugnant and who campaigned for an end to the practice. It was, first of all, "a disgrace to the civilized world" and "something that no nation ought to have." [46] Furthermore, it contributed to the widespread disorder in the province. The ranks of the bandits and pirates, they said, were filled with gamblers down on their luck. Consequently the solution to the problem of brigandage in Kwangtung was to prohibit gambling. In a curious (perhaps forged?) letter to the Canton Newspaper Association in 1910, the notorious bandit chief Lu Lan-ch'ing confirmed that "We, being poor, are obliged to try our luck by gambling and when we have lost our money, we have been driven to robbery." He promised that "As soon as the Imperial Edict is issued for the total suppression of gambling, we robbers, one and all, will surrender ourselves." [47] Licensed gambling, in short, was shameful and it produced crime.

The anti-gambling forces began earnestly in 1909 to petition the provincial officials and the throne to do something about the gambling problem in Kwangtung. They brought up the question at the first session of the provincial assembly in November 1909. Governor-General Yüan Shu-hsün, though favoring abolition in principle, insisted that alternate sources of revenue must be found before gambling could be suppressed. The assemblymen brushed aside his objections. As they declared in their first resolution of the session, licensed gambling was uncivilized and should be abolished without delay and without consideration for substitute funding.[48] Governor-General Yüan then went along with the assembly's resolution part way. He ordered an early termination of the two least productive gambling concessions, the ts'ai-p'iao and the wei-hsing, whose revenue loss of 350,000 taels was met by retrenchment of the Reserve Forces. He refused, however, to abolish the fantan or the chi-p'u shan-p'iao until he had developed other sources of income to offset the four million taels they brought in annually.[49]

Shortly afterwards, early in December 1909, a group of merchants headed by Ch'en Pao-ch'en made a timely offer to the provincial government of 10 million taels a year for the Kwangtung salt monopoly. The offer was almost three times as much as the 3.7 million taels a year that the former concessionarire had paid. Yet Ch'en promised that under his administration the price of salt would rise at most 60 percent to 5.6 candareens per catty, which was generally regarded as high but not exorbitant. Reassured by the promise, the governor-general conferred the concession on Ch'en on December 28. In a separate proclamation, he happily announced that the additional 6 million taels from the salt monopoly would be used to replace the revenue from gambling.[50]

Contrary to expectations, the gentry and merchants of Canton reacted to Yüan's announcement with considerable misgivings. They feared that despite Ch'en's assurances the price of salt would rise precipitously, for otherwise how would the new concessionaire be able to turn a profit or make the rental payment of 10 million taels? They were also suspicious about Ch'en Pao-ch'en and his associates. Most of them allegedly were gambling merchants who were only interested in offsetting *their* losses should gambling be suppressed.[51] The critics communicated their apprehensions to Peking.

In March 1910 the Ministry of Finance sent Yen An-lan, a salt official, to Canton to investigate the controversy. Yen subsequently worked out a compromise solution. The salt monopoly was taken away from Ch'en Pao-ch'en and given back to the old concessionaire, who in return agreed to a scaled increase in the annual rental over the next several years. During the first year he was to pay 5.8 million taels (as opposed to his previous 3.7 million); during the second year, 6.2 million. Thereafter, if increased salt consumption warranted, he was liable to a maximum rent of 7.8 million taels a year. However, as Yen An-lan pointed out to the resident assemblymen before he returned to Peking, the salt concession under the revised terms would produce only 2.1 million taels in additional revenue during the first year, an insufficient amount to cover the revenue loss should gambling be proscribed.[52]

The provincial assembly returned to the attack. In May, when it reconvened in an extraordinary session, it insisted that all additional income from the salt monopoly be earmarked for meeting the loss of gambling revenue, and it repeated its request for an immediate ban on gambling.[53] Governor-General Yüan again denied the request as premature. In October, at its second regular session, the assembly, after first clashing with Yüan over the budget, brought up the gambling question once more. On October 12 the assemblymen demanded that the governor-general memorialize the throne within three days to plead for an immediate prohibition of licensed gambling in the province. With an unprecedented boldness that was characteristic of the second session, they threatened to resign en masse should he fail to memorialize within the prescribed three days or should the court refuse to give heed to their plea. On October 17, after Governor-General Yüan had disregarded their threat, they stopped their deliberations. Three days later, he memorialized the throne. Although the imperial response was only to direct its officials to study their petition, the assemblymen were satisfied that they had made their point. They resumed deliberations on October 22.[54] A week later, confounded and humbled, Yüan Shu-hsün resigned as governor-general. Chang Ming-ch'i was appointed to succeed him, but pending his arrival in Canton Tseng-ch'i, the Tartar-general, took over as acting governor-general.

The assemblymen's elation was short-lived. Fresh from their stunning victory over the governor-general, they fell almost at once to quarreling among themselves. The issue, ironically, was again gambling. On November 9 the assembly took up for discussion an application by the An-jung Company, owned by assemblyman Su Ping-shu, to operate the *p'u-p'iao* gambling concession. In a brief but acrimonious debate, proponents of the application defended the *p'u-p'iao* as a relatively harmless form of gambling, while opponents, led by Ch'en Chiung-ming and Ch'iu Feng-chia, attacked all forms of gambling as harmful. When the motion to reject the application was put to a recorded vote, there were 20 "ayes" and, to the surprise of most observers, 35 "nays." In an apparent reversal of its long-standing opposition to all gambling, the assembly had allowed the *p'u-p'iao*.[55]

A wave of indignation swept through Canton. The 35 assemblymen who had voted "nay" were accused of having been bribed by Su Ping-shu and the gambling interests. They were burnt in effigy; their photographs were displayed and circulated as objects of scorn.[56] Stirred by the protests, Acting Governor-General Tseng-ch'i quickly ordered a halt to the An-jung Company's *p'u-p'iao* operation. On November 14, at the Ming-lun hall of the Confucian Temple in Canton, a mass meeting of the gentry, merchants, and representatives of the charitable halls (chaired curiously by the Hong Kong merchant Li Yü-t'ang) applauded Tseng-ch'i's action against the An-jung Company but called on him to go further and expel the pro-gambling members from the assembly. Only then, the meeting insisted, could the credibility of the provincial assembly as a representative institution be restored and the public indignation pacified. In the meantime, the assembly itself ground to a halt, as both anti-gambling and pro-gambling assemblymen resigned, the former to vent their anger and the latter to protest their innocence. When the second session of the assembly adjourned on schedule on November 16, less than one third of its membership was intact.[57]

Sensing their opportunity, the anti-gambling forces, with the gentry-dominated Association for the Study of Self-Government at the forefront now, pressed once more for an immediate and total prohibition of gambling in the province. At the urging of leading members of the upper gentry, including Ch'en Po-t'ao (a former director of education in Kiangnan), Teng Hua-hsi, and Chiang K'ung-yin, the governor-general on November 19 sent a telegram to the Grand Council expressing his support for prohibition. He suggested in his telegram that the revenue needed to offset the loss from gambling might come from additional levies on salt, opium, and wine. Referring to the public spiritedness of the people of Kwangtung—what a change this was from Ou Chü-chia's complaints about their selfishness and apathy!—he also suggested that if there should still be a deficit, the people would make it up through voluntary contributions. The first step, however, was for the court to set a date for the prohibition to go into effect.[58]

The following day, about eight hundred "eligible voters," led by Ch'en Po-t'ao, met again at the Confucian Temple in Canton. Claiming to speak for the people of Kwangtung in place of the assembly, which had been shattered by mass resignations and loss of public confidence, they resolved to send a telegram of their own to the Grand Council. The telegram, with Teng Hua-hsi heading the list of signatories, refuted the main argument against an immediate ban on gambling. It pointed out that the court, when it earlier banned the use of opium, had not then set the developing of alternate sources of revenue as a prior condition. The meeting agreed that should the court deny their plea it would follow the recent example of the petitioners for a parliament and send a delegation to Peking to present its appeal directly.[59]

In the following weeks the anti-gambling campaign developed additional public support. In late November the gentry and merchants in Canton met at the Wen-lan Academy and proposed the establishment of an anti-gambling society (chin-tu hui). Early in December, the one hundred twenty guilds of Canton issued a circular forbidding their members from gambling and threatening joint action against employees of gambling establishments if they did not give up their harmful occupations within three months. At about the same time, the Canton Merchants' Self-Government Society sent a telegram of its own, signed by more than five hundred persons, requesting the throne for an immediate ban.[60]

When Chang Ming-ch'i arrived in Canton at the beginning of January 1911 to take up his post as governor-general, he was committed to the anti-gambling position. On January 9 he accepted the resignation of the 35 pro-gambling assemblymen, though not of their rivals, and he called for new elections to fill the vacancies. While it is not clear whether, or when, these special elections were held, the stage was set for the reconvening of the assembly, which met in an extraordinary session in March. Next, Governor-General Chang conferred with the leaders of the gentry to work out specific plans for the prohibition of gambling. On January 10, at a mass welcome planned for him by the Association for the Study of Self-Government, he expressed agreement with their demand for prohibition, but he, like his predecessors, cautioned that it must await the finding of substitute revenue. Li Yü-t'ang, the Hong Kong merchant, once more stated the need for immediate action.[61]

In consultations with the gentry, Chang looked, as Tseng-ch'i had suggested, to additional levies on salt, opium, and wine for the revenue to offset the loss from gambling. However, even with the new revenue generated by these concessions, there remained a deficit of between 0.5 and 1.2 million taels. The gentry leaders assured Chang, as they had Tseng-ch'i, that voluntary contributions by the people would make good the deficit. With the revenue problem ostensibly solved, the governor-general summoned the gentry leaders to his official compound on January 21 and together they agreed on March 30 as the date for the gambling prohibition to go into effect. Two days later, he submitted his plan to the throne, which gave its approval on February 12.[62]

When the ban on gambling went into effect on March 30, it was celebrated with a huge procession through the streets of Canton. Like the earlier anti-opium parades, it included exhibits intended to impress upon the populace the evil consequences of the gambling habit: "A man covered from head to foot with pawn tickets, or clad in most beggarly garments; a man leading his child to be sold to bring cash for gambling; criminals with cangue, chain and handcuffs, and sometimes followed by an executioner with sword and the official coming on to give the orders." The parade was so lengthy that it took about two hours for it to pass any given point. "The streets were literally packed for miles, and everybody in the best of spirits and good-will. Never has anything like it been seen in Canton." [63]

The ban on gambling was fairly effective. The evidence at hand, though far from conclusive, suggests that the ban was enforced and that gambling in public was in fact sharply curtailed. "Public gambling has practically ceased," according to one report from the Swatow–Ch'ao-chou region in late August. "Even in markets and fairs far removed from governing centers where booths once stood by the score, well-patronised by villagers too, the business has folded its tents and silently stolen away." However, it is likely that gambling continued surreptitiously in the countryside, away from the cities, and where official enforcement was lax. [64]

The imposition of the gambling ban was the culmination of two years of bitter struggle. It was a many-sided triumph—a triumph of the deliberative assembly over the provincial administration, of the native residents over the outsider officials, of mobilized public opinion over the entrenched bureaucracy, of moral principles over fiscal considerations. Above all, as the American consul in Canton, Leo Bergholz, commented perceptively in January 1911, the provincial assembly, by extra-constitutional means such as stoppage of debate, mass resignations, and appeal to public feeling, had won a great deal of power from "those who theoretically enjoy it." [65]

Self-Government at the Local Level

The provincial assembly was not the only achievement of the court's constitutional program. There were similar efforts at the subprovincial level. The court had declared its policy of encouraging self-government at the local level in October 1907, but it did not approve the set of detailed regulations regarding the formation of self-government bodies in cities, towns, and rural areas until January 1909. According to its Nine-Year Plan, the establishment of self-rule at the subdistrict level was to be completed by 1913. The court also issued regulations for self-government assemblies in prefectures, subprefectures, departments, and districts, with the completion date scheduled for 1914. In Kwangtung some representative assemblies were created at the subdistrict level before the outbreak of the revolution; none apparently at the level of prefecture and district. Under the circumstances, it is remarkable that any had been established at all. [66]

In Kwangtung the constitutional program at the local level was put into effect by the provincial Commission for the Organization of Local Self-Government (Ti-fang tzu-chih ch'ou-pan ch'u) and its local counterparts in the various districts.[67] One of the first tasks of the local self-government offices was to take a census of their district in preparation for the local elections, as no census had been taken for the provincial assembly elections. The census, which was China's first modern census, was ordered by the Commission for the Organization of Local Self-Government at the end of 1909. It was carried out hastily, where it was carried out at all, in 1910. Its results generally were not very accurate.[68]

Another early task, presumably undertaken after the completion of the census, was to divide each district into three types of self-governing units, cities, towns, and rural areas. According to the official regulations, a "city" (ch'eng) was the administrative center of the district together with its suburbs; a "town" (chen), a place which had a population of 50,000 or more and was not an administrative center; and a "rural area" (hsiang), a place or a combination of places with a population of less than 50,000. For example, as a result of consultations between the magistrate and the gentry and elders of the district on December 27, 1909, P'an-yü district was carved up into one "city" (that is, its half of Canton), five "towns," and twenty-six "rural areas." Similarly, Ch'ing-yüan district was divided up in June 1910 into one "city," eight "towns," and two "rural areas."[69]

Each district was also supposed to set up a Self-Government Instruction Office (Ti-fang tzu-chih yen-chiu so), which offered a six-to-eight months' course of instruction in the principles and practices of self-government. Persons possessing the franchise in the local elections were encouraged to enroll in the course. A number of districts, including Shun-te, Yang-chiang, Le-ch'ang, En-p'ing, Shih-ch'eng, and Hsinning, offered the course in 1909 and 1910.[70]

The census, the districting and the self-government instruction courses were all aimed toward the election in each city, town, and rural area of two local self-government bodies. One was the deliberative council (i-shih hui), which was elected directly by the eligible voters. The other was the executive council (known as tung-shih hui in cities and towns and hsiang tung in rural areas), which was elected by the deliberative council from the ranks of the voters. The franchise for these local elections was significantly broader than for the provincial assembly elections earlier. In place of the several options by which one might qualify to vote in the provincial elections, there was only a single and universal financial requirement, which furthermore was considerably less restrictive than before. Whereas in the provincial elections the minimum financial requirement had been ownership of a business or property worth at least $5,000, for these local elections it was payment of only $2 a year in taxes or public contributions. However, the eligible voters were divided into two classes, with the first class composed of only the largest taxpayers and contributors. Since each class voted separately to fill one half of the deliberative council, the wealthy were thus assured of greater representation.[71] As before, only males were entitled to vote.

In Kwangtung, deliberative councils are known to have been founded in Swatow, Cheng-hai, Yang-chiang, Kao-yao, and Fo-shan, while an executive council was reportedly set up in Kao-yao city.[72] The only one of these councils on which there is much information is the Swatow deliberative council. It was probably not a representative example, partly because Swatow, which lies in Cheng-hai district, was not a "city" but a "town" and partly because the port was a highly commercial place. It bears comparison with the city council in Shanghai.[73]

The Swatow town council was popularly elected in August 1910. Altogether 1,656 people were registered to vote in that election. In a town of about 50,000, they amounted to slightly more than 3 percent of the total population or 12 percent of adult males, which is six times larger than the electorate for the provincial election the year earlier.[74] Of the 1,656 registered voters, 367 belonged to the first class, which was limited to those who had paid at least Mex. $30 a year in taxes or charitable contributions; the remaining 1,289 were assigned to the second class, those who paid between $2 and $30. (In Shanghai, where a city election was held in 1910 also, the number of registered voters totaled 3,644, or about 2 percent of the city's population; they were divided between 334 first-class and 3,310 second-class voters.) In the election itself, where each class voted for eleven councilmen and five alternates, "almost all" the first-class voters in Swatow voted, while "little more than half" of the second class did so. (Similarly in Shanghai the turnout among the first-class voters was twice as high as among the second class.) Thus, despite the broadened franchise, the local deliberative council was hardly any less a creature of the well-to-do than the provincial assembly.

However, it was the well-to-do merchants and not the gentry who were most likely in control of the deliberative council in Swatow (and in Shanghai too). The president of the Swatow council was a certain Hsiao Hong K'wei, described as the vice-chairman of the Chamber of Com-

merce (perhaps Hsiao Yung-hua, though he was already a provincial assemblyman); the vice-president was Wu Tzu-shou, editor of the *Illustrated News* (*T'u-hua pao*). The rest of the membership is unknown, but
given the commercial character of Swatow, it is likely that many of the
remaining twenty councilmen were merchants. Moreover, the actions of
the council during its month-long session in March and April 1911
reflected the unique problems of the city as opposed to the countryside.
For example, in the interest of public health it forbade the carriage of
human refuse through the city streets in open topless buckets. It also
limited awnings and signs that projected into the streets and obstructed
pedestrian traffic.

Like the provincial assembly, the Swatow council tried to wrest additional authority from the officials, particularly with respect to finances.
According to the American consul, its members had "a ready apprecia-
tion of the fact that the control of the revenue is the key to securing the
adoption of their recommendations." This was evident in their demand
to be allowed to audit the accounts of the local police force in return for
helping it out of its financial difficulties. The council also claimed the
right to levy taxes for local purposes and in general to act as the final authority on all local matters in Swatow.

The other deliberative councils in Kwangtung probably were not
dominated by merchants as the Swatow council was.[75] But since the financial requirement for the right to vote in the local elections was relatively low and since there was no need for a complete financial disclosure, the merchants were undoubtedly better represented in the local
councils than they were in the provincial assembly.

This possibility of merchant domination was perhaps why Canton,
which was the leader in practically every other contemporary reform, did
not organize a deliberative council of its own. Canton, like most provincial capitals, was divided administratively between two districts, Nan-
hai and P'an-yü. Under the self-government regulations the two halves
of the city could either form two separate city councils or join together
to form a single municipal council. The leading gentry and merchant organizations in Canton, including the Association for the Study of Self-
Government, the Chamber of Commerce, and the Self-Government Society, all favored a union of the two parts of the city. Only the local
scholar-gentry of P'an-yü, fearful of being outnumbered and outvoted by
the merchants entrenched in the city's Nan-hai half, particularly the
Western Suburbs, objected to the proposal. Their opposition prevented
the formation of a single municipal council. At the same time, presum-

ably while negotiations continued between P'an-yü and Nan-hai, neither half of the city formed its own separate council.[76]

Apart from the official self-government councils, apparently informal associations for the study of self-government (*ti-fang tzu-chih yen-chiu she*) existed in many districts. These associations were formed as early as 1909 in some districts, for example, Hui-chou and Hsiang-shan, and were distinct from the similarly named self-government instruction offices (*ti-fang tzu-chih yen-chiu so*), most of which were not started until 1910.[77] They were perhaps the local counterpart of the provincial Association for the Study of Self-Government founded in November 1907. They seem to have been advisory groups to the local officials. As such they may not have been very different from the deliberative councils except that they were not popularly elected. For example, the Association for the Study of Self-Government in Shao-chou, in northern Kwangtung, was described in February 1910 by a visiting foreign correspondent as an advisory body "to which the influential citizens were invited to discuss what reforms were necessary." Its membership was composed of "scholars," including persons who had purchased the necessary "scholarly" qualifications for $20. Included among the reforms that it discussed were proposals that shop signs overhanging the street be removed and that night-soil buckets be provided with tops. Except that its membership was apparently appointed by the magistrate, the Shao-chou association was thus very much like the Swatow town council.[78]

The self-government movement at the subdistrict level had not progressed very far before the republican revolution intervened. Indeed, in many districts there had been little or no progress at all. The gazetteer for K'ai-p'ing frankly admits that in 1909, when the district was supposed to have been divided into ten "self-government wards," each with a "self-government bureau," the various villages merely created a "bureau," called themselves a "ward," and left it at that.[79] Nevertheless, it might still have been possible, if there had been no interruption, for many cities and towns to have achieved self-government by the target date of 1913. Clearly, during the first two years of the plan, something more than superficial progress had been made in at least a handful of districts.

Peasant Resistance to Gentry Domination

The self-government program, like the modern schools earlier, benefited mainly the gentry and to a lesser extent the merchants; it benefited the peasant majority hardly at all. Indeed it worked considerable hardship on the peasants. As before, they were the ones who ultimately bore the costs of the reforms directly through higher taxes on a variety of goods and services and indirectly through higher land rents. In Shun-te district, for example, after 1900 hardly a year went by without the imposition of a new tax or an additional surtax.[80] Moreover, as the gentry's role in government grew at the expense of the officials at both the provincial and the local level, so did their opportunity to dominate and exploit the peasantry. The result was growing peasant resistance.

Whereas in earlier years of the dynasty the peasants had often joined with the local gentry in opposing the outsider magistrate and the yamen clerks, now their wrath was turned against the gentry themselves.[81] When the pattern of gentry domination first became apparent during the middle years of the decade with the promotion of the modern schools, the peasants had protested with occasional school burnings and anti-tax riots. Later in the decade, as gentry demands became more far-reaching with the proliferation of new schools and the initiation of the self-government program, peasant resistance stiffened and spread. Harassment of the new schools continued. In Kwangtung, for example, the school at Sung-t'ang, upriver from Swatow, was wrecked in the spring of 1908 "because the villagers objected to their monastery being annexed for school purposes"; and in February 1911, in a country town near Canton, opponents of the local schools gathered to insult the students as they went to school and to throw stones upon the schoolhouse roof to disrupt classes.[82] But increasingly the peasants' discontent was directed toward other targets than the schools. They began attacking the various features of the self-government program and the taxes levied to support the program. In doing so, they were in fact attacking the whole system of gentry domination.[83]

During 1910 and early 1911, there were at least twelve serious riots against gentry self-government in widely scattered parts of Kwangtung. In some instances, the imposition of a new tax or the increase of an old one provoked the riot. For example, on June 12, 1910, about three hundred persons in Hsiang-shan city rose up against the tax-farmer who had just been granted the right of levying a head tax on all shamans, priests, monks, and nuns in the district. Rallied by the disgruntled monks, they destroyed the tax-farmer's office. They also set fire to the office of a second tax-farmer, who collected the "coast defence" and the "rice cauldron" tax. Finally, they looted and burned the local salt depot.[84] The registration of houses and the taking of the census occasioned other riots. These were steps preparatory to the local council elections, but in many minds they were thought to be laying the foundation for future tax increases. In 1910 anti-census riots broke out in Loting in June, Hsin-an in July, Ta-p'u in August, and Lei-chou prefecture in October.[85]

There was a particularly persistent disturbance in 1910 in Lien-chou, in northern Kwangtung, about which exists an unusual amount of information coming from several widely different sources. In addition to newspaper reports, there are accounts by the American Presbyterian missionaries who had re-established themselves in the city after the 1905 massacre and the diary of the Shao-chou taotai who made an official investigation of the uprising. These accounts clearly reveal the gentry's exploitation of self-government for their own purposes and the peasants' hostility to gentry domination.[86]

Early in September 1910 the subprefect of Lien-chou, following instructions from the provincial Commission for the Organization of Local Self-Government, directed some of the local elite to take a census of the department. Unfortunately, neither he nor they made any attempt to explain to the people the reasons for the census or the procedure for the registration of houses. As a result, nearly everybody, including the American missionaries, was convinced that the census foreshadowed a tax increase. It provoked a riot. On September 15 some villagers in the suburbs broke into Lien-chou city and went on a rampage, attacking the city's single government primary school, some private schools, the gentry's meeting hall, and the homes of some of the gentry leaders. Altogether ten buildings, every one of them closely associated with the gentry, were destroyed.

The riot ended when night fell. The next day the city gates were reopened and business was almost back to normal. But beneath the surface calm Lien-chou continued to seethe with the peasants' discontent. Their hostility against the elite flared up intermittently in different parts of the department during the following month and a half. On September 23 a group of people from the outside again surged through the streets of Lien-chou city, burning four gentry homes and kidnaping three gentry members for ransom. The main target of this foray was evidently the P'an family. One of the P'an brothers was an official investigator assigned to take the census; another P'an brother was a colporteur with the Presbyterian mission. Afterwards posters appeared in the city calling for the seizure of additional gentry members. They also called for a halt to the collection of various taxes, including specifically the wine tax, the rice cauldron tax, the butcher tax, and the lumber tax. On October 12 a group of villagers destroyed a village school to the north of the city. On October 31 another group destroyed the school buildings and some gentry homes at the market town of San-chiang; they also plundered and burned the Presbyterian chapel, school, and parsonage at San-chiang.

With the situation getting out of the control of the local officials, the provincial authorities in Canton dispatched detachment commander Wu Tsung-yü and his Reserve Forces to Lien-chou to crush the insurrection. Early in December Wu's troops routed the rebel force, composed now of secret society members and local bandits in addition to the original rioters, and forced them to retire to the nearby mountains. By January 1911 they had more or less restored order to Lien-chou. The insurrection had lasted about four months.

Obviously there had been more to the Lien-chou rebellion than simply opposition to the taking of the census. The American missionary J. S. Kunkle and the investigating taotai Tso Shao-tso agreed independently of each other that the basic cause of the troubles was the peasants' hostility to the elite's self-serving manipulation of the various reform programs. For example, "The gentry in charge of the schools were said to have appropriated the funds largely for their own use," Kunkle wrote. "The schools, anyhow, were available only for the rich." [87] When Taotai Tso asked to see the records of the government school and of the taxes that supposedly went toward its upkeep, they were conveniently unavailable. Gentry members charged with taking the census similarly exploited their position for their own benefit. When they went out to the villages to register houses, they demanded money from the people, claiming that the twelve dollars they received from the government was inadequate to cover their expenses. When the people complained about these exactions, the subprefect paid no heed. Tax farming was another fruitful field for gentry manipulation, since many of the department's tax-farmers were only frontmen for local gentry members. Nor did the rapacity of the gentry cease with the attacks against them. When putting in their claims for compensation, they all inflated the amount of property damage ten times over.

The peasants' response to the elite's abuse of power in Lien-chou was by no means indiscriminate. The plunder, burning, and destruction were directed only at those institutions identified with gentry domination, such as the schools, the granaries, the gentry's meeting hall, and gentry homes. The Presbyterian mission evidently came under attack also because of its association with the hated gentry. One of the four gentry members named by Taotai Tso Shao-tso as responsible for provoking the peasants to rebellion, a man named Mo, was a Christian convert; in addition, there was the colporteur P'an whose brother was a census taker. Aside from the establishments linked to the gentry, almost nothing else in Lien-chou was touched by the rioters. Selective destruction was true of other anti-tax, anti-census riots too.

The gentry's success in 1911 in forcing the Kwangtung government to declare an immediate halt to licensed gambling upset the peasants even more than before and helped spark at least two more riots in the early months of 1911, both of them directed against the new tax on wine that had been devised to offset the revenue loss from gambling. They took place in Hsin-hui and Ch'ing-yüan in April. In Ch'ing-yüan, the riot began with an attack on the offices of the wine tax-farmer but quickly broadened out to include a number of other hated institutions, such as old clothes shops, pawn shops, the salt depot, rice shops, and the homes of well-known merchants and gentry members. The attack, though broad, was again selective. [88]

The anti-tax, anti-census riots were widespread but sporadic and isolated. There was no link-up either among themselves or with outside forces (except in the case of the anti-tax riot in 1907 in Ch'in-chou and Lien-chou in West Kwangtung). Therefore, they posed no great threat to the regime. They seem not even to have moderated the acquisitiveness of the gentry or altered the course of the self-government program. In the end, the riots were primarily expressive of the plight of the peasants under the growing domination of the gentry.

Once inaugurated, the self-government program became a movement with a momentum of its own. Instead of curbing the considerable amount of unauthorized political activity already going on, as the court had hoped they would do, the provincial assemblies and the other newly formed deliberative bodies enlarged the scope of activities. The nationalist demonstrations had politicized the merchants; the self-government movement now politicized the gentry. As the court gave way before the joint demands of the gentry and merchants to hasten the summoning of Parliament, China was seemingly close to being transformed into a constitutional monarchy.

8

Final Years of the Post-Boxer Decade, III: Revolution

As nationalism and constitutionalism flourished, revolution waned. After 1907 the level of revolutionary activity within China dropped sharply and remained at a low point until 1911.[1] In contrast to the feverish doings of the middle years, the only revolutionary uprisings in all of China during these years were the two New Army mutinies at Anking, Anhwei, in November 1908 and Canton in February 1910 and the Canton revolt in April 1911. Moreover, the revolutionary movement was in great disarray. The resurrection of the Restoration Society (Kuang-fu hui) by T'ao Ch'eng-chang in 1909 and Chang Ping-lin's defection to it from the Revolutionary Alliance in 1910 destroyed the unity of the anti-Manchu forces. The Alliance itself was deeply split between the Yangtze faction at its Tokyo headquarters and the Kwangtung faction centering on the peripatetic Sun Yat-sen.[2] Sun's own faction was divided over future strategy as Wang Ching-wei in 1910 personally abandoned the mass revolt approach favored by the Alliance and took up political assassination instead. The Alliance thus lost whatever organizational coherence it formerly had. It also lost its principal organ when the Japanese authorities closed down the *People's Report* in October 1908.

As in the middle years, Kwangtung was a focus of attention for Sun Yat-sen's revolutionaries. It was the scene of both revolts they organized. (The Anking New Army mutiny was carried out independently of the

Alliance.) However, even in Kwangtung the revolutionary movement was hardly as vigorous as it appeared.

The Revolutionaries and the Reforms

The revolutionaries' decline after 1907 stemmed from the court's success in appealing to the reformers and also from the irrelevance of their own ideology. They had difficulty both in attracting new supporters and in holding on to their old ones. While some individuals who were ostensibly revolutionaries occupied important positions in the emergent new society, most were unwilling or unable to make use of their influential connections to further the revolution, as the abortive "Protect Asia" revolt made clear. In short, many revolutionaries had been coopted by the court's reforms.[3]

If in the past the revolutionaries had thrived on the frustrated hopes of reformers, then the last years of the post-Boxer decade would not have been a propitious time for them. These were the years when the court's programs enjoyed extensive support among both constitutionalists and nationalists. The constitutionalists and the nationalists did not always get what they wanted, but they nevertheless had reason to think that the court was not unresponsive to organized public opinion. They were not so frustrated as to resort to revolution.

The revolutionaries, furthermore, failed to adjust to the new climate of opinion in China and were often at odds with it. They continued to denounce the constitutional program as a sham and to blame all of China's ills primarily upon the alien origins of the Ch'ing rulers.[4] Their narrow interpretation of nationalism was particularly out of step with the rest of the politicized elite, for they viewed nationalism primarily in anti-Manchu terms. Thus, in the midst of the West River patrol agitation in Canton late in 1907, a revolutionary speaker, trying to redirect the anti-British sentiments that had been generated into an anti-dynastic channel, did so not by condemning the Manchus for their weak foreign policy (as he might well have done) but by equating them to the hated British simply because both were foreigners: "China at present is weak and helpless [like India]. Why? Because she, too, is groaning under alien rule."[5]

Their anti-Manchu emphasis sometimes led the revolutionaries to do what they accused the Manchus of doing, selling out China's national interests in order to further their own selfish interests. During the *Tatsu Maru* controversy in 1908, every newspaper but one in south China denounced the Japanese government's high-handed dealings with China and vigorously supported the retaliatory boycott. The exception was the *China Daily News,* which condemned the anti-Japanese agitation because it threatened to disrupt Japan's support for the revolutionary cause and also to interfere with the revolutionaries' running arms into Kwangtung.[6] (This was consistent with Sun Yat-sen's later stand in 1915, when he again ran counter to Chinese public opinion by not joining in the almost universal condemnation of Japan's Twenty-one Demands.) [7] In the face of the court's tangible accomplishments in the constitutional field and the rights recovery movement, the revolutionaries' propaganda about the Manchus was not immediately relevant.

In Kwangtung the principal revolutionary activity after the termination of the uprisings along the Vietnam border in the spring of 1908 was once again propaganda, some of which reflected these ideological preoccupations and shortcomings. The organ of the Revolutionary Alliance continued to be Feng Tzu-yu's *China Daily News.* As before, the paper was plagued by financial problems and managed to survive in 1908 and 1909 only through timely subsidies from Feng's wealthy father-in-law, Li Yü-t'ang, and sympathetic merchants such as Lin Chihmien.[8] In addition to the *China Daily News,* the revolutionaries published at least three other journals in Kwangtung during 1908 and 1909, one each in Hong Kong, Swatow, and Canton. The Hong Kong publication was a revival of the *Current Events Pictorial,* which previously had been published in Canton. Founded in the fall of 1909 by the journalists Hsieh Ying-po and P'an Ta-wei, both of whom were new members of the Alliance, the magazine lasted for only ten or so issues.[9]

The other two new publications, both daily newspapers, were more durable. One was the *China New Journal (Chung-hua hsin pao)* of Swatow. It was started in the summer of 1908 by a group of Hakka businessmen headed by Hsieh I-ch'iao; it was edited by Yeh Ch'u-ts'ang. Both were members of the Revolutionary Alliance. Hsieh I-ch'iao, a brother of Hsieh Liang-mu, is supposed to have joined the Alliance in Tokyo in 1905; earlier in 1900 he had been the contact in East Kwangtung for the T'ang Ts'ai-ch'ang rebellion. It was the two Hsieh brothers who introduced Yeh Ch'u-ts'ang into the Alliance in the spring of 1909. Under Yeh's editorship the *China New Journal* was known for its support of modern education and for its criticism of official abuses and corruption; it was also the spokesman for the Hakkas of East Kwangtung, a disproportionately large number of whom, it may be recalled, belonged to the

Alliance. Until the spring of 1911, however, the paper was extremely careful about what it printed lest it be interfered with by the officials. In order to survive it had to be discreet.[10] The other newspaper in Kwangtung founded by revolutionaries was the *South Viet News* (*Nan Yüeh pao*) of Canton. It began in June 1909 and was published by Lu Po-lang and Su Leng-feng; Lu Po-lang is known to have joined the Alliance in Hong Kong in 1909. The *South Viet News* too attacked the officials without straying beyond the bounds of permissible criticism. It was still circulating at the beginning of 1911.[11]

Apart from newspapers, the revolutionaries also appealed to the people through popular novels and drama. During these years Huang Shih-chung, a member of the Alliance since 1906, published several novels in Hong Kong which helped spread the ideas of the revolutionaries. One was *The Romance of Hung Hsiu-ch'üan* (*Hung Hsiu-ch'üan yen-i*), a popular biography of the leader of the Taiping Rebellion; published in 1908, it reputedly was "rich in revolutionary thought." Another, with a punning title *Ta-ma-p'ien* (that is, *ta-p'ien,* the great swindler), was a diatribe against K'ang Yu-wei. A third, published in 1909, was a contemporary bureaucratic exposé entitled *Rise and Fall in the Sea of Officialdom* (*Huan-hai sheng-ch'en lu*); it focused on the meteoric career of Yüan Shih-k'ai. By stressing Yüan's rapid rise to power following the Sino-Japanese war and then his abrupt fall from grace after the death of the Empress Dowager in November 1908, presumably attributed to the machinations of jealous Manchus, Huang Shih-chung was able to underscore the un-trustworthiness of the Manchus, their hostility toward Han Chinese, and their unwillingness to concede to Han Chinese any measure of independent power. These were basic themes in the revolutionaries' critique of the Manchu constitutional program.[12]

At the same time, the veteran revolutionary Ch'en Shao-pai and a recent convert, Mo Chi-p'eng, organized theatrical troupes to take similar anti-Manchu ideas to the illiterate masses. These troupes traveled about the populous Pearl River delta performing plays that "ridiculed superstition, satirized the government, cultivated the sense of loyalty and denounced foreign races." [13] Plays fitting the last two categories include *Yüeh Fei Avenges the Country* (*Yüeh Fei pao kuo-ch'ou*) and *Hsiung Fei's Uprising* (*Hsiung Fei ch'i-i*). Both eulogized Han Chinese loyalists who resisted conquest by barbarian invaders. Yüeh Fei, of course, led the fight against the Jurcheds at the end of the Northern Sung period; Hsiung Fei was equally well known in his native Kwangtung for resisting the Mongols. Obviously, by "loyalty" the plays meant loyalty not to the Chinese state but to the Chinese cultural tradition, and by "foreign races" they meant not the imperialists but the Manchus. One wonders whether those who saw these plays performed were really aware of their subversive intent. But according to the reminiscences of a woman who was a schoolgirl at the time, many of her fellow students spotted the parallel between Yüeh Fei's struggle against the Jurcheds and the contemporary one against the Manchus.[14]

Partly because of these efforts at propaganda but mostly because of concurrent preparations for the two military revolts in Canton, the Hong Kong Alliance enrolled many new members during these years. According to Feng Tzu-yu, who was still its head, "several hundred" joined the organization in 1908 and "about two thousand" in 1909, though only a hundred are listed by name.[15] Among those who are listed by name, the largest group were soldiers recruited for the military uprisings, especially the New Army mutiny. The next largest group were journalists, including Hsieh Ying-po, P'an Ta-wei, Ho Chien-shih, Lu O-sheng, Huang Hsüan-chou, Li I-heng, and Li Wen-fu. Several were merchants: T'an Min-san, Lin Chih-mien, and perhaps Li Wen-ch'i, Li Yü-t'ang's younger brother. Other new recruits were Ma Ta-ch'en, former leader of the anti-American boycott, Mo Chi-p'eng, organizer of revolutionary theatrical troupes, and Ch'en Chiung-ming, the provincial assemblyman. Also joining the Alliance at this time were four women—all of them medical doctors in the mold of the early feminist Chang Chu-chün and all of them converted to the revolutionary cause in 1909 by Hsü Tsung-han, who was later to marry Huang Hsing.[16] These were impressive gains for the Alliance in Hong Kong. But in other parts of the country, where there were no preparations for revolts, the Alliance probably attracted few new adherents.

Meanwhile, even in Kwangtung, the Alliance was having trouble retaining the allegiance of its old supporters. Many of its early members, who had joined the organization before the court had inaugurated its sweeping constitutional program, undoubtedly returned to the path of reformism once it was implemented. In particular, it is probable that a majority of the student radicals who had been original members of the Tokyo Alliance in 1905–06 quietly drifted away from the revolutionary cause after their return to China, especially as they settled down to the comfortable jobs to which their overseas training had entitled them.

In the Kwangtung contingent of 112 members, for example, leaving aside those who had stayed abroad to become professional revolutionaries such as Hu Han-min and Wang Ching-wei, only a few are known to have engaged in any revolutionary activities in China during these years. It may be recalled that there is information for only about 30 of the 112, which alone suggests how few may have been involved in the subsequent revolutionary movement, since anyone who was involved would probably have rated a mention in the voluminous records of the revolution. But even among those for whom there exists some information, not all were active.

Consider the experience of the five or six revolutionaries who were hired to teach at the College of Law and Administration in Canton. They were Chang Po-ch'iao, Chu Chih-hsin, Ku Ying-fen, Li Wen-fan, and Tu Kung-shih, all of whom had joined the Alliance in Tokyo in 1905; to them may be added Yeh Hsia-sheng, who had written for the *People's Report* though he apparently did not join the Alliance. Of these six, only two took an active part in the revolutionary movement in Canton after their return in 1906 until 1910. The two were Chu Chih-hsin and Chang Po-ch'iao, who as we have seen were involved in Liu Ssu-fu's unsuccessful attempt to assassinate Li Chun in 1907. Chang Po-ch'iao's death not long afterwards left Chu as the lone activist. Two other teachers, Li Wen-fan and Ku Ying-fen, are said to have been active revolutionaries too, but it is unspecified what their activity consisted of.[17] According to Tsou Lu, who was a student at the school from 1907 to 1909, "Of the teachers at the college . . . not a few had joined the revolutionary organization. But those who actually participated in the revolutionary movement from first to last included only Chu Chih-hsin among the teachers."[18]

As members of the tiny elite with a modern education, the covert revolutionaries were in great demand to staff the new institutions and lead the new social movements of post-Boxer China. From these positions they had excellent opportunities for recruitment and agitation on behalf of the revolutionary cause, but apparently only a few made good use of such opportunities. One activist in Kwangtung was Kuo Kung-chieh, who was an original member of the Tokyo Alliance. From 1907 until his resignation in 1910, Kuo taught physics, chemistry, and physical education at the Hui-chou Prefectural Middle School. At the same time, he reportedly indoctrinated his students assiduously with revolutionary ideas. With his student converts in turn spreading these ideas among their friends at home during school vacations, "no fewer than ten thousand" persons throughout the prefecture eventually took the revolutionary oath.[19] Two others like him were Kan Hui-ju and Wang Po-ch'ün. A teacher at the Tzu-chin district primary school in the hills of East Kwangtung, Kan Hui-ju "disseminated revolutionary ideas, encouraged his pupils to participate in revolutionary activity, and persuaded them to enroll in the Alliance."[20] Similarly, Wang Po-ch'ün, a primary school teacher in Hua-chou in West Kwangtung, incorporated revolutionary propaganda among the "new books and journals" that he assigned to his pupils, so that later when a secret cell of the Alliance was set up at the school at least 60 percent of the pupils joined.[21]

Such claims of recruitment success, however, must be viewed with considerable skepticism, especially in the light of some better documented cases. At the College of Law and Administration, for example, the revolutionary teachers were singularly unsuccessful in gaining new recruits for the cause. Out of over a thousand students at the school, only two, Ch'en Chiung-ming and Tsou Lu, are known for sure to have joined the revolutionary movement. Wu Han-ch'ih, a Western-style medical doctor who attended the college from 1906 to 1908, may have been a third; it was he who took care of Liu Ssu-fu's wounds after his accidental bomb blast in 1907.[22]

In addition to the new schools, the revolutionaries also infiltrated the provincial assembly. Vice-president Ch'iu Feng-chia and resident assemblyman Ch'en Chiung-ming were both members of the Alliance. Ch'iu, whose anti-dynastic feelings may have taken shape when Taiwan was ceded in 1895 to the Japanese, was reportedly in 1908 the "oath administrator" for the Alliance in eastern Kwangtung.[23] His colleague Ch'en joined the Alliance in Hong Kong in 1909 after the end of the assembly's first session. Both were frequent and vigorous critics of the officials and both were involved in the movement to petition the court for the early summoning of Parliament. But until early 1911 they evidently did nothing within the assembly that was particularly revolutionary except perhaps in a very oblique way, as when Ch'en Chiung-ming, objecting to the transfer of a piece of public land to the bannermen, warned in 1909 that if the transfer went through, "the future course of China may not be such as would be desired by the bannermen."[24] Apart from the two assemblymen, the chief secretary of the assembly's chancery, Ku Ying-fen, was a member of the Alliance also, as was one of his four assistant secretaries, Tsou Lu.[25]

The revolutionaries were associated with other institutions and movements too, but were similarly unwilling or unable to use their associations to advance the revolutionary cause significantly during these years. The head of the self-government instruction office set up in 1909 by the Canton Merchants' Self-Government Society was Tu Kung-shih, and one of its two instructors was Tsou Lu.[26] Two of the four men who drafted the constitution of the Macao Boundary Delimitation Society in 1909 were Tu Kung-shih and Yeh Hsia-sheng.[27] Three of the eleven-man directorate of the Society to Recover the Nation's Rights founded in Canton during the West River patrol agitation late in 1907 were Yeh Hsia-sheng, Ch'en Chiung-ming, and Wu Han-ch'ih.[28] Two of the leaders of the Canton Red Cross Society were Wu Han-ch'ih and Ma Ta-ch'en.[29] Finally, Li Yü-t'ang was active in the anti-gambling movement. Though all these opportunities were dazzling, they simply did not pan out for the revolutionaries.

This was particularly so of the revolutionaries' associations with the Kwangtung New Army. Until the spring of 1909, the First Infantry Regiment of the New Army, its core unit, was commanded by Chao Sheng, a member of the Alliance since 1907. Yet when the Canton revolutionaries attempted a military uprising in the fall of 1908, Chao was not of much assistance. This was the abortive "Protect Asia" mutiny, prompted by the sudden and mysterious deaths of the Kuang-hsü Emperor and Empress Dowager Tz'u-hsi on successive days in November 1908. It was obviously an opportune moment for a revolt. (In Anhwei, Hsiung Ch'eng-chi took advantage of it to mount the New Army mutiny at Anking.) As soon as news of the imperial deaths reached Canton, several revolutionary leaders, including Chu Chih-hsin, Chao Sheng, and Tsou Lu, met hurriedly to see about preparing a revolt. Since there was no time to put together an attack force of their own, they decided to try to instigate a military mutiny. Chao Sheng's First Regiment, however, was judged to be "not ready," so they had to turn instead to the old-style Reserve Forces. They entrusted the task of preparing them for the revolt to two army men, Ko Ch'ien and T'an Fu.[30]

Ko and T'an were natives of the same district in Hunan, but they had come to the revolutionary movement by quite different paths. Ko Ch'ien was introduced to the cause in the winter of 1905–06 during Huang Hsing's visit with detachment commander Kuo Jen-chang at Kweilin; at that time Ko was a student in the "instruction command" (*sui-ying hsüeh-t'ang*) attached to Kuo's Reserve Forces. He later went to Japan for further study. Afterwards he apparently rejoined Kuo Jen-chang's army, which had since moved from Kweilin to Ch'in-chou in Kwangtung. It was probably there that Ko met T'an Fu, whose background is more obscure. A member of the Elder Brothers Society (Ko-lao hui), the secret society in the Yangtze valley, T'an had enlisted in the army and come with it to Kwangtung. Both joined the Alliance in Hong Kong in 1907. They were chosen to lead the revolt because most of the soldiers in the Reserve Forces were Hunanese and many of them also belonged to the Elder Brothers Society.

In preparing the Reserve Forces for the projected mutiny, Ko Ch'ien and T'an Fu appealed to the soldiers' secret society connections and their mercenary instincts. On the one hand, they drew upon the traditional hostility of the Elder Brothers Society toward the Manchus. On the other, they issued certificates, called "Protect Asia" certificates (Pao-Ya p'iao), offering material incentives for supporting the revolution. Each certificate promised its holder certain stated benefits once the revolution was victorious. (A familiar device for the Elder Brothers Society, it was also hardly different from the "revolutionary army bonds" that Sun Yat-sen was selling then to the overseas Chinese.) [31] Furthermore, to encourage the dissemination of the certificates, a schedule of rewards was set up whereby, for example, someone who distributed fifty certificates would be rewarded with the position of platoon chief in the post-revolutionary army.

Unfortunately, because of careless distribution, some of the certificates were discovered, and with them, the plot. On December 7 Ko Ch'ien and a number of his fellow conspirators were arrested. In his written deposition, Ko made no attempt to hide his affiliation with the Revolutionary Alliance nor his confidence that the Chinese revolution was historically inevitable. Citing the "great revolutions of Europe and America," he declared that before the revolution in China could succeed, much blood would have to be shed, that before there could be a successful liberator like George Washington, there might be countless failures like himself.[32] Thus, in contrast to the traditionalist ideology which he and T'an Fu had been propagating among the troops, Ko's own personal outlook was self-consciously modern. Ten days later, he and a companion were beheaded. T'an Fu managed to elude arrest for about a year before he too was captured and executed. Three other convicted ringleaders were imprisoned. As for the rest of the Reserve Forces who had been implicated in the projected revolt, Li Chun, who in addition to being the naval commander-in-chief was also the commander of the Reserve Forces in central Kwangtung, was inclined at first to deal drastically with them, but he eventually allowed them to surrender their certificates without penalty.

Since the revolt was quashed even before final plans were drawn up, it is difficult to judge how serious a threat it really had been. According to Tsou Lu, 70 to 80 percent of the Reserve Forces in Canton had accepted the "Protect Asia" certificates. However, acceptance of the certificates did not necessarily represent a commitment by the holder to revolutionary action. Furthermore, Ko Ch'ien in his deposition admitted that it had been difficult to appeal to the residual anti-Manchu attitude of the secret society members among the soldiers. "Most members," he explained, "were uneducated and were lacking in historical consciousness; they had long ago forgotten the deep and great enmity that divided the Han and the Manchu people." [33] It is therefore understandable why Li Chun could have afforded to treat his men so leniently.

The New Army Mutiny

In February 1910, after close to two years of subdued activity in Kwangtung, the revolutionaries organized the Canton New Army mutiny. It was, however, not quite the revolutionary feat that is often portrayed. Its failure was a further setback to the Alliance and plunged many revolutionaries into the deepest gloom, even as its aftermath caused a backlash of popular sympathy for the mutinous troops.

The initiator and principal organizer of the mutiny was Ni Ying-tien. A native of Anhwei, Ni in his youth had turned his back on his father's profession in traditional medicine to seek a career in the Kiangnan New Army, rising eventually to command an artillery division (*ying*). He lost his command, however, when he was implicated in Hsiung Ch'eng-chi's conspiracy among the New Army troops at Anking. When the Anking revolt broke out in November 1908, Ni was already on his way to Hong Kong, where he formally enrolled in the Alliance. Not long afterwards, under an assumed name, he went to Canton and applied for a position in the New Army there. The Kwangtung officials were just then expanding their two infantry regiments into a mixed brigade; they badly needed artillerymen with experience. Ni was promptly appointed to be a platoon (*p'ai*) chief in the Second Artillery Division.[34]

In Canton Ni Ying-tien set about on his own initiative organizing an uprising similar to Hsiung Ch'eng-chi's in Anking. However, even during Chao Sheng's term as commander of the First Infantry Regiment, the revolutionaries had not occupied a very strong position in the Kwangtung New Army. That position was further weakened when Chao was dismissed from his post in the spring of 1909, after the provincial officials finally began to question his loyalty. Ni arrived in Canton just about the time that Chao left. He thus had to work from scratch. He started by recruiting a few associates from among his fellow lower-level officers, many of whom were graduates of the Canton Short-term Officers' School, where there had been some prior revolutionary agitation in 1907, and the Whampoa Military Primary School, where from 1909 to 1911 Teng K'eng, a revolutionary sympathizer, was an instructor.[35] They in turn recruited additional supporters within their own units. Proceeding in this fashion, Ni Ying-tien succeeded after about three months in creating a network of revolutionaries that allegedly extended through most units in the First Infantry Regiment (Chao Sheng's old command) and the four noninfantry battalions, all of them quartered at Yen-t'ang, a distant suburb of Canton. Ni evidently had less success with the Second Infantry Regiment and the training battalion stationed at the North Parade Ground just outside the city.[36]

In contrast to their traditionalist and mercenary approach to the Reserve Forces for the abortive "Protect Asia" revolt, the revolutionaries capitalized on the high educational level and political sophistication of the New Army soldiers. In their discussions with the soldiers and in their literature they focused on both old and new issues. They dwelt on the anti-Manchu theme; they complained, for example, about how the Manchus had occupied China for over 250 years, how they favored their own people and slighted the Han Chinese, and how this situation was unjust and why a revolution was therefore necessary. But they also dealt with more current problems. Among the pamphlets that the *China Daily News* in Hong Kong had prepared for use among the troops, one was on the "foreign question," another on the "constitutional question," and a third was entitled "The Revolutionary Vanguard," an appeal perhaps to the New Army to play the leading role in the coming revolution.[37]

The revolutionaries' activities within the New Army did not escape the attention of the military officials. In June and July more than ten soldiers were dismissed on suspicion of subversive behavior; in October and November several more were let go. Among the latter was Ni Ying-tien himself. It is, however, indicative of the porousness of the Ch'ing security system and the complacence of the Kwangtung officials in treating the suspected plot that Ni was able to remain in Canton after his discharge and to continue his secret work.[38]

By then Ni Ying-tien's efforts had become sufficiently promising to attract the notice of the Alliance leadership. Sometime in October or November Hu Han-min left Southeast Asia to come to Hong Kong to set up a new body called the South China Bureau to assume overall charge of the projected revolt. The bureau decided that in addition to the New Army mutiny that Ni had been planning there should be a number of coordinated secondary uprisings in the surrounding countryside. Leaving Ni in charge of preparations in Canton, it delegated responsibility for the secondary uprisings to other revolutionaries. Thus, Chu Chih-hsin and Hu I-sheng sought the support of bandit chiefs in the Pearl River delta, such as Li Fu-lin in P'an-yü and Lu Ling in Shun-te. Li Fu-lin, who had met Sun Yat-sen in Haiphong in November 1907, promised to cooperate; so did Lu Ling. The New Army soldier Hsü Wei-yang went home to Hua-hsien, north of Canton, to organize a supporting attack force that would march on the provincial capital once the revolt broke out. Tsou Lu even went to Swatow to notify the bandit chiefs in East Kwangtung about the revolt. To finance the uprising, the South China Bureau wired Sun Yat-sen, then in America, to remit HK$ 20,000. After repeated delays Sun was able to send only $8,000. A sympathetic merchant in Hong Kong, Li Hai-yün, finally embezzled the needed $20,000 from a family-owned money shop of which he was the manager. Wealthy Lin Chih-mien also contributed to the costs of the revolt.[39]

Toward the end of January 1910 the pace of activity quickened. More and more soldiers in the New Army were persuaded to join the plot. One by one the other leaders of the Alliance flocked to Hong Kong to take part. Huang Hsing, who had been living in Japan since 1908, arrived on January 29; T'an Jen-feng, on February 5. Chao Sheng, who had gone home to Kiangsu after his dismissal from the Kwangtung New Army, also returned to Hong Kong. In early February they joined Hu Han-min and Ni Ying-tien, who had come up from Canton, to make their final plans and to set the date.[40]

They agreed to make the revolt sometime during the New Year holidays beginning on February 10, when it would be more difficult than at other times for the Canton authorities to maintain tight security. But they could not agree on a specific date. One group, including Huang Hsing and Chao Sheng, favored an attempt sometime within the first week of the New Year. Another group, including Hu Han-min and his cousin Hu I-sheng, favored a date closer to the middle of the month in order to await further deliveries of funds and military supplies from Sun Yat-sen and others. Huang and Chao protested against any delay, lest the plot be discovered by the authorities.[41]

As the two groups were arguing inconclusively in Hong Kong, a trivial dispute involving a soldier and a shopkeeper had broken out in Canton on New Year's Eve that, unknown to the Alliance leaders, was to wreck all their plans and hopes within the next four days.[42] The soldier, an infantryman in the Second Regiment of the New Army, was trying to buy a box of calling cards when he quarreled with the shopkeeper. After a while, when the quarrel had not abated, the Canton police intervened and took the soldier to a nearby police station for questioning. The Kwangtung New Army and the Canton police, however, had never been on the best of terms. Proud of their elite status, the New Army had nothing but contempt for the police, an opinion which was shared by many residents of the city because of the generally unruly behavior of the police. News that one of their comrades had been arrested spread quickly among the soldiers of the Second Regiment. They flocked to the police station to demand that he be released immediately. The police at first refused. Finally, after consultations with an army officer, they agreed to release the soldier into the custody of the military authorities. The other soldiers then retired without further trouble. But they were unappeased. During the night, in their barracks outside the city, they evidently nursed their hostility and resentment against the police. The next day, February 10, New Year's Day, the soldiers went back into the city and sought their revenge. They brawled with the police and managed to destroy two police stations. Now satisfied, they returned to camp.

At this juncture, the Canton officials, fearing further disturbances, proceeded to disarm the soldiers, although as a matter of fact there had been until then no recourse to arms. They also canceled all military leave and confined the entire New Army to barracks. The latter move turned out to be a serious mistake. Up to this point only the Second Infantry Regiment and perhaps the training battalion, both camped at the North Parade Ground just outside the walls of the city, had been involved in the disturbances. The First Infantry Regiment and the four noninfantry battalions, stationed away from the city at Yen-t'ang, had not been involved at all. These units were furious when they learned, on February 11, that their leave too had been canceled. (They may have had an additional reason to be resentful: their monthly pay reportedly had been reduced.) [43] Their officers tried, but failed, to calm their wrath. They mutinied. Seizing arms that had not yet been confiscated, they marched on Canton city, probably with the intention of presenting their grievances to the high officials. When they went by the North Parade Ground, they called on the Second Regiment for support. Surprisingly they found none. The regiment, totally disarmed, refused to join them.

As the mutineers approached the city wall, Huang Shih-lung, Director of the Military Primary School at Whampoa, who happened to be in Canton for the holidays, ventured out to try to conciliate them. He had personally recruited and trained many of the men in the New Army and was popular among them. Promising to plead their case before Governor-General Yüan Shu-hsün, he persuaded them to return to camp. It appeared that his bold move had succeeded in averting a fight. However, as Huang was returning into the tense city, a nervous bannerman atop the city wall defending the city gates mistook him for a rebel; he opened fire, wounding him. The shooting of Huang Shih-lung ended all hope of conciliation. The soldiers regarded it as an act of betrayal on the part of the other officials. At their barracks that night they anxiously awaited the coming of loyalist troops to disarm and punish them.

Through these three days of unpremeditated but escalating violence, the revolutionary leaders, all of whom were gathered in Hong Kong, had looked on in utter helplessness. Because the regular steamer service did not operate on New Year's Day, no one was able to reach Canton until the evening of the eleventh, that is, not until after Huang Shih-lung had been shot. In the absence of their leaders, a few revolutionary soldiers at Yen-t'ang had tried to make the mutineers rise above their grievances about the canceled leave, but they had had no success.

Ni Ying-tien was the first revolutionary leader to arrive back in Canton. He realized at once that the coordinated revolt that had been planned was no longer feasible. There could be no delay. The only possibility of success now was to take charge of the mutiny and redirect it forcibly toward revolutionary ends. The next morning, February 12, Ni appeared among his former comrades, the artillerymen, and urged them to revolt. He assured them (falsely) that reinforcements were on their way from Hong Kong. He also called upon the commander of the First Artillery Division to join the insurrection. When the commander refused, Ni, in full sight of the men, shot him down. The commander of the Second Division was then cowed into submission. Whatever they may have felt personally, the mutineers were now irrevocably committed to Ni's course.

With Ni Ying-tien in the lead, the soldiers marched once more toward Canton, and toward a confrontation with Li Chun's loyalist forces. There was a brief, inconclusive parley between the two sides, each calling on the other to surrender. Then came the clash. The rebels, undermanned and underarmed, were no match for Li's Reserve Forces; they were easily defeated. Ni was among the first to be killed. Most of the rebellious soldiers, shedding their uniforms and weapons, fled in confusion. Ironically, the force which dispersed the New Army rebels was the very same force on which the revolutionaries had pinned their hopes in December 1908. Because the mutiny had broken out prematurely, there were, of course, no responsive uprisings by the bandit chiefs in the Pearl River delta and no supporting attack from Hua-hsien. All the elaborate plans of the Alliance had gone for nought.

In its wake the New Army mutiny left another stormy controversy pitting the populace of Canton against their officials. The dispute centered on the extent to which the mutiny had been a revolutionary revolt and on the appropriate punishment for the mutinous troops. Soon after the uprising Governor-General Yüan Shu-hsün characterized it as a revolutionary attempt from beginning to end. In a memorial to the throne he claimed to have had advance knowledge of the revolutionaries' plans and to have been taking precautionary measures such as disarming the troops when the revolt broke out on New Year's Day. He cited the confessions of the captured rebels, many of whom admitted that the revolutionaries had been preparing the New Army for a revolt.[44]

As punishment, three ringleaders, all confessed revolutionaries, were executed; another thirty-three soldiers were given varying terms of imprisonment. Regarding the others, Yüan contended that there was no alternative but to disband the guilty units, the First Infantry Regiment and the four noninfantry battalions, and to send the mutinous soldiers home, where they were to be subject to three years' probation. Discharged under this arrangement were 1,362 soldiers; 1,127 more "went home of their own accord." Paradoxically, the units that had initiated the fighting on New Year's Day, the Second Regiment and the training battalion, were left intact because they had refused to join the outright mutiny two days later.[45]

Many people in Kwantung, however, disagreed with the governor-general's conclusion that the mutiny had been a premeditated revolt.

The censor Ch'en Ch'ing-kuei, a native of P'an-yü, pointed out for example that Yüan, in his haste to blame only the revolutionaries, had neglected to mention the accidental shooting of Huang Shih-lung and its possible bearing on the uprising. Censor Ch'en himself was inclined to attribute the mutiny more to mismanagement on the part of the officials than to forethought on the part of the revolutionaries.[46] Similarly, the various popular associations in Canton, such as the Merchants' Self-Government Society, the Nine Charitable Halls, the Seventy-two Guilds, the Chamber of Commerce, the Red Cross Society, and the newspapers, almost unanimously criticized the officials and sympathized with the mutinous troops. Even after they had been defeated, it was observed, the New Army troops had behaved faultlessly, whereas Li Chun's Reserve Forces had acted like scavengers, picking up the discarded uniforms and weapons.[47] Unlike Governor-General Yüan, the popular organizations tended to overlook the revolutionaries' involvement in the mutiny; instead they saw it primarily as a spontaneous protest by some of the soldiers against the sudden and unjustified cancellation of their leave. As a matter of fact, such nonpolitical mutinies were not at all unusual among the new armies at this time.[48]

The people in Canton therefore deplored the harsh punishments handed out to the soldiers, and they regretted that the New Army, which had been training for so long and of which they were so proud, should be largely disbanded. On February 22, ten days after the fateful clash, the gentry "in a body" visited Commander Li Chun to urge that the troops be pardoned for their "slight and unintentional offense" and that they not be discharged. They protested that the soldiers were not "revolutionary mutinous troops," as Governor-General Yüan had characterized them. According to the newspapers, Li "appeared greatly in favour of the gentry's suggestions" and promised to speak to the governor-general about it.[49] On March 5 the Merchants' Self-Government Society similarly suggested that the discharged soldiers, all of whom were said to be sons of good families, be allowed to rejoin the army, partly to keep the army intact and partly to give the soldiers an opportunity to rehabilitate their reputation.[50] The reason for these expressions of sympathy for the accused revolutionaries clearly was not any feeling of solidarity with the revolutionary cause but simply disgust for the ineptitude of the officials.[51] Governor-General Yüan evidently refused to reconsider the case.

As the controversy persisted, the throne finally directed the former

Canton governor-general, Chang Jen-chün, to make a special investigation into the causes of the uprising. Chang's findings, published at the end of May, were generally critical of the officials, without however denying the involvement of revolutionaries in the uprising. The revolutionaries, Chang concluded, unquestionably had been planning a revolt. Nevertheless, the initial incident in the four days of troubles had been unpremeditated. It was only through the repeated mistakes and cowardly behavior of both the civil and military officials that the troubles had got out of hand and developed into a riot, which the revolutionaries then exploited.[52] This conclusion, incidentally, was similar to that reached by a Singapore newspaper sympathetic to the revolutionary cause. It acknowledged candidly that while the revolutionaries had been agitating among the New Army, the revolt itself was not really their work.[53] As a result of Chang Jen-chün's report, the commanders of the Mixed Brigade and the First Infantry Regiment were cashiered, and various other officials, including Governor-General Yüan, were reprimanded.[54]

The failure of the New Army mutiny was a serious blow to the work of the Alliance and a bitter disappointment to the local revolutionaries. In Kwangtung the premature revolt and the subsequent partial disbandment of the army shattered the revolutionary network within the New Army that Ni Ying-tien had laboriously built up. In Hong Kong the departure in 1910 of Feng Tzu-yu for another newspaper job in Vancouver, Canada, greatly weakened the Alliance; he had been the mainstay of the movement in the colony since his arrival from Tokyo in 1905. The newspaperman Hsieh Ying-po succeeded Feng as head of the local branch. Meanwhile, enrollment of new members declined sharply from two thousand in 1909 to less than two hundred in 1910, of whom only two are listed by name.[55]

Many of the older members became quite discouraged in 1910. Some in desperation followed the lead of Wang Ching-wei in turning away from mass action to individual action. When Wang's attempt to assassinate the Prince Regent Tsai-feng failed in April 1910, a Chinese Assassination Corps (Chih-na an-sha t'uan) was founded in Hong Kong to carry on his mission. The corps had about ten regular members, most of them also members of the Alliance, including Hsieh Ying-po, Ch'en Chiung-ming, Kao Chien-fu, and Liu Ssu-fu, who had only just been released from prison following his 1907 attempt to assassinate Li Chun.

The corps' first target was the Prince Regent, but unfortunately their assassin was not up to the task. A few months after he disappeared into the mainland, it was learned that he had gone over to the government side.[56]

One of the few positive signs in an otherwise gloomy year for the revolutionaries in Kwangtung was the founding of the *Democrat* (*P'ing-min pao*) in Canton in late October by a group of newspapermen headed by Teng Mu-han and P'an Ta-wei, both members of the Alliance. Described by a foreign correspondent as "somewhat Socialistic" and devoted to "the preaching of the equality of mankind," the *Democrat* joined the *South Viet News* to become the second pro-revolutionary newspaper in the capital.[57]

Sun Yat-sen and other leaders of the Alliance abroad, however, seem not to have shared the doubts and pessimism of the revolutionaries in Kwangtung. After their setback in February they returned to Southeast Asia to raise funds for yet another revolt. Despite the disorganization within the revolutionary movement, they were, remarkably enough, ready to try again nine months later.

The Canton Revolt

In November 1910 Sun Yat-sen summoned Huang Hsing, Chao Sheng, and Hu Han-min to Penang, Malaya, to meet with representatives from various Chinese communities in Southeast Asia to plan the new attempt.[58] They agreed to make the revolt this time with their own personnel rather than depend on external allies, who in the past had proven to be less than completely reliable. The result was the Canton revolt of April 27, 1911. It was the most sensational of the revolutionaries' numerous attempts; it was also the most costly.

The strategy for the revolt resembled Sun Yat-sen's very first attempt in 1895. It called for an uprising within Canton city by a force of revolutionaries smuggled into the city beforehand. The major difference was that in 1895 Sun had hired secret society members to do the fighting for him, whereas he now planned to organize his own fighting force of five to eight hundred volunteers. As the revolutionary leaders fanned out from Penang to raise funds for the new attempt, they signed up people for the fighting force too. The volunteers thus recruited turned out to be a heterogeneous lot. They included natives of Kwangtung, extraprovincials, and overseas Chinese. There were intellectuals, tradesmen, workers, and peasants. Some were veterans of previous revolts; most, however, were not. The one common denominator was that they all "dared to die" for the revolution.[59]

Early in 1911 Huang Hsing and Chao Sheng returned to Hong Kong to set up a "general planning board" to take charge of the revolt. Hu Han-min joined them in March. They decided tentatively to schedule the uprising for April 13. In preparation the revolutionaries smuggled a great quantity of arms and ammunition into Canton from Hong Kong, and they set up close to forty secret cells in different parts of the city where these were stored and where the volunteers could assemble and hide out. The several women members in the Alliance were particularly useful in the smuggling operations. Posing as brides on the way to join their husbands, they hid the weapons and explosives in their dowry and conveyed them from place to place without detection.[60]

The revolutionaries also notified other groups in Kwangtung and beyond of the upcoming effort and sought their cooperation. According to their calculations, the "dare-to-die" volunteers could only initiate the revolt; if they were to seize and hold Canton they would need the prompt support of the nearby military units and bandit gangs. After Canton had been secured, Huang Hsing and Chao Sheng would lead separate armies northward through Hunan and Kiangsi to link up with the revolutionaries in the Yangtze valley. Consequently, Yao Yü-p'ing contacted his former associates in the New Army and the Reserve Forces in and near Canton. Chu Chih-hsin and Hu I-sheng got in touch again with bandit chiefs such as Lu Lan-ch'ing in San-shui and Lu Ling in Shun-te. Hsü Wei-yang went home to Hua-hsien once more to organize a supporting force. And T'an Jen-feng traveled all the way to the Yangtze valley provinces to alert the revolutionary groups there.[61]

Finally, the revolutionaries wanted to prepare Canton public opinion for the revolt. Through Ch'en Chiung-ming they subverted a publication of the Kwangtung provincial assembly and turned it into their mouthpiece. During the last stages of the gambling controversy, when the provincial assemblymen had been split between the pro-gambling and the anti-gambling bloc, each side started a newspaper in order to publicize its own views and to combat the other's.[62] The anti-gambling bloc's newspaper was called *Aye* (*K'o pao*), in reference to the "aye" (*k'o*) votes that they had cast on the question that had precipitated the split. Since Ch'en Chiung-ming had been a leader of the anti-gambling forces in the assembly, it was not difficult for him to turn the operation of the newspaper over to his fellow revolutionaries, among them Chu Chih-hsin and Yeh Hsia-sheng. *Aye* began publication on March 30, the day the ban on licensed gambling went into effect in the province.[63]

Unfortunately, five days before the scheduled outbreak of the revolt there occurred an accident of the sort that had plagued the revolutionary movement since its inception. On April 8 a Chinese worker from Singapore named Wen Sheng-ts'ai, operating alone, assassinated the new Tartar-general in Canton, Fu-ch'i. Captured immediately by the police, Wen admitted that he was a follower of Sun Yat-sen and gave as his motive for killing the Tartar-general a bitter hatred for the Manchus. He was summarily executed a week later. On the way to his execution, he fearlessly called upon the spectators lining the streets to take up where he had left off.[64]

Although Wen Sheng-ts'ai had not been a part of the planning for the Canton revolt and knew nothing about it, his shooting of Fu-ch'i seemed to confirm earlier rumors about a possible uprising in the city. (In February, for example, an English-language newspaper had reported the presence in Canton of a group of revolutionaries led by "a graduate from Japan" named Wong, meaning perhaps Huang Hsing.) [65] The officials immediately increased their vigilance. They instituted house-to-house searches in the city for concealed revolutionaries and weapons. They removed the firing pins from arms belonging to what was left of the Kwangtung New Army, whose loyalty was still in doubt because of the mutiny the year before. They summoned several battalions of the more trusted Reserve Forces from outlying districts to reinforce the defense of the capital.[66]

Fu-ch'i's assassination forced the revolutionaries to reconsider their plans. The general planning board met hurriedly in Hong Kong and decided not to cancel the revolt, but to delay it a couple of weeks. Perhaps in line with this decision, the revolutionaries in Canton who were in charge of publishing *Aye* threw all caution to the wind and seized upon Wen Sheng-ts'ai's act as a propaganda issue. On April 10, two days after the shooting, the paper hailed the assassin Wen as a "hero." On the fifteenth, it praised the uses of political terrorism, citing as an example the assassination of Governor En-ming of Anhwei. En-ming's murder in 1907 had resulted in the issuance of the constitutional decrees; what, *Aye* asked, will Fu-ch'i's bring? In another issue, it accused the Ch'ing rulers of lacking in patriotism and revived the old charges that they were treating their foreign "friends" better than they treated their "household slaves," the Han Chinese. The police finally suppressed the paper on Apirl 22. Undoubtedly they had hesitated until then to take action against *Aye* for fear of offending the provincial assembly, by whom the paper was thought to be published.[67] The Canton officials now had additional reasons to anticipate an uprising.

Huang Hsing arrived in Canton for the revolt on April 23, the day after *Aye* ceased publication. Earlier the general planning board had decided that the uprising would consist of ten separate but simultaneous attacks upon various governmental offices in Canton, with each attack force composed of fifty to one hundred volunteers. It had also designated Chao Sheng and Huang Hsing to direct and coordinate the attacks. Since Chao was well known in Canton from his recent stint as regimental commander in the New Army, Huang had arrived ahead of him. Huang was to choose the new date for the uprising. He chose the twenty-seventh.[68]

Vacillation and confusion marked the course of the revolt from beginning to end. Almost as soon as Huang Hsing arrived in Canton, some of the local revolutionaries advised him that because of the officials' precaution the uprising had little chance of success. They urged him to postpone it indefinitely. So, on April 26, one day before its scheduled outbreak, Huang told the volunteers who had already slipped into Canton to return to Hong Kong for the time being; he also wired Chao Sheng and Hu Han-min in Hong Kong to tell the rest of the volunteers not to come to Canton. However, as soon as he had done this, other revolutionaries pressed him to mount the attack regardless of the consequences. They contended that a postponement now was tantamount to cancellation and that this would gravely disappoint the overseas Chinese who had invested so generously in the revolt and would undermine their confidence in the revolutionary movement. As Huang wavered, Yao Yü-p'ing, who was in touch with the government forces, arrived to announce that some units of the Reserve Forces that the officials had brought into Canton as reinforcements were sympathetic to the revolutionary cause. They would support an uprising, Yao said. As a result, Huang Hsing swung back to his original plan to have the revolt on the twenty-seventh, which was the next day. He wired Chao Sheng again and asked that he send the volunteers back to Canton.

Huang's request stunned Chao and Hu Han-min. With the Canton–Kowloon railway several months from completion, the quickest way to get to Canton from Hong Kong was still by ferry, which operated only twice a day. They decided to put only half the volunteer force aboard that night's ferry and to send the other half aboard the next day's. Since the second group would not arrive until nightfall of the twenty-seventh, Chao and Hu asked Huang for a one-day delay. They sent T'an Jen-feng to Canton with the first group of volunteers to explain the matter to him.

T'an arrived in Canton on the morning of April 27 in time to give Huang Hsing the message. Huang, however, was now against any delay. The plans were set; he would not wait for the remainder of the volunteer force. Unfortunately, the last minute changes in plans had thoroughly confused the various attack forces, scattered in different parts of the city and not in close touch with Huang. For example, Ch'en Chiung-ming and Hu I-sheng, who were each to lead one of the ten assault columns, both thought that the revolt had been postponed. Yet, amidst all this confusion, Hsü Wei-yang and Mo Chi-p'eng somehow managed to bring a group of peasants and workers from Hua-hsien to Canton in time for the start of the revolt.

The revolt began in the late afternoon with an attack on Governor-General Chang Ming-ch'i's official compound in the middle of the city. One hundred and sixty volunteers, led personally by Huang Hsing, captured it easily from the ineffectual guards. They failed, however, to find the governor-general, who had escaped to another part of the compound. So they set the building ablaze, and then divided into several smaller groups. One group attacked the Little North Gate, through which they hoped to establish contact with the New Army stationed at the North Parade Ground outside the city. Another group attacked the arsenal at Kuan-yin-shan at the northern edge of the city. A third group attacked the offices of Commander Li Chun. Government troops beat off all three of these groups with ease. A fourth group, led by Huang, headed for the Great South Gate. There it clashed with a unit of the Reserve Forces and was scattered. This last action may have ruined whatever chance of success the revolt had, for it is claimed that the commander of this Reserve Force unit, who was killed in the encounter, was one of the revolutionary sympathizers of whom Yao Yü-p'ing had spoken. He and his troops were supposedly on their way to take part in the attack on Li Chun's offices, but in order to avoid a premature battle with loyalist government troops, they had postponed putting on their identifying white armband. Huang Hsing and his men were, of course, unaware of this when they attacked them.

When Chao Sheng and Hu Han-min arrived in Canton at nightfall with the second boatload of volunteers, the city had been sealed up and the revolt suppressed. Unable to help, they returned to Hong Kong aboard the same boat. Some of the defeated rebels trapped inside the city, including Huang Hsing, managed to get out with the assistance of sympathetic soldiers, policemen, and bystanders. Others were captured by the authorities and executed. Altogether eighty-six rebels, not the fabled seventy-two, died as a result of the revolt.

Because of the last-minute confusion of plans and the rapidity with which the revolt was put down, few of the supporting uprisings outside the city took place and none was of any help to the rebels in the city. Revolutionaries in the New Army, who might have rearmed themselves, especially if the arsenal at Kuan-yin-shan had been taken, were caught completely off guard by the revolt. No one had informed them of the final plans. Only one unit of the Reserve Forces made a move to join the revolt, and it was neutralized by Huang Hsing's mistake. With one exception, none of the bandit bands rose up either. The exception was Lu Ling in Shun-te district. He and his men rose on April 28, the day after the Canton revolt, and captured the market town of Le-ts'ung. They drove off the local guards and seized the weapons and ammunition stored in the office of the militia bureau. Afterwards, they proceeded toward Canton by way of Fo-shan. Three days later, near Fo-shan, they were met by a detachment of Reserve Forces under the command of Wu Tsung-yü. (Wu was back in Canton after putting down the anti-gentry disturbances at Lien-chou.) No match for Wu Tsung-yü's soldiers, Lu Ling and his men were quickly scattered.[69]

The Canton revolt, a hopeless cause once the officials were alert to it, was a devastating defeat for the Kwangtung revolutionaries. It was not only that they had lost close to a hundred lives or that they had suffered another disappointment. More important, they had thrown practically all their resources, including their underground in Canton, into the revolt, and they had lost everything. Ch'en Chiung-ming, Chu Chih-hsin, Teng K'eng, Tsou Lu—all had been exposed and forced to flee. The Alliance in south China had been so weakened that by its own admission it was incapable of making another revolt for five years.[70]

However, even as the Canton revolt was going down to costly defeat, the political situation in China had begun to change. The reappearance of Yeh Hsia-sheng within the revolutionary ranks after five years of apparently unrevolutionary conduct and the willingness of Ch'en Chiung-ming and Chu Chih-hsin to sacrifice their substantial careers under the Ch'ing and blow their cover after years of underground revolutionary work may have signaled the change. They had gambled that the demise of the Ch'ing was imminent, and lost. But they were only slightly premature. If the revolt had been postponed even a month, its chances of success would have been greatly increased. For a revolutionary situation had been developing very rapidly in China since the end of 1910.

9

The Revolution in 1911

Manchu rule in China came abruptly to an end in a revolution of rising expectations. At the end of 1910 the Ch'ing dynasty was still a viable regime; six months later, it was doomed; eight months after that, it had been overthrown. The revolutionaries did not cause this quick turnabout in the Manchus' fortunes. They were more disorganized in 1911 than at any time since the founding of the Alliance six years earlier. Although there was an upsurge of revolutionary activities throughout China as the year progressed, it was more the product than the cause of the changed situation. Instead, the Manchu rulers themselves were to blame for the revolution. Until the end of 1910 they had managed reasonably well to defuse the threat of revolution by means of timely reforms and concessions to organized public opinion. But thereafter they failed to keep pace with the political expectations that their reforms had created. In disappointment and frustration, the reformers once more withdrew their active support from the dynasty. This produced a new revolutionary situation, a far more serious one than in 1900. Under such circumstances, it did not take a highly organized revolutionary movement to topple the dynasty.

On the Eve of the Revolution

The revolutionary situation that doomed the dynasty developed rapidly between November 1910 and May 1911. Various actions by the court during these six critical months gravely disappointed many reformers and generated widespread opposition to the government in Kwangtung and other provinces. Afterwards, although the revolutionary movement itself was in a shambles, individual revolutionaries were emboldened by the change in the climate of opinion to step up their attacks. Notwithstanding official countermeasures, public confidence in the regime sagged even further. By the time the revolution broke out in October, it hardly came as a surprise.

The revolution may well have begun on November 4, 1910, with the court's response to the third petition for the immediate summoning of a parliament. It had agreed then to advance the date for the opening of parliament from 1916 to 1913, but no earlier, and it had ordered the petitioners to disband their organization and cease their activities. While perhaps most constitutionalists were satisfied with the court's partial acceptance of their demands, others were distressed that it had not responded more fully. Some of the petitioners reportedly were so unhappy with what they termed "the hopeless political condition of the government" that they secretly decided then and there to return to their respective provinces to organize a revolution.[1]

The court's decision in late December on the far less substantial but symbolically significant question of the queue also disappointed the reformers. With the spread of the post-Boxer reforms, many Chinese, particularly the reformist urban elite, had come to dislike this style of wearing the hair that the Manchu rulers had imposed upon their Chinese subjects. Opponents of the pigtail objected not only because it was an inappropriate reminder of the dynasty's alien origins (which was of course how the revolutionaries viewed it exclusively) but also because it was a symbol of China's backwardness and outlandishness in the modern world.[2]

In the last half of 1910, there was a concerted move, led within the court by Tsai-t'ao, the reform-minded brother of the Prince Regent, and outside it by the Western-educated Wu T'ing-fang, to persuade the rulers to sanction a change in hair style.[3] At this time, large numbers of Chinese, especially students, began cutting off their queue; some did so in anticipation of a favorable ruling from the court, others to demonstrate popular support for the reform. In Kwangtung, for example, queue-cutting associations were organized in numerous communities across the province. The movement in the province reached its peak with a mass demonstration in Hong Kong on December 4, when six old and conservatively dressed gentlemen led several hundred people in shedding their plaits.[4] Nevertheless, the court in late December ruled against changing the custom. It contended that, contrary to the assurances of its supporters, abandonment of the queue would encourage people to change also to foreign-style clothes imported from abroad, which could ruin China's own textile industry.[5] Despite the appeal to economic nationalism, the decision was taken by some reformers as another indication of the court's unresponsiveness to organized public opinion.

In the wake of such actions by the court, a revolutionary situation began to emerge. It was perhaps apparent by March 1911, when followers of Liang Ch'i-ch'ao informed him of their intentions "to return to the old idea." The "old idea" was revolution, which they had abandoned as unnecessary after the inauguration of the post-Boxer reforms; they were returning to it because of the court's recalcitrant stands. Liang himself published an article in March renouncing his former views regarding the threat of partition by the imperialists in the event of a revolution in China. He now thought that it was possible for China to undergo a revolution without necessarily inviting foreign intervention. Moreover, Liang thereafter proceeded to try to initiate a coup d'etat which would have replaced the Prince Regent Tsai-feng with his more enlightened brother Tsai-t'ao. Liang however did not go so far as to advocate the overthrow of the Ch'ing and the establishment of a republic.[6] Clearly, when the advocates of gradualism and reformism began to repudiate their cause, the dynastic rulers were in serious trouble.

Ignoring the danger signals, the Manchu court dug its own grave with three decisions taken within two weeks of one another in May. On May 8, it named a cabinet that was dominated by Manchus. On the tenth it ordered the nationalization of all private trunk railway lines. Finally, on the twentieth it concluded the four-power Hu-kuang railway loan agreement. These actions deeply shocked both the constitutionalists and the nationalists and produced a revolutionary situation from which there was to be no reprieve.

The constitutionalists were, first of all, upset by the court's desregard of their well-known desire for a greater sharing of power between the Manchu rulers and their Han Chinese subjects. They had wanted the immediate summoning of a parliament and the creation of a cabinet responsible to the parliament. When they failed to get all this in November 1910, most had been willing to accept the good faith of the court when it promised to name a cabinet soon. One can therefore imagine their dismay when the composition of the new cabinet was disclosed: eight Manchus, including five imperial princes, one Mongol, and only four Han Chinese! What hope was there left for constitutional reform with such a cabinet? [7]

Moreover, those constitutionalists who were active in the local self-government movement and favored greater devolution of authority from the central government to the local communities were disappointed with the nationalization of the railways also. From the court's point of view, the arguments in favor of nationalization were compelling. In south China, merchant management and provincial administration of the railways had, without question, failed. In Szechwan, Hupeh, and Hunan, the private railway companies had been unable, either through voluntary subscription or compulsory taxation, to raise more than a fraction of the required capital. Furthermore, partly because of inadequate capitalization but also because of mismanagement, corruption, and discord among the directors, these companies had made practically no progress in the construction of railroads. In 1911, not a single mile of the two projected trunk lines was open in either Szechwan or Hunan, and only 9 miles were open to traffic in Hupeh. Even in Kwangtung, the most successful operation, only 66 miles had been laid and the construction costs were twice what had been estimated. [8]

The local autonomists, however, were not reconciled by such arguments to accept either this or the other centralizing measures of the time, such as currency reform. They resisted any move by the central government that curbed the trend toward greater local control, whether in political or economic matters. Thus, when Governor-General Chang Ming-ch'i called a meeting of the Kwangtung Railway Company shareholders on June 6 to allow them to state their preference among three suggested plans for redeeming their shares, the shareholders, led by Huang Ching-t'ang, a former vice-president of the company, rejected all three plans and voted instead for continued merchant control of railway affairs in the province. [9]

The central government's plan for compensating the private railway shareholders, announced on June 17, intensified the localists' opposition to railway nationalization. The criticisms were most bitter in Szechwan, where the shareholders were to be compensated entirely in government bonds. Beginning with the formation of the Railway Protection Society (Pao-lu hui) on June 21, the opposition there escalated steadily into a province-wide rebellion against the central government by early September.[10] In Kwangtung, where the government's compensation scheme was much more generous to the shareholders (60 percent in cash and only 40 percent in bonds), the opposition was considerably less violent. In mid-August a branch of the Railway Protection Society was organized in Hong Kong, with the merchant (and revolutionary sympathizer) Li Yü-t'ang as head. (It was set up in the British colony because the officials in Canton were prohibiting unauthorized public discussions of the railroad question.) At a mass meeting in Hong Kong on September 3, attended by representatives from the Kwangtung provincial assembly, the Canton Chamber of Commerce, the Nine Charitable Halls, the Seventy-two Guilds, the Association for the Study of Self-Government, and the Hong Kong and Canton newspaper associations, the society reiterated its opposition to railway nationalization and its preference for continued merchant control. But unlike Szechwan, there was no revolt.[11]

Finally, the anti-imperialist nationalists were angered by the Hukuang loan from the four-power consortium of banks representing Great Britain, France, Germany, and the United States. However necessary the loan may have been for financing the Hunan and Hupeh sections of the two trunk lines, most people outside the central government objected to it simply because it was a *foreign* loan. Even those who favored nationalization of the railways opposed the loan. As a Szechwanese pamphleteer put it, "The people of Szechwan will tolerate redeeming the railway for their own nation, but to redeem it on behalf of other nations is something they will never tolerate." [12] The government was charged with "gratuitously selling the interests of the country" out to the foreign powers. At its meeting in Hong Kong on September 3, the Kwangtung branch of the Railway Protection Society expressed as much opposition to the foreign loan as to nationalization.[13] Noting these developments, the Canton governor-general advised the central government not to use the loan to redeem the railway shares in Kwangtung. "Otherwise, traitorous people will more easily use 'Oppose the loan; protect the railways' as a pretext to oppose nationalization itself." [14]

The conclusion of the Hu-kuang loan with the four-power consortium also revived fearful rumors of impending dismemberment. These rumors evidently were based upon the meetings of the consortium members to draw up the loan agreement before it was presented to the Ch'ing government, for in late April and early May the Canton newspapers were full of reports "that representatives of the Powers had met at Paris and discussed the partition of China." On at least two occasions in late April, the students in Canton gathered to talk about these reports and to consider forming their own militia "to save China from ruin at this critical moment." [15]

The revolutionary situation as it thus developed in 1911, especially after May, was far more critical than the earlier one in 1900 in at least three ways. First of all, as a consequence of the phenomenal growth of the politicized elite in the intervening decade, the estrangement from the government in 1911 involved many more people, who furthermore were far better organized than in 1900. Second, in 1911 there was an established and recognized alternative to the regime that had been lacking in 1900. The court's various actions confirmed what the Revolutionary Alliance had always maintained: the Manchu rulers would never give up any measure of real power to their Han Chinese subjects; they would sooner sell China out to the imperialists than see the Han Chinese take over from them. Finally, and probably most important, the dynastic leaders in 1911 were far less flexible than in 1900. Unlike Tz'u-hsi during the earlier crisis, they refused to make the necessary concessions to their estranged subjects until after the revolution had already broken out. By then, of course, it was too late.

As the court blundered its way toward a revolution, the revolutionary movement itself was in paradoxical shape. On the one hand, the Alliance, after the Canton revolt in April, was more disorganized than ever before. The Yangtze faction of the Alliance, tiring of Sun Yat-sen's preoccupation with his native Kwangtung, in effect defied his leadership in order to work on a revolt of its own in central China.[16] In Kwangtung the once promising underground in Canton had been uprooted, while the movement in Hong Kong drifted aimlessly for lack of leadership. Hu Han-min, the head of the dormant South China Bureau, was back in Southeast Asia raising money. Hsieh Ying-po, who had only recently succeeded Feng Tzu-yu as head of the Hong Kong branch, left for a teaching position in Honolulu in the summer. The *China Daily News* ran through three editors in about as many months.[17] In short, neither nationally nor locally in Kwangtung was the Alliance offering much direction to the revolutionary movement.

On the other hand, despite the lack of leadership, the revolutionaries were extraordinarily active. Not only were reformers newly converting to the revolutionary cause, but also former revolutionaries who had ceased to be active in the movement were making their reappearance. Acting on their own and with little or no coordination among themselves, individuals and small groups began with increasing boldness to engage in openly revolutionary activities. This was the case, at least, in Kwangtung.

The revolutionary press began to cast aside its inhibitions. In Swatow the *China New Journal,* hitherto content with cautious criticism of the officials, was suppressed on June 26 for being too outspoken in its comments on recent events, including the assassination of Tartar-General Fu-ch'i, the Canton revolt, and the Szechwan railway troubles. The paper, however, was silenced for only a month. Through the mediation of an American-Chinese businessman, L. K. Goe (Liang Chin-ao, also known as Liang Kuan-san), who operated the local Singer sewing machine agency, it was registered with the American consulate in Swatow under a slightly different name, the *New China Journal* (*Hsin Chung-hua pao*), but with essentially the same staff. Now beyond the reach of the Chinese officials, the paper resumed publication on July 26.[18]

In Canton three new revolutionary papers made their appearance. One was the *Celestials* (*T'ien-min pao*), which was edited by Lu O-sheng and others. It began publication on June 21. Two days later the officials shut it down for "irritating the Emperor and defaming the dynastic government." Another was the *Central Plain News* (*Chung-yüan pao*), which appeared in late September and, like the *Celestials,* was suppressed after two days of publication; it was charged with "throwing the government in confusion and advocating revolution." The third paper founded in Canton at this time, the *Human Rights News* (*Jen-ch'üan pao*) edited by the Alliance member Ch'en Keng-fu, was more durable than the other two. Along with the previously founded *South Viet News* and *Democrat,* it was one of three pro-revolutionary papers being published at the time of the revolution.[19] Similarly, when the revolution began, three of the nine Chinese-language newspapers in Hong Kong actively favored the republicans, one of them, of course, being the *China Daily News.* Of the remainder, five were neutral and only one, the *Commercial News,* organ of K'ang Yu-wei and Liang Ch'i-ch'ao, opposed the republican revolution. Significantly, the pro-Ch'ing *Commercial News* was the one paper excluded from membership in the Hong Kong Newspaper Association.[20]

Not only were the newspapers more daring than ever before in opposing the dynasty, so were individual revolutionaries. In Macao, where the revolutionary movement had been dormant for most of the post-Boxer decade, a group of Alliance members established a reading room and stocked it with revolutionary materials along with current books and periodicals. In the French enclave of Kwangchowwan, "anarchists" were reported to be "delivering anti-Manchu lectures and inducing the people to join their party." In many places, revolutionaries sold or passed out pamphlets (sometimes disguised as Christian tracts) and gave street-corner talks, their activities coming to light only if they were caught. Thus, four lecturers were arrested at Fo-shan in late May for inciting the people to revolt against the government as they talked of "the approaching partition of China." Four others were seized at Shih-wan, near Canton, in early August for speaking at temples and marketplaces on "race distinction and dynastic revolutions and selling books on revolutionary topics." Yet another was detained at Tan-shui, in Kuei-shan district, for discussing "the overthrow of the present dynasty and revolutionary matters." However, countless other revolutionary speakers undoubtedly escaped official notice.[21]

The most spectacular revolutionary action during these months was the nearly successful assassination of Commander Li Chun in August. Among the revolutionaries, Li was easily the most hated official in Kwangtung. His forces had been involved in the suppression of every one of their uprisings since 1907, including the recent attempt in Canton. After the April revolt, two separate groups plotted his death. One group designated Ch'en Ching-yüeh as the assassin; the other, the Chinese Assassination Corps formed in 1910, designated Lin Kuan-tz'u. The two assassins joined forces when they became aware of their common cause while tracking their quarry. On August 13, as Li Chun was making his way to his office, Lin Kuan-tz'u rushed up and tossed a home-made bomb at him. The bomb killed some of his guards, but only wounded Li. Lin was shot to death on the spot. Ch'en Ching-yüeh was arrested as he waited at a second location with another bomb; he was later executed. The assassination attempt, though a failure, put Li Chun out of action for a couple of months while he convalesced from his wounds.[22]

In the meantime, while the revolutionaries were individually stepping up their pace of activity, the Canton authorities, fearing a repetition of the April revolt, undertook various countermeasures. In May Governor-General Chang Ming-ch'i transferred nine battalions of troops from Kwangsi to Canton and put their commander Lung Chi-kuang in overall charge of the defense of the capital in place of Li Chun.[23] (Even before the April revolt, Li Chun's dismissal as commander of the Reserve Forces in central Kwangtung had been rumored. It was said that the new governor-general objected to his corruption and his ostentatious style of living. Li remained, however, as commander-in-chief of the naval forces. Prior to his transfer to Canton, Lung Chi-kuang was the provincial commander-in-chief in Kwangsi, where Chang Ming-ch'i had recently been governor.) [24]

A few months later, near the time of the attempted assassination of Li Chun in mid-August, Governor-General Chang broke up the politically suspect New Army and scattered it far from Canton. (As a matter of fact, the commander of the Kwangtung brigade at this time, Chiang Tsun-kuei, was an original Tokyo member of the Alliance; however, he had not been active in the revolutionary movement for some time.) [25] Three infantry battalions under the command of Huang Shih-lung, who had since recovered from his accidental shooting during the New Army mutiny, were sent to Kao-chou, to help quell an anti-tax rebellion in West Kwangtung. Another infantry battalion and two newly recruited artillery battalions were sent to Ch'ien-shan, at the head of Macao peninsula, ostensibly as a show of force during a minor flare-up of the ongoing border dispute with the Portuguese. Only a few battalions of the New Army were retained at Canton. [26]

Apart from building up the military defenses of Canton, the authorities were actively hunting down the revolutionaries. In the wake of the April revolt, they instituted a strict house-to-house search in Canton. They also searched Chinese passengers and cargo arriving by ferry from Hong Kong. In addition, throughout these months, as we have seen, the police and the newly created Detective Bureau (Chen-chi chü) were on the lookout for suspected revolutionary speakers and agitators.

Some of these official precautions, especially the police measures, aroused considerable popular opposition. The house-to-house searches in Canton, carried out by the police and the Reserve Forces, were so arbitrary and disorderly that they created a public scandal similar to the aftermath of the New Army mutiny the year before. The bankers, for example, finally "decided that they will not allow [their] premises to be entered, unless they first search those who are about to enter, the assumption being that these men will themselves bring in arms and then will 'discover' them." [27] The arrest of suspected revolutionaries created much resentment across the province too, because in many instances anyone who had discarded the queue and wore Western-style clothes was automatically suspect. Such arrests were reported so frequently in the newspapers that a foreign observer in late August concluded that "there is positively a reign of terror in Canton." On at least a couple of occasions, once in June at Kung-i, the American-style model town in Hsin-ning, and once in September at Tan-shui, in Kuei-shan, protesting mobs attacked the local authorities as they attempted to arrest queueless youths as revolutionaries.[28]

These measures were thus counterproductive. Instead of curbing the revolutionary threat, they antagonized many people and caused them to regard sympathetically those who the officials said were revolutionaries. The state of public opinion in Kwangtung in the summer of 1911 was such that, as the censor Wen Su put it, rebels are glorified as belonging to the "people's party" (*min-tang*) and those who are executed are honored as "men of determination."[29] Moreover, the officials' efforts did not succeed in reassuring the populace. Throughout these months Canton was in a state of perpetual unrest because of recurring rumors that the revolutionaries were plotting a second uprising. In mid-May, as a result of one such scare, so many people flocked to Hong Kong that the cost of overnight lodging in the British colony reportedly quadrupled.[30] At the beginning of August, when the discovery of a cache of nitroglycerin aboard one of the Hong Kong–Canton ferries produced another scare, "almost all families of the officials and of the wealthy class were seen leaving Canton." On August 2, the day of the rumored uprising, the city appeared to be deserted. An estimated 40,000 had fled to Hong Kong and another 10,000 to Macao.[31] Although there was no trouble on the second, the rumors continued to fly. Then, on the thirteenth came the attempted assassination of Li Chun. Public confidence plummeted. According to one "careful estimate," altogether 150,000 had left the city by then: "Trade is almost paralyzed."[32]

The anarchic situation in the Kwangtung countryside during these months was not conducive to public confidence either. In addition to the usual banditry, piracy, and secret society activity, there were six more instances of anti-gentry tax resistance at widely separated places across the province between June and September. Several were directed at the new wine tax, collected since the beginning of the year to finance the prohibition on licensed gambling; one was opposed to the taking of the census.[33] According to Governor-General Chang Ming-ch'i himself in mid-August, the only prefectures which were more or less peaceful were

Hui-chou in the east and Lien-chou and Ch'in-chou in the west. "In the rest of the province, there is not a place where bandits do not freely roam." [34]

To cope with these rural disorders, particularly in the region around Canton, the governor-general in early May set up a General Office for Rural Pacification and Reconstruction (Ch'ing-hsiang shan-hou tsung kung-so) for Kuang-chou prefecture. He appointed the prominent upper gentry member Chiang K'ung-yin as its head with the authority to command the services of all the military and naval forces within the prefecture in order to suppress the bandits. Each district within the prefecture was directed to form a similar office. [35] However, as with the measures to cope with the revolutionaries, these plans to pacify the countryside generated considerable opposition. The gentry in particular objected to the governor-general's reliance upon the Reserve Forces. These forces were widely hated because they were usually ineffectual and, like the police in Canton, disorderly. During the Canton revolt, for example, detachment commander Wu Tsung-yü's troops reportedly stripped the governor-general's yamen bare of its furnishings after it had been vacated by the revolutionaries. Later on, when they were sent to oppose Lu Ling's bandit gang which had risen at Le-ts'ung, they again looted freely and furthermore opened fire recklessly upon innocent civilians. As the Kwangtung gentry leaders protested, in a number of memorials to the throne during the summer, the peasants and gentry both dreaded the soldiers more than they did the bandits. [36]

Clearly, by the end of the summer of 1911 most groups in Kwangtung, gentry, merchants, students, and peasants, had become disenchanted with their government. The recurrent panics in Canton, the growing number of peasant anti-tax riots, the frequent criticism of the officials in the press and in memorials to the throne, the sometimes blatant sympathy for accused revolutionaries all indicated that public confidence in the government had practically vanished. At the end of September a couple of students in Kuei-shan district, arrested for not paying their debts, explained, "The revolution is already here. Why bother to pay?" [37]

The Revolution in Canton

On October 10, 1911, sixteen years after Sun Yat-sen's first attempt, the republican revolution finally broke out. It took the form that Ou Chü-chia had once recommended, as province after province seceded from the Ch'ing empire in order to regroup later in February 1912 under new leadership. But contrary to what both Sun and Ou had wanted, Kwangtung was not the first but the eleventh province to join the revolutionary side. The revolution began instead at Wuchang under the direction of the schismatic Yangtze faction of the Alliance. Canton, on the other hand, did not follow suit until a month later, on November 9. In Canton, as probably in the other provincial capitals, the dynasty's fate was sealed by the hopeless estrangement of the nonrevolutionary elite from the regime.

The revolutionaries in Kwangtung were remarkably slow to respond to the Wuchang revolt. For the first two weeks they hardly stirred. There are several reasons for this. In the first place, they had not been forewarned about the revolt, which in any case broke out prematurely. Second, even if they had known about it, they had no reason to think that it would be any more successful than their own revolts had been. It was not until October 18 or 19 that the Hupeh revolutionaries consolidated their initial victories by driving the government forces seven miles outside Hankow; and it was not until the twenty-second that revolutionaries first took power in another province (Hunan).[38] Third, since the Canton revolt in April, the Kwangtung revolutionaries had been disorganized and leaderless. Hu Han-min, the head of the South China Bureau of the Alliance, was in Saigon at the time of the Wuchang uprising; he did not sail for Hong Kong until the twenty-ninth. Finally, as a result of Governor-General Chang Ming-ch'i's recent military buildup, Canton was too well defended for the scattered revolutionaries within and without the city to have taken action by themselves.

Popular opinion in Kwangtung, however, favored the revolutionaries from the start. There was hardly any public support for the Manchu regime. The celebration of Confucius' "birthday" on October 18 in Hong Kong and Macao was notable for the scarcity of yellow imperial dragon flags on display. The day before, an angry crowd mobbed the offices of the *Commercial News,* the lone pro-Ch'ing newspaper in Hong Kong.[39] In Canton a bank run that started on October 14 revealed an ominous lack of public confidence in the continued existence of the government, as people anxiously cashed in their paper banknotes for silver coins. The city's three government banks fortunately had large reserves of coins on hand and were able to satisfy the demand and to exchange the notes for coins at par.[40]

Since the revolutionaries were not immediately active in Kwangtung, the initiative during the first two weeks of the revolution lay entirely with the officials, particularly the young, reform-minded governor-general, Chang Ming-ch'i. A provincial graduate from Shantung, Chang was then only in his mid-thirties, the youngest provincial ruler in all of China at this time. He had begun his brief but brilliant official career as an adviser and secretary to Ts'en Ch'un-hsüan, the former Canton governor-general. He had come with Ts'en to Kwangtung–Kwangsi, where he held a variety of administrative posts during most of the post-Boxer decade. From 1907 until 1910, he was governor of Kwangsi, which he tried to make into a model for reform and development. He succeeded Yüan Shu-hsün as governor-general in Canton at the beginning of 1911.[41]

Chang Ming-ch'i's strategy for dealing with the revolutionary crisis, as pieced together from his subsequent actions, was to steer a middle course between the revolutionaries and the court. On the one hand, he took a neutral position on the fighting in Hupeh and denied material assistance to the Ch'ing forces there. This of course greatly benefited the revolutionaries. On the other hand, he refused to join the revolutionaries. Instead, he initiated certain political reforms that he hoped would appeal to the reformers and coopt the revolutionaries. In essence, his aim was provincial autonomy within a new federal Ch'ing empire with himself continuing as governor. This plan was strikingly similar to what Liang Ch'i-ch'ao was privately advocating to his friends at this time. He too was anxious to find some middle ground between the court and the revolutionaries. Since Liang was evidently in touch with Chang Ming-ch'i, the similarities between the two plans were probably not coincidental.[42]

Chang Ming-ch'i's allies in this delicate maneuver were Chiang K'ung-yin and Ch'en Ching-hua. One was his contact with the reformist gentry in Kwangtung; the other, his contact with the revolutionaries in Hong Kong. Chiang K'ung-yin, the metropolitan graduate from Nanhai, was undoubtedly the most active member of the gentry in Kwangtung during the post-Boxer decade. He had taken part in practically every aspect of the merchants' nationalist movement as well as the gentry's self-government movement. He had been a leader, though a controversial one, in the anti-American boycott. A member of both the Merchants' Self-Government Society and the Macao Boundary Delimitation Society, he had spoken out successively on the West River patrol, the *Tatsu Maru* case, the *Fatshan* incident, and the Macao question. He had helped organize the provincial assembly and, though he declined the election, he had been elected to the assembly. He had also been a leader of the campaign to abolish licensed gambling. Finally, when Governor-General Chang Ming-ch'i inaugurated the rural pacification and reconstruction program in the Canton area in May 1911, he had chosen Chiang K'ung-yin to head it up.

It may have been Chiang who introduced Ch'en Ching-hua to the governor-general. A provincial graduate from Hsiang-shan, Ch'en Ching-hua was serving as a magistrate in Kwangsi when early in the decade Governor-General Ts'en Ch'un-hsüan indicted him for the ruthless way he administered his district. To escape punishment, Ch'en had fled to Bangkok, Thailand, where he founded a Chinese-language newspaper. More important, he had joined the Revolutionary Alliance there and was one of its leaders. In 1909 he had returned to Hong Kong and become a comprador for Olof Wijk & Co. How Ch'en Ching-hua knew Chiang K'ung-yin is not clear, but it was through the latter's intercession that Ch'en managed to have his fellow townsman and revolutionary Liu Ssu-fu released from prison in 1909. It may also have been on Chiang's recommendation that Governor-General Chang Ming-ch'i memorialized the throne early in October 1911 requesting a pardon for Ch'en's previous misconduct in Kwangsi. Thus, even before the outbreak of the revolution, a web of personal relationships already bound together the three men. [43]

Governor-General Chang Ming-ch'i began to put his plan into effect during the second week of the Wuchang revolt, when it was apparent that the revolutionaries would not be readily defeated. He sent Chiang K'ung-yin to Hong Kong to ask the editors of the Chinese-language newspapers there to tone down their coverage of the revolt and "wait patiently for the result of the rebellion." In the course of the talks, Chiang later reported, "The question came up of Kwangtung declaring its independence. I told them that this was not so satisfactory as using the government to improve upon independence." By this he apparently meant that government-initiated reforms were preferable to the drastic recourse to secession, particularly when the revolutionaries were still struggling to hold Wuchang. Chiang agreed "that if two or three of the provincial capitals should capitulate to the rebels, Kwangtung might declare itself an independent republic." Until then, however, the editors should wait and see and give reform a chance. The editors, by his account, were unimpressed: "Many naturally agreed, but not surprisingly there were also those who thought it a devious stratagem." [44]

On October 19, a day or two later, Ch'en Ching-hua, accompanied by Chiang K'ung-yin, visited Governor-General Chang at his office in Canton. According to the brief, cryptic news report, the three men talked about "political reforms." [45] Since the governor-general was considering reforms that might coopt the revolutionaries, he perhaps asked Ch'en for his estimate of the plan's feasibility. Ch'en's response is unknown, but as he evidently went along with the plan later on, he may well have encouraged the governor-general to try it out. In view of the disorganization among the Hong Kong revolutionaries, Ch'en was probably acting on his own.

With Chiang K'ung-yin's help, Governor-General Chang next sought out the views of the gentry leaders, who closely identified themselves with his plan; whether deliberately or through neglect, he apparently did not consult the merchants. Thus, he went before the provincial assembly, which reconvened on October 22 for its third annual session, to ask it for "suggestions as to the best ways of reorganizing affairs in the province." In addition, he encouraged the gentry to call a public meeting in Canton for the afternoon of the twenty-fifth to discuss ways "to maintain public order." On his own initiative the governor-general abolished the wine and butcher taxes on the twenty-fourth; both taxes were highly unpopular and had been the cause of several anti-tax riots in the province. [46]

On the morning of October 25, as the gentry prepared to meet and discuss the crisis, the revolution was brought home to Canton. The new Tartar-general, Feng-shan, named to succeed the murdered Fu-ch'i, was himself assassinated within minutes after his arrival in the city. This was the work of a handful of revolutionaries grouped around Huang Hsing and the Chinese Assassination Corps; it was carried out by two brothers, Li Ying-sheng and Li P'ei-chi, both of whom escaped. The assassination, however, was an isolated action unrelated to any general insurrection. Planned before the Wuchang uprising, it had been delayed in execution only by Feng-shan's own fearful procrastination in getting to Canton. [47]

The assassination of Feng-shan gave the gentry's meeting on the afternoon of the twenty-fifth an added sense of urgency. Moreover, by then the provincial capitals of Changsha and Sian as well as the city of Kiukiang had declared for the revolutionaries. The gentry met at the Wen-lan Academy with the retired officials Teng Hua-hsi and Liang Ting-fen as co-chairmen and the provincial assemblyman Mo Jen-heng as moderator. Governor-General Chang was not present, but Chiang K'ung-yin was there, acting perhaps as his spokesman.[48]

After brief opening remarks by Teng Hua-hsi, Liang Ting-fen, recently the provincial judge in Hupeh, spoke of the need for greater self-government for the province.[49] "Kwangtung belongs to the people of Kwangtung. The officials govern it on our behalf. That's all. If the officials are worthy, we commend them. If they are unworthy, we dismiss them. Where their authority does not reach, we assist them. The principle espoused by the revolutionary party is reformation of the political system. If our system is all right, the revolutionaries ought not come and bother us. Or if they should come, we will be in a position to deal with them. What we are discussing today is the realization of self-government. Let us not mince words. Everyone knows that the general situation is critical, but it can be remedied. Because of the disorders in our neighboring provinces, Kwangtung has now the impetus to reform its political system."

Chiang K'ung-yin issued a similar plea. "In the past few days several provinces have responded to the outbreak in Hupeh. A cataclysmic force has been released. No matter how loyal and devoted we are, with regard to the general situation and popular attitudes, we must speak without inhibitions even though it may be unbearable. Today there are only two solutions to the crisis. One is quickly to set in motion the policy of confederation and allow the twenty-two provinces each to govern itself. We should do this in order to curb the revolutionary agitation . . . . The other solution is for the central government to give the provincial rulers authority to act as the circumstances require and reform the political system. We should do this in order to stop our citizens from opting for independence." The two solutions boiled down to provincial autonomy and internal political reforms.

Chiang continued, "The question before us today, to speak of Kwangtung only, is as Mr. Liang put it, 'Kwangtung belongs to the people of Kwangtung.' Surely we cannot depend on other people; we cannot allow ourselves to become entangled in the affairs of other provinces. Each province has its peculiarities . . . In other provinces bandits are not numerous; in Kwangtung they are. Should we be the least bit careless, then though our citizens themselves do not rise up, the bandits may yet take advantage of the crisis. And if the foreigners should intervene, then the mess will really be difficult to clean up." At that moment, eight foreign gunboats were moored off Canton, two of them British, two French, two American, one Japanese, and one German.[50] The possibility of foreign intervention was never very far from anyone's thoughts.

Chiang then mentioned his visit with the Hong Kong newspaper editors and elaborated on his stratagem of using the provincial government "to improve upon independence." "All those aspects of the political system that formerly distressed the people of Kwangtung can be eliminated one by one by the government. Take, for example, the abolition yesterday of the butcher tax and the wine tax. This will satisfy fully the hearts of the people. Since the aim of the revolutionary party does not go beyond this, how then can they use it as an excuse for their destructive activities?"

Next to speak was Su Leng-feng, editor of the *South Viet News,* one of three newspapers in Canton sympathetic to the revolution. He made no effort to disabuse Liang and Chiang of their stated hope that last-minute reforms would satisfy and deter the revolutionaries. Instead, Su moved that the meeting take up the resolution that was on the agenda, namely, that as Kwangtung itself was in sore need, it absolutely would not answer the requests of other provinces for soldiers, funds, or arms but would "temporarily" retain all these for its own defense. The resolution, which amounted to a declaration of fiscal autonomy and neutrality in the civil war in central China, passed.

T'an Li-yüan, editor of the nonrevolutionary *Canton Daily News,* next proposed the creation of something called the "general organ for the supervision of the officials and the reform of the political system." It too passed. This general supervisory organ was a representative body to oversee the operations of the provincial government; it lay at the heart of the proposals of the governor-general and the gentry to keep the peace in Kwangtung. Essentially, it was an informal auxiliary to the provincial assembly. It was designed to overcome two principal shortcomings of the assembly. Its main purpose was to back up the assembly in its dealings with the provincial administration. Should the administration, as it often had in the past, ignore the advice of the assembly, then the supervisory organ would mobilize public opinion behind the assembly. As T'an Li-yüan described it, "All petitions will be forwarded [to the provincial administration] by the provincial assembly. If they are not granted, then the supervisory organ will back the assembly up. And if they are still not granted, then the thirty million people of Kwangtung will back it up."

The other principal purpose of the supervisory organ was to broaden popular representation in the provincial government. It was far larger in size and much less restricted in membership than the gentry-dominated assembly. All those present at the Wen-lan Academy meeting were automatically designated as members of the organ. In addition, the various popular associations in the province, such as the guilds, charitable halls, *hui-kuan,* and newspapers, were each asked to send at least five representatives to manage the affairs of the organ.

Finally, before the meeting adjourned, Lu Nai-chuang, vice-president of the provincial assembly, suggested that the Canton Newspaper Association send a delegation to meet with the popular associations in Hong Kong and get their acquiescence to the peace-keeping proposals just adopted. The suggestion was accepted, and a six-man delegation appointed. It included representatives from all three revolutionary newspapers in Canton, Su Leng-feng of the *South Viet News,* P'an Ta-wei of the *Democrat,* and Lao Wei-meng of the *Human Rights News;* it also included three from nonrevolutionary papers, Lo Shao-ao of the *Seventy-two Guilds' Commercial News,* Li P'ei-shih of the *Cultural Daily News,* and T'an Li-yüan of the *Canton Daily News.*

Governor-General Chang Ming-ch'i readily accepted the gentry's proposals. That same night, he commended them for their concern for the peace and safety of Kwangtung and declared that "the resolutions were all quite satisfactory and could all be put into practice." He agreed to retain all troops, funds, and weapons within the province and thus turned down an urgent request of the Ministry of Finance for remittance of money to Peking. He promised that "hereafter the maintenance of order in the province was the joint responsibility of the officials and the citizens." [51] At the same time, Chang also informed the Manchu garrison in Canton of what had transpired. Mindful that the anti-Manchu revolutionaries had murdered their last two Tartar-generals, the bannermen were anxious to cooperate with the peace-keeping efforts, which promised to forestall a revolutionary takeover. On the advice of the governor-general, they announced that their representatives would meet with the leaders of Canton on October 29 to work out the details of their cooperation. [52]

Meanwhile, the delegation of newsmen had conveyed the views of the Canton gentry to the Chinese newspapers and commercial organizations in Hong Kong. On at least one occasion, when appearing before a group of merchants on the night of October 29, Chiang K'ung-yin and Ch'en Ching-hua accompanied the delegation. The merchants received their views skeptically. They expressed strong doubts as to whether the governor-general would in fact be able to steer a middle course between the republican revolutionaries and the imperial government. Chiang and some of the newsmen, and maybe also Ch'en Ching-hua, reportedly returned to Canton on the thirtieth.[53]

By the time they arrived, however, the political situation in the capital city had undergone two rapid and drastic changes. With the revolution still unchecked in central China and revolutionary sentiment gaining ground locally, a rumor swept through Canton after October 25 that the famous bandit chief Lu Lan-ch'ing, who was allied to the revolutionaries, would attack the city on the thirtieth. A second rumor claimed that the Manchu garrison had vowed to "make the whole city die with them rather than be murdered by the revolutionaries." [54] The rumors produced another panic. Many of the wealthy residents fled again for the relative safety of Hong Kong, Macao, or the countryside, while shopkeepers closed their stores in the city and removed their stocks to the suburbs. The officials tried to refute the rumors and called on the populace to remain clam and the merchants to carry on normally. But it was to no avail. The city braced for trouble.[55]

On the morning of October 29, the day before the rumored attack, some of the merchants, led by Ch'en Hui-p'u of the Self-Government Society and perhaps T'an Min-san, a member of the Revolutionary Alliance, met at the Ai-yü Charitable Hall to consider the worsening situation. The merchants of Canton, like those in Hong Kong, had grave doubts about the adequacy of Governor-General Chang's peacekeeping plans. These were plans that they had had little or no part in formulating; only the gentry had been consulted. They were particularly dubious about the calculated equivocation in choosing between the republicans and the court. As the possibility of an attack by Lu Lan-ch'ing loomed before them, the merchants, who were of course the ones most likely to suffer from any fighting in the city, sought desperately to remove the revolutionary threat. As the moderator for the meeting, probably T'an Min-san, put it, "Kwangtung right now is faced with a crisis that threatens its very existence. We absolutely cannot equivocate any longer. The power of the republican regime is now an established fact. And it stands in direct opposition to the despotic regime of former days. The despotic regime simply cannot be supported any longer." The assembled merchants were asked to consider "the feelings of the people of Kwangtung and our own long-term protection" and decide "which ought we recognize: the despotic or the republican regime?" They opted for the republican.[56]

Ch'en Hui-p'u and several other merchants then went over to the Wen-lan Academy to announce their decision to the previously scheduled conference between the gentry and the bannermen. To the anxious bannermen they promised that, in the words of one of their leaflets, "When the troops of the new government arrive in Canton, we will insist that they treat the Manchus as they do the Han. The Hupeh Military Government has already declared that theirs is a political and not a racial revolution and that they look upon Manchus with equal regard. Therefore, what we have pledged will certainly be recognized by the new government." [57]

It is not clear from the newspaper accounts, perhaps because of subsequent press censorship, what the gentry at the Wen-lan Academy thought about the merchants' decision. On the one hand, they were probably upset that *their* plan for keeping peace in Canton had been found wanting. On the other, they must have realized that since the formulation of their plan on October 25 the situation in Canton had deteriorated considerably. In the end, the gentry went along with the merchants and voted also to join the republicans. They called on the various popular associations in the city to form a delegation to notify the governor-general of their decision. As the meeting ended, a huge banner was dramatically unfurled declaring the independence of Kwangtung.

Suddenly relieved that the changeover of regime had been effected without bloodshed, the people of Canton went wild with joy. A parade formed immediately and wound its way from the Wen-lan Academy in the Western Suburbs along the new bund into the Old City to the governor-general's compound. Signs and banners welcoming the new era were produced hurriedly and put on display throughout the city. "Firecrackers blazed and spluttered by hundreds for hours." As the celebrations wore on into the night, festive lanterns were also brought out.

Canton's declaration of independence, however, proved to be premature. Later that same night, Governor-General Chang Ming-ch'i abruptly halted the celebrations. He announced that independence had not been declared. He claimed instead that a handful of agitators had acted falsely in the name of the charitable halls and had hired vagrants to

stage the demonstrations. He ordered that the agitators be arrested and
that all signs, lanterns, and other displays be removed immediately.[58]
The merchants and gentry had acted without his prior approval, and
they apparently were unable to persuade him afterwards that so drastic a
step was absolutely necessary to maintain peace in the city. Indeed, the
last-minute news of a major Ch'ing victory over the republicans at
Hankow may have convinced him otherwise. On October 29 it was still
not certain that the revolution would succeed. The governor-general
chose to wait and see.

October 30 passed without the attack on Canton by Lu Lan-ch'ing. In
the week that followed, Governor-General Chang tried to calm the city
and conciliate public opinion. He announced that he still favored the
gentry's original proposals for provincial autonomy and political reforms.
He also released from prison the editors of the *Celestials* and the *Central
Plain News,* the two papers that had been shut down a few months earlier for advocating revolution. And he disbanded the Detective Bureau,
whose indiscriminate arrests of queueless youths had stirred up much
criticism.[59]

At the same time, the authorities and leading organizations in Canton
issued a number of reassuring statements. The officials declared that the
capital's defenses were strong, that the Manchus and Han were reconciled, that the revolutionaries had not attacked the city and indeed were
not likely to attack since they were preoccupied with Hupeh. The Newspaper Association announced, after the six-man press delegation had returned from Hong Kong, that the newspapers and commercial organizations in the colony agreed with the course of action proposed by the
governor-general and the gentry. (This was not entirely true.) The
Chamber of Commerce called on the merchants to keep their shops open
for business; it assured them that "the officials will not go deeply into
the incident" of the declaration of independence and that "all merchants
can therefore relax." [60] Nevertheless, the city remained tense. Merchants, ignoring the Chamber of Commerce, continued to board up
their shops. Those who could afford it, including relatives of all the high
officials, fled the city. In the first days of November business ground to a
halt. Canton became almost a deserted city.

Governor-General Chang Ming-ch'i's disavowal of Canton's declaration of independence on October 29 actually worked to the advantage of
the revolutionaries. During the preceding three weeks, the revolutionaries in Kwangtung had been relatively inactive, except for the assas-

sination of Feng-shan. Although a few individuals, such as Ch'en Ching-hua, Su Leng-feng and the other two newsmen who went to Hong Kong, and perhaps T'an Min-san, had taken part in some of the emergency planning sessions in Canton, there had been no organized effort by the revolutionaries. If the merchants and gentry had had their way on the twenty-nineth, they and not the revolutionaries would have come to power in Canton. They might then have been able to forestall the entry of the revolutionaries into the city except on their own terms. As it happened, Chang's actions gave the revolutionaries the opportunity to organize their forces and to mount an attack that established beyond dispute their right to be in Canton.

The revolutionaries finally seized the initiative from the officials at the beginning of November, probably following Hu Han-min's arrival in Hong Kong from Saigon. Even as the Canton officials were reassuring the city's inhabitants that the revolutionaries were fully occupied in Hupeh and would not bother Kwangtung, various bandit bands allied with the Alliance (now redesignated as "people's armies," *min-chün*) were stirring in the delta east and south of the capital. Lu Lan-ch'ing, instead of attacking Canton, rose up at Ma-ning in Shun-te; Lu Ling, at Le-ts'ung, also in Shun-te, scene of the revolt in April; and Li Chiu, at Hsiao-lan in Hsiang-shan.[61] The revolutionaries themselves took the field in areas closer to their extraterritorial bases in Macao and Hong Kong. On November 5 a group from Macao captured Shih-ch'i, the capital of Hsiang-shan district. The next day, revolutionary agents convinced the New Army garrison at Ch'ien-shan, the fortified town adjacent to Macao, to defect en masse.[62] From Hong Kong, Wang Hsing-chung formed a people's army in early November and took Hsin-an city on the sixth.[63] In neighboring Kuei-shan, Ch'en Chiung-ming and Teng K'eng rose up at Tan-shui on the third; a couple of days later they began a siege of Hui-chou city, which they finally captured on the nineth.[64] Since the officials had organized their defense around the capital, they were virtually incapable of dealing with these uprisings in the countryside, which furthermore all occurred more or less simultaneously.

As the Ch'ing forces in the outlying areas crumbled under the attacks of the revolutionaries, the center of activity shifted back to Canton. On November 5, the day the revolutionaries captured their first district capital in Kwangtung, Hu Han-min sent a message from Hong Kong to the guilds and charitable halls of Canton, applauding the merchants' attempt at a peaceful declaration of independence on October 29. He regretted that as a result of the officials' obstinacy the takeover could no longer be bloodless; he called on the people not to oppose the entry of the revolutionary army into Canton.[65] On November 7 the merchants from the guilds and charitable halls met to discuss Hu's warning. As a result, they decided to convey their anxieties to each of the high officials, Governor-General Chang, Commander Lung Chi-kuang and Naval Commander-in-Chief Li Chun, and to question them about their plans for defending the city from attack.[66]

It so happened that on the same day that the merchants came to talk to him Li Chun was, incredibly enough, working out an accommodation with the revolutionaries.[67] Li had two reasons for coming to terms with his enemies, who twice had tried to kill him. One was to spite Governor-General Chang, who earlier had stripped him of his command over the Reserve Forces in central Kwangtung and replaced him with Lung Chi-kuang. After he was wounded in the August assassination attempt, Li retired to his headquarters at Hu-men and took his time about convalescing. When the revolution broke out, he repeatedly ignored the governor-general's summons to come to Canton and help with military preparations. His excuse was that he still had not recovered from his injuries. The other reason was, of course, to compensate for his past actions against the revolutionaries. He was thus doubly receptive when on October 25 his adviser Hsieh Chih-wo, whose nephew Hsieh Liang-mu was active in the Alliance, discreetly inquired about the possibility of his collaboration with the revolutionaries.

When Hu Han-min arrived in Hong Kong, he doubted that Li Chun was seriously interested; nevertheless, he wrote Li on November 4 assuring him in general terms that should he cooperate he would be forgiven his counterrevolutionary past. Li responded promptly by sending his younger brother to the Hong Kong Legislative Councillor Wei Yuk, who in turn put him in touch with Hu Han-min. (Ch'en Ching-hua may have had a hand in this too, for Wei Yuk and he, together with a Swede, were partners in an export-import firm, perhaps the same Olof Wijk & Co. for which Ch'en was the comprador.) [68] As a result, on November 7, with his brother acting on his behalf, Li Chun signed a secret pact with the revolutionaries pledging to cooperate with them in capturing the forts at Hu-men in return for a guarantee of safety for himself and his family.

Lung Chi-kuang, however, refused similar enticements to defect.[69] With his support, Governor-general Chang could have defended Canton against the revolutionaries indefinitely. But it would have cost a number of lives. And it probably would have been futile in the long run, for despite the success of the Ch'ing counteroffensive at Hankow, the revolution had resumed its progress elsewhere in the country. By November 7 it had spread to Yunnan, Shansi, Kweichow, Kiangsu, and Chekiang.

Moreover, armed resistance to the revolutionaries at Canton might have led to foreign intervention. In a special interview with the English-language *South China Morning Post* of Hong Kong on October 28, the governor-general had called attention to this specifically. "Rumours have reached me," he said then, "that there might be intervention on the part of the Powers. This would not be right. Every nation had internal trouble at one time or another in its history, which is allowed to settle itself. It would not be fair to interfere with China in her present trouble . . . China, in my opinion, is quite capable herself of settling all this trouble." [70] As revolutionary agitation increased in the Pearl River delta, so did the threat of intervention. On or about November 6, according to a newspaper report, the British consul at Canton, James Jamieson, warned Governor-General Chang that unless "piracy" on the West River were checked, his government "would be compelled to take action independently." At the same time, at Jamieson's request, the British added two torpedo boats and two torpedo boat destroyers to their naval force at Canton. [71]

Realizing the futility of resistance and fearful of foreign intervention, Governor-General Chang Ming-ch'i bowed to the anxieties of the merchants. He agreed to recognize the republican regime. [72] As he did so, the gentry, who had been closely associated with his abortive scheme to achieve provincial autonomy, receded into the background, while the merchants, who were early advocates of republicanism, stepped forward to manage the changing of the regimes. On the morning of November 8 Governor-General Chang sent his secretary Hu Ming-p'an, together with Chiang K'ung-yin, to the Chamber of Commerce to meet with representatives of the guilds and charitable halls to make the necessary decisions, which were ratified later that afternoon at a sparsely attended public meeting at the provincial assembly. The governor-general and the merchants agreed that pending the formation of the republican government, the existing authorities would keep control of the troops; Chang Ming-ch'i and Lung Chi-kuang were accordingly named as provisional military governor (*tu-tu*) and lieutenant governor. At the same time, they invited the revolutionary leaders, Wang Ching-wei, Hu Han-min, and Ch'en

Ching-hua, to come to Canton to set up the new government. They also designated the provincial assembly as the new "general deliberative organ" for the province; but it was to be enlarged by five delegates from each popular association in the province and was thus similar to the "general supervisory organ" that the gentry had proposed earlier. Finally, they scheduled the formal declaration of independence for early next morning, at which time Chang and Lung would be presented their temporary seals of office.[73]

In the course of the night, however, Chang Ming-ch'i secretly fled Canton.[74] If he had been the head of a province where the revolutionaries had not been so active as they had been in Kwangtung, he might have been able to stay on indefinitely under the new regime. But in Kwangtung his tenure as provisional military governor would have been a short one. The revolutionaries would never have accepted him despite his reformist views. Indeed, the Hong Kong Newspaper Association and other revolutionary supporters abroad lost no time in cabling their refusal to recognize Chang as governor.[75] Practically all of the civil officials in Canton followed the governor-general in flight. Lung Chi-kuang, however, stayed behind to negotiate a modus vivendi with the revolutionaries.

On the morning of November 9 Canton finally succeeded in declaring its independence of the Ch'ing. As previously arranged, several thousand people jammed the provincial assembly, where for the first time in the month-old crisis, the revolutionaries were in charge.[76] Chairmen of the meeting were Ch'en Ching-hua and Teng Mu-han, editor of the *Democrat*. The assembly first passed a set of ten resolutions. (1) It invited the "people's party" to form the provisional organs of the new government. (2) It proclaimed its adherence to republicanism and independence and announced it to all the provinces and to the world. (3) It permitted all the old Ch'ing officials to stay in their positions but required them to pledge their loyalty to the new Republic of China. (4) It vowed not to discriminate against the Manchus. (5) It recalled to Canton the various units of the New Army, which Governor-General Chang had previously dispersed in order to reduce the threat of revolution from that quarter. It also allowed the soldiers and officers who had been discharged after the mutiny in 1910 to rejoin the New Army. And it urged all the police and Reserve Forces to remain at their posts. (6) It asked all social groups to carry on as usual and gave assurances that the new government would provide for their safety. (7) It ordered all officials dealing in financial affairs to remain at their posts until relieved by appointees of the new government. (8) It released all prisoners. (9) It called on the secret societies to give up their illegal activities. And last (10) it authorized the formation of people's militia.

Afterwards, the assembly deputized Ch'en Ching-hua and two others to take the seal of office to the governor-designate. Only then did Chang Ming-ch'i's flight become known. The three deputies next offered the position to Lung Chi-kuang, who earlier had been chosen as lieutenant governor. Lung demurred. Finally, Ch'en Ching-hua and Teng Mu-han put forward Hu Han-min for the vacant post. Hu was quickly elected. But as he was still in Hong Kong, the assembly nominated Chiang Tsun-kuei, the brigade commander of the New Army and a member of the Alliance, to act as governor until Hu arrived the next morning.

For the second time in ten days, the city of Canton celebrated its independence. The second celebration, not surprisingly, lacked the spontaneity and fervor of the first; it was, after all, anticlimactic. Nevertheless, all over the city shops were closed, and people entered the new age by cutting off their queue. Signs everywhere hailed the "New Han" and firecrackers blazed well into the night.[77]

In retrospect, the least important player in the revolutionary drama just concluded in Canton had been the Ch'ing dynasty. From the start of the Wuchang revolt, no one, not even its own officials, had worked very hard on its behalf. However, though the dynasty was left for dead, the republican revolutionaries did not automatically inherit its mantle. The governor-general and the provincial scholar-gentry, who were bound by common class origins, worked closely together to produce a third course, an alternative between the dynasty and the revolutionaries. The alternative was provincial autonomy, which would have continued and extended the gentry's traditional control of society. This was why their plan did not meet with the approval of the merchants. The merchants, now politicized, were not anxious to see perpetuated the old social system under which they were at best second-class citizens. They looked for more radical changes; they were thus more sympathetic than the gentry were to the revolutionaries, who were ideologically, if not in class origins, "bourgeois."[78] But the merchants, even in so commercial a city as Canton, were too weak to challenge the gentry by themselves; in the end, they were able to give only limited assistance to the revolutionaries, who thus had to overcome the gentry's resistance by themselves. This they succeeded in doing after they finally managed to get their forces organized. But the revolutionaries were not always so powerful in the other provinces, or even in other parts of Kwangtung province.

Elsewhere in the Province

When Canton declared for the revolution, other cities in the province followed suit quickly. Apart from the Pearl River delta in the vicinity of the provincial capital, the only other area in Kwangtung where the revolutionaries personally seized control was the Swatow–Ch'ao-chou area.[79] Swatow had been the center of a certain amount of revolutionary activity prior to the revolution. The *China New Journal,* for example, had been publishing in the city since the summer of 1908. It had been suppressed in June 1911 for its immoderate criticism of the government, only to reappear a month later, under American consular protection, as the *New China Journal.* The revolutionaries at Swatow, however, were few in number. Moreover, they were divided, partly along ethnolinguistic lines, into at least three different independent groups. One group was centered on Chang Lu-ts'un, a Hakka, who had been a member of the Alliance since 1907. Another, on Sun Tan-yai, a Teochiu, who had recently returned from Japan. The third, on L. K. Goe (Liang Chin-ao), publisher of the *New China Journal;* though he himself was a Punti, the paper was an organ of the Hakkas.[80] (Hsü Hsüeh-ch'iu, the Teochiu organizer of the 1907 revolt in nearby Huang-kang, was in Southeast Asia at the time of the revolution; he did not return to Swatow until after it had succeeded.)

The revolution in Swatow closely followed and indeed almost paralleled developments in Canton. As in the provincial capital, the first response to the Wuchang revolt came not from the revolutionaries but from the incumbent officials and the nonrevolutionary gentry and merchants. In late October, when Canton seemed to be on the verge of declaring its independence before the revolutionaries had even taken to the field, the head of the Swatow police, whose force of seven hundred policemen was the principal military force in the port, let it be known that he was willing to relinquish his authority without a fight. He advised the chairman of the Chamber of Commerce, Kao Ping-chen, to call together people from various walks of life to devise measures for their own protection. (It is not clear why he did not simply go before the Swatow town council, which had been formed within the past year.) The result was the tentative formation of a self-defense force, which was to be financed by the local merchants, and a self-government society, which was headed by Yeh Ch'u-ts'ang, editor of the *New China Journal,* and Wu Tzu-shou, editor of the *Illustrated News* (and, incidentally, vice-president of the town council). But, of course, Canton's declaration of independence turned out to be premature. Following the governor-general's lead in Canton, the Ch'ao-chou prefect, Ch'en Chao-t'ang, stepped in to put an end to Swatow's plans for self-government.[81]

As in Canton, the revolutionaries benefited most from the collapse of this last-minute movement toward local autonomy. During the next ten days or so, the revolutionaries in Swatow, scattered and disorganized, lay low and awaited the outcome of the struggle in the provincial capital. They bestirred themselves only on November 9, when Canton formally declared for the republic. That evening, perhaps at the initiative of Chang Lu-ts'un, who had just returned from a quick trip to Hong Kong, the three main revolutionary groups in Swatow got together and decided to stage an uprising the next morning. The rising on the morning of the tenth turned out to be a walk. The revolutionaries were "a poor looking lot," according to a British eyewitness, but they met no resistance from either the police or the small detachment of Reserve Forces in the city. The people reportedly "rejoiced greatly" at the take-over.[82]

With the port of Swatow in hand, the revolutionaries turned their attention toward Ch'ao-chou city. On November 12 an army under the joint command of the Hakka Chang Lu-ts'un and the Teochiu Sun Tan-yai set out from Swatow for the prefectural capital. There they encountered a problem in the person of Prefect Ch'en Chao-t'ang. Instead of fleeing, as most of his associates had done, Ch'en had remained at his post and, apparently with the support of the gentry and merchants of the city, had declared for the republic. Although he welcomed their arrival and arranged quarters for their army, the revolutionaries were far from pleased with Ch'en. They recalled that he had been the prefect at Hui-chou at the time of the 1907 revolt, which he presumably helped suppress. They demanded that he disarm his Reserve Forces and surrender his authority to them. Ch'en Chao-t'ang, however, refused and cited the resolution of the Canton assembly on November 9 allowing incumbent officials like himself to serve the new regime so long as they pledged loyalty to it. He in turn accused the revolutionaries of behaving like bandits. After about a week of indecisive negotiations and maneuverings, the revolutionaries lost their patience and attacked Ch'en. His troops, whose pay was three months in arrears, offered little resistance. He then tried to escape, but was captured. A couple of days later, on November 21, Prefect Ch'en was executed. And so in Ch'ao-chou city too, the revolutionaries took power.[83]

With the revolutionaries concentrating practically all their effort on taking Canton and Swatow–Ch'ao-chou, the rest of the province made the transition from Ch'ing to republican rule on its own. In some districts, local bandit groups, under the name of "people's armies," converged on the market towns and centers of administration. In Shao-chou, on the North River, an army of four thousand armed robbers besieged the prefectural city and compelled its chief military official to switch his allegiance on November 13. In K'ai-p'ing, on the edge of the Pearl River delta, a people's army invaded the district capital on November 11, and released all prisoners and destroyed official files. In neighboring En-p'ing, another people's army, which had gathered at the town of Sheng-t'ang on November 13, overran the district city about a week later and occupied it for a month. In Ch'ih-hsi, the Hakka subprefecture on the coast of Central Kwangtung, a people's army captured the capital city on November 12.[84]

In other districts, the incumbent officials themselves managed the transfer of allegiance, as Prefect Ch'en Chao-t'ang had tried to do at Ch'ao-chou. In Ch'in-chou, at the other end of the province, Taotai Kuo Jen-chang, whose flirtation with the Alliance had encouraged the series of revolutionary attempts in that region in 1907–08, declared for the republic on November 14. With fifteen battalions of Reserve Forces in Ch'in-chou and three in Lien-chou supporting him, Kuo quickly set up an independent military government for the region with himself as governor and a subordinate commander as the head of a branch government in Lien-chou. Similarly, in Chao-ch'ing, in the West River valley, it was the regiment commander of the Reserve Forces who took the prefectural city over to republican side; and in Ch'ing-yüan, in the North River valley, it was a major in the Army of the Green Standard.[85]

Probably in all districts, as in Canton, the gentry and merchants played a significant, if sometimes backstage, role. They arranged for prompt declarations of independence in order to forestall the people's armies. They elected and sanctioned the new officials. Perhaps most important, they financed the new government. In Lo-ting, in the West River valley, soon after Canton's capitulation to the republicans, the local elite "publicly elected" a triumvirate composed of the incumbent magistrate, the local Reserve Forces commander, and a member of the gentry to handle the department's civil, military, and financial affairs respectively. In Ch'ih-hsi, after the people's army had driven off the subprefect and the local military official, the gentry and merchants took over the responsibility of maintaining order for the next several months. In Hoihow, the treaty port on Hainan island, the Five Guilds financed and provisioned the local Reserve Forces for close to two months. In the treaty port of Pakhoi, after all the officials had absconded without warning, the Chamber of Commerce paid off their mutinous troops and then formed a self-defense force of its own.[86]

Thus, to judge from the fragmentary reports that one finds in the local gazetteers and contemporary newspapers, all the districts in Kwangtung made the transition from Ch'ing to Republic within a matter of days after Canton's declaration of independence on November 9. Furthermore, the change usually took place without the direct involvement of the revolutionaries. It also met with very little opposition from the Ch'ing officials, most of whom, from the governor-general on down, fled or switched sides rather than put up a fight. The revolution was therefore carried out with remarkably little bloodshed.

The ease with which Kwangtung passed from empire to republic may be attributed to two factors. One was the fear of foreign intervention. Both the revolutionaries and the nonrevolutionaries scrupulously avoided molesting foreigners and their establishments. One hysterical account by a Westerner of the soldiers' pillaging in Pakhoi ended with an illuminating aside: "Foreign houses are the only safe refuges here."[87] The other factor was the estrangement of the people from the dynasty. As a result of developments since the end of 1910, the regime had become so discredited that practically nobody, not even its own officials, thought that it was worth the effort and the risks of defending. Under the weight of sheer indifference the Ch'ing dynasty simply crumbled away.

10

Revolution and Counterrevolution

Nationally, the heirs of the revolution were the old imperial elite, the scholar-officials, whose estrangement from the Manchu regime had made it all possible. This was symbolized by Sun Yat-sen's resignation of the presidency of the new republic on April 1, 1912, in favor of Yüan Shih-k'ai. In many provinces, therefore, the effects of the revolution were minimal, perhaps no more than the discarding of the queue and the realization of home rule. Kwangtung was an exception. Along with An-hwei, Kiangsi, and Hunan, it was one of the few provinces where the revolutionaries had played an important role in the revolution and where they were in control afterwards. The effects of the revolution upon the province were truly revolutionary. The revolutionaries, however, were in power in south China less than two years. In the summer of 1913 they were goaded by President Yüan Shih-k'ai into launching the "Second Revolution," which failed for lack of popular support. They were driven into exile once more, and practically all their reforms were undone.[1]

The Revolutionaries in Power

When Canton declared its independence of the Ch'ing on November 9, 1911, it inaugurated the rule of the revolutionaries in Kwangtung. During their twenty-one months in power, the revolutionaries' most pressing tasks were to create a new administration, to maintain military and economic order, to overcome their domestic opposition, and to appease the foreign powers. These were formidable problems, but the revolutionaries coped with them reasonably well.

The mass exodus of the Ch'ing officials just as the revolutionaries entered Canton greatly simplified the task of forming a new government. Practically all the old civil officials had fled; so had many of the military officials. The most prominent holdovers were the two military commanders, Lung Chi-kuang and Li Chun. Li Chun, despite his eleventh hour defection to the revolutionary side, lasted only a week in Canton. The former naval commander-in-chief departed in haste on November 18, after one of the revenge-seeking people's armies in the city ransacked his headquarters.[2] Lung Chi-kuang, however, was more successful. Although he had helped crush the Chen-nan-kuan and Ho-k'ou uprisings along the Vietnam border in 1907 and 1908, the revolutionaries nevertheless found it useful to work with him. Lung and his army remained in Kwangtung until January 1913, when they returned to Kwangsi.

The revolutionaries thus had little difficulty in staffing the new administration with their own appointees, who (like the original membership of the Revolutionary Alliance) were typically young men, in their twenties and early thirties, usually of gentry background, with a modern (often foreign) education. The military governor (tu-tu) who headed the new provincial government was alternately Hu Han-min or Ch'en Chiung-ming. Hu was 32 years old in 1911; Ch'en, 33. Hu was a graduate of the Tokyo College of Law and -Administration; Ch'en, a graduate of the Kwangtung College of Law and Administration and a former provincial assemblyman. Both qualified for membership in the scholar-gentry and both had been active members of the Alliance. Hu Han-min was governor from November 10 until December 20, 1911, when he suddenly left Canton to accompany Sun Yat-sen to Nanking. Ch'en Chiung-ming, the lieutenant governor, then took over as acting governor until Sun's resignation from the presidency in April 1912, when Hu returned to Canton and resumed his duties as governor. A year later, in June 1913, when Hu was dismissed, Ch'en again succeeded him and was governor until the regime was overthrown in August. Although relations between Hu Han-min and Ch'en Chiung-ming were by no means cordial, they nevertheless cooperated with one another during these two years. There was no serious disagreement between them over the conduct of the Kwangtung government.[3]

Men of the same breed headed the various ministries and commissions into which the new provincial administration was divided. Liao Chung-k'ai, 33 years old in 1911, a graduate of Waseda and Chūō, was minister of finance. Chu Chih-hsin, 26, a graduate of the Tokyo College of Law and Administration, was auditor general. Teng K'eng, also 26, a graduate of the Canton Military Officers' School, was army minister. Li Shu-fen, 24, a medical graduate of the University of Edinburgh, was health commissioner. Lo Wen-kan, 23, a graduate of Oxford, was minister of justice. Ch'ien Shu-fen, an American-returned student, was minister of civil affairs. Lo P'an-hui, a Chicago-educated lawyer, was minister of foreign affairs. Wang Ch'ung-yu and Kuan Ching-shen, both U.S.-trained, succeeded one another as minister of industry. Ch'eng T'ien-tou, also U.S.-trained, was commissioner of public works. Of this group, only four, Liao, Chu, Teng, and Li, are known to have been members of the Alliance.[4]

Three of the remaining ministers belonged to the earlier generation of Westernized Chinese revolutionaries: Ch'en Shao-pai, 42 years old, the former head of the Alliance in Hong Kong, who preceded Lo P'an-hui as minister of foreign affairs; Li Yü-t'ang, the wealthy Hong Kong merchant and member of the Alliance, who preceded Liao Chung-k'ai as minister of finance; and Chung Jung-kuang, 45, the "Chinese dean" at the Canton Christian College, who was minister of education. Though not a member of the Alliance, Chung had been sympathetic to the revolutionary cause.[5] Among the ministry and commission heads in the Kwangtung revolutionary government, the only one who stands out as unusual was Li Kuo-lien, Ch'ien Shu-fen's predecessor as minister of civil affairs. Li was an old-style provincial graduate who was famous for leading the popular opposition to the attempted official takeover of the Canton–Hankow railroad in 1906; he was not known to be a revolutionary.

The new regime was in name and in fact a military government; its power rested upon its control over the armed forces. Lung Chi-kuang, who commanded a 5,000-man army, was none too dependable. As late as December 1, 1911, he confided to the British consulate that "if the Manchus win in the north, Kwangtung would again quietly change its coat." [6] Nevertheless, for reasons of his own, he cooperated well enough with the revolutionary government up to the time of his voluntary withdrawal from Kwangtung in January 1913. The regime, fortunately, was not dependent upon Lung. It relied principally upon the Kwangtung Army, formerly the New Army, which had been recalled to Canton after the revolution. When Huang Shih-lung, its popular but nonrevolutionary chief of staff, fled Canton after a month, the government evidently reorganized the army and put it under the command of men who favored the revolution.[7] The commander of the First Division, Chung Ting-chi, was a Japanese-trained artillery officer who was at least sympathetic to the revolution in 1911. The commander of the Second Division, Su Shen-ch'u, had taken part in the April 1911 revolt in Canton. The commander of the Fifth (Independent) Brigade, Li E, was a member of the Alliance; he had been imprisoned by the Ch'ing for complicity in the abortive "Protect Asia" revolt in Canton in 1908. Li E's successor as commander of the Fifth Brigade in 1913, Chang Wo-ch'üan, had also belonged to the Alliance.[8] In addition to the regular army, the new regime could also rely on the various people's armies that had risen in the course of the revolution and on the provincial police, which was in the hands of the Alliance member Ch'en Ching-hua.

Control over the provincial administration and the Kwangtung Army gave the revolutionaries control over Canton; this in turn gave them control over the rest of the province. Specifically, they were able to make civil and military appointments across the province. However, their control elsewhere was less direct than in Canton. In Swatow, for example, the military commander after April 1912 was not a revolutionary but an old Ch'ing official.[9] The original commander had been Chang Lu-ts'un, a veteran Hakka revolutionary, but he had left Swatow in December 1911 to join the fighting in central China. The Canton government then appointed Ch'en Hung-e, a nonrevolutionary New Army officer, as his successor. Ch'en was a Teochiu and was well liked by the Swatow merchants. Indeed, he may have identified himself so closely with Swatow as to have opposed the extension of financial and police authority from Canton. The Canton government soon replaced him with another Hakka revolutionary, Lin Chi-chen. The Swatow merchants, however, hated Lin; they accused him of discrimination and other "barbarous actions" against Teochius and demanded his immediate removal.

The Canton government was in a quandary because of this Hakka–Teochiu rivalry. Practically all the leading revolutionaries in East Kwangtung were Hakkas from the Chia-ying region, like Chang Lu-ts'un and Lin Chi-chen. They, however, were unacceptable to the Swatow merchants, who preferred a native Teochiu. But like Ch'en Hung-e, few Teochius were revolutionaries. The leading Teochiu revolutionary was Hsü Hsüeh-ch'iu, organizer of the 1907 uprising at Huang-kang, but afterwards he had abandoned the Alliance and joined the rival Restoration Society instead. He was not acceptable to the Canton government. So in the end, in April 1912, it appointed Wu Hsiang-ta, a former brigade-general in the Ch'ing Reserve Forces and, as a native of Chekiang, a complete outsider. Wu was no revolutionary. Indeed, he had made his reputation in 1900 when, as a captain in the Reserve Forces, he had put down the Hui-chou revolutionary uprising. However, despite his counterrevolutionary past, he (like Lung Chi-kuang) was evidently responsive to the Canton government. (One of his first acts was to execute Hsü Hsüeh-ch'iu as a "trouble-maker.") At the same time, Wu Hsiang-ta was apparently acceptable to the Swatow merchants.

The new government, once it was established, faced two immediate problems, one military and one financial. The military problem was what to do with the people's armies; related to it was the question of banditry. In the early days of the revolution, the people's armies had played an important role. Rising up everywhere and marching on the administrative centers, they had neutralized the Ch'ing forces and overawed the gentry and merchants into supporting the revolutionaries. After the revolution had succeeded, however, they became a burden to the regime. By the beginning of December 1911, 140,000 people's army soldiers had flocked to Canton, augmenting the city's population by about one quarter. Some of the larger units belonged to such former bandit leaders as Lu Lan-ch'ing, Li Fu-lin, Lu Ling, and Wang Ho-shun, each with between two and five thousand men. The armies were expensive to maintain. Since each soldier was supposed to be paid $10 a month, their monthly bill in Canton alone ran to $1,500,000, which the government could ill afford. Moreover, the armies were not so disciplined as the authorities and the merchants would have liked. They tangled frequently with former supporters of the Ch'ing, seeking revenge. On December 9, for example, serious street fighting broke out between some of the people's armies and Lung Chi-kuang's troops.[10]

The regime's solution was to disband the people's armies, especially since it had assumed control of the regular army and was no longer dependent upon them. After first ordering a stop to their further recruitment in late November 1911, it began the difficult process of disbandment under Acting Governor Ch'en Chiung-ming in early February 1912.[11] When the leaders of the people's armies objected, the regime turned to the regular army to enforce its decision. The first to resist was Shih Chin-ch'üan. On February 24 the Kwangtung Army surrounded and disarmed his army of one to two thousand men. Shih himself was arrested, charged with disobedience, and shot. More serious opposition came two weeks later from Wang Ho-shun, organizer of the 1907 Fang-ch'eng rebellion, and his army of three to four thousand. He had the sympathy of most people's army leaders; Lu Lan-ch'ing reportedly threatened that "in the event of the people's army not getting the upper hand against the Government, he would send a few shells on to the Shameen [the Anglo-French settlement] to induce foreign intervention." [12] But in the showdown that began on March 10, Wang had the active support of only a couple of the smaller armies. After four days of savage street fighting with the Kwangtung Army, he fled Canton in defeat. Half of his army was disbanded immediately.

The overpowering of Wang Ho-shun ended all overt resistance to disbandment from the people's armies. When Hu Han-min returned to Canton as governor in late April, he continued Ch'en Chiung-ming's program. (Thus, contrary to the impression created by hostile writers, disbandment was not the work of Ch'en alone.) During the rest of 1912 the people's armies were cut back one by one. The peasant-soldiers, handing in their arms, received "a gratuity, a medal and certificate and travelling expenses home." [13] Eventually, most of the armies were eliminated, while the remainder were reorganized into Picket Guards (Ching-wei chün). Lu Lan-ch'ing's army, for example, was cut back repeatedly until finally he himself was charged with gross corruption and forced to flee the province and the rest of his army was disbanded completely. By the end of the year, the only important people's army left in Canton was Li Fu-lin's, which was entrenched on Ho-nan island opposite the city, where they remained until at least the early 1920's. According to Governor Hu Han-min in December 1912, of the 148,440 peasant-soldiers raised at the time of the revolution a year ago, only 39,600 remained.[14] Further cutbacks were made early in 1913.

People's armies were disbanded in other parts of the province too. When Governor Ch'en Chiung-ming dispatched Wu Hsiang-ta to Swatow in April 1912, one of the tasks assigned to Wu was to curb the people's armies that had similarly converged on Swatow. Thus, Sun Tan-yai's army was eliminated in May. Later on, the retrenchment campaign reached into Wu's own army, as his four battalions of Picket Guards were reduced in March 1913 to two. In Ying-te, north of Canton, about a thousand soldiers were disbanded also in March 1913.[15]

Disbandment, however, had the effect of aggravating Kwangtung's endemic unrest, as many of the disbanded peasant-soldiers took to banditry. In 1912 the province was more disturbed than it had been in years. In many outlying areas, bandit gangs operated freely and fearlessly. To deal with the problem, Governor Hu Han-min in May 1912 appointed Ch'en Chiung-ming and Lung Chi-kuang as heads of the Pacification Commission (Sui-ching ch'u) and charged them with ridding the province of all bandits and pirates within a year. Ch'en and Lung, supported by Ch'en Ching-hua's police, proceeded with merciless severity. In May and June 1912, to take a not too extreme example, hundreds of accused "criminals" were summarily executed in the Canton area; on May 7 alone, about a hundred were shot. Mere possession of firearms and explosives was liable to severe punishment. These draconian measures, it may be imagined, had a dampening effect upon the banditry. In West Kwangtung, where near anarchy had reigned in the early months of 1912, it was reported in late October that "the inland of Pakhoi is now more quiet than a few weeks ago, and it seems that business is progressing everywhere . . . The roads are safe to a certain degree, and it is now an exception if one meets robbers." This was a return to the nearly normal state of unrest that had existed before the revolution.[16]

The other immediate problem facing the Kwangtung revolutionary government was finances. From the beginning, partly because of the expenses of maintaining the people's armies, the government's expenditures had outstripped its income. At first it had, through the good offices of its initial minister of finance Li Yü-t'ang, borrowed heavily from the merchants in Canton and Hong Kong.[17] But such "patriotic loans" were inadequate to meet its continuing needs. Neither were taxes, because of Canton's uneven control over the province, especially in the early months. Consequently, the government had resorted to issuing paper currency without sufficient backing. By September 1912 it had pumped close to eighteen million dollars worth of new paper notes into the province, at a rate of roughly two million dollars a month.[18]

The result, of course, was a marked depreciation in the value of the Kwangtung notes, relative to both the twenty-cent silver coins produced by the Canton Mint and the paper notes issued by the Hong Kong banks. During the bank run that preceded the revolutionary takeover in Canton, the Kwangtung government notes had been exchanged at parity for silver coins. In early April 1912 they were discounted 9 to 10 percent, a relatively modest drop. In June, however, the paper dollars declined sharply in value and remained at a low level throughout the summer. In early August they were discounted 27 to 28 percent.[19] The government tried to stem the tide in various ways. It reduced its expenditures by disbanding the people's armies. It made the discounting of notes a criminal offense punishable by fines. It encouraged the use of notes by allowing a premium of 2 percent on payment of taxes in notes. It tried to discourage the hoarding of silver coins by minting them as fast as its supply of silver permitted. But these and similar measures had at most a temporary effect upon the money market.[20]

In September the government was forced to work out with the merchants of Canton a more drastic set of measures to restore public confidence in its money. It agreed to cut back further on its expenditures in order to reduce or eliminate its budgetary deficit, which at this time was still running between half a million and a million dollars a month. Thus it curtailed many of its operations and services and reduced all official salaries by 10 to 20 percent. It also tried to increase its income by reintroducing many of the miscellaneous taxes that in earlier, more optimistic days it had abolished. And it agreed to stop issuing new paper notes and indeed had one of the money presses taken apart piece by piece and shipped back to Shanghai. In return, the merchants agreed at once to accept its notes at par.[21]

These measures finally succeeded. From a discount rate of 28 percent in August the value of the notes bounded upward to parity with the silver coins by the end of September. It remained nominally at parity for the next two or three months. When it began to slip again, because of the government's continuing, though diminished, budgetary deficits, it nevertheless stopped at a level that was at least temporarily tolerable. In mid-February 1913, the discount rate stood at 10 percent, far above the critical level of the previous summer.[22]

This relative stability in the money market, however, was achieved at some expense to the revolutionary government and to the people. To satisfy the requirements of the merchants for fiscal responsibility, the government had to give up some of its reform projects. It had also to reintroduce the hated miscellaneous taxes, against which many people had rioted in the last years of the old regime. Finally, in accepting parity of exchange between the paper notes and the silver coins, the merchants in effect raised prices to their customers, for those who paid in coins no longer received a preferential discount.[23]

Like any new revolutionary regime, the Canton government faced the possibility of a counterrevolution. The threat from partisans of the old regime was slight. Liang Ch'i-ch'ao and some of his followers made a half-hearted effort to establish a foothold in their native Kwangtung soon after the revolution. When the plot was discovered the Canton government dealt with it swiftly and ferociously. On December 18 and 19 at least forty-four persons were found guilty of associations with the Society to Protect the Emperor and executed; in some cases, their bodies were dismembered and their internal organs sacrificed to the spirits of the revolutionary martyrs of the Canton uprising.[24] In general, however, the Ch'ing dynasty had been too discredited to pose a danger to the new government, especially since most of its officials in Kwangtung had fled. The Manchus and Chinese bannermen in Canton offered no opposition either; left alone by the revolutionaries, they soon disappeared into the general population.

The most serious threat to the regime came instead from two of its own erstwhile military supporters, Huang Shih-lung and Wang Ho-shun, in collaboration with Sun Yat-sen's independent-minded older brother, Sun Mei. In January 1912 Sun Mei publicly condemned the Canton government for its "arbitrary and often unlawful action" during the recent reign of terror against the monarchists. Accompanied by Huang Shih-lung, Sun later went to Nanking to complain personally to his brother about the alleged misgovernment in Kwangtung. Sun and Huang also organized the Upright Alliance (Fu-cheng t'ung-meng hui) in opposition to the ruling Revolutionary Alliance (Ko-ming t'ung-meng hui).[25]

After his defection from the regime in mid-March, Wang Ho-shun joined forces with Huang Shih-lung to foment a "second revolution" in Kwangtung. They hoped to capitalize on the merchants' unhappiness with monetary depreciation, the peasant-soldiers' discontent with the disbandment of the people's armies, and the widespread conservative opposition to the government's radical reforms. Throughout the late spring and early summer of 1912 there were frequent rumors in Canton of an imminent revolt by Wang and Huang. In late June, Pacification Commissioners Ch'en Chiung-ming and Lung Chi-kuang disclosed that they had smashed a conspiracy by confederates of Wang Ho-shun to stir up an uprising. Nevertheless, sporadic fighting in the name of either Huang Shih-lung or Wang Ho-shun continued to take place in K'ai-p'ing and Hsin-ning districts and in Hui-chou prefecture in the following months. By then, however, the two leaders themselves had gone to Peking to seek the support of Yüan Shih-k'ai.[26]

Finally, the revolutionary government had to cope with the hostility of the foreign powers, particularly Great Britain. From the start the British consul at Canton, James Jamieson, was scornful of practically the entire administration. Governor Hu Han-min was "incompetent and time-serving," while his associates "when not quarrelling amongst themselves, on the strength of their so-called foreign education are endeavoring to carry out the crude notions of practical government and economics which they have brought from abroad." The only officials for whom Jamieson had any respect were Lung Chi-kuang, who maintained close contact with the consulate, and the police superintendent, Ch'en Ching-hua, whose "efficiency" was praised often.[27] His dealings with the rest of the government were so obviously antagonistic that he earned the rebuke of his own minister more than once. The American consuls at Canton were hardly any more sympathetic to the new regime. F. D. Cheshire especially criticized its inexperience.

Lacking confidence in the government, the foreign powers did not hesitate from direct intervention. When Lin Chi-chen arrived at Swatow by ship on February 15, 1912, to take over from Ch'en Hung-e, the British consul there personally prevented him and his troops from landing, presumably to forestall fighting that might have damaged British property. When Lin finally captured Swatow from Ch'en a month later, Japanese and American warships in the harbor each landed a party of soldiers. While they reportedly "took no active part" in the transfer of power from Ch'en to Lin, their mere presence in Swatow caused considerable consternation among the local soldiers and the populace. When Wu Hsiang-ta arrived at Swatow in April to take over from Lin, British, Japanese, and American warships sent guard parties ashore once more, with no doubt the same effect upon the Chinese as before.[28] Another, and more lasting, instance of foreign intervention in the internal affairs of Kwangtung was the reactivation of the British naval patrol on the West River. It followed a piratical attack on the river steamer *Shiu On* on November 23, 1911, in which the British captain was killed. The patrol was maintained up through at least March 1912.[29]

Notwithstanding such provocations, the Canton government, fearful of even more massive intervention, tried diligently to maintain good relations with the foreign powers. It was strict about protecting foreign lives and property. Although unrest was widespread, foreigners, including the missionaries in the interior of the province, were remarkably safe from attacks. The murder aboard the *Shiu On* was clearly an exception.

The government even treated the British patrol of the West River cautiously. Despite popular pressure for a more vigorous response, it "resolved that everything be done to avoid offending British susceptibilities." [30] At the same time, however, the Canton government did not willingly give up any of China's sovereign rights. In August 1912 it successfully challenged Consul Jamieson's attempt to deny its authority to try and punish Chinese nationals accused of crimes committed in the Anglo-French settlement of Shameen. [31]

As a byproduct of its commitment to anti-imperialist nationalism, the new regime, unlike the Ch'ing, looked favorably upon the anti-colonial movement across the border in Vietnam. It was in revolutionary Canton, where they were given a free rein to pursue their anti-French activities, that Phan Boi Chau and other Vietnamese nationalists shed their lingering commitment to monarchism and embraced republicanism. They regrouped themselves into the Vietnam Restoration Society (Viet-Nam Quang Phuc Hoi), which despite its name was "unabashedly and to the smallest detail" modeled on the Chinese Revolutionary Alliance. Canton in 1912–13 became the center of the Vietnamese revolutionary movement, as it was again to be in the mid-1920's. The movement at this time, however, was disorganized and on the defensive. Chau and the Restoration Society were able to do little more than to dispatch several generally unsuccessful teams of assassins into Vietnam. [32]

Thus, in spite of the strictures and ridicule of the foreign consuls, the youthful revolutionary government in Kwangtung, for all its inexperience, managed in fact to cope with its major problems. It did not succeed entirely in much of what it had to do, such as maintaining the value of the paper currency or suppressing banditry or keeping the foreign powers in check. But as time went on, it had these problems increasingly under control. Moreover, it was supreme over its internal enemies. It was, in short, a viable government.

Home Rule

In Kwangtung, as in probably most other provinces, the revolution strengthened certain tendencies of the late Ch'ing local self-government movement: popular participation in public affairs, popular representation in government and, most striking, home rule. These broadly political reforms were not radically new; their roots reached back to the reforms of the post-Boxer era. But they were implemented far more widely than before. The level of politicization thus rose to a new high.

One immediate consequence of the revolution was a spectacular proliferation of popular associations. Although the Ch'ing dynasty's ban on associational activities had been relaxed in its last years, it by no means
had been discarded. It was only when the dynasty was overthrown that
the ban disappeared. In Canton, one month after the revolution, 38 organizations had been recognized by the new government. On April 23,
1912, at a reception for Sun Yat-sen, over 60 groups were represented.
A month later, 82 societies sent delegates to a ceremony commemo-
rating the martyrs of the 1911 Canton revolt.[33] This was a sharp break
quantitatively with the post-Boxer decade.

Only a few of these organizations were old ones, such as the Chamber
of Commerce and the Red Cross Society. One old association which did
not survive the transition to republican rule was, curiously, the Canton
Merchants' Self-Government Society. Its former head Ch'en Hui-p'u,
who had played a crucial role in persuading the Ch'ing officials to turn
Canton over to the revolutionaries without a fight, later founded the Citizens' Union (Kuo-min t'uan-t'i hui), whose aim was to organize a bank
to finance commercial and industrial development.[34] The role of the
Self-Government Society as spokesman for the local merchants seems to
have been assumed by a new organization, the Canton Merchants' Society for the Maintenance of Public Peace (Yüeh-shang wei-ch'ih kung-an
hui). It was the parent organization of the Merchants' Volunteer Corps,
a merchants' militia which the new government, unlike the old, readily
sanctioned. The corps included among its officers some of the leading
bankers and merchants in the city.[35] Like the volunteer corps, most of
the organizations were new. They included professional associations, like
the Society of Engineers (Chung-hua kung-ch'eng-ssu hui) and the Society of Telegraph Operators (Tien-pao hui); study groups, like the Society
to Study the Salt Laws (Yen-fa yen-chiu hui) and the Society to Promote
the Study of Medicine (I-hsüeh kung-chin hui); "lecture societies" (*yen-
shuo hui*), founded to popularize new ideas and enlighten public opinion;
as well as a second press association, known as the Newspaper Society
(Pao-yeh kung-she), in opposition to the established Newspaper Association (Pao-chieh kung-hui).[36]

The most significant of the organizations to be founded after the revolution were the political parties, which had not been allowed even in the
post-Boxer era. The several political parties in Canton in 1912 included
the Democratic Party (Min-chu cheng-tang), the People's Rule Party
(Min-chih tang), the Republican Party (Kung-ho tang), the Socialist

Party (She-hui tang), the Progressive Party (Chin-pu tang, not to be confused with the party of the same name founded in 1913 by Liang Ch'i-ch'ao), and of course the Revolutionary Alliance.[37] In March 1912 the Alliance shed its former secrecy to become an open political party. It dominated the government of Kwangtung and had branches in many cities across the province. It was later reorganized and renamed the Nationalist Party (Kuo-min tang).[38] Ranged against the political parties were two anarchist groups, the Cock-Crow Study Society (Hui-ming hsüeh-she) and the Conscience Society (Hsin she), both founded by Liu Ssu-fu in Canton in 1912; among the twelve regulations of the Conscience Society were prohibitions against becoming an official or a deliberative assemblyman, joining a political party, and enrolling in the army or navy.[39] It is clear that the associations of the new era differed greatly from those of the old not only in number but also in variety.

Newspapers similarly multiplied. In Canton the number of daily newspapers jumped from sixteen in 1911 to close to thirty in 1912; in addition, another thirty or so journals were published on a less frequent basis. Among the additions was the *China Daily News,* the long-established organ of the revolutionary movement in south China, which moved from Hong Kong to Canton after the revolution; it was edited by Lu Hsin, a veteran revolutionary journalist. In the Swatow–Ch'ao-chou area, the number of daily newspapers in 1913 seems also to have doubled since 1911. With the press again as an indicator, the level of popular concern for public affairs rose sharply after the revolution.[40]

The republican government continued and extended the Ch'ing experiments with popularly elected deliberative assemblies. When the revolutionaries took power in Canton in November 1911, the provincial assembly established by the Ch'ing in 1909 had virtually disintegrated, partly because of the mass resignations during the gambling controversy the year before and partly because of the nearly total absenteeism at the time of the revolution. Deprived of a functioning provincial assembly, the new government at first solicited popular support for its policies at a series of mass meetings (perhaps the "general deliberative organ" considered at the time of the changeover of regime), but this proved to be too unwieldy. Therefore, early in December, it agreed to a request of the Canton merchants to convene a new, provisional provincial assembly.[41]

The resultant assembly was a larger, less narrowly constituted body than the Ch'ing assembly.[42] The minimum requirements for election to the new assembly were significantly lower than those for the old. Anyone who was a native of Kwangtung or had been a resident for five (not ten) years, who was twenty (not thirty) years old, who was of good character, and who was not then serving in the government, army, or police was eligible. There were no property qualifications of any sort. The assembly was to be composed of one representative from each of the province's ninety-odd departments and districts, exclusive of Canton, which formed a separate electoral unit from the rest of Nan-hai and P'an-yü districts and was allotted twenty representatives of its own. Because of the press of time and the unsettled conditions in most parts of the province, the elections were necessarily informal. Each of the district representatives was elected by natives of the district then resident in Canton. The twenty representatives from Canton were elected at a mass meeting attended by one delegate from each of the guilds, nine delegates from the Nine Charitable Halls, five from the Society for the Study of Self-Government, and five from unspecified "workers' associations."

In addition to the geographical representation, the provisional assembly also included representation by special groups: twenty representatives for the Revolutionary Alliance; twenty for the Association of Military Corps (Chün-t'uan hsieh-hui), an Alliance-dominated group composed of the leaders of the various regular and people's army units; [43] twelve for the different overseas Chinese communities (for example, three from Hong Kong, one from the United States); six for college students and teachers; one for the "Self-Government Corps" (Tzu-chih t'uan), possibly the Canton Merchants' Volunteer Corps; an unspecified number for the popular associations that were then springing up everywhere; and, most remarkably, ten for women. When the assembly met for the first time on December 18, 1911, at least 140 representatives were on hand. [44]

The new provisional assembly apparently was composed mostly of the "new gentry" and merchants, as the administration itself was, and not the classically educated scholar-gentry, as the Ch'ing assembly had been. (As there is no membership list, it is impossible to be precise.) Among the few identifiable assemblymen were Li Kuan-hua, Huang Chih-ch'ang, and Wu Yüan-chang, all recent graduates of one or another of the new higher schools in Canton; Yang Yung-t'ai, a graduate of the Peking Methodist University Law School and a returned student; and Ch'en Chien-ch'ih, vice-chairman of the Canton Chamber of Commerce, and Feng I-ch'i, a director of the Bankers Guild, both of whom were also associated with the Merchants' Volunteer Corps. [45] The president of

the assembly was Huang Hsi-ch'üan, who held the rank of taotai under
the Ch'ing. The vice-presidents were Sung I-mei and Lu Hsin, two returned students; aside from editing the *China Daily News,* Lu headed the
Revolutionary Alliance in Kwangtung.[46]

The provisional assembly met from December 1911 to February
1913. It was, like the Ch'ing assembly, basically a deliberative body
with no legislative authority. It however possessed the power of im-
peachment, which it used against both Ch'en Chiung-ming and Hu
Han-min. The assembly, for example, denounced Hu in June 1912 as
one who "despotically enforces the martial law, tramples the statute law,
refuses to put into execution most of the bills passed by the Provincial
Assembly." (Hu brushed the accusation aside.) The assembly also claimed
a right to confirm the selection of the governor.[47]

In December 1912 elections were held to replace the provisional assembly with a regular provincial assembly. The voting requirements for
the regular assembly, which were set nationally, were more restrictive
than those for the Kwangtung provisional assembly. The age and residence requirements were largely identical—twenty-one years of age and
five years' residence in the province—but property or educational qualifications were once again imposed: ownership of real property valued at
$500; graduation from middle school or its equivalent; or payment of a
direct tax of $2 a year. Moreover, women were not permitted to vote or
serve on the assembly. Nevertheless, the requirements were still considerably more liberal than those for the Ch'ing provincial assembly. The
financial requirement, in particular, was reduced from $5,000 worth of
property to $500. As a result, the number of enfranchised voters in
Kwangtung in 1912 reached 1,906,516, about 30 percent of the adult
male population. This was a thirteen-fold expansion of the electorate
since the Ch'ing provincial assembly elections in 1909.[48]

The elections in 1912, unlike those in 1909, were waged with open
electioneering. The political parties campaigned actively for their can-
didates. In Kwangtung the revolutionaries so overshadowed the other
parties that they apparently competed against themselves, with the moderates supporting the recently organized Nationalist Party and the radicals, who had opposed the concessions required to form the Nationalist
Party, clinging to the banner of the Alliance. In East Kwangtung, the
ethnolinguistic rivalry between the Hakkas and the Teochius assumed a
new form as the Hakkas rallied behind the Alliance and the Teochius

backed the Nationalist Party. The Alliance won in the major urban areas; the Nationalist Party, in the rural districts.[49]

The 120-man provincial assembly thus elected appears to have been a more conservative group than the provisional assembly; it represented a partial return to the Ch'ing assembly. (There is only an incomplete listing of its membership.)[50] It had few merchants, who as in the Ch'ing may have been put off by the need to disclose their wealth. It had more classically educated scholar-gentry, including three who had served in the Ch'ing assembly: Ch'en Nien-tien, Lin Yü, and Hsieh T'ao. However, it also had many members of the new gentry, such as the two representatives from Ch'ing-yüan, Liu Kung-kuan and Fan Hung-ch'ou. The president of the assembly, Hsieh Chi-yüan, had been a member of the Alliance since 1906.[51] This provincial assembly began its sessions in February 1913. It too was a deliberative and advisory body. Like its two predecessors, it struggled, generally without success, to gain some authority as a legislature. It demanded, for example, to pass on the provincial budget.[52]

The provincial assembly was complemented at the local level by district assemblies. In the final years of the post-Boxer decade, a few representative assemblies had been organized at the subdistrict level of city and town. After the revolution, many more were founded, but now at the district level. At first, like the provincial assembly, only provisional assemblies were established, usually without any regular pattern. In Ch'ing-yüan, for example, a 32-member assembly was formed in January 1912 with 6 representatives from each of the district's 4 wards, 6 from educational circles, and 2 from commercial circles. In Lo-ting each of the 6 wards elected 12 representatives to form a 72-member assembly, with a 12-man standing committee. Provisional assemblies were also established in at least seven other districts: Le-ch'ang, Kao-yao, K'ai-p'ing, Ch'ih-hsi, Hsin-hui, San-shui, and Cheng-hai.[53] In 1913 new regulations were issued, evidently by the central government, regarding district assemblies. They followed the regulations decreed by the Ch'ing and provided for the creation of a deliberative assembly (*i-shih hui*) and a smaller advisory council (*ts'an-shih hui*). Consequently, in many districts the provisional assembly was abolished and the new bicameral body founded, as was done in Kao-yao, Lo-ting, and K'ai-p'ing.[54]

The district assemblies were, in all likelihood, dominated by the landed, scholarly elite. The 20-member provisional assembly in K'ai-p'ing included 2 provincial graduates (both new-style) and 3 senior licentiates (2 old-style and 1 new-style). The 10-member advisory council in Kao-yao had 2 provincial graduates. The 30-member deliberative council in Lo-ting included 6 "irregular" senior licentiates.[55] The district assemblies, which were less urban-oriented than the late Ch'ing city and town councils (such as the Swatow council), seem to have included few merchants. The district assemblies worked much like the provincial assemblies. They were primarily deliberative and advisory bodies. In some cases, as in P'an-yü and San-shui, they elected their own district magistrate. They also had the authority to impeach the magistrate.[56]

The greatest departure from the late Ch'ing political order was provincial home rule. At various times in the recent past, gentry, merchants, and revolutionaries all had agitated for greater autonomy under the slogan, "Kwangtung belongs to the people of Kwangtung." But so long as the Ch'ing remained in power, the central authority was predominant and the provinces continued to be ruled from Peking. When the dynasty fell, Kwangtung finally became independent of the rest of the country. It remained so, both financially and administratively, until well into 1913. During this period, the Kwangtung government contributed rarely to the financial needs of the central government; it in turn received little or no financial assistance from the center, not even during its money crisis in the summer of 1912. Administratively it made its own official appointments, with the central government exercising no more authority than confirming its choices.

Moreover, practically all the officials were natives of Kwangtung and not, as under the Ch'ing with its law of avoidance, extraprovincials. Hu Han-min, Ch'en Chiung-ming, and the heads of all the provincial ministries and commissions were, without exception, natives of the province. There were, however, some exceptions among the holdover military officials, like Lung Chi-kuang (a native of Yunnan) and Wu Hsiang-ta (Chekiang). Home rule was characteristic also at the district level, where the magistrates were almost always natives of the province and somtimes of the district as well. In Lo-ting, for example, after the departure of the Ch'ing holdover (a Hunanese) in March 1912, the next four magistrates, who served through the summer of 1913, were all natives of Kwangtung, though none was a native of the department. In Kao-yao, the first two magistrates, who served until September 1913, were both natives of the district. In K'ai-p'ing, four of the five magistrates between November 1911 and August 1913 were natives of

Kwangtung, two of whom were also natives of the district. (There is no information on the origins of the fifth magistrate.) [57]

As the authority of the central administration came to end, so did the use of Mandarin, the spoken language of the external administrators. It was replaced by Cantonese. "Mandarin is nowhere heard or tolerated," a visitor to a government office in Canton commented soon after the revolution; "plain Cantonese will do." [58] This change was perhaps more than simply an expression of cultural provincialism. It may also have reflected the changed social composition of the new administration, with its influx of the non-scholar-gentry, many of whom were probably unfamiliar with Mandarin.

The passing of Mandarin and other features of the Ch'ing control system, however, opened the way for the assertion of subprovincial regionalism as well, particularly from the Swatow–Ch'ao-chou area. If Kwangtung was to be ruled by natives of Kwangtung, why should not Ch'ao-chou be ruled by natives of Ch'ao-chou too? Thus, when the Canton government removed the popular Teochiu commander Ch'en Hung-e from Swatow in March 1912 and replaced him with a "foreigner," the Teochiu *Illustrated News* raised the cry of "Ch'ao-chou for the people of Ch'ao-chou!" Similarly, if Cantonese was to be the language of administration in Canton, then why should not Teochiu be used and taught officially in the Swatow area, as some students of the Ch'ao-chou Middle School demanded of their principal early in 1913? [59] But Canton would no more allow Swatow to go its separate way than the Ch'ing had allowed Kwangtung. It denied the claims of Teochiu "nationalism" and, as we have seen, adopted the Ch'ing technique of appointing a complete outsider, Wu Hsiang-ta, to exercise its rule over the region.

Politically, the revolution thus produced a considerable enlargement of the area of popular activity. It also brought that activity out into the open and, through home rule, made it more directly relevant to the citizens of the province. Although by no means a democratic revolution, as shown by the limitations on the legislative authority of the provincial assembly, it nevertheless produced a regime that was considerably more democratic than its predecessor.

Cultural Transformation

The revolution also intensified the social and cultural changes that had been set in motion by the post-Boxer reforms. This was perhaps more evident in Kwangtung than in most other provinces. In Kwangtung,

ruled by young men with a modern education and a Western orientation, the changes were so numerous and extensive that they added up to
a radical recasting of the traditional value system, almost a cultural revolution. The social and cultural effects of the revolution were strongest in
the provincial capital; they were less keenly felt in the rest of the province.

The first cultural innovation of the revolution was undoubtedly the
discarding of the queue, for which many reformers had agitated unsuc-
cessfully in the last years of the Ch'ing. A month after the revolution,
hardly anyone in Canton still wore his queue. Those who had not removed it voluntarily had had it shorn off forcibly by the police or the
people's armies. In Swatow too, most queues were discarded quickly.
But in the rural areas, queue-cutting proceeded more slowly. In Ch'ao-
yang and Hui-lai districts, just west of Swatow, less than 10 percent of
the inhabitants had taken off their queue as of February 1912. A year
later, so many people in Ch'ao-chou prefecture still had not shaved it off
that the local pacification commissioner set a time limit for its removal.[60]

Queue-cutting led many, particularly students, to abandon the traditional mode of dress as well. They replaced the long gowns and skull
caps with suits and hats of Western design, sometimes with uninten-
tionally comic results: "Sartorially Young China displays its eagerness to
be 'right up to date' by combining the hats, boots and trousers of New
York with the coats of London and the waistcoats of Berlin." Foreign
hats were particularly popular. Even the poor who could not afford a suit
of new clothes sported "some semblance of a European cap or hat." Such
new fashions were observed not only in Canton and Swatow but also in
places like Ying-te, where in February 1913 "hats of many foreign kinds
are in evidence, and occasionally there are full suits of Western clothing
to be seen." [61]

The new regime recast the calendar according to Western lines. On
January 1, 1912, it dropped the lunar calendar, which the Ch'ing had
followed, and adopted instead the Gregorian solar calendar. Also, under
the old regime there were no holidays except for the long lunar New
Year celebration and occasional festivals during the rest of the year. The
new government set Sunday aside as an official weekly holiday and,
beginning in 1913, it discouraged celebration of the lunar New Year.
The latter measure, however, was not very successful. Most people in

Canton continued to observe the traditional holiday on February 6, 1913; only the government offices were open for business.[62]

The Kwangtung government inaugurated an unprecedented and wide-ranging program of public health and sanitation in Canton. Its health commission, headed by Dr. Li Shu-fen, systematically screened and registered all medical schools, doctors, and midwives. It segregated lepers and prohibited them from begging in the streets. It disinfected plague-infected premises and quarantined suspected plague carriers. It barred night-soil collectors from busy city streets during the daytime. It registered births and deaths. These measures, not always welcomed by the people, were enforced by Ch'en Ching-hua's police department, of which the health commission was a part. Unfortunately, the health program was one of the casualties of the regime's retrenchment late in 1912.[63]

The new government followed up on the anti-opium and anti-gambling campaigns inaugurated by the Ch'ing. It set December 31, 1912, as the deadline for all opium smokers to give up the habit. Those who continued to smoke after the deadline were fined or jailed. In March 1913 a score of well-to-do opium smokers, most of them "clad in furs and long silk coats but in fetters and chains," were seen doing scavengers' work on the bund in Canton. The ban on smoking was vigorously carried out in Swatow and Hoihow too.[64] The regime also enforced the ban on gambling.[65]

The regime updated the legal system of the province. This followed the lines of the tentative reforms of the post-Boxer decade, which provided for an independent judiciary. The new courts utilized Western legal procedures too. "Evidence is taken in a manner resembling [the] European system, after which the judge weighs up the pros and cons of each case and give[s] his judgment on its merits." The use of torture to extract confessions from the accused was disallowed. Also, according to an early pronouncement by the minister of justice, parties to lawsuits were permitted to employ counsel.[66] In the same spirit, the new regime modernized the government's office procedures. As a visitor to a government office in Canton was told, "By the American system of indexing, classifying and filing, labelling and docketing it is now possible to turn up and deal in a few minutes with a subject which formerly took weeks, perhaps months and years." Moreover, "every magistrate's yamen throughout the province will be required to adopt the new system."[67]

The revolutionary government in Kwangtung rejected the hierarchical values of the Confucian past and embraced the egalitarianism of the modern West. It eliminated the social distinctions that previously had separated the common people from the officials, and it decreed a new democratic form of address, "Mister" (*hsien-sheng*). "Kowtowing is a thing of the past," a reporter observed in Canton in December 1911. "There is no more 'Your Excellencies' [*ta lao-yeh*]. Everyone connected with the yamen is plain 'Mr. So-and-so,' and they are all approachable. There is none of the old ceremonial. All that has been done away with." [68]

The government also espoused the principle of sexual equality and women's rights. Its inclusion in the provisional provincial assembly of ten women representatives, who moreover were elected by the women themselves, was an action far ahead of its time. Unfortunately, when the Alliance was reorganized as the Nationalist Party in 1912, it was forced by its more conservative coalition partners to drop its insistence on sexual equality. Women were subsequently denied the right to participate in the December 1912 elections for the parliament and the provincial assembly. The women representatives in the Kwangtung provisional assembly twice protested this retraction of their rights, but on both occasions they lost, once by a vote of 65 to 38. [69]

Outside the government, the women of Canton organized associations to promote their own interests and encourage greater solidarity among themselves, including one association to improve women's education and another to "further and consolidate women's rights." They also founded a weekly newspaper in June 1912 "to cultivate morality and protect the rights and privileges of womankind." [70] The anti-footbinding movement continued to make substantial gains, as the Kwangtung government threatened to deprive parents and husbands of bound-footed girls of their civil rights. In Ting Hsien, Chihli, among the girls born during the 1910–14 period, the proportion with natural feet doubled again, from 40.3 percent in the previous half-decade to 80.5 percent. In other words, in Ting Hsien at least, the pernicious custom of footbinding had been practically wiped out even before the May Fourth movement. [71]

The new regime disestablished Confucianism as the ideology of the state. The modern schools of the post-Boxer era had greatly reduced the Confucian content of education, but had not eliminated it. The revolutionary government completed the process. In June 1912 the minister of education Chung Jung-kuang issued a set of regulations prohibiting all government-registered schools from teaching the classics or venerating

Confucius. The intention was not to destroy Confucianism, as many accused the government of doing, but to deprive it of official support and so abolish its privileged status in society.[72]

Toward China's other two religious traditions, Taoism and Buddhism, the regime and its followers were unambiguously hostile. As a later Chinese writer noted approvingly, Canton "was the first to set an example in eradicating superstitious practices by taking idols from the temples and dumping them into the river." Thus, on December 15, 1911, in the first flush of revolutionary success, a group of overseas Chinese Christians known as the Bomb Throwing Brigade (Cha-tan tui) rampaged through the temple of the city god and at least two other well-known Canton temples, smashing all the shrines and decapitating the statuary. The government itself in June 1912 ordered the closing of thirty nunneries in Fo-shan and the dispersal of more than three hundred young nuns. It claimed that "nuns deceive people and get the women to give them money and food in return for promised help and protection which they are unable to provide." In addition to such outright iconoclasm, the regime extended the late Ch'ing practice of appropriating temples and converting them into schools and offices. As a result, traditional religious observances lapsed. What most impressed a French correspondent early in 1912 was "the complete disappearance of the city's ritualistic character," for example, "the protective divinities posted at the gates of the various quarters, the incense sticks burning in their little niches at the entrance of all the shops." [73]

However, unlike its successor regime in the mid-1920's, the Canton government of 1911–13 was not opposed to all religions. To the contrary, as part of its pro-Western orientation, it looked with favor upon Christianity, especially Protestantism. The administration itself included many Christians, such as the minister of finance Li Yü-t'ang, the minister of education Chung Jung-kuang, the minister of civil affairs Ch'ien Shu-fen, the health commissioner Li Shu-fen, and the president of the provincial assembly Hsieh Chi-yüan. Indeed, according to one report, "In 1912 in Kwangtung sixty-five per cent of the provincial officials were Christians or had been in mission schools." [74] Moreover, the new government dropped the Ch'ing policy of not accepting mission schools for official registration.[75] The regime's attitude, no doubt, stimulated a further rapid increase in Christian missionary activity and another sharp rise in the number of converts.

In contrast to the wide-ranging cultural reforms, the economic reforms of the revolutionary government were rather limited. Most were intended to foster commercial and industrial growth, which was of benefit primarily to the merchants and entrepreneurs. One of the first acts of the new government was to tear down the Canton city walls, which it denounced as a remnant from the "age of autocracy." (Earlier, the Canton gentry and merchants had asked in vain for the removal of the walls; according to the Ch'ing officials, the walls were a useful defense against attack such as during the New Army mutiny.) In place of the walls the government proposed to build a sixty-foot-wide carriage road in order to facilitate traffic in and around the congested city. Demolition of the massive walls began on February 1, 1912. The project, however, proved to be prohibitively expensive and was soon suspended, probably in the summer, when various programs were cut back or stopped altogether in order to alleviate the money crisis. It was not to be resumed until 1918.[76]

Not all was destruction, however. Along the newly completed bund in Canton, many buildings were erected. Among them was the city's first modern multi-storied department store, a branch of the Sincere Company (Hsien-shih kung-ssu) of Hong Kong, which was so popular when it opened in the spring of 1912 that it charged 10¢ admission in order to prevent crowding in the store. As a foreign reporter commented in 1912 on the changes along the waterfront, "Modern Canton has grown up on land reclaimed from the Pearl River in little more than ten years. Hardly more than a decade ago the journey from Hong Kong ended between mud banks. Today the traveller steams up between long lines of factory chimneys and godowns, 'European-style' hotels, 'European-style' shops, and semi-Chinese stores." [77]

The regime encouraged the further development of economic nationalism. In 1912 it restricted the export of limestone from Kwangtung to the British-owned Green Island Cement Company in Hong Kong to protect and encourage its own Canton Cement Factory. This action, much criticized by British officials, almost put the Green Island Company out of business.[78] Similarly, the provincial army in 1912 led a campaign to replace foreign cigarettes with cigarettes made locally from tobacco grown in Hao-shan district. In addition, one of the popular associations active in Canton after the revolution was the Society to Support Native Products (Wei-ch'ih t'u-huo hui).[79]

Despite the political instability, the period of revolutionary rule was one of continued commercial and industrial growth. According to an observer in Canton in November 1912, "Sound enterprises are making the city an important manufacturing centre." The progress of the Canton–Hankow railroad may be indicative. Opened for 66 miles at the time of the revolution, it was extended another 50 miles by August 1913. It reached north of Ying-te to Sha-k'ou, more than halfway to the Hunan border.[80] Unfortunately, the road made little progress thereafter and was not completed until 1936.

Certainly the most interesting, though not the most successful, economic reform of the Kwangtung regime was its attempt to carry out the pledge of the Alliance to equalize land rights. It was, according to Sun Yat-sen, the one piece of unfinished business for the Alliance. As he yielded the presidency to Yüan Shih-k'ai in April 1912, Sun declared, "Today with the abdication of the Manchus and the founding of the Chinese Republic, the two principles of nationalism and democracy have been achieved; only the principle of people's livelihood has yet to be realized." [81] At the heart of the latter principle was equalization of land rights. Spurred by Sun's subsequent homecoming visit to Canton, his first since 1895, the Kwangtung government, supported by the provisional provincial assembly, inaugurated the equalization measure in June 1912.[82]

Land rights equalization aimed to prevent speculation in or monopoly of land by confiscating all future unearned increments in land value. The necessary first step was obviously to determine the current value of the land. Therefore, every landowner in the province was ordered to exchange his old title deed for a new one issued by the republican government. At this time he himself would assess the value of his land. Since the government reserved the right to purchase the land at his self-imposed price, the landowner was not likely to set it too low. Nor was he likely to set it too high either, because his annual land tax would be based upon it. The renewal of the title deeds and the assessment of the land began at the end of July and were expected at first to take no more than six months. But they took much longer, partly because much of the land in Kwangtung was owned by absentee landlords, some of them overseas Chinese, who could not return home at once. Consequently the period for deed renewal and land assessment had to be extended several times, until finally the counterrevolution intervened. Thus, the Kwangtung regime never completed the first stage of land rights equalization, but it clearly had tried.[83]

Taken altogether, the regime's reforms brought to a head the post-

Boxer tendencies toward a repudiation of traditional Chinese social practices and cultural values in favor of modern Western ones. Thus, the
gentry-officials' monopoly of political power gave way to greater popular
participation and involvement in political affairs. The Confucian classical
education yielded to a modern education based on science and technology. The subordination of women to men and of youth to age bowed to
more egalitarian relationships. Notwithstanding the geographical limitations on their effectiveness, the reforms approximated a cultural revolution. It was indeed a "new" Kwangtung.

The various reforms implemented by the new regime in Kwangtung
were distinctly "bourgeois," conforming to the ideals of political democracy, social equality, and economic development. This is particularly
reflected in the regime's preoccupation with the city and its neglect of
the countryside. Even the equalization of land rights, the one reform
directed at the countryside, was, it may be recalled, concerned not with
current agrarian problems but with future urban problems to be created
by industrialization. However, although the merchants were the group
that benefited most directly from the revolution, they remained a small
and weak social force. Nothing so epitomized the bourgeois aspirations
of the revolution as the hasty tearing down of the Canton city walls,
much as the walls of European cities had been torn down in the course of
the bourgeois revolution in the West. At the same time, nothing so epitomized the pathetic weakness of the Canton bourgeoisie as its inability
to see the job through.[84]

In contrast to the bourgeoisie, with its "precocious" ideology and its
underlying fragility, the gentry had been stripped of its Confucian ideological justification but was perhaps stronger than ever. With the demise
of the Ch'ing and, along with it, the traditional civil service system, the
gentry had lost its claims to authority as the scholarly elite. However, it
remained after the revolution as the landlord class and, even in
Kwangtung, the dominant group in society. In part, this was because
most of the leaders of the Kwangtung regime, despite their bourgeois
ideology, originated from the gentry. More important, it was because of
the regime's unconcern for and insensitivity to agrarian problems. The
government's failure to replace the countervailing power that the extraprovincial officials had exercised under the Ch'ing freed the land-
lord-gentry of most external restraints and left it more firmly in control at
the local level than ever before. Even more so than under the Ch'ing,

the gentry manipulated "self-government" and home rule in such a way as to maximize its power over the peasantry.

The Kwangtung government, characteristically, ignored the peasants' grievances against the gentry's growing domination as expressed in sporadic attacks of "revenge" upon the local gentry similar to the anti-tax riots at the end of the Ch'ing.[85] Even the workers received an unprecedented if small measure of recognition from the regime when it allowed "workers' associations" to participate in the election of Canton's twenty representatives to the provisional provincial assembly in December 1911. The peasants received nothing.

In short, the revolution in Kwangtung was not a social revolution. It was instead an urban-oriented political and cultural revolution catering to the merchants. But unfortunately the merchants were not so strong nor so numerous as to form a solid foundation for the regime. When the foundation cracked, the regime was easily toppled.

The Counterrevolution

In the summer of 1913, after less than two years in power, the revolutionary regime in Kwangtung came to a sudden end. In July, along with several other provinces in south China, it was provoked by the increasingly hostile actions of Yüan Shih-k'ai's central government into attempting the "Second Revolution." Unfortunately, the revolutionaries in 1913 had lost the critical support of the merchants and the army which they had had two years earlier. With even less fighting than in 1911, the ruling revolutionaries were routed. Kwangtung's independence was terminated. So were many of its radical reforms.[86]

The demise of the independent and revolutionary government in Kwangtung began perhaps in early 1913, when, to cope with its continuing money crisis, it allowed the central government to reassert itself into the province. Ever since he became president, Yüan Shih-k'ai had been anxious to reduce the autonomy of the former secessionist provinces and to recentralize authority. In Kwangtung all that he had managed to do at first was to claim nominally his right to make provincial appointments. Thus, in December 1912, on the "recommendation" of Governor Hu Han-min, he "confirmed" the appointment of various incumbents to their posts.[87] President Yüan's opportunity, however, came not long afterwards.

Early in 1913 the Kwangtung government still had not solved its money crisis. Despite earnest efforts to reduce expenditures and increase taxes, it was still running a budgetary deficit of half a million dollars a month, which it was meeting by pumping ever more unsecured notes into circulation. The result, as before, was to depreciate the value of its paper notes. Although the discount rate remained at about 10 percent— it was 11 percent in mid-April—it could not continue like this indefinitely without a serious loss of business confidence.[88]

The only solution was outside help. The Kwangtung government first contracted for a five million dollar loan from an American group at the end of 1912.[89] But when this fell through in February or March 1913, Canton was obliged to turn to the central government, which was about to conclude its own foreign loan, the huge Reorganization Loan from the five-power consortium of banks. On the occasion of a personal visit to Canton in March, Liang Shih-i, who was Yüan Shih-k'ai's chief secretary and general manager of the Bank of Communications, negotiated an agreement between the Kwangtung government and the central government regarding the finances of the province. Liang announced that Peking would earmark twenty-two million dollars of the Reorganization Loan for the purpose of redeeming the debased Kwangtung government notes and floating an entirely new currency issue. In return, Canton would cooperate closely with the central government in financial matters.[90] Thus, even while Liang Shih-i was still in Canton, the Kwangtung minister of finance, Liao Chung-k'ai, went to Peking to work out a proper division between provincial and national taxes.[91] The central government was beginning to cut into Kwangtung's autonomy.

Almost at once, relations between Peking and Canton became openly antagonistic. Yüan Shik-k'ai's assassination of the Nationalist Party leader Sung Chiao-jen on March 20, followed by his signing of the Reorganization Loan agreement on April 26 in disregard of the Nationalist-dominated Parliament, outraged the revolutionaries. In Kwangtung the provincial government, supported by a majority of the provincial assembly and by the Nationalist Party, condemned both the president's failure to submit the loan to Parliament for prior approval and his hypothecation of China's salt revenue to the foreign consortium as security for the loan.[92] The Canton government also resisted Yüan's attempt to appoint his own nominees to several financial posts within the province, including a new salt commissioner.[93] Kwangtung's opposition to Yüan took on a bellicose tone, as military preparations were made under the guise of mounting a patriotic expedition to expel the growing Russian presence in Mongolia.[94]

Strengthened immeasurably by the Reorganization Loan, Yüan Shih-k'ai moved toward an early confrontation with the recalcitrant provinces in south China. On June 9 he dismissed the revolutionary governor of Kiangsi province, Li Lieh-chün. Five days later, he removed Hu Han-min as governor of Kwangtung. Hoping perhaps to split the revolutionaries, he replaced Hu with Ch'en Chiung-ming. Ch'en however took over from Hu without difficulty; moreover he retained Hu's administration practically intact. A month later, with no other alternative except to submit to him, the revolutionaries in south China rose up against Yüan Shih-k'ai. On July 12 Li Lieh-chün in Kiangsi declared war on Yüan. After some apparent hesitation, Ch'en Chiung-ming followed suit. On July 18 he went before the Kwangtung provincial assembly to accuse the president of twelve major "crimes" and secured its approval for a declaration of war.[95] In all, seven provinces declared their independence of Peking. Thus began the abortive Second Revolution.

In Canton, apart from the Nationalist-dominated provincial assembly, there was scarcely any popular enthusiasm for the anti-Yüan revolution. (The same was true in Shanghai.) The merchants strongly opposed it; those in Hong Kong, freed from Canton's censorship, telegraphed their support for Yüan.[96] Public confidence in the regime, as reflected in the value of its paper currency, plummeted. On July 22, four days after the declaration of independence, the government notes were discounted 24 percent, a big drop from the 11 percent in mid-April. On July 23 the discount rate was 30 percent; on the twenty-eighth, 53 percent.[97] As in previous crises, thousands of well-to-do people flocked to Hong Kong and Macao for safety, while business in Canton came to a virtual stand-still.

For lack of popular support, the Second Revolution collapsed quickly throughout south China; in Kwangtung it lasted less than one month. Responding to the insurrection in Kwangtung, President Yüan Shih-k'ai appointed Lung Chi-kuang as the new military governor in place of Ch'en Chiung-ming and authorized his troops to invade Kwangtung. (They had left it only in January.) Coming down the West River from Kwangsi, Lung and his four thousand troops occupied Chao-ch'ing by August 1. Ch'en Chiung-ming then called upon the Kwangtung Army to repel the invasion. According to the American consulate, "his words practically fell on deaf ears." The army urged Ch'en to rescind the declaration of independence instead. When he refused, artillery troops in the army's Second Division mutinied. On August 4 they drove Ch'en from the city, set up their divisional commander Su Shen-ch'u in his place, and canceled Kwangtung's independence. Others in the army, however, were not pleased with the choice of Su Shen-ch'u. One day later they forced Su out and nominated as governor Chang Wo-ch'üan, commander of the Fifth (Independent) Brigade.[98]

By driving Ch'en Chiung-ming out and revoking the declaration of independence, the Kwangtung Army may have hoped to stop Lung Chi-kuang from proceeding further down river. If so, the stratagem did not work. Lung continued his drive toward Canton and arrived outside the city on August 11. His entry into the capital was resisted by some units of the Kwangtung Army, notably the artillerymen. It was several days before Lung's troops, fighting their way through the city streets, succeeded in taking control of the city.[99]

The defeat of the Canton revolutionary regime clearly had been facilitated by the defection of the merchants and the army, whose support it had enjoyed during the first revolution. How had that support slipped away? It was the revolutionary government's inability to solve the money crisis which alienated the merchants, who of course were the ones most vulnerable to the instability in the money market. The regime had tried earnestly and at great cost to its own reform program to maintain the value of its paper money, but the best that it had been able to do was to keep the money market from collapsing completely. The solution to the money crisis depended upon the twenty-two million dollars from the Reorganization Loan that President Yüan had set aside for redeeming the Kwangtung currency. The Canton government's objections to the loan and its antagonistic relationship with Yüan jeopardized this arrangement.

It was then that the merchants withdrew their support from the revolutionary regime. In May the Canton Chamber of Commerce, the Merchants' Society for the Maintenance of Public Peace, and the Seventy-two Guilds—all the leading merchant organizations in the city—publicly defied the Canton government to telegraph their support for the president and for the loan, which they said was "indispensable" for saving the country. Some merchants may even have called on Yüan to dismiss Hu Han-min as governor, as a Peking newspaper reported in late May.[100] Thus, weeks before the outbreak of the Second Revolution, the merchants had indicated their willingness to abandon the revolutionaries in order to secure relief from the money crisis. (The relief, incidentally, was long in coming. The value of the Kwangtung notes did not recover after the expulsion of the revolutionaries. In November 1913 they were discounted 30 percent; in May 1914, 67 percent.) [101]

It is more difficult to explain how the regime lost the support of its own army, especially since all three commanders of the Kwangtung Army, Chung Ting-chi, Su Shen-ch'u, and Chang Wo-ch'üan, had been revolutionary sympathizers. Perhaps like Yen Hsi-shan in Shansi, who also had supported the Alliance in the past, the Kwangtung commanders "admired the realistic and military-minded Yüan more than the dreamy and less effectual Sun Yat-sen." [102] In addition, they undoubtedly realized the futility of the anti-Yüan cause in view of the president's superior financial and military resources and the already evident erosion of popular support for the revolutionaries. This probably explains why Ch'en Ching-hua's police in Canton and Li Fu-lin's army on Ho-nan island did not actively support the Second Revolution either.

At the same time, the army commanders, all of whom were also natives of Kwangtung, may have rebelled against their own government, whose cause was lost anyway, in a last-ditch effort to save themselves and their province from Lung Chi-kuang's "foreign" troops. They sacrificed the revolutionaries in order to salvage what they could of provincial autonomy. Their coup, however, did not stop Lung Chi-kuang. Finally, the army commanders may simply have been subverted by agents of Yüan Shih-k'ai, notably Huang Shih-lung, who had returned to Canton for that very purpose. Huang was formerly Su Shen-ch'u's superior, and it was Su's troops that initiated the rebellion against the Ch'en Chiung-ming government. [103]

Lung Chi-kuang's forced entry into Canton in August 1913—a bitter foretaste of warlordism—ended the two-year rule of the revolutionaries in Kwangtung. As in November 1911, there was a wholesale turnover of officials. Practically all the officials of the revolutionary regime in Canton were forced to flee the province and seek asylum abroad. As the British consulate observed with unconcealed joy, the "foreign-educated young men of ultra-radical tendencies . . . have all been superseded and their departure is a distinct gain to the province. No official of Kuo-Min-Tang tendencies remains in office today and the principal senior posts are held by men who have served in one capacity or another under the Empire." [104] The only leading official to stay behind was the police superintendent, Ch'en Ching-hua, who evidently thought that Lung valued his cooperation and perhaps former friendship enough to overlook his revolutionary associations. On September 16, after a Lucullan feast at Lung's headquarters, the unsuspecting Ch'en was murdered.[105]

Lung Chi-kuang began at once to dismantle most of the reforms of the revolutionary regime. He terminated Kwangtung's autonomy and reimposed central control over the province. With the return of the old imperial officials—including, incidentally, the return of the last Ch'ing governor-general, Chang Ming-ch'i, as civil governor in July 1915—came the reestablishment of the old rule of avoidance. The officials in Kwangtung were once again extraprovincials, from the military governor (*tu-tu*), Lung Chi-kuang, and the civil governor (*min-cheng chang*), Li K'ai-shen (a native of Hupeh), down to the magistrates of the three previously cited districts of Kao-yao, Lo-ting, and K'ai-p'ing.[106] The long-evolving movement toward greater popular participation in public affairs was halted. The provincial assembly was dissolved almost at once. The district assemblies were abolished in January 1914, following President Yüan's dissolution of Parliament itself on January 10. All other programs designed to promote local self-government were terminated four months later.[107]

Numerous newspapers were suppressed. In the single month of November 1913 at least twelve papers were closed down in Canton. In Swatow the number of daily newspapers in 1914 was reduced once again to two. Various associations were banned. The offices of the Nationalist Party throughout Kwangtung were closed down on November 11, 1913. Its organ, the *China Daily News,* which had survived numerous crises since its founding in 1899, was among the Canton newspapers suppressed. Liu Ssu-fu's anarchist Cock-Crow Study Society was also banned, along with its magazine.[108]

Moreover, Lung Chi-kuang put a stop to the previous regime's incipient cultural revolution. Instead, traditional ideas and practices were reinstated. The cult of Confucius revived.[109] The incense sticks reappeared in the wall niches along the streets.[110] The traditional garb returned to favor, as the fad of Western-style clothes passed.[111] Licensed gambling, in the form of the *p'u-p'iao* and *shan-p'iao* lotteries, was reintroduced in October 1914.[112] The anti-opium drive ground to a halt.[113] The restrictions on the export of limestone to the Green Island Cement Company were lifted, in return for past British help for Yüan Shih-k'ai.[114] In another retreat from anti-imperialism, the support previously given to the Vietnamese nationalist movement was withdrawn and its leader Phan Boi Chau imprisoned in Canton.[115] Finally, in December 1915, the monarchy was reestablished with Yüan as the new dynast.

However, Yüan Shih-k'ai's counterrevolution, which tried to crush not only the revolutionary reforms but many of the late Ch'ing reforms as well, turned out to be even less of a success than the revolution. The various movements which had been gathering force during the nearly two decades from 1895 to 1913 did not remain suppressed for long. When the restraints weakened after the death of the strongman Yüan in 1916, the result was the cultural explosion of the May Fourth movement.

Conclusion

In more than just the geographical sense, Kwangtung's place in China has always been peripheral. This is probably because of its setting, in particular, its isolation and, more important, its seaward orientation so that Kwangtung literally turns its back on the rest of the country. As a result, Kwangtung has never commanded the influence that Hunan, for example, has had, nor has Canton or Hong Kong approached the importance of Shanghai as a center for the diffusion of modern ideas and movements.[1] The overseas Chinese organizers of the 1905 anti-American boycott, for example, chose Shanghai for the start of their effort even though Canton would have been the more logical place since practically all the Chinese emigrants to the United States were natives of the Pearl River delta. Shanghai was central; Canton was not. For the same reason the Yangtze faction within the Revolutionary Alliance objected to Sun Yat-sen's preoccupation with his native Kwangtung. It was perhaps not just a coincidence of timing that the Alliance achieved its long-sought success only after it had shifted its operations from south to central China.

Although Kwangtung is thus not a typical province, its experiences during the era from 1895 to 1913 were not necessarily all untypical. A great deal more revolutionary agitation took place within its borders than in any other province, though the other provinces were by no means free of revolutionary activities. Its cultural transformation during the brief post-revolutionary period was probably more extensive than most or all other provinces, but it was not the only province where the revolutionaries came to power after the revolution. The nationalist movement was probably more fully developed in Kwangtung too than in most provinces, though in its initial development it lagged behind that in the Shanghai area. But with respect to the imperialist challenge, the post-Boxer program of reforms from above, and the late Ch'ing constitutionalist movement, Kwangtung seems not to have been markedly different from the other provinces. Where differences existed, they may have been ones of degree and not of kind.

As we have seen in the case of Kwangtung, China's paramount concern throughout these nearly two decades was imperialism, as the foreign presence in China increased sharply both in scope and in intensity in the sordid aftermath of the war with Japan. Imperialism became an omnipresent, inescapable condition of life in China; it affected, directly or indirectly, every action, big or small, taken by the Chinese. The effects of imperialism, while pervasive, were ambiguous.[2] Foreign investments, for example, financed the construction of the Canton–Kowloon and the Canton–Samshui railroads in Kwangtung, while foreign trade fostered the growth of Hong Kong, Swatow, and most of the other treaty ports and foreign territories in the province. More important than its contributions to the economy was the role of imperialism as a catalyst of social, political, and intellectual change. The onslaught of imperialism after 1894 jarred the Chinese out of their traditional way of life, which until then was still essentially intact, and brought about various forms of social mobilization. Without the threat of partition, nationalism, constitutionalism, and revolution certainly would not have developed as rapidly as they did.

The baneful effects of imperialism, however, outweighed its supposed benefits. In the economic sphere, the growth of the treaty ports often took place at the expense of other nearby cities. Thus, Swatow and Hoihow prospered, while the older administrative cities inland, Ch'aochou and Kiungchow, apparently decayed. (As Hong Kong grew, Canton too declined, but Canton's former prosperity probably had also come from foreign trade.) Moreover, the opening of the treaty ports in central China had put large numbers of transport workers in Kwangtung out of work and so greatly increased the already extensive unrest in the province. As for foreign investment, the building of the Canton–Samshui branch line in no way justified the incompetence and rapaciousness of the American China Development Company, owner of the Canton–Hankow railroad concession. The company not only failed to build a single mile of the main line but also charged the Chinese government the outrageous sum of US$6,750,000 for the right to redeem the concession. This averages out to $200,000 for each mile of the 32-mile Samshui line. For the Chinese it was indeed "an expensive lesson in international finance." [3] Unfortunately the powers were not content with just one lesson; the Germans, for example, charged similarly inflated prices for the redemption of their concessions in Shantung too. [4] In any case, whatever foreign investments there were in China were more than offset by the huge outflow of funds resulting from the 1895 and 1900 war indemnities along with many smaller indemnities. The indemnity payments necessitated the levying of numerous additional taxes and helped double the cost of living (in Kwangtung at least) over the course of the post-Boxer decade. [5]

If imperialism was a catalyst of change, it was also an inhibitor of change. One positive response to imperialism, for example, was the campaign to eradicate the opium habit in China, a habit that the foreigners had helped create in the first place. But the campaign might have been even more successful than it was if the Chinese government had not been stopped by the unequal treaties from decreeing a complete and immediate ban on the importation of Indian opium into China; instead it had to accept a British plan that promised to phase out the opium shipments gradually over a period of ten years. More important, the possibility of foreign intervention, and ultimately of partition, was never far from people's thoughts at any time throughout this period. Nor was this merely paranoia on the part of the Chinese as the allied expedition against the Boxers in 1900 and the foreign support for Yüan Shih-k'ai in 1913 or, locally, the British naval intervention in the West River in 1907 and again in 1912 proved. This was a threat that, while it mobilized the Chinese in unprecedented ways, also inhibited them from acting as they otherwise might have. The Ch'ing government, for example, was nearly helpless in dealing with revolutionaries who operated from the safety of Hong Kong and the numerous foreign enclaves inside China or who sought foreign consular protection. Later, when the revolution broke out, all parties were forced to curtail their operations lest they invite foreign intervention. Locally, in Kwangtung, Governor-

General Chang Ming-ch'i yielded to the Alliance without a last-ditch stand in Canton, while nationally the revolutionaries accepted an early compromise with Yüan Shih-k'ai.

The fear of intervention and the resulting inhibitions produced a widespread sense of shame and inferiority among the Chinese that ultimately was perhaps the most pernicious effect of imperialism upon China. The Chinese became their own worse critics, magnifying every perceived weakness, whether it was the opium habit or gambling or lack of patriotism, into a source of "national shame" and a cause for self-flagellation. To Ou Chü-chia and many other radicals and revolutionaries indoctrinated with the ideas of Social Darwinism, their fellow countrymen were no better than dumb animals doomed to extinction in the international struggle for survival. As the essayist and anti-Manchu revolutionary Su Man-shu put it in 1903, "Foreigners and people from other provinces are fond of saying that if China is enslaved at all she will be enslaved thanks to us Cantonese . . . We have a natural instinct for cringing to foreigners, which is, no doubt, why the profession of houseboy is a Cantonese speciality." [6] The psychological costs of such despair and self-doubt are incalculable.

Challenged from without and also from within, the Manchu court in the post-Boxer era was far from the creature that is often portrayed, submissive abroad and reactionary at home. It, in fact, vigorously combatted imperialism through the rights recovery movement, which, costly as it may have been, resulted in the redemption of a number of railroad and mining concessions. The court's new nationalistic stance was partly responsible for the appreciable diminution of the foreign threat to China soon after the Boxer Rebellion. This, however, should not be overstressed, for the relaxation of the imperialist pressures upon China stemmed more from the rivalry among the foreign powers than from any actions by the court. The Ch'ing government, for example, would not have had such striking success in curbing Germany's sphere of interest in Shantung if the Germans had not been diplomatically isolated and opposed by the British and the Japanese. Thus, it was able to assert customs control over the German leasehold of Tsingtao, but it was unable to do the same in the Japanese leasehold of Dairen. [7] The court's only option, which to its credit it exercised with great effect, was to capitalize upon the splits among the powers. This was why there was so much nervous commotion in China in late 1907 when the foreigners decided to resolve their differences among themselves. It remains to be investigated how well the Ch'ing was able to cope with the foreigners' united front after 1907.

The court had greater latitude in dealing with domestic affairs and was able to display greater initiative. Its program of reforms in the post-Boxer era was a serious, comprehensive, and often successful attempt at radical social transformation; it was not a sham nor mere window-dressing, as partisans of the revolutionary movement have charged.[8] The new school system and the constitutional program both made substantial progress before the end of the decade, while the military reforms were probably more advanced than the case of Kwangtung would suggest. Other reforms, such as the creation of an independent judiciary, had not had time to develop before they were interrupted by the revolution. Most of the credit for the success of these reforms belongs to the court. It not only decreed that the reforms be initiated but, just as important, it ensured that they were carried out by its appointments to the high provincial posts. In Kwangtung as in Shantung conservatives and reactionaries like T'an Chung-lin and Kang-i were replaced by reform-minded, nationalist officials like Ts'en Ch'un-hsüan and Chang Ming-ch'i.[9] The post-Boxer reforms, moreover, did not end with the overthrow of the dynasty. In most instances, the republican government continued and extended them. Many, though not all, of the apparently new institutions of republican China thus actually originated in the late Ch'ing.

The court's inept performance at both the beginning and the end of the post-Boxer decade, therefore, should not blind us to its considerable achievements in between. When compared with its immediate successors, the governments of Yüan Shih-k'ai, the warlords, and Chiang Kai-shek, the post-Boxer regime stands up well in many respects: the geographical extent under its control, its administrative effectiveness, its economic stability and financial solvency, its control over the military, its success at rights recovery, its willingness to experiment with constitutional reform and popular representation in government. It was, in retrospect, the best national government China was to enjoy for the rest of the half-century.

Unquestionably, the most astounding aspect of social change after 1895 was the extent to which a large segment of the Chinese population was politicized. The process of politicization, which was a radical departure from the governmentally enforced tradition of popular noninvolvement in political affairs, began shortly after the war with Japan with the formation of the gentry-led study societies; it picked up momentum during the post-Boxer decade and continued through the revolution without interruption until the counterrevolution in 1913. (Here, as with the reforms from above, the early Republic was the heir to the late Ch'ing.) In the course of these two decades, the traditional ban on popular societies fell by the wayside as all sorts of voluntary associations were formed. Even though most of these organizations during the Ch'ing were nonpolitical or only marginally political in nature, they nevertheless contributed to the politicization of their members because such nonpolitical groups "tend to acquire a political tinge, particularly in countries where more open outlets for political activities are not available," as was the case in China before the revolution.[10] They paved the way for the explicitly political parties that appeared almost at once after the revolution.

In addition, newspapers, an innovation of the late nineteenth century, became institutionalized in this era. They not only increased numerically in the major cities but were founded in more and more communities. They helped create a popular opinion where before it had scarcely existed.[11] Mass demonstrations, beginning with the anti-Russian controversy over Manchuria in 1903 and the anti-American boycott in 1905, occurred with increasing frequency and effectiveness. Nationalism was no longer a state of mind among a few far-seeing individuals like Wang T'ao [12] nor an official program of rights recovery carried out by the government. It was truly a mass movement. To deny the existence of a mass nationalism in China before 1937 simply because it did not comprehend the peasantry is to restrict the meaning of "mass" unnecessarily.[13] Mass protests also played an important part in the constitutional movement. They prodded the court to inaugurate the self-government program in the first place; they later forced it to speed up its constitutional timetable. The political process, which until 1895 had been largely dominated by the court and its officials, had by the time of the revolution become a two-way process with much interaction between the rulers and the ruled.

As a result, several new social groups entered the public arena.[14] The merchants, whose associations were accorded formal official recognition for the first time through the chambers of commerce, quickly became a significant and independent force in politics; in the more commercialized places like Canton they began to challenge the traditional dominance of

the gentry. They were particularly active as organizers of the various nationalist demonstrations. Soldiers, hitherto even more despised than
merchants, achieved a new standing in society with the formation of the
New Armies, as popular awareness of the foreign military threat to
China's sovereignty grew. Students and youths, because of their adapt-
ability to the rapidly changing conditions of post-1895 China and because of the great demand for their expertise in the modern fields of
learning, similarly acquired a new importance in what was formerly a
gerontocratic society. From the postwar reform movement of K'ang Yu-
wei and Liang Ch'i-ch'ao to the revolutionary government of Hu Han-
min and Ch'en Chiung-ming, the politics of the era was youth-
dominated to an unusual extent. Women too began to emancipate themselves from their traditional seclusion and bondage to men, as the practice of footbinding declined sharply and the opportunities for formal
public education increased. They played a significant if auxiliary role in
both the nationalist and the revolutionary movement. This early campaign for women's rights culminated in the suffrage movement of 1912,
which however was generally unsuccessful except in Kwangtung.[15]

Such extensive social change did not leave the gentry unaffected.
Unlike the other groups, the gentry already enjoyed the right of participation in politics under the old regime either as officials in distant governmental posts or as directors of a variety of self-government programs
in their home community. But these were essentially administrative duties. The gentry's activities after 1895 extended far beyond mere participation in government. Like the other groups, they too became involved
in extra-governmental politics, beginning with the formation of the
study societies in the postwar period and reaching its peak in the petition movement organized by the gentry-dominated provincial assemblies
to speed up the summoning of parliament. The one major group that
was largely unaffected by the events of 1895–1913, except in a negative
way, was the peasantry. The social mobilization of this period was thus
essentially an urban process, as it was to remain until the anti-Japanese
war of resistance thirty years later.

In these and other respects—the political and social activism, the
merchants' independence, the social egalitarianism as exemplified by the
rising status of youth and women, the anti-imperialist nationalism, the
ideological orientation toward the modern West, the cult of the new,
the urban basis—the period 1895–1913 clearly prepared the way for the
May Fourth movement of 1919. So also did the overthrow of the mon-

archy and, perhaps most important, the remarkably quick decline of Confucianism. As late as 1898 Confucianism was still a vital matter for both K'ang Yu-wei and his conservative critics. By 1905 it was no longer so; otherwise the traditional Confucian-based examination system could not have been abolished with such ease. By 1909 special schools were being founded in a losing effort to keep alive the classical studies of antiquity. By the time of May Fourth all that was left for the opponents of "Confucius & Sons" to do was to administer the coup de grace. The period 1895–1913, which witnessed the demise of the old order and the emergence of the new, may thus justifiably be considered as the watershed between traditional and modern China.[16]

The revolutionary movement was only one element in this much larger process of politicization and social mobilization. It shared many points of contact with the other, nonrevolutionary movements. The revolutionaries generally came from the same social elite as the nationalists and constitutionalists and shared their anxieties about the foreign threat to China as well as their commitment to a radical transformation of Chinese society. The nationalists and constitutionalists often opposed the Ch'ing with no less vigor than the revolutionaries. In the case of the railroad protection movement in 1911, their opposition even developed into an open rebellion. On numerous occasions, reformers abetted the revolutionary cause, as when the newspapers in Chekiang and Shanghai voiced sympathy for the revolutionary martyr Ch'iu Chin in 1907 [17] or when the Canton gentry and merchants publicly supported the New Army mutineers in 1910. Revolutionaries aided the reform causes too, as when Sung Chiao-jen worked as a translator for the court's constitutional study mission in 1906–07 or when he later assisted the Ch'ing Foreign Ministry during China's territorial dispute with Japan over a stretch of the Korean border.[18]

The reform movements and the revolutionary movement were so intertwined that they sometimes seemed to be indistinguishable from each other. However, practically all the opposition to the Ch'ing expressed by the nationalists and constitutionalists was not "revolutionary" (as defined in the Introduction) because its purpose was peaceful, not violent, change. Even the railroad protection rebellion that broke out in Szechwan in September 1911 was nonrevolutionary, despite its violence, because it basically sought a change in government policy—the cancellation of the Hu-kuang loan agreement and restoration of the railroad to local management—and not a change of the government itself. Therefore, notwithstanding extensive superficial resemblances, the post-Boxer radicalism was not, strictly speaking, revolutionary.

There was a further connection between the revolutionary and the reform movements: the strength of the revolutionaries varied in inverse proportion to the reformers' confidence in the Ch'ing. This was because the revolutionary movement from beginning to end found its basic support among disenchanted, frustrated reformers. Thus, the Society to Restore China's Prosperity was active among the Westernized Chinese reformers after the Sino-Japanese war and again after the Boxer Rebellion, while the Society to Protect the Emperor flourished among the Confucian-educated gentry reformers following the coup d'etat against the "hundred days of reform." The Revolutionary Alliance similarly drew upon the radical new students uncertain about the future of the post-Boxer reforms. Conversely, when substantial reforms were being carried out and public confidence in the regime was high, the revolutionary movement then lost much of its support. Thus, the Society to Restore China's Prosperity was inactive during the 1895–1898 postwar reforms. Later, when the post-Boxer reforms were inaugurated, the Society to Protect the Emperor dropped its former insistence on revolutionary change. Finally, when the constitutional reforms were implemented in the last years of the post-Boxer decade, many members of the Alliance ceased for all practical purposes to be revolutionaries. Contrary to the mythology of the revolution, the Alliance did not gain steadily in strength from its formation in 1905 until the Wuchang uprising in 1911.

The chances of revolutionary success, therefore, depended less upon the efforts of the revolutionaries themselves than upon the climate of opinion within China. There could not have been a revolution without a revolutionary situation, a condition characterized in large part by the estrangement of the elite from the incumbent regime. Such a situation had existed in 1900, at the time of the Boxer Rebellion and the allied expedition against Peking, when many provincial leaders had ignored even so important a matter as the court's declaration of war. Only the prompt initiation of the post-Boxer reforms had restored public confidence and defused the explosive situation. As a result, the court was able to withstand the attacks of the Alliance in 1907 and early 1908. However, loyalty to the regime was never again as deep as it had been before the Boxer troubles; it was now conditional on the court's implementation of its reform program and on its responsiveness to the demands of the politicized elite. When the court faltered again in the spring of 1911, a second revolutionary situation quickly developed. So eroded was public confidence in the court after this that when it was toppled a little later, practically no one, not even its own officials, came to its defense.

The role of the Alliance in the making of the 1911 Revolution thus was much more modest than is usually claimed for it, though it was by no means insignificant. If a revolutionary situation had not arisen in 1911 independently of its efforts, the Alliance would probably have been no more successful then than it had been in 1907–08. On the other hand, if the Alliance had not taken advantage of the revolutionary situation in 1911, the court might well have weathered the storm as it had done in 1900. For a revolutionary situation does not automatically result in a revolution; it is a necessary but not a sufficient precondition of revolution. This, then, was the role of the Alliance in 1911: to convert a revolutionary situation into a revolution. It accomplished this not only by precipitating the revolution with its Wuchang uprising but just as much by demonstrating through its past efforts that it was a credible alternative to the Ch'ing. It thereby forced the nonrevolutionary elite, deeply alienated from the Ch'ing, either to accept the Alliance, as a few of them (like the Canton merchants) did, or else to search for a middle course between it and the Ch'ing, as most of them (like the Canton gentry and Yüan Shih-k'ai) tried to do. (Yüan succeeded where the Canton gentry failed.) In either case, the Alliance, even though it was too weak and disorganized to have carried out the revolution by itself except in certain areas like Canton, was instrumental in bringing about the collapse of the Ch'ing.

There is much in the demise of the Ch'ing that resembles the traditional process of dynastic collapse.[19] One classical feature of the 1911 Revolution was the decline in power of the central government and the corresponding increase in power of the provinces, or what has been misleadingly termed "regionalism."[20] Such military-bureaucratic machines as Li Hung-chang's in Chihli or Chang Chih-tung's in Hupeh were in reality based more on personalities than on geographical regions; it was more personalism than regionalism. In Kwangtung, for example, even though the province would appear to be geographically conducive to such a development, no "regionalist" organization emerged at any time during the late Ch'ing. Instead, what developed, especially after 1895, were diverse attempts by a variety of individuals and groups, ranging in

Kwangtung from revolutionaries like Ou Chü-chia to reformist gentry members like Liang Ting-fen and Chiang K'ung-yin and to imperial officials like Li Hung-chang and Chang Ming-ch'i, to achieve some sort of provincial autonomy. These efforts, neatly expressed in slogans such as "Kwangtung for the natives of Kwangtung!" finally bore fruit in the 1911 Revolution, as many provinces got rid of their centrally appointed officials and achieved home rule. Yüan Shih-k'ai's attempt to recentralize authority, which provoked the abortive Second Revolution in the south, was only momentarily successful. When he died in 1916 the nation plunged headlong into the anarchy of warlordism, the ultimate in the "regionalization" of power.

Two other classical features of the revolution were the growth of gentry power and the attendant immiseration of the peasantry. The main beneficiaries of the decentralization of power in the aftermath of the Taiping Rebellion were the gentry. Decentralization in the post-Taiping period often took the form of the gentry-led and officially sanctioned local defense associations; in the post-Boxer era, it took many forms, such as the education associations, the offices to arrange for self-government, and the provincial and subdistrict deliberative assemblies. The gentry, adapting to the abolition of the traditional examination system with surprising ease, dominated these new institutions and used them to wrest ever more power from the officials, as they did for example with the provincial assembly. As the power of the outsider officials waned, so the power of the local gentry waxed. The revolution gave the gentry yet additional opportunities to increase their power. They were the ones who were most anxious during the revolutionary crisis to find an alternative to both the Ch'ing and the Alliance. The hoped-for alternative was more self-government, for "self"-government meant essentially gentry government. In many provinces the gentry apparently achieved their aim right away; even in Kwangtung, where they were prevented by the revolutionaries from taking power directly, they soon gained much of what they wanted through home rule.

If the gentry were ultimately the chief gainers from the post-Boxer reforms and the revolution, the peasants were the primary losers. They bore in added taxes and rents the costs of the new schools and the various self-government programs of the late Ch'ing, even though they themselves derived no benefits from these reforms. Moreover, they were subject to increasing domination by the gentry, as the latter gained power steadily at the expense of the outsider officials, who correspondingly were less and less able to restrain the exploitative tendencies of the gentry-landlords. This growing gentry domination produced in reaction a remarkable upsurge of anti-gentry riots by the hard-pressed peasants. The situation worsened after the establishment of the Republic, when home rule prevailed and the local officials were often in league with the gentry. Whereas at the end of the Ch'ing the peasants still had been able to get a measure of redress from the officials, now this was no longer likely. There was no redress from the revolutionaries either, who even where they were in power were indifferent to the plight of the peasantry. This was the beginning of the rampant landlordism of the republican era.

However, the 1911 Revolution, for all its traditionalist features, was more than just another turn of the dynastic cycle, and the Republic was more than just another dynasty in different guise.[21] Because of the great social, cultural, and intellectual changes that had occurred in China since 1895, which affected the gentry as much as they affected the other groups, it was impossible for tradition simply to repeat itself in 1911. It was symptomatic of the fundamentally changed ethos of post-1895 China that a typical end-of-dynasty phenomenon like the increase in gentry power, which had begun in the late nineteenth century in a traditional way with the formation of local defense associations, ended up in a distinctly modern form, that is, the popularly elected assemblies. The proof came during the counterrevolution with the crushing defeat of Yüan Shih-k'ai's attempt to resurrect the monarchy. Thus, if the 1911 Revolution accomplished nothing else, it showed that the dynastic system was gone for good and that the republic was here to stay.

In short, the 1911 Revolution was, despite its shaky aftermath, a revolution. It was, specifically, not one but two revolutions. One was the narrowly political revolution of 1911–12 that overthrew the system of monarchical rule. The other was the broader cultural revolution of 1895–1913 which destroyed the Confucian system of values. Both of these were permanent achievements as proven by Yüan Shih-k'ai's failure to revive either the monarchy or Confucianism. The 1911 Revolution, it is true, failed to bring forth a new society to replace the one it had swept aside. It was more successful at destruction than at reconstruction. Nevertheless, in its embrace of nationalism, egalitarianism, and popular participation in social and political affairs, it clearly pointed the way to the creative achievements of May Fourth and beyond.

Notes, Bibliography, Glossary, and Index

Abbreviations used in the notes

DR   China, Imperial Maritime Customs, *Decennial Reports on the Trade, Navigation, Industries, etc., of the Ports Open to Foreign Commerce in China and Corea . . . ,* by years

DS/CD   United States, General Records of the Department of State, Despatches of U.S. Consuls, 1901–1906, by consulate

DS/DF   ————, Records of the Department of State, 1910–1929, the decimal file

DS/NF   ————, Numerical File of the Department of State, 1906–1910

FO   Great Britain, Foreign Office archives

HC   *hsien-chih* (also *hsien hsü-chih* or *chih*)

HHKM   *Hsin-hai ko-ming*

HIL   *Hsin-hai ko-ming hui-i lu*

HKT   *Hong Kong Telegraph*

HLHCC   *Ko-ming hsien-lieh hsien-chin chuan*

HT   Hsüan-t'ung

HTJP   *Hua-tzu jih-pao*

KH   Kuang-hsü

KKWH   *Chung-hua min-kuo k'ai-kuo wu-shih-nien wen-hsien*

KMWH   *Ko-ming wen-hsien*

NCH   *North China Herald*

SCMP   *South China Morning Post*

TFTC   *Tung-fang tsa-chih*

TR   China, Imperial Maritime Customs, *Returns of Trade and Trade Reports,* by year and port

WWP   China, Wai-wu pu archives

Notes

Introduction

1. Chalmers Johnson, *Revolutionary Change* (Boston, 1966), pp. 3, 5.

2. For a recent example, see Ta-ling Lee, *Foundations of the Chinese Revolution, 1905–1912 (An Historical Record of the T'ung-meng Hui)* (New York, 1970). Chün-tu Hsüeh, *Huang Hsing and the Chinese Revolution* (Stanford, 1961), is a revisionist work that nevertheless falls within the orthodox tradition; it deemphasizes the role of Sun Yat-sen but continues to stress that of the Alliance. Mary Clabaugh Wright, ed., *China in Revolution: The First Phase, 1900–1913* (New Haven, 1968), was the first major study to question the entire orthodoxy, but it did not offer a fully worked out alternative version of its own. For what purports to be, already, a *re*-revisionist interpretation, see Roger V. Des Forges, *Hsi-liang and the Chinese National Revolution* (New Haven, 1973).

3. Lawrence Stone, "Theories of Revolution," *World Politics,* 18:159 (1966).

4. Johnson, pp. 60, 70–71.

5. Johnson, pp. 80–87.

6. Crane Brinton, *The Anatomy of Revolution* (New York, 1952), pp. 44, 52.

7. Johnson, pp. 71, 88–97, 106.

8. Johnson, p. 97.

9. Harry Eckstein, "On the Etiology of Internal Wars," *History and Theory,* 4:160 (1965).

10. Brinton, p. 40.

11. Eckstein, p. 160; Stone, p. 167; Brinton, p. 41.

12. Stone, p. 172; see James C. Davies, "Toward a Theory of Revolution," *American Sociological Review,* 27:1–19 (1962).

13. Brinton, p. 53.

14. Johnson, pp. 98–99; cf. Eckstein, pp. 140–143.

15. Brinton, p. 78; see also Vidya Prakash Dutt, "The First Week of the Revolution: The Wuchang Uprising," in Wright, ed., *China in Revolution*, pp. 383–416.

16. See Charles Tilly, "The Analysis of a Counter-Revolution," *History and Theory*, 3:30–58 (1963).

17. See Mary Backus Rankin, *Early Chinese Revolutionaries: Radical Intellectuals in Shanghai and Chekiang, 1902–1911* (Cambridge, 1971); Charles H. Hedtke, "Reluctant Revolutionaries: Szechwan and the Ch'ing Collapse, 1898–1911," Ph.D. diss., University of California at Berkeley, 1968; Joseph W. Esherick, "Reform, Revolution and Reaction: The 1911 Revolution in Hunan and Hupeh," Ph.D. diss., University of California at Berkeley, 1971; and Samuel Yale Kupper, "Revolution in China: Kiangsi Province, 1905–1913," Ph.D. diss., University of Michigan, 1973. See also three papers prepared for the 1965 Wentworth, New Hampshire, conference on the 1911 Revolution: Charlton M. Lewis, "Foreign Encroachment, Reform and Revolution, 1900–1907: The Response of the Hunan Gentry," and William R. Johnson, "Revolution and Reconstruction in Kweichow" and "Revolution and Reconstruction in Yunnan: A Sketch."

18. Frederic Wakeman, Jr., *Strangers at the Gate: Social Disorder in South China, 1839–1861* (Berkeley, 1966); and Ezra F. Vogel, *Canton under Communism: Programs and Politics in a Provincial Capital, 1949–1968* (Cambridge, 1969).

19. For a succinct survey of economic developments during this period, see Albert Feuerwerker, *The Chinese Economy, ca. 1870–1911* (Ann Arbor, 1969).

1. On the Eve of Change

1. This discussion of the geography of Kwangtung is based upon the following works: George Babcock Cressey, *China's Geographic Foundations: A Survey of the Land and Its People* (New York, 1934); Theodore Shabad, *China's Changing Map: National and Regional Development, 1949–71* (New York, 1972); Great Britain, Naval Intelligence Division, *China Proper* (1944–45); *The Christian Occupation of China* (Shanghai, 1922), pp. 157–174; B. C. Henry, *Ling-Nam, or Interior Views of South China* (London, 1886); J. Thomson, *The Straits of Malacca, Indo-China and China* (London, 1875), pp. 179–288; N. B. Dennys, *The Treaty Ports of China and Japan* (London, 1867), pp. 1–242; and Vogel, chap. 1. See also Liang Jen-ts'ai, *Economic Geography of Kwangtung* (JPRS/DC-389 [1958]).

2. C. K. Yang, *A Chinese Village in Early Communist Transition* (Cambridge, 1959), pp. 43–45.

3. Cressey, p. 354.

4. *Christian Occupation of China*, p. 158; cf. Cressey, p. 359.

5. See Ho Ke-en, "The Tanka or Boat People of South China," in F. S. Drake, ed., *Symposium on Historical, Archeological and Linguistic Studies on Southern China, South-East Asia and the Hong Kong Region* (Hong Kong, 1967), pp. 120–123; T'ung-tsu Ch'ü, *Law and Society in Traditional China* (Paris, 1965), pp. 129–133; Chung-li Chang, *The Chinese Gentry: Studies on Their Role in Nineteenth-Century Chinese Society* (Seattle, 1955), p. 183, n. 74; and *Christian Occupation of China*, pp. 158, 367.

6. These comments about the levels of development for the different regions and

subregions of Kwangtung at the turn of the century are based on G. William Skinner, "Marketing and Social Structure in Rural China, Part II," *Journal of Asian Studies,* 24:207–208 (1965); note however that Skinner's identification of the regions differs slightly from mine.

7. Ta Chen, *Emigrant Communities in South China: A Study of Overseas Migration and Its Influence on Standards of Living and Social Change* (New York, 1940), pp. 82–84.

8. See R. A. D. Forrest, "The Southern Dialects of Chinese," appendix to Victor Purcell, *The Chinese in Southeast Asia* (London, 1965), pp. 569–571; Adele M. Fielde, *Pagoda Shadows: Studies from Life in China* (Boston, 1884), pp. 39–47; Wan Lo, "Communal Strife in Mid-Nineteenth-Century Kwangtung: The Establishment of Ch'ih-ch'i," *Papers on China,* 19:112–113, n. 9 (1965).

9. *Nan Shina sōran* (Taihoku, 1943), pp. 389–390; cf. *Christian Occupation of China,* p. 158.

10. For a rough mapping of the language groups, see *Christian Occupation of China,* p. 173; and Herold J. Wiens, *China's March to the Tropics* (Hamden, 1954), map 23.

11. See Henry, pp. 180, 492.

12. See Lo Hsiang-lin, *K'o-chia yen-chiu tao-lun* (Hsin-ning, 1933).

13. Cf. Lo Hsiang-lin, *K'o-chia yen-chiu tao-lun,* pp. 5–6; Tsou, Lu, *Hui-ku lu* (Nanking and Taipei, 1947–51), 1:26–28.

14. *Christian Occupation of China,* p. 352.

15. See Wan Lo.

16. G. B. Endacott, *A History of Hong Kong* (London, 1964), pp. 243, 252–253.

17. Hosea Ballou Morse, *The International Relations of the Chinese Empire* (Taipei, n.d.), 1:43–46, 337–341; 2:386–388; Dennys, pp. 202–229; *China Proper,* 2:340–349; *NCH,* March 12, 1897, p. 437.

18. Arnold Wright and H. A. Cartwright, *Twentieth Century Impressions of Hong Kong, Shanghai, and Other Treaty Ports of China* (London, 1908), pp. 784, 787–788; *HKT,* Sept. 25, 1909, p. 3.

19. *China Proper,* 3:266–271; Dennys, pp. 230–242; Thomson, pp. 279–288; Lord Charles Beresford, *The Break-up of China* (New York, 1900), p. 177; Wright and Cartwright, pp. 829–836.

20. Henry, p. 339; *China Proper,* 3:237–240; Morse, *International Relations,* 1:562–563.

21. Paul King, *In the Chinese Customs Service: A Personal Record of Forty-seven Years* (London, 1924), p. 170; *China Proper,* 3:235–237; Morse, *International Relations,* 2:302.

22. For Protestant activity, see *Christian Occupation of China,* pp. 160–162; for Catholic activity, see Adrien Launay, *Histoire des missions en Chine: Mission du Kouang-tong, monographies des districts par les missionnaires* (Paris, 1917).

23. Kenneth Scott Latourette, *A History of Christian Missions in China* (New York, 1932), pp. 324–325.

24. See *The China Mission Hand-book* (Shanghai, 1896); D. MacGillivray, *A Century of Protestant Missions in China, 1807–1907* (Shanghai, 1907); and *Christian Occupation of China,* pp. 160–162.

25. Yen-p'ing Hao, *The Comprador in Nineteenth Century China: Bridge between East and West* (Cambridge, 1970), p. 99; Morse, *International Relations,* 2:231–233; Thomson, p. 284.

26. Chi-ming Hou, *Foreign Investment and Economic Development in China, 1840–1937* (Cambridge, 1965), pp. 82, 84; Endacott, pp. 196, 259.

27. *China Mission Hand-book,* part 2, p. 210.

28. Charles Hodge Corbett, *Lingnan University* (New York, 1963), pp. 7–28.

29. Endacott, pp. 241–242.

30. Lindsay Ride, "The Early Medical Education of Sun Yat-sen," in Jen Yu-wen and Lindsay Ride, *Sun Yat-sen: Two Commemorative Essays* (Hong Kong, 1970), pp. 25–27; Endacott, pp. 249–250.

31. Endacott, p. 240; *China Mission Hand-book,* part 2, pp. 54–61; Ride, p. 26.

32. See Daniel H. Bays, "The Nature of Provincial Political Authority in Late Ch'ing Times: Chang Chih-tung in Canton, 1884–1889," *Modern Asian Studies,* 4:325–347 (1970).

33. Knight Biggerstaff, *The Earliest Modern Government Schools in China* (Ithaca, 1961), pp. 36–43; Nancy Evans, "The Banner-School Background of the Canton T'ung-wen kuan," *Papers on China,* 22A:89–103 (1969).

34. On the arsenal and shipyard, see Wang Erh-min, *Ch'ing-chi ping-kung-yeh ti hsing-ch'i* (Taipei, 1963), pp. 111–113; Bays, pp. 333–335; Biggerstaff, pp. 49–50, n. 68.

35. William Ayers, *Chang Chih-tung and Educational Reform in China* (Cambridge, 1971), pp. 108–113; Biggerstaff, pp. 48–49, 54–57, 64–65, 80; John L. Rawlinson, *China's Struggle for Naval Development, 1839–1895* (Cambridge, 1967), pp. 155–156; Bays, pp. 333–335.

36. Ayers, p. 105, n. 17.

37. Albert Feuerwerker, *China's Early Industrialization: Sheng Hsüan-huai (1844–1916) and Mandarin Enterprise* (Cambridge, 1958), pp. 190–207; *China Proper,* 3:596–597; FO 371/1663, Canton intelligence report for the fourth quarter, 1908; Ayers, p. 106, n. 18; Biggerstaff, pp. 65–68.

38. Frank H. H. King, *Money and Monetary Policy in China, 1845–1895* (Cambridge, 1965), pp. 225–228.

39. Thomas E. LaFargue, *China's First Hundred* (Pullman, 1942), pp. 33–34, 111–113; on Chan T'ien-yu, see Howard L. Boorman and Richard C. Howard, *Biographical Dictionary of Republican China* (New York, 1967–71), 1:12–15.

40. See Lü Shih-ch'iang, *Chung-kuo kuan-shen fan-chiao ti yüan-yin, 1860–1874* (Taipei, 1966), especially the appendix, pp. 202–260; *History of the South China Mission of the American Presbyterian Church, 1845–1920* (Shanghai, 1927); Lloyd Eastman, "The Kwangtung Anti-foreign Disturbances during the Sino-French War," *Papers on China,* 13:131 (1959).

41. Joseph R. Levenson, *Liang Ch'i-ch'ao and the Mind of Modern China* (Cambridge, 1959), p. 16.

42. Jung-pang Lo, *K'ang Yu-wei: A Biography and a Symposium* (Tucson, 1967), p. 36.

43. Hsiao I-shan, *Ch'ing-tai t'ung-shih* (Taipei, 1962–63), 4:2263–2264; Jen Yu-wen, "The Youth of Dr. Sun Yat-sen," in Jen Yu-wen and Lindsay Ride, *Sun Yat-sen: Two Commemorative Essays,* pp. 20–22.

44. Jung-pang Lo, pp. 3, 45, 53; Levenson, pp. 17–18.

45. Kenneth E. Folsom, *Friends, Guests, and Colleagues: The Mu-fu System in the Late Ch'ing Period* (Berkeley, 1968), pp. 76, 138–139.

46. Lloyd E. Eastman, "Political Reformism in China Before the Sino-Japanese War," *Journal of Asian Studies,* 27:695–710 (1968); Kwang-Ching Liu, "Nineteenth-Century China: The Disintegration of the Old Order and the Impact of the West," in Ping-ti Ho and Tang Tsou, eds., *China in Crisis* (Chicago, 1968), vol. 1, bk. 1, pp. 138–149; Harold Z. Schiffrin, *Sun Yat-sen and the Origins of the Chinese Revolution* (Berkeley, 1968), pp. 20–22; Yen-p'ing Hao, "Cheng Kuan-ying: The Comprador as Reformer," *Journal of Asian Studies,* 29:15–22 (1969); Feuerwerker, *China's Early Industrialization,* pp. 116–117.

47. See James R. Townsend, *Political Participation in Communist China* (Berkeley, 1969), pp. 11–20.

48. A map of the districts appears in *Christian Occupation of China,* p. 157; a list of the districts, in G. M. H. Playfair, *The Cities and Towns of China: A Geographical Dictionary* (Taipei, 1967), appendix, pp. xiv–xv.

49. See T'ung-tsu Ch'ü, *Local Government in China under the Ch'ing* (Cambridge, 1962), pp. 169–173; Ping-ti Ho, *The Ladder of Success in Imperial China: Aspects of Social Mobility, 1368–1911* (New York, 1962), pp. 17–41; Chung-li Chang, part 1; Maurice Freedman, *Lineage Organization in Southeastern China* (London, 1958), pp. 52–59; John Watt, "Leadership Criteria in Late Imperial China," *Ch'ing-shih wen-t'i,* 2.3:17–39 (1970); and Philip A. Kuhn, *Rebellion and Its Enemies in Late Imperial China: Militarization and Social Structure, 1796–1864* (Cambridge, 1970), pp. 3–4.

50. Kung-chuan Hsiao, *Rural China: Imperial Control in the Nineteenth Century* (Seattle, 1960), p. 242.

51. See Kuhn; also Wakeman, *Strangers at the Gate,* esp. chaps. 6, 15, and 17.

52. Jung-pang Lo, p. 39.

53. P'an-yü *HC,* 12:32–32b; *Shina shobetsu zenshi* (Tokyo, 1917), 1:973–982; *DR,* 1892–1901, p. 198; Ho Ping-ti, *Chung-kuo hui-kuan shih-lun* (Taipei, 1966), pp. 51–52.

54. Sybille van der Sprenkel, *Legal Institutions in Manchu China: A Sociological Analysis* (London, 1962), p. 91; Hosea Ballou Morse, *The Gilds of China* (Taipei, 1960), pp. 53–57; *DR,* 1882–91, pp. 537–540. See also John Stewart Burgess, *The Guilds of Peking* (New York, 1928).

55. J. G. Kerr, "The Native Benevolent Institutions of Canton," *China Review,* 2.2:88–95 (1873) and 3.2:108–114 (1874); Nan-hai *HC,* 6:10b–12; John Henry Gray, *Walks in the City of Canton* (Hong Kong, 1875), pp. 167–168; Thomson, pp. 271–273; Endacott, pp. 155–157, 246–248; Feng Tzu-yu, *Ko-ming i-shih* (Taipei, 1953–65), 3:161; Henry James Lethbridge, "The Evolution of a Chinese Voluntary Association in Hong Kong: The Po Leung Kuk," *Journal of Oriental Studies,* 10:33–50 (1972). On the charitable halls, see also Wellington Kam-kong Chan, "Merchants, Mandarins and Modern Enterprise in Late Ch'ing China, 1872–1911," Ph.D. diss., Harvard University, 1972, pp. 77–82.

56. Van der Sprenkel, p. 90; Morse, *Gilds,* pp. 18–21, 25–28.

57. Jean Chesneaux, *Les Sociétés secrètes en Chine, XIXe et XXe siècles* (Paris, 1965), pp. 23–54; Frederic Wakeman, Jr., "The Secret Societies of Kwangtung, 1800–1856" and Boris Novikov, "The Anti-Manchu Propaganda of the Triads, *ca.* 1800–1860," in Jean Chesneaux, ed., *Popular Movements and Secret Societies in China, 1840–1950* (Stanford,

1972), pp. 29–63; W. P. Morgan, *Triad Societies in Hong Kong* (Hong Kong, 1960). On the revolutionaries' experience with the Triads, see, for example, Ch'en Shao-pai, "Hsing-Chung hui ko-ming shih-yao," *HHKM*, 1:23.

58. Chesneaux, *Sociétés secrètes*, pp. 38–43.

59. Roswell S. Britton, *The Chinese Periodical Press, 1800–1912* (Shanghai, 1933), pp. 3–15; Ko Kung-chen, *Chung-kuo pao-hsüeh shih* (Peking, 1955), chap. 2.

60. Lin Yu-tang, *A History of the Press and Public Opinion in China* (New York, 1968), chap. 8; also Britton and Ko Kung-chen.

61. Frank H. H. King and Prescott Clarke, *A Research Guide to China-Coast Newspapers, 1822–1911* (Cambridge, 1965), pp. 20–28; Britton, pp. 38–47, 80; Ko Kung-chen, pp. 73–75, 119–120; Lo Hsiang-lin, *Hong Kong and Western Cultures* (Tokyo, 1963), pp. 201–209; Yen-p'ing Hao, *Comprador*, p. 199.

62. Ko Kung-chen, p. 121; Britton, p. 79; Feng, *I-shih*, 1:113; *DR*, 1882–91, p. 579.

63. Endacott, pp. 208–209.

2. The Postwar Period, 1895–1900

1. Rawlinson, chap. 9.

2. Westel W. Willoughby, *Foreign Rights and Interests in China* (Baltimore, 1920), pp. 120–129; *TR*, 1896, Canton, pp. 437–438; 1897, Canton, p. 447.

3. Willoughby, pp. 161–163.

4. *TR*, 1898, Canton, pp. 457, 459–461; 1899, Canton, pp. 559–560.

5. MacGillivray, p. 485; see also Paul A. Varg, *Missionaries, Chinese and Diplomats: The American Protestant Missionary Movement in China, 1890–1952* (Princeton, 1958), pp. 3, 52–63.

6. Morse, *International Relations*, 3:112–113; J. Silvestre, "La France à Kouang-Tchéou-Ouen," *Annales des sciences politiques*, 17:473–493 (1902); Alfred Bonningue, *La France à Kouang-Tchéou-Wan* (Paris, 1931).

7. Morse, *International Relations*, 3:119–120; R. G. Groves, "Militia, Market and Lineage: Chinese Resistance to the Occupation of Hong Kong's New Territories in 1899," *Journal of the Hong Kong Branch of the Royal Asiatic Society*, 9:38, 60 (n. 25) (1969).

8. Morse, *International Relations*, 3:90–91, 120–121; Willoughby, pp. 275–281; Percy Horace Kent, *Railway Enterprise in China: An Account of Its Origins and Development* (London, 1908), pp. 161–162; Li En-han, *Wan-Ch'ing ti shou-hui k'uang-ch'üan yün-tung* (Taipei, 1963), p. 27; *TR*, 1899, Pakhoi, p. 690; 1900, Kiungchow, p. 658; 1901, Kiungchow, p. 684; Paul King, p. 170.

9. William R. Braisted, "The United States and the American China Development Company," *Far Eastern Quarterly*, 11:147–149 (1952); Morse, *International Relations*, 3:120; Willoughby, p. 240.

10. Willoughby, pp. 488–494; Chi-ming Hou, pp. 42–43.

11. *NCH*, Dec. 4, 1899, pp. 1134–1135.

12. On the resistance at Kwangchowwan, see *NCH*, Nov. 21, 1898, p. 952; Oct. 20, 1899, p. 1018; Dec. 4, p. 1123; Dec. 18, p. 1207; Dec. 27, p. 1255. On the resistance in the New Territories, see Groves; Endacott, pp. 263–265; *NCH*, April 17,

1899, p. 672; May 1, p. 767; May 8, p. 817. See also Chao Yung-liang et al., "1897–1899-nien Chung-kuo jen-min ti fan-ti fan-feng-chien tou-cheng," *Li-shih chiao-hsüeh,* 1960, no. 9, pp. 7–14.

13. Kwang-Ching Liu, pp. 150–169; "The Chinese Reform Movement of the 1890's: A Symposium," *Journal of Asian Studies,* 29:7–53 (1969); Wolfgang Franke, *The Reform and Abolition of the Traditional Chinese Examination System* (Cambridge, 1963), pp. 32–47; Benjamin Schwartz, *In Search of Wealth and Power: Yen Fu and the West* (Cambridge, 1964), esp. chaps. 3–5.

14. Kwang-Ching Liu, p. 164.

15. *Wu-hsü pien-fa* (Shanghai, 1957), 4:403–405; see also John Schrecker, "The Pao-kuo Hui: A Reform Society of 1898," *Papers on China,* 14:50–69 (1960).

16. Howard S. Levy, *Chinese Footbinding: The History of a Curious Erotic Custom* (New York, 1966), p. 71; for the regulations of the society, see *Wu-hsü pien-fa,* 4:433–436. A list of the society's members appears in *Shih-wu pao,* no. 31 (KH 23/6/1), and subsequent issues; I wish to thank Marianne Bastid for drawing my attention to this list. See also Roxane Heater Witke, "Transformation of Attitudes towards Women during the May Fourth Period of Modern China," Ph.D. diss., University of California at Berkeley, 1970, pp. 23–28.

17. Ting Wen-chiang, *Liang Jen-kung hsien-sheng nien-p'u ch'ang-pien ch'u-kao* (Taipei, 1962), p. 38; Jung-pang Lo, p. 76; Ko Kung chen, p. 125; Feng, *I-shih,* 4:75–76. Texts of eight articles are reprinted in *Wu-hsü pien-fa,* 3:287–316.

18. Feng, *I-shih,* 4:76; cf. *Wu-hsü pien-fa,* 4:396.

19. *Wu-hsü pien-fa,* 4:395–396, 514–515; T'an Li-yüan, "Ssu-shih-ch'i-nien-lai pao-yeh shih kai-lüeh," pp. 3–4, in *Hua-tzu jih-pao ch'i-shih-i chou-nien chi-nien k'an* (Hong Kong, 1934); *NCH,* Oct. 17, 1898, pp. 736–738.

20. Jung-pang Lo, pp. 76–77.

21. Jung-pang Lo, pp. 107–108; cf. *HKT,* April 28, 1900, p. 2. See also Wellington Chan, pp. 234–242.

22. Biggerstaff, p. 42; P'an-yü *HC,* 42:9b; *NCH,* Oct. 10, 1898, p. 677.

23. Beresford, p. 278.

24. Ayers, p. 143; Jung-pang Lo, pp. 114, 163 (n. 60).

25. John Howard Fincher, "The Chinese Self-Government Movement, 1900–1912," Ph.D. diss., University of Washington, 1969, p. 74.

26. Charlton M. Lewis, "The Hunanese Elite and the Reform Movement, 1895–1898," *Journal of Asian Studies,* 29:41 (1969).

27. Franke, p. 46; *NCH,* Dec. 12, 1898, pp. 1099–1100; Jung-pang Lo, pp. 137–139.

28. P'an-yü *HC,* 12:32b; Feuerwerker, *China's Early Industrialization,* p. 47; *TR,* 1899, Samshui, p. 532; Canton, p. 562; 1900, Canton, p. 550; cf. *NCH,* Sept. 25, 1899, p. 621; Oct. 16, p. 749.

29. Just when the Chinese Chamber of Commerce in Hong Kong was founded is in dispute. *NCH,* Feb. 7, 1896, p. 208, says January 1896; Yen-p'ing Hao, *Comprador,* p. 189, says 1900; Endacott, p. 251, says 1887.

30. *History of the South China Mission,* pp. 92–95.

31. *NCH,* Oct. 17, 1898, pp. 736–738; Nov. 7, pp. 877–878; *HKT,* Aug. 31, 1900, p. 3; *DR,* 1902–11, 2:154; Feng, *I-shih,* 1:113; T'an Li-yüan, p. 3. See also

Ch'ing-i pao, no. 100 (KH 27/11/11), pp. 6489–6498 of the 1967 Taiwan reprint by the Ch'eng-wen ch'u-pan she.

32. FO 228/1203, Bristow to O'Connor, July 19, 1895. I owe this reference to Linda Shin.

33. For a list of the early members of the society in Hong Kong, see *KMWH,* 3:343–345, 369. On Sun and on the society in general, see Schiffrin, *Sun Yat-sen,* chaps. 2–3. On Yang, see Feng, *I-shih,* 1:4–6; 5:8–15; Chün-tu Hsüeh, p. 27. On Hsieh (Tse), see his autobiographical account, *The Chinese Republic: Secret History of the Revolution* (Hong Kong, 1924). On Cheng, see *HLHCC,* pp. 20–24; Feng, *I-shih,* 1:24–25. On Ch'en, see Boorman and Howard, 1:229–231; Ch'en Te-yün, "Ch'en Shao-pai hsien-sheng nien-p'u," *KKWH,* 1.10:510–520; *HLHCC,* pp. 495–496. On Lu, see *HLHCC,* pp. 1–7. Finally, on Huang, see Feng, *I-shih,* 1:6.

34. Schiffrin, *Sun Yat-sen,* pp. 34–40, 70–72. On the Fu-jen Literary Society, see Wang Hsing-jui, "Ch'ing-chi Fu-jen wen-she yü ko-ming yün-tung ti kuan-hsi," *Shih-hsüeh tsa-chih,* 1:35–45 (1945).

35. Schiffrin, *Sun Yat-sen,* pp. 42–44, 49–53; Chün-tu Hsüeh, pp. 28–29.

36. The best account of the 1895 Canton revolt is Schiffrin, *Sun Yat-sen,* chap. 4. Other accounts are Feng Tzu-yu, *Chung-hua min-kuo k'ai-kuo ch'ien ko-ming shih* (Taipei, 1954), 1:17–29, and *I-shih,* 4:10–13; Tsou Lu, *Chung-kuo Kuo-min-tang shih-kao* (Taipei, 1965), pp. 655–664; Ch'en Shao-pai, pp. 28–32; and Teng Mu-han, "Kuo-fu i-wei Kuang-chou chü-i shih-mo chi," *Kuang-tung wen-wu,* pp. 1–5.

37. For a list of members, see *KMWH,* 3:343–348, 369–370.

38. Schiffrin, *Sun Yat-sen,* pp. 73, 77–79.

39. See DS/CD, Canton, Seymour to Uhl, Nov. 18, 1898.

40. Beresford, p. 220.

41. Feng, *Chung-hua,* 1:171–172; *I-shih,* 1:66; Ch'en Shao-pai, p. 65; Schiffrin, *Sun Yat-sen,* p. 171; *HKT,* Jan. 19, 1900, p. 2.

42. The best account of this weird episode linking Sun Yat-sen and Li Hung-chang is Schiffrin, *Sun Yat-sen,* chap. 7. Other accounts include Marius B. Jansen, *The Japanese and Sun Yat-sen* (Cambridge, 1954), pp. 86–90; Feng, *I-shih,* 1:76–80; 4:92–100.

43. The strategy is set forth in Sun's letter to Liu Hsüeh-hsün in September 1900, quoted in Feng, *I-shih,* 4:88. Most accounts of the uprising, colored by what subsequently occurred, imply that the Hui-chou operations were the central focus of the revolutionaries' strategy. However, the revolt as it unrolled was not necessarily the revolt as it was planned.

44. See *KMWH,* 3:354–358, 359–362. On Li Chi-t'ang, see Huang Ta-han, "Hsing-Chung hui ko t'ung-chih ko-ming kung-tso shih-lüeh," *KKWH,* 1.9:470–475; *HLHCC,* pp. 515–527; and Feng, *I-shih,* 3:160–169.

45. The 1900 Hui-chou revolt is described in Schiffrin, *Sun Yat-sen,* chap. 8; Jansen, pp. 94–96; Feng, *Chung-hua,* 1:90–101, and *I-shih,* 5:16–25; Tsou, *Tang shih-kao,* pp. 665–672; Ch'en Ch'un-sheng, "Keng-tzu Hui-chou ch'i-i chi," *HHKM,* 1:235–244; Miyazaki Torazō, "Hui-chou chih ko-ming," *KKWH,* 1.9:564–568; Chang Yu-jen, "Keng-tzu Hui-chou San-chou-t'ien ch'i-i fang-wen lu," *HIL,* 2:263–280; Ch'en Shao-pai, pp. 65–73; and Chuang Chi-fa, "Keng-tzu Hui-chou ko-ming yün-tung shih-mo," *Ta-lu tsa-chih,* 41:124–131 (1970). On the endemic unrest of the Hui-chou region, see Winston Hsieh, "Triads, Salt Smugglers, and Local Uprisings: Observations on the

Social and Economic Background of the Waichow Revolution of 1911," in Chesneaux, ed., *Popular Movements and Secret Societies*, pp. 145–164.

46. Chang Yu-jen, pp. 274, 279; Tsou, *Tang shih-kao*, p. 670, quoting the memorial of Governor Te-shou. My understanding of the initial engagements of the Hui-chou revolt differs from Schiffrin's. I have relied heavily on Chang Yu-jen's article; he, on Ch'en Ch'un-sheng's, which in turn is based on Feng Tzu-yu's. Both Feng and Ch'en date the first battles erroneously. Thus, Schiffrin, following Feng, dates the battle of Chen-lung as October 15, while Chang dates it the seventh. Why should it have taken the rebels nine days, from the sixth to the fifteenth, to go the short distance from Sha-wan to Chen-lung, especially when they had the element of surprise? Again, Schiffrin, following Feng, says that the rebels left Yung-hu on October 17, while Chang says the tenth. Here Miyazaki corroborates Chang's dating. He says that the rebels rested at Yung-hu on the fifth day after Sha-wan, that is, October 11. Moreover, Schiffrin, following Feng, says that Cheng Shih-liang arrived with Sun's directive to head for Amoy the day after the rebellion got underway. If so, why then did the rebels waste ten days fighting their way toward Hui-chou city instead of going toward Amoy along the coastal route via Tan-shui? It seems more likely that Sun's message arrived several days after the initial uprising, when the rebels, following original plans, had already gone toward Hui-chou.

47. The best accounts of the assassination attempt are Feng, *Chung-hua*, 1:102–110, and *I-shih*, 5:26–33; and Ts'ui T'ung-yüeh, "Wo chih ko-ming ching-kuo," *KKWH*, 1.9:629–638. Other accounts are Tsou, *Tang shih-kao*, pp. 673–675; Ch'en Shao-pai, pp. 71–73; Liao P'ing-tzu, "Shih Chien-ju an shih-i," *HHKM*, 1:249–250; Schiffrin, *Sun Yat-sen*, pp. 248–251; and *HLHCC*, pp. 8–16. On Teng Yin-nan, see Huang Ta-han, pp. 459–461; *HLHCC*, pp. 513–515.

48. See Paul King, pp. 214–215.

49. DS/CD, Canton, McWade, Nov. 14, 1900.

50. Jung-pang Lo, pp. 180–181, 258–261 (nn. 8–11).

51. Li Shao-ling, *Ou Chü-chia hsien-sheng chuan* (Taipei, 1960), p. 20.

52. Feng, *I-shih*, 4:76; Li Shao-ling, pp. 21–23.

53. Feng, *I-shih*, 2:195–196. On the T'ang Ts'ai-ch'ang revolt, see E. Joan Smythe, "The Tzu-li Hui: Some Chinese and their Rebellion," *Papers on China*, 12:51–68 (1958); Jung-pang Lo, pp. 184–188. See also Philip C. Huang, *Liang Ch'i-ch'ao and Modern Chinese Liberalism* (Seattle, 1972), pp. 94–96; cf. Schiffrin, *Sun Yat-sen*, pp. 218–224.

54. *Hsin Kwangtung* is reprinted in Chang Nan and Wang Jen-chih, eds., *Hsin-hai ko-ming ch'ien shih-nien chien shih-lun hsüan-chi* (Hong Kong, 1962), vol. 1, bk. 1, pp. 269–311; it is briefly summarized in Y. C. Wang, *Chinese Intellectuals and the West, 1872–1949* (Chapel Hill, 1966), pp. 231–232. On Ou Chü-chia, see Li Shao-ling, pp. 1–40; also Feng, *I-shih*, 2:119–121; 3:40.

55. See Schiffrin, *Sun Yat-sen*, chap. 7.

56. Hao Chang, *Liang Ch'i-ch'ao and Intellectual Transition in China, 1890–1907* (Cambridge, 1971), pp. 126–127.

57. Feng, *I-shih*, 1:122.

58. Schiffrin, *Sun Yat-sen*, pp. 157–165.

3. *Early Years of the Post-Boxer Decade*

1. On the post-Boxer reform movement, see Meribeth E. Cameron, *The Reform Movement in China, 1898–1912* (Stanford, 1931), and Mary Clabaugh Wright, "Introduction: The Rising Tide of Change," in *China in Revolution,* pp. 1–63.

2. On T'ao Mo, see *Ch'ing-shih lieh-chuan* (Taipei reprint, 1962), 61:39–43b; also *HKT,* mail supplement, Oct. 20, 1902, p. 7. On Ts'en Ch'un-hsüan, see Boorman and Howard, 3:305–308; also his autobiographical *Lo-chai man-pi* (Taipei, 1962) and the appended biography by Wu Hsiang-hsiang. Ts'en's membership in the reformist organizations is mentioned in Ko Kung-chen, p. 121, and Jung-pang Lo, p. 77.

3. Franke, pp. 48–53; Cameron, pp. 67–68; Ayers, pp. 200–216.

4. P'an-yü *HC,* 42:11b; *HKT,* April 23, 1902, p. 3; mail supplement, Oct. 6, p. 7; John G. Kerr, *A Guide to the City and Suburbs of Canton* (Hong Kong, 1904), pp. 14–15; Chang Wen-po, *Chih-lao hsien-hua* (Taipei, 1952), p. 13.

5. P'an-yü *HC,* 11:10–10b; "Ts'ang-hai hsien-sheng Ch'iu kung Feng-chia nien-p'u," in *Ling-yün-hai jih-lou shih-ch'ao* (Taipei, 1960), p. 402.

6. See Nan-hai *HC,* 6:23–38.

7. *HKT,* mail supplement, Aug. 16, 1902, p. 4.

8. Chang Wen-po, p. 13; Hu Han-min, "Tzu-chuan," *KMWH,* 3:380–381; Feng, *I-shih,* 1:113–114, 186; *TFTC,* 1.1: Chiao-yü, pp. 23–27 (KH 30/1). Fang Chao-ying, *Ch'ing-mo Min-ch'u yang-hsüeh hsüeh-sheng t'i-ming lu, ch'u-chi* (Taipei, 1962), pp. 51–52, has what appears to be a list of the students sent, but the date of their entry into the school, given as 1898, is clearly wrong.

9. P'an-yü *HC,* 11:10b–12b.

10. Franke, pp. 54–67; Ayers, pp. 237–242; Cameron, pp. 71–74; H. S. Brunnert and V. V. Hagelstrom, *Present Day Political Organization of China* (Taipei, n.d.), nos. 574–627.

11. P'an-yü *HC,* 11:1–1b.

12. Ch'ing-yüan *HC,* 15:14–14b; *TFTC,* 1.7: Chiao-yü, p. 172 (KH 30/7); 1.8: Chiao-yü, p. 195 (30/8); Brunnert and Hagelstrom, nos. 829 and 829A; P'an-yü *HC,* 11:7.

13. P'an-yü *HC,* 11:7–7b, 10b; *TFTC,* 1.1: Chiao-yü, p. 35 (KH 30/1); 1.7: Chiao-yü, p. 172 (30/7); Ch'ing-yüan *HC,* 15:13b–14.

14. *TFTC,* 1.9: Chiao-yü, p. 217 (KH 30/9), which gives the names of the scholars. See also 1.1: Chiao-yü, pp. 23–27, 39 (30/1).

15. *TFTC,* 1.2: Chiao-yü, pp. 44–46 (KH 30/2); 1.7: Chiao-yü, pp. 173–174 (30/7). See also Michael Gasster, *Chinese Intellectuals and the Revolution of 1911: The Birth of Modern Chinese Radicalism* (Seattle, 1969), pp. 31–32, n. 11.

16. Nan-hai *HC,* 6:23–38; P'an-yü *HC,* 11:5b–6, 13–16; Shun-te *HC,* 2:27–29; K'ai-p'ing *HC,* 21:20b–21; Ch'ih-hsi *HC,* 3:17b–18; Lo-ting *HC,* 4:2b; Lung-men *HC,* pp. 194–194b.

17. P'an-yü *HC,* 42:11b.

18. Franke, p. 69.

19. *TFTC,* 1.8: Chiao-yü, p. 194 (KH 30/8); 1.10: Chiao-yü, p. 240 (30/10); 2.6: Chiao-yü, pp. 161–162 (31/6); 2.9: Chiao-yü, p. 245 (31/9).

20. Feng, *I-shih,* 2:41–43; Chiang Yung-ching, "Hu Han-min hsien-sheng nien-p'u

kao," *Chung-kuo hsien-tai-shih ts'ung-k'an,* 3:89–90, 92 (1961); cf. *HKT,* Oct. 11, 1902, p. 6; March 24, 1903, p. 8.

21. *TFTC,* 1.1: Chiao-yü, p. 35 (KH 30/1); 1.2: Chiao-yü, pp. 41–42 (30/2).

22. Ralph L. Powell, *The Rise of Chinese Military Power, 1895–1912* (Princeton, 1955), pp. 133–135.

23. *TFTC,* 1.10: Chiao-yü, p. 240 (KH 30/10); 1.12: Chiao-yü, p. 281 (30/12); 2.12: Chiao-yü, pp. 332–333 (31/12); *HKT,* June 6, 1902, p. 2; Feb. 16, 1905, p. 4; *NCH,* Jan. 27, 1905, p. 209; Yao Yü-p'ing, "Chui-i keng-hsü ch'i-i ho hsin-hai san-yüeh erh-shih-chiu-jih chih i," *HIL,* 2:287. *Saishin Shina kanshin roku* (Tokyo, 1918), pp. 392–405 of the supplement, lists the Chinese cadets who graduated from the Japanese Army Officers' School; it includes thirty from Kwangtung.

24. *TFTC,* 1.4: Chiao-yü, p. 102 (KH 30/4); 1.5: Chiao-yü, pp. 123–124 (30/5); 1.8: Chiao-yü, p. 195 (30/8); FO 371/13480, Report by G. Pereira, Feb. 7, 1906.

25. Kerr, *Guide to Canton,* pp. 60–61; Ayers, p. 105, n. 17.

26. P'an-yü *HC,* 8:1; FO 371/13480, Report by G. Pereira, Feb. 7, 1906; 371/1225, Pereira, Distribution of provincial troops in China, July 17, 1907; *HKT,* April 14, 1909, p. 4; Beresford, p. 278. On the Tartar Quarter, see Henry, pp. 45–46; Dennys, pp. 142–143.

27. FO 371/17902, Report by G. Pereira on an overland journey from Canton to Foochow, Dec. 31, 1906, to Feb. 4, 1907; 371/1225, Pereira, Distribution of provincial troops in China, July 17, 1907; Brunnert and Hagelstrom, nos. 749–751.

28. Powell, pp. 134–135; *TFTC,* 1.5: Chün-shih, pp. 216–218 (KH 30/5); 1.7: Chün-shih, p. 283 (30/7); 1.10: Chün-shih, pp. 386–387 (30/10); 3.1: Chün-shih, p. 23 (32/1).

29. FO 371/314, Ts'en to Mansfield, Aug. 2, 1906; 371/17902, Pereira, Report of an overland journey from Canton to Foochow, Dec. 31, 1906, to Feb. 4, 1907; P'an-yü *HC,* 8:2–3. See also Stephen R. MacKinnon, "The Peiyang Army, Yüan Shih-k'ai, and the Origins of Modern Chinese Warlordism," *Journal of Asian Studies,* 32:408–409 (1973).

30. Feuerwerker, *China's Early Industrialization,* pp. 70–71; Brunnert and Hagelstrom, no. 774; *Nung-kung-shang-pu t'ung-chi piao* (Peking, 1908–09), 1st ser., section on chambers of commerce. See also Wellington Chan, chap. 10.

31. *TFTC,* 1.7: Shih-p'ing, p. 42 (KH 30/7).

32. Cameron, p. 63; P'an-yü *HC,* 8:5; 42:13; Brunnert and Hagelstrom, nos. 520–521; *NCH,* Aug. 5, 1904, p. 293; Shih-ch'eng *HC,* 10:37; 40:61.

33. *TR,* 1905, Canton, p. 396; Wu Hsiang-hsiang, "Ts'en Ch'un-hsüan," pp. 5–6, in *Lo-chai man-pi.*

34. Shun-te *HC,* 23:17; En-p'ing *HC,* 12:15–15b; 14:33b; K'ai-p'ing *HC,* 21:20b; Yang-shan *HC,* 10:17b–18. On the establishment of the Chinese Imperial Post, see Ying-wan Cheng, *Postal Communication in China and Its Modernization, 1860–1896* (Cambridge, 1970).

35. *HKT,* mail supplement, Dec. 12, 1903, p. 6; *China Proper,* 3:596.

36. Kent, p. 117; *HKT,* mail supplement, Nov. 21, 1903, pp. 6–7.

37. Ling Hung-hsün, *Chung-kuo t'ieh-lu chih* (Taipei, 1954), pp. 399–400; Kent, p. 172.

38. Kent, pp. 176–177.

39. *HKT,* Oct. 17, 1901, p. 8.

40. G. T. Bishop et al., *Hong Kong and the Treaty Ports: Postal History and Postal Markings* (London, 1949), pp. 165–175.

41. *HKT,* Sept. 25, 1909, p. 3.

42. Latourette, p. 527; MacGillivray, pp. 248, 249, 485, 530–531, 538–539, 677; *History of the South China Mission,* pp. 140, 151–155.

43. *TFTC,* 1.3: Tsung-chiao, pp. 15–16 (KH 30/3); 1.7: Tsung-chiao, p. 46 (30/7); 2.5: Tsung-chiao, p. 39 (31/5); 2.12: Tsung-chiao, p. 69 (31/12); *HKT,* Dec. 10, 1904, p. 5. See also Holmes Welch, *The Buddhist Revival in China,* pp. 163–165; Iriye Akira, "Chūgoku ni oketu Nihon Bukkyō fukyō mondai," *Kokusai seiji,* no. 28, pp. 87–100 (1964).

44. *HKT,* Oct. 16, 1907, p. 4; see also *HKT,* July 26, 1901, p. 3; Dec. 17, p. 3; July 11, 1902, p. 5; July 12, p. 5; Hsüan-t'ung Kao-yao *HC,* 10:44b; Tung-kuan *HC,* 36:8b; see also Des Forges, pp. 27–30.

45. John E. Schrecker, *Imperialism and Chinese Nationalism: Germany in Shantung* (Cambridge, 1971), esp. chap. 5; Werner Levi, *Modern China's Foreign Policy* (Minneapolis, 1953), pp. 83–98.

46. Cameron, pp. 84–85.

47. En-han Lee, "China's Response to Foreign Investment in Her Mining Industry, 1902–1911," *Journal of Asian Studies,* 28:55–76 (1968); Braisted, "The United States and the American China Development Company"; E-tu Zen Sun, *Chinese Railways and British Interests, 1898–1911* (New York, 1954), pp. 74–84.

48. As quoted in Li En-han, *Wan-Ch'ing ti shou-hui k'uang-ch'üan yün-tung,* pp. 98–100.

49. Mary Backus Rankin, "The Manchurian Crisis and Radical Student Nationalism, 1903," *Ch'ing-shih wen-t'i,* 2.1:87–106 (1969); Feng, *Chung-hua,* 1:129–130.

50. Feng, *Chung-hua,* 1:55; *I-shih,* 1:104–107; 5:34–39.

51. *HKT,* mail supplement, May 30, 1903, p. 6.

52. DS/CD, Canton, Cheshire, Oct. 20 and Oct. 26, 1904; *NCH,* Nov. 4, 1904, pp. 616–617; Chang Chih-tung, *Chang Wen-hsiang kung ch'üan-chi* (Taipei, 1963), 65:21b–29; 66:1–16; 191:14b–15; E-tu Zen Sun, *Chinese Railways,* pp. 80–84.

53. Schrecker, *Imperialism and Chinese Nationalism,* pp. 126, 153.

54. DS/CD, Canton, Cheshire, Oct. 20, 1904; J. G. Lay, April 20, 1905; *HKT,* Sept. 28, 1904, p. 5; Oct. 19, p. 5; *NCH,* Oct. 28, 1904, p. 960.

55. *DR,* 1902–11, 2:154; FO 228/1627, Mansfield to Carnegie, May 29, 1906; Kerr, *Guide to Canton,* pp. 12, 16; Feng, *I-shih,* 1:113–114; T'an Li-yüan, p. 4.

56. FO 371/221, Memorandum by Garnett, Dec. 18, 1906; Lin I-han, " 'Hsin-hai Ch'ao-chou ko-ming chi-lüeh' ting-cheng shu," *KKWH,* 2.4:482; *TR,* 1902, Kiung-chow, p. 771; 1903, p. 828; *DR,* 1902–11, 2:263–264; *TFTC,* 2.4: Chiao-yü, p. 94 (KH 31/4).

57. See, for example, *TFTC,* 1.10: Chiao-yü, p. 242 (KH 30/10); 2.3: Chiao-yü, pp. 50, 51 (31/3); Feng, *I-shih,* 4:76.

58. *TFTC,* 1.10: Chiao-yü, p. 242 (KH 30/10).

59. Cameron, p. 62; Levy, pp. 85–92; Sidney Gamble, *Ting Hsien: A North China Rural Community* (Stanford, 1968), pp. 46–48, 60 (table 9).

60. Schiffrin, *Sun Yat-sen,* pp. 251–253 and chap. 11.

61. Feng, *I-shih*, 3:227–228; on Cheng, see 1:82–85.

62. Feng, *I-shih*, 1:67–68; 3:228; *Chung-hua*, 1:172–173; Ch'en Ch'un-sheng, "Ch'en Shao-pai hsien-sheng yü Hsiang-kang *Chung-kuo jih-pao* chi *Chung-kuo jih-pao* yü Chung-kuo ko-ming chih kuan-hsi," *KKWH*, 1.10:506–508.

63. Feng, *I-shih*, 1:69, 84; *Chung-hua*, 1:173–174.

64. On the 1903 attempted revolt, see Ch'en Ch'un-sheng, "Jen-yin Hung Ch'üan-fu Kuang-chou chü-i chi," *HHKM*, 1:315–321; Feng, *Chung-hua*, 1:118–125, and *I-shih*, 4:106–114; Tsou, *Tang shih-kao*, pp. 676–678; Liao P'ing-tzu, "Hung Ch'üan-fu ch'i-i shih-mo," *KKWH*, 1.9:667–670; Wu Jui, " 'Ta-Ming shun-t'ien kuo'—Hsing-Chung hui ti wai-i chang," *Ch'ang-liu*, 32.4:11–13 (1965); Schiffrin, *Sun Yat-sen*, pp. 305–306; Tse Tsan Tai, pp. 16–17, 22–23; Huang Ta-han, pp. 472–473.

65. Tse Tsan Tai, p. 16; *HHKM*, 1:322–327; *KKWH*, 1.9:671–677.

66. *HKT*, mail supplement, Jan. 31, 1903, p. 4; Feb. 9, 1903, p. 7.

67. Schiffrin, *Sun Yat-sen*, p. 305.

68. *HKT*, mail supplement, Feb. 23, 1903, p. 7; March 24, p. 8; May 16, p. 7.

69. Feng, *Chung-hua*, 1:173–174; *I-shih*, 1:68.

70. Feng, *Chung-hua*, 2:147–149; *HHKM*, 2:550–551; cf. *KKWH*, 1.13:59–60.

71. Gasster, pp. 21–26; Hao Chang, pp. 220–224.

72. Ting Wen-chiang, pp. 193–194; Hu Ying-han, *Wu Hsien-tzu hsien-sheng chuan-chi* (Hong Kong, 1953); pp. 5–11; Feng, *Chung-hua*, 1:174; *I-shih*, 1:69; Jung-pang Lo, pp. 195–196, 200. On Wu Hsien-tzu, see Boorman and Howard, 3:433–436.

73. Tse Tsan Tai, p. 24.

74. Feng, *I-shih*, 1:44, 94–95; 3:164–166.

75. See Rankin, *Early Chinese Revolutionaries*, esp. chaps. 3, 4, and 7; Schiffrin, *Sun Yat-sen*, chaps. 9–10; Chün-tu Hsüeh, chap. 2; Robert A. Scalapino, "Prelude to Marxism: The Chinese Student Movement in Japan, 1900–1910," in Albert Feuerwerker et al., *Approaches to Modern Chinese History* (Berkeley, 1967), pp. 190–215.

4. Middle Years of the Post-Boxer Decade, I: Reform

1. For a brief biographical sketch of Chou Fu, see Folsom, pp. 141–142; also Boorman and Howard, 1:410.

2. Franke, pp. 69–71.

3. *TFTC*, 2.11: Chiao-yü, p. 296 (KH 31/11); 2.12: Chiao-yü, p. 349 (31/12); Shun-te *HC*, 23:17; Yang-chiang *HC*, 37:14b–15; 18:50–51.

4. *NCH*, Nov. 24, 1905, p. 429.

5. *Chiao-yü t'ung-chi t'u-piao* (Peking, n.d.), 1st ser., section on Kwangtung, p. 2; cf. Brunnert and Hagelstrom, no. 829A.

6. P'an-yü *HC*, 11:6–9b; Brunnert and Hagelstrom, nos. 608, 618–618B, 623A, 626; *The National Sun Yat-sen University: A Short History* (Canton, 1937), pp. 1–2; *Chiao-yü t'ung-chi t'u-piao*, 1st. ser., section on Kwangtung, pp. 2–3; Biggerstaff, pp. 42–43.

7. Hsüan-t'ung Kao-yao *HC*, 12:14b; P'an-yü *HC*, 11:3b; Nan-hai *HC*, 6:23–38; *Chiao-yü t'ung-chi t'u-piao*, 1st ser., section on Kwangtung, p. 1.

8. Nan-hai *HC*, 6:23–38; Shun-te *HC*, 2:27–29; Hsü-wen *HC*, 5:4b; Le-ch'ang *HC*, 19:16; Ch'ing-yüan *HC*, 3:44b; Jen-hua *HC*, 2:45; Yang-chiang *HC*, 18:50–51;

37:14b–15; Kan-en *HC,* 5:6; *Chiao-yü t'ung-chi t'u-piao,* 1st ser., section on Kwangtung, p. 1.

9. Ch'ing-yüan *HC,* 15:14–14b; En-p'ing *HC,* 9:13–13b; 14:34–35; Yang-chiang *HC,* 18:50–51; 37:14b–15; Brunnert and Hagelstrom, no. 618A; *Chiao-yü t'ung-chi t'u-piao,* 1st ser., section on Kwangtung, p. 1.

10. Scalapino, p. 192; Gasster, pp. 31–32, n. 11; see also Philip Huang, pp. 37, 41, 175 (n. 11).

11. *Chiao-yü t'ung-chi t'u-piao,* 1st ser., section on Kwangtung, p. 1; P'an-yü *HC,* 11:14–14b.

12. Lewis, "The Hunanese Elite," p. 42.

13. Brunnert and Hagelstrom, nos. 829–829B; *TFTC,* 4.2: Chiao-yü, p. 24 (KH 33/2); 4.4: Chiao-yü, pp. 127–128 (33/4); 4.9: Chiao-yü, pp. 225, 227 (33/9); cf. Marianne Bastid, *Aspects de la réforme de l'enseignement en Chine au début du 20ᵉ siècle, d'après des écrits de Zhang Jian* (Paris, 1971), pp. 71–72, 163–165.

14. *Chiao-yü t'ung-chi t'u-piao,* 1st ser., section on Kwangtung, p. 1.

15. *NCH,* June 20, 1907, p. 734.

16. Welch, pp. 11–13, 164–165.

17. *NCH,* June 29, 1906, p. 774; Sept. 20, 1907, p. 664; for yet another example, see Sept. 13, 1907, p. 640.

18. Lo Shou-chang, "Ch'in-hsien San-na fan-k'ang t'ang-chuan tou-cheng yü Ch'in-Fang chih i," *HIL,* 2:392–394; Feng, *Chung-hua,* 2:174–175; *SCMP,* May 14, 1907, p. 7; DS/NF, 215/56–58, Report by the British consul at Pakhoi, V. L. Savage, May 25, 1907, and letter from A. H. Bach, Pakhoi, to Bergholz, June 11; *TFTC,* 4.7: Chün-shih, p. 83 (KH 33/7); *TR,* 1907, Pakhoi, p. 611.

19. Powell, pp. 172–184; Brunnert and Hagelstrom, nos. 655–656F; Ch'en Hsü-lu and Lao Shao-hua, "Ch'ing-mo ti hsin-chün yü hsin-hai ko-ming," *Hsin-hai ko-ming wu-shih chou-nien chi-nien lun-wen chi* (Peking, 1962), pp. 154–156.

20. *TFTC,* 2.9: Chiao-yü, p. 245 (KH 31/9); 2.12: Chiao-yü, pp. 332–333 (31/12); 3.10: Chiao-yü, p. 280 (32/9); 4.3: Chiao-yü, p. 60 (33/3); P'an-yü *HC,* 11:17–17b; Yao Yü-p'ing, pp. 287–288; Brunnert and Hagelstrom, nos. 711A, 711C; FO 371/13480, Report by Pereira, Feb. 7, 1906; Chang Lu-ts'un, "Keng-hsü hsin-chün ch'i-i ch'ien-hou ti hui-i," *HIL,* 2:282; Wen Kung-chih, "Hsin-hai ko-ming yün-tung chung chih hsin-chün," *HHKM,* 3:337.

21. Ch'en Hsü-lu and Lao Shao-hua, p. 154; *TFTC,* 5.4: Chün-shih, pp. 49–52 (KH 34/4); FO 371/13480, Report by Pereira, Feb. 7, 1906; D. Clayton James, *The Years of MacArthur* (Boston, 1970), 1:93–94.

22. *TFTC,* 4.5: Chün-shih, pp. 49–54 (KH 33/5); 5.4: Chün-shih, pp. 49–52 (34/4); FO 371/13480, Report by Pereira, Feb. 7, 1906; 371/1040, Extracts from a "Changes Report" by Pereira, Nov. 15, 1907.

23. *TFTC,* 4.5: Chün-shih, pp. 49–54 (KH 33/5); *SCMP,* March 19, 1908, p. 7; Ch'en Hsü-lu and Lao Shao-hua, pp. 158–160.

24. *TFTC,* 5.4: Chün-shih, p. 76 (KH 34/4).

25. *Nung-kung-shang-pu t'ung-chi piao,* 1st. ser., 4:9b–10b, 32b–33b, 44–46; 2nd ser., 4:24–24b. See also Wellington Chan, pp. 266–270.

26. *TFTC,* 1.12: Shang-wu, pp. 154–157 (KH 30/12); cf. *NCH,* Dec. 23, 1904, p. 1404. See also Wellington Chan, pp. 17–28, 258–262.

27. *TFTC,* 2.3: Chiao-yü, p. 52 (KH 31/3); 2.11: Chiao-yü, p. 298 (31/11); Britton, p. 125.

28. See *Nung-kung-shang-pu t'ung-chi piao,* 1st ser., 4:9b–10b, 32b–33b, 44–46; 2nd ser., 4:24–24b.

29. On Chang Pi-shih, see Boorman and Howard, 1:90–92; on Hsiao Yung-hua, *Nung-kung-shang-pu t'ung-chi piao,* 1st ser., 6:21b; 2nd ser., 2:16. See also Wellington Chan, pp. 28–30, 228–229, 266–275.

30. *TFTC,* 3.7: Tsung-chiao, p. 37 (KH 32/6); 3.10: Tsung-chiao, p. 49 (32/9); *SCMP,* Aug. 6, 1906, p. 7; *NCH,* Aug. 17, p. 379; cf. *HLHCC,* pp. 319–320.

31. *NCH,* July 14, 1905, p. 73.

32. *NCH,* Dec. 29, 1905, pp. 704–705; June 29, 1906, pp. 749–750.

33. *NCH,* Dec. 21, 1906, p. 650; April 12, 1907, p. 74; cf. Rankin, *Early Chinese Revolutionaries,* pp. 61–64, 114, 143; Ayers, pp. 189–195. On the "student tides," see John Israel, *Student Nationalism in China, 1927–1937* (Stanford, 1966), p. 89.

34. *SCMP,* March 19, 1908, p. 7.

35. Marie-Claire Bergère, "The Role of the Bourgeoisie," in Wright, ed., *China in Revolution,* p. 241.

36. *DR,* 1902–11, 2:132, 154; FO 228/1627, Mansfield to Carnegie, May 29, 1906; 371/4385, Memorandum by Garnett, Dec. 18, 1906; *TFTC,* 3.5: Chiao-yü, p. 103 (KH 32/4); 3.10: Chiao-yü, p. 283 (32/9); 4.3: Chiao-yü, p. 64 (33/3); *HHKM,* 2:551.

37. *TFTC,* 3.13: Chiao-yü, p. 413 (KH 32/12).

38. *TFTC,* 3.8: Tsa-tsu, p. 39 (KH 32/7); *SCMP,* July 11, 1906, p. 7; July 29, p. 2.

39. See Mary Roberts Coolidge, *Chinese Immigration* (New York, 1909), esp. part 2; Paul A. Varg, *Open Door Diplomat: The Life of W. W. Rockhill* (Urbana, 1952), p. 61.

40. On the anti-American boycott, see Chang Ts'un-wu, *Kuang-hsü sa-i-nien Chung-Mei kung-yüeh feng-ch'ao* (Taipei, 1966); Ting Yu, "1905-nien Kuang-tung fan-Mei yün-tung," *Chin-tai-shih tzu-liao,* 1958, no. 5, pp. 8–52.

41. DS/CD, Canton, Lay, May 20, 26, and 31, 1905; Chang Ts'un-wu, p. 108.

42. Howard K. Beale, *Theodore Roosevelt and the Rise of America to World Power* (Baltimore, 1956), pp. 211ff; Warren I. Cohen, *America's Response to China: An Interpretative History of Sino-American Relations* (New York, 1971), pp. 70–71.

43. Ting Yu, pp. 11–12; DS/CD, Canton, Lay, Aug. 16, 1905; *HKT,* Aug. 10, p. 3; *NCH,* Aug. 11, pp. 346–347; Sept. 8, pp. 543, 580–581; *Nan-yang hsiung-ti yen-ts'ao kung-ssu shih-liao* (Shanghai, 1958), pp. 1–4; cf. Y. C. Wang, "Free Enterprise in China: The Case of a Cigarette Concern, 1905–1953," *Pacific Historical Review,* 29:395–414 (1960). On Chien Chao-nan, see Boorman and Howard, 1:364–366.

44. Chang Ts'un-wu, pp. 110, 114–115; Ting Yu, pp. 13–14; *HKT,* Aug. 3, 1905, p. 5.

45. *Foreign Relations of the United States,* 1905, pp. 215, 218, 225.

46. *NCH,* July 14, 1905, p. 85; Sept. 8, p. 581; DS/CD, Canton, Lay, Aug. 24, 1905; Lay to Ts'en, Aug. 30, in Lay, Sept. 12; Ting Yu, p. 38.

47. DS/CD, Canton, Lay, Sept. 12, 1905, enclosures; Chin Tsu-hsün, "1905-nien Kuang-tung fan-Mei yün-tung ti p'ien-tuan hui-i," *Chin-tai-shih tzu-liao,* 1958, no. 5, pp. 54–55. A copy of the poster is reprinted in James A. Le Roy, "The Outcome of the Taft Commission," *The World To-day,* 10.1:55 (Chicago, Jan. 1906).

48. Ting Yu, p. 43; DS/CD, Canton, Lay to Ts'en, Aug. 30, 1905, in Lay, Sept. 12.

49. Ting Yu, pp. 45–47.

50. *HKT,* Sept. 20, 1905, p. 5; *NCH,* Oct. 20, p. 166; DS/CD, Canton, Lay, Sept. 28, and Lay to Ts'en, Oct. 27, in Lay, Oct. 30.

51. DS/CD, Canton, Lay to Ts'en, Oct. 27, 1905, in Lay, Oct. 30; W. W. Rockhill papers, Lay to Rockhill, Oct. 17; cf. *NCH,* Nov. 3, pp. 249–250. On Feng Hsia-wei, see Ting Yu, pp. 33–35.

52. *NCH,* July 14, 1905, p. 73; Dec. 22, p. 659; Ting Yu, p. 28.

53. Chang Ts'un-wu, pp. 134–136; Ting Yu, pp. 28–29; *HKT,* Aug. 14, 1905, p. 5; Aug. 15, p. 4; *NCH,* Sept. 8, p. 545; Sept. 15, p. 603.

54. Chang Ts'un-wu, pp. 136–137; Ting Yu, pp. 29–30; *HKT,* Sept. 29, 1905, p. 4; Nov. 2, p. 5.

55. Ting Yu, pp. 24–28; DS/CD, Canton, Heintzleman, Sept. 28, 1905.

56. *NCH,* Oct. 13, 1905, p. 67; Lingnan University archives, Box 11, Graybill to Grant, Sept. 6, 1905.

57. On the Lien-chou murders, see Edward J. M. Rhoads, "Nationalism and Xenophobia in Kwangtung (1905–06): The Canton Anti-American Boycott and the Lienchow Anti-Missionary Uprising," *Papers on China,* 16:167 ff. (1962).

58. Beale, pp. 239–245; William Reynolds Braisted, *The United States Navy in the Pacific, 1897–1909* (Austin, 1958), pp. 187–188; Lingnan University archives, Box 11, Journal of C. K. Edmunds, entry of Nov. 28, 1905; Presbyterian Board of Foreign Missions Papers, 47/24, Noyes, Canton, March 6, 1906.

59. DS/CD, Canton, Heintzleman, Dec. 4, 1905.

60. DS/CD, Canton, Ts'en to Lay, Nov. 14, 1905, in Heintzleman, Dec. 4; Chang Ts'un-wu, p. 115.

61. DS/CD, Canton, Heintzleman, Dec. 4, 1905, and enclosures; Lay, Dec. 19, and enclosures; HKT, Nov. 11, p. 5.

62. DS/CD, Canton, Lay, Dec. 19, 1905, and enclosures; Chang Ts'un-wu, p. 234.

63. *HKT,* Dec. 19, 1905, p. 5; DS/CD, Canton, Lay, Feb. 1, 1906.

64. DS/CD, Canton, Lay, March 5, 1906; June 19, enclosure.

65. *SCMP,* July 30, 1906, p. 7; Aug. 6, p. 7; *NCH,* Aug. 10, p. 314.

66. Ting Yu, pp. 49–50; *SCMP,* Dec. 12, 1906, p. 7.

67. *NCH,* Jan. 11, 1907, p. 90; Sept. 13, p. 606; DS/NF, 785/10–15, Bergholz, Canton, Jan. 4, 7, and 8; 785/21–24, clipping from the Hong Kong *Daily Press,* Jan. 24; *SCMP,* Jan. 11, p. 6. On Chou Fu's lukewarm attitude toward nationalism, see also Schrecker, *Imperialism and Chinese Nationalism,* pp. 151, 160–161, 201–202.

68. *TFTC,* 3.1: Tsa-tsu, p. 4 (KH 32/1); 3.4: Chiao-t'ung, p. 118 (32/4); Chang Chih-tung, 195:11b–13, Chang to Ts'en, 31/11/15 and 11/18.

69. Chang Chih-tung, 195:11b–30b, Chang to Ts'en, KH 31/11/15 and 12/20, Chang to Wang Ping-en, 12/22 and 32/1/3, Chang to Yang Wei-pin et al., 1/11.

70. *SCMP,* Jan. 18, 1906, p. 7; Jan. 19, p. 7; Jan. 22, p. 7; *NCH,* Jan. 24, p. 177; Feb. 2, pp. 218, 227; *TFTC,* 3.1: Tsa-tsu, p. 10 (KH 32/1). On the Ming-lun hall, see Chung-li Chang, pp. 201–202.

71. Chang Chih-tung, 195:30b–31b, Chang to Ts'en, KH 32/1/11; *SCMP,* Feb. 16, 1906, p. 7; Feb. 21, p. 7; *TFTC,* 3.6: Tsa-tsu, p. 32 (32/5); *Tung-hua lu* (Taipei, 1968), KH 33/5/26, pp. 5667–5668, memorial of the Ministry of Posts and Communications.

72. *TFTC*, 3.4: Chiao-t'ung, p. 118 (KH 32/4); *NCH*, April 6, 1906, p. 17; *SCMP*, July 11, p. 7; Aug. 11, p. 7.

73. See T'ung-tsu Ch'ü, *Local Government*, pp. 183, 313 (n. 6).

74. *SCMP*, April 20, 1906, p. 7; April 28, p. 7; Aug. 10, p. 7; *NCH*, May 4, p. 252; June 22, p. 691; *TFTC*, 3.5: Tsa-tsu, p. 28 (KH 32/#4); 3.6: Tsa-tsu, pp. 32–33 (32/5).

75. *SCMP*, June 16, 1906, p. 7; June 20, p. 7. For a similar split between the gentry and merchants in Hunan, see Esherick, "Reform, Revolution and Reaction," pp. 153–156.

76. See *TR*, 1907, Canton.

77. Kent, p. 172.

78. Ling Hung-hsün, pp. 232–234; E-tu Zen Sun, *Chinese Railways*, pp. 84–88; *DR*, 1902–11, 2:147–148, 162–163; *NCH*, Dec. 7, 1906, p. 552; Dec. 28, p. 729.

79. Ling Hung-hsün, pp. 400–401.

80. See *TR*, Canton, for these years.

81. On the anti-opium movement, see Cameron, chap. 7; see also DS/NF, 774/576–581, Hull, Canton, Jan. 12, 1909. See Des Forges, pp. 93–102, for the movement in Yunnan. For a brief history of opium in China, see Leonard P. Adams II, "China: The Historical Setting of Asia's Profitable Plague," appendix to Alfred W. McCoy, *The Politics of Heroin in Southeast Asia* (New York, 1972), pp. 365–383.

82. DS/NF, 774/576–581, Hull, Canton, Jan. 12, 1909; *SCMP*, Feb. 9, 1906, p. 7; Feb. 14, p. 7; Aug. 21, p. 7; Aug. 22, p. 7.

83. Cameron, pp. 141–143.

84. *TR*, 1907, Canton, p. 483; *SCMP*, July 27, 1907, p. 7; July 30, p. 7; Aug. 8, p. 7; Aug. 12, p. 7; *HKT*, Nov. 29, 1907, p. 5; DS/NF, 774/576–581, Hull, Canton, Jan. 12, 1909.

85. FO 371/40880, Mansfield to Jordan, Oct. 7, 1907; 371/976, Report on opium by Leach, enclosed in Jordan to Grey, Nov. 27; *TR*, 1903, Canton, p. 694; 1908, Canton, p. 542.

86. DS/NF, 774/143–145, Baugh to Bergholz, in Bergholz, Canton, Nov. 14, 1907; *SCMP*, Aug. 22, 1907, p. 7; Aug. 31, p. 7; Sept. 20, p. 7; see *TR*, Swatow, 1903, p. 651; 1908, p. 506.

87. Cameron, pp. 144–146.

88. Cameron, p. 58; see also Samuel C. Chu, *Reformer in Modern China: Chang Chien, 1853–1926* (New York, 1965), pp. 59–63.

89. As quoted in Fincher, "Chinese Self-Government Movement," p. 76; cf. Samuel Chu, p. 61.

90. Cameron, pp. 101–105; Samuel Chu, pp. 63–64. See E-tu Zen Sun, "The Chinese Constitutional Missions of 1905–1906," *Journal of Modern History*, 24:251–268 (1952).

91. *SCMP*, Sept. 11, 1906, p. 7; Sept. 12, p. 7; *NCH*, Sept. 28, pp. 746, 748–749; Bergère, p. 255.

92. *TFTC*, 4.5: Nei-wu, p. 233 (KH 33/5); 4.10: Nei-wu, p. 509 (33/10); *SCMP*, July 27, 1907, p. 7; July 30, p. 7.

93. *TFTC*, 4.1: Nei-wu, p. 32 (KH 33/1); 4.3: Nei-wu, p. 148 (33/3).

94. Cameron, pp. 108–112.

95. On the Shanghai municipal council, see Mark Elvin, "The Gentry Democracy in Chinese Shanghai, 1905–14," in Jack Gray, ed., *Modern China's Search for a Political Form* (London, 1969), pp. 41–65.

96. This recalls the Ch'ing's legitimization of the gentry's local defense associations (*t'uan*) in the late nineteenth century lest they become a threat to the state's military monopoly. See Kuhn, pp. 206–211.

5. Middle Years of the Post-Boxer Decade, II: Revolution

1. On the Revolutionary Alliance, see Schiffrin, *Sun Yat-sen*, pp. 293–366; Chün-tu Hsüeh, chap. 4; George T. Yu, *Party Politics in Republican China: The Kuomintang, 1912–1924* (Berkeley, 1966), chap. 2; K. S. Liew, *Struggle for Democracy: Sung Chiao-jen and the 1911 Chinese Revolution* (Berkeley, 1971), pp. 43–48; Ta-ling Lee; and Shelley Hsien Cheng, "The T'ung-meng-hui: Its Organization, Leadership and Finances, 1905–1912," Ph.D. diss., University of Washington, 1962.

2. On the ideology of the Alliance, see Gasster; Robert A. Scalapino and Harold Schiffrin, "Early Socialist Currents in the Chinese Revolutionary Movement: Sun Yat-sen versus Liang Ch'i-ch'ao," *Journal of Asian Studies*, 18:321–342 (1959); Harold Schiffrin, "Sun Yat-sen's Early Land Policy: The Origin and Meaning of 'Equalization of Land Rights,' " *Journal of Asian Studies*, 16:549–564 (1957).

3. Chün-tu Hsüeh, p. 44. The membership list is reproduced in *KMWH*, 2:158–210; the section on Kwangtung is on pp. 193–199. On the history of the list, see Ta-ling Lee, p. 36, n. 28.

4. The following members have individual biographies. Chu Chih-hsin: Boorman and Howard, 1:440–443; Wu Hsiang-hsiang, "Chu Chih-hsin chih hsing ho-i," *Chuan-chi wen-hsüeh*, 6.6:30–33 (1965); *HLHCC*, pp. 428–451.

Chu Shao-mu: Feng, *I-shih*, 1:181–184.

Feng Tzu-yu: Boorman and Howard, 2:30–32; *HLHCC*, pp. 535–549.

Ho Hsiang-ning: Boorman and Howard, 2:67–68.

Ho T'ien-chiung: *HLHCC*, p. 897.

Hsieh Liang-mu: *HLHCC*, pp. 1022–1023.

Hu Han-min: Boorman and Howard, 2:159–166; *HLHCC*, pp. 639–721; and Chiang Yung-ching.

Kao Chien-fu: Boorman and Howard, 2:235–237.

Ku Ying-fen: Boorman and Howard, 2:259–261; *HLHCC*, pp. 932–934; Wu Hsiang-hsiang, "Ku Ying-fen ch'i-jen ch'i-shih," *Chuan-chi wen-hsüeh*, 9.2:29–30 (1966).

Kuo Kung-chieh: *HLHCC*, pp. 188–189.

Li Wen-fan: *HLHCC*, pp. 934–935.

Liao Chung-k'ai: Boorman and Howard, 2:364–367; *HLHCC*, pp. 473–482.

Liu Ssu-fu: Boorman and Howard, 2:413–416; *HLHCC*, pp. 889–891.

Wang Ching-wei: Boorman and Howard, 3:369–376.

5. Herbert A. Giles, *From Swatow to Canton: Overland* (London, 1877), pp. 16–17; see also Ssu-yü Teng, *The Taiping Rebellion and the Western Powers: A Comprehensive Survey* (Oxford, 1971), pp. 18–19.

6. For a list of the government scholars sent in 1904, see *TFTC*, 1.9: Chiao-yü, p. 217 (KH 30/9).

7. For a list of the Chinese graduates of the Japanese Army Officers' Academy, see *Saishin Shina kanshin roku*, pp. 392–405 of the supplement.

8. See Maurice Meisner, *Li Ta-chao and the Origins of Chinese Marxism* (Cambridge, 1967), pp. 4–5.

9. See Hao Chang; also Levenson.

10. Cf. Chün-tu Hsüeh, pp. 44–45.

11. On Ch'iu Chin, see Rankin, *Early Chinese Revolutionaries,* pp. 38–46. See also Witke, pp. 52, 57.

12. *KMWH*, 3:357.

13. Feng, *I-shih,* 1:134; *KMWH,* 3:363–366.

14. Feng, *I-shih,* 3:237; *HLHCC,* pp. 465–469.

15. Gasster, p. 171.

16. On Yeh Hsia-sheng, see *Shin-matsu Minsho Chūgoku kanshin jimmeiroku* (Peking, 1918), p. 605.

17. Chün-tu Hsüeh, pp. 57–58; Feng, *I-shih,* 3:290–291; Feng, *Chung-hua,* 1:176, 179; Liu K'uei-i, *Huang Hsing chuan-chi* (Taipei, 1953), p. 9.

18. Feng, *I-shih,* 2:150–151; T'ien T'ung, "T'ung-meng hui ch'eng-li chi," *KMWH,* 2:142–144.

19. Feng, *Chung-hua,* 1:197.

20. See Gasster.

21. K. S. Liew, p. 58.

22. Feng, *Chung-hua,* 1:175–178; *I-shih,* 1:69–72; 3:228–232.

23. See *KMWH,* 2:217; Feng, *I-shih,* 3:229; *Chung-hua,* 1:176.

24. On Ch'en Shu-jen, see Boorman and Howard, 1:234–235; Feng Tzu-yu, "Ch'en Shu-jen shih-lüeh," *Kuo-shih-kuan kuan-k'an,* 1:101–103 (1948); *HLHCC,* pp. 988–989. On Huang Shih-chung, see Feng, *I-shih,* 2:46–51. On Li Shu-fen, see his autobiographical *Hong Kong Surgeon* (London, 1964). On Liao P'ing-tzu, see Feng, *I-shih,* 3:258–264.

25. Feng, *I-shih,* 1:193–201; Woo Sing Lim, *The Prominent Chinese in Hong Kong* (Hong Kong, 1937), pp. 7–8 of the supplement.

26. *NCH,* May 4, 1906, p. 275.

27. Feng, *I-shih,* 1:69–72; *Chung-hua,* 1:177–178. On Feng's article, see Schiffrin, "Sun's Land Policy," pp. 551–553; Scalapino and Schiffrin, pp. 326–329; Gasster, pp. 144–145.

28. Feng, *I-shih,* 1:70, 84–85; 3:142–143; *Chung-kuo ko-ming yün-tung erh-shih-liu-nien tsu-chih shih* (Shanghai, 1948), pp. 102–103, 116; "Ch'en Shu-jen shih-lüeh," p. 101; *SCMP,* Aug. 22, 1906.

29. Feng, *Chung-hua,* 1:174–175.

30. Feng, *I-shih,* 3:139–159; cf. 1:70, which adds the *Ya-chou pao* to the list, but practically nothing is known about this paper.

31. *NCH,* Aug. 10, 1906, p. 314.

32. *DS/NF,* 1879/4–5, Bergholz, Canton, Oct. 5, 1906, which contains a copy of the twenty-fourth issue.

33. *KKWH,* 1.12:538; FO 228/1627, Mansfield to Carnegie, May 29, 1906.

34. T'an Li-yüan, pp. 4–5; *KKWH*, 1.12:539; Feng, *I-shih*, 3:142; FO 228/1627, Mansfield to Carnegie, May 29, 1906; *NCH*, Feb. 15, 1907, p. 347.

35. For an overview of these uprisings, see Chün-tu Hsüeh, pp. 56–72.

36. Jansen, pp. 122–123, 125; see also J. Kim Munholland, "The French Connection That Failed: France and Sun Yat-sen, 1900–1908," *Journal of Asian Studies*, 32:88–95 (1972).

37. Chün-tu Hsüeh, pp. 57–58.

38. On Chao Sheng, see *HLHCC*, pp. 559–580.

39. Cf. Feng, *Chung-hua*, 2:150, 166, 175.

40. Feng, *Chung-hua*, 2:175; Teng Mu-han, "Shu ting-wei Fang-ch'eng ko-ming chün-shih," *HHKM*, 2:546–547; Ch'en Ch'un-sheng, "Kuang Ching-ch'uan Ch'en Shou-t'ien so-shu Ch'in-Fang Chen-nan-kuan Ho-k'ou chu i ch'i-i hsiang-ch'ing," *KKWH*, 1.13:131–133; *HLHCC*, pp. 563–564, 577–578; *TFTC*, 4.7: Chün-shih, p. 83 (KH 33/7); see also Lo Shou-chang, pp. 392–394.

41. Feng, *I-shih*, 2:200–201; *Chung-hua*, 2:90, 149–150; Tsou, *Tang shih-kao*, pp. 726–727; Huang Chen-wu, *Hua-ch'iao yü Chung-kuo ko-ming* (Taipei, 1963), pp. 106–108; "Ting-wei Ch'ao-chou Huang-kang erh i pieh-chi," *KKWH*, 1.13:76–77.

42. On the Huang-kang revolt, see Feng, *Chung-hua*, 2:150–164, and *I-shih*, 2:201–202; Tsou, *Tang shih-kao*, pp. 727–730; "Ting-wei Ch'ao-chou Huang-kang erh i pieh-chi"; Huang Chen-wu, pp. 102–116; Huang Fu-luan, *Hua-ch'iao yü Chung-kuo ko-ming* (Hong Kong, 1954), pp. 126–140; *KKWH*, 1.13:103–110, quoting from Chang Yung-fu, *Nan-yang yü ch'uang-li min-kuo* (Southeast Asia and the establishment of the Republic); Ch'en Ch'un-sheng, "Ting-wei Huang-kang ch'i-i chi," *KKWH*, 1.13:64–72; DS/NF, 215/54–55, Hausser, Swatow, to Bergholz, June 13, 1907; *TR*, 1907, Swatow, pp. 458–459; *SCMP*, May 30, 1907, p. 7; *NCH*, June 7, p. 589.

43. On the Ch'i-nü-hu revolt, see Feng, *Chung-hua*, 2:166–170; *I-shih*, 4:182–185; 5:111–116; Tsou, *Tang shih-kao*, pp. 733–735; *SCMP*, June 7, 1907, p. 7; June 13, p. 7.

44. *SCMP*, June 13, 1907, p. 7.

45. See Huang Chen-wu, p. 117.

46. Feng, *Chung-hua*, 2:166.

47. On the attempt to assassinate Li Chun, see Feng, *Chung-hua*, 2:84–101; *I-shih*, 2:207–213; Chiang Yung-ching, pp. 104–105.

48. On the Fang-ch'eng revolt, see Feng, *Chung-hua*, 2:175–180, and *I-shih*, 5:213–215; Teng Mu-han, "Shu ting-wei Fang-ch'eng ko-ming chün-shih," pp. 547–549; Liu K'uei-i, pp. 15–17; Ch'en Ch'un-sheng, "Ting-wei Fang-ch'eng ch'i-i chi," *KKWH*, 1.13:126–130; Ch'en Ch'un-sheng, "K'uang Ching-ch'uan Ch'en Shou-t'ien so-shu Ch'in-Fang Chen-nan-kuan Ho-k'ou chu i ch'i-i hsiang-ch'ing," pp. 133–134; Lo Shou-chang, pp. 392–395; *KKWH*, 1.13:136–137, 164–165; Ling-shan *HC*, p. 110; Tsou, *Tang shih-kao*, pp. 744–748; *TFTC*, 4.10: Chün-shih, pp. 118–119 (KH 33/10); *SCMP*, Sept. 24, 1907, p. 7; DS/NF, 215/81, Bergholz, Canton, Oct. 21, 1907. On Wang Ho-shun, see Feng, *I-shih*, 2:216–221, and Winston Hsieh, "Triads, Salt Smugglers and Local Uprisings," pp. 150–151.

49. *KKWH*, 1.13:137.

50. On the Shan-wei smuggling attempt, see Feng, *Chung-hua*, 2:181–190, and *I-*

shih, 2:202–206; 5:211–213; Teng Mu-han, "Ting-wei Shan-wei chü-i shih-mo chi," *KKWH*, 1.13:349–352.

51. On the invasion of Ch'in-chou, see Feng, *Chung-hua*, 2:201–204, and *I-shih*, 5:144–156, 222–224; Liu K'uei-i, pp. 18–19; Chün-tu Hsüeh, pp. 68–70; T'an Jen-feng, "Shih-sou p'ai-tz'u hsü-lu," *Chin-tai-shih tzu-liao*, 1956, no. 3, pp. 37–38; Tsou, *Tang shih-kao*, p. 755.

52. Feng, *I-shih*, 3:233–237; *Chung-hua*, 1:179–180; FO 371/3364, Lugard to Moore, Dec. 24, 1907; 371/14849, WWP to Jordan, April 4, 1908.

53. Feng, *I-shih*, 3:233, 291–292; *Chung-hua*, 2:86, 90; Tsou Lu, *Kuang-chou san-yüeh erh-shih-chiu ko-ming shih* (Taipei, 1953), pp. 28–29.

54. Feng, *I-shih*, 2:200–201.

55. Feng, *I-shih*, 3:233.

56. Cf. Rankin, *Early Chinese Revolutionaries*, pp. 155–157, 174–175, 192; Kupper, pp. 35, 101.

57. See Schiffrin, "Sun's Land Policy."

6. *Final Years of the Post-Boxer Decade, I: Nationalism*

1. There is a biography of Yüan Shu-hsün in *Pei-chuan chi pu* (A supplementary collection of funerary inscriptions; Peiping: Kuo-hsüeh yen-chiu so, Yenching University, 1931), which I have not consulted; there is, to my knowledge, no biography of Chang Jen-chün.

2. P'an-yü *HC*, 11:9b–10; Brunnert and Hagelstrom, nos. 621B, 627A; *Chiao-yü t'ung-chi t'u-piao*, 3rd ser., section on Kwangtung, p. 2; Ayers, pp. 248–251.

3. *Chiao-yü t'ung-chi t'u-piao*, 3rd ser., section on Kwangtung.

4. *Chiao-yü t'ung-chi t'u-piao*, 1st and 3rd ser., section on Kwangtung; Gasster, p. 32, n. 11; Bastid, p. 52, n. 62.

5. *Chiao-yü t'ung-chi t'u-piao*, 1st and 3rd ser., section on Kwangtung; Hsüan-t'ung Kao-yao *HC*, 2:14b–16b; Ling-shan *HC*, pp. 148–151; Shun-te *HC*, 2:27–28b.

6. *Nung-kung-shang-pu t'ung-chi piao*, 2nd ser., section on chambers of commerce, 4:19b–21b; K'ai-p'ing *HC*, 12:9b; Nan-hai *HC*, 6:8b; Shun-te *HC*, 3:12–12b.

7. *SCMP*, Nov. 25, 1908, p. 7; K'ai-p'ing *HC*, 21:23; Ch'ing-yüan *HC*, 3:46; 13:22.

8. FO 371/634, Report respecting the reform movement in Canton, Jan. 28, 1909; *SCMP*, July 14, 1908, p. 7; June 22, 1909, p. 6; *HKT*, Jan. 18, 1910, p. 3; see also *TR* for these ports for these years.

9. Cf. Wright, pp. 14–15.

10. *TFTC*, 5.4: Chün-shih, pp. 49–52 (KH 34/4); FO 371/1148, Changes report for the Chinese army, 1909, Dec. 23, 1909; *HKT*, Dec. 12, 1910, p. 5; Great Britain, War Office archives, 33/509, "Field Notes on China. 1.-The Army," 1910: Jean Rodes, *Le Céleste empire avant la révolution* (Paris, 1914), pp. 49–50; Mo Ch'ang-fan et al., "I-chiu-i-ling-nien Kuang-tung hsin-chün ko-ming chi-shih," *Chin-tai-shih tzu-liao*, 1955, no. 4, p. 85.

11. See *TR*, Canton, for these years; also *DR*, 1902–11, 2:146.

12. *SCMP*, April 1, 1912, p. 8.

13. *TR*, Canton, 1908–1911.

14. Ling Hung-hsün, pp. 400–401; *NCH*, Jan. 10, 1908, p. 76; Jan. 24, p. 218; Feb. 28, p. 516; Jan. 2, 1909, pp. 13–14; April 22, 1911, p. 211; *SCMP*, June 7, 1909, p. 3; *DR*, 1902–11, 2:188; *China Proper*, 3:490.

15. Brunnert and Hagelstrom, no. 770; Nan-hai *HC*, 6:8b–9; P'an-yü *HC*, 12:3–4b; *National Sun Yat-sen University*, p. 2; Tseng-ch'eng *HC*, 3:57; Le-ch'ang *HC*, 19:16; Shih-ch'eng *HC*, 4:63.

16. Brunnert and Hagelstrom, nos. 758–761; Cameron, p. 174; P'an-yü *HC*, 4:4; *SCMP*, July 29, 1911, p. 7; *KKWH*, 1.12:542–543; see also Wright, p. 13.

17. Brunnert and Hagelstrom, nos. 766–767; P'an-yü *HC*, 11:7; *SCMP*, April 11, 1908, p. 7; June 6, 1910, p. 6.

18. *TFTC*, 5.3: Tsa-tsu, p. 10 (KH 34/3); 5.6: Chiao-yü, p. 150 (34/6); *SCMP*, April 2, 1908, p. 7; cf. *HKT*, Dec. 7, 1908, p. 4.

19. *Chung-kuo lao-kung yün-tung shih* (Taipei, 1959), 1:51–52; Boorman and Howard, 1:15; *HKT*, May 11, 1911, p. 3.

20. *HKT*, Oct. 12, 1908, p. 4; Jan. 15, 1909, p. 4; *HLHCC*, pp. 320, 323; WWP, Macao file, Canton newspaper clippings, *Yang-ch'eng jih-pao*, HT 1/10/20; *HTJP*, HT 3/9/9.

21. *SCMP*, Feb. 6, 1911, p. 7; Oct. 19, p. 6; *HKT*, Sept. 16, 1910, p. 4; Oct. 7, 1911, p. 5; *NCH*, April 15, 1911, p. 151; Rodes, *Céleste empire*, p. 42.

22. *Chiao-yü tsa-chih*, 3.2: Chi-shih, p. 16 (HT 3/2); 3.5: Chi-shih, p. 37 (3/5); 3.6: Fu-lu, p. 1 (3/6); Bastid, pp. 73–74.

23. *TFTC*, 7.9: Chi-tsai III, pp. 243–246 (HT 2/9).

24. *TFTC*, 7.8: Chang-ch'eng, pp. 15–18 (HT 2/8); Wellington Chan, pp. 281–282.

25. *DR*, 1902–11, 2:132; *TFTC*, 5.6: Chiao-yü, p. 150 (KH 34/6); *HLHCC*, p. 880; Lin I-han, pp. 480–484.

26. *DR*, 1902–11, 2:132, 191–192; *Ch'en Ching-ts'un hsien-sheng nien-p'u* (Hong Kong, n.d.), p. 12; T'an Cho-yüan, "Kuang-chou ting-ch'i k'an-wu ti tiao-ch'a," *Ling-nan hsüeh-pao*, 4.3:2 (1935).

27. *DR*, 1902–11, 2:154; *HKT*, Nov. 4, 1910, p. 5; cf. FO 371/634, Report respecting the reform movement in Canton, Jan. 28, 1909.

28. *Chiao-yü t'ung-chi t'u-piao*, 1st and 2nd ser., section on Kwangtung; *SCMP*, July 13, 1908, p. 10; Gamble, pp. 48, 60 (table 9); Rodes, *Céleste empire*, p. 42.

29. Levi, p. 101; *SCMP*, Dec. 25, 1907, p. 7.

30. Wright, pp. 4–19.

31. *NCH*, Nov. 29, 1907, p. 532; *SCMP*, Dec. 4, p. 7. For the West River patrol agitation, see the FO 371/314 file; see also Paul King, pp. 195–201.

32. Paul King, p. 197; *NCH*, Dec. 6, 1907, pp. 580–581.

33. *HKT*, Nov. 21, 1907, p. 4; Nov. 22, p. 5; Nov. 25, p. 4; Nov. 27, p. 5; *SCMP*, Nov. 22, p. 7; *HTJP*, KH 33/10/15, p. 2; 10/16, p. 2; 10/17, p. 2; 10/20, p. 2; 10/22, p. 2; and WWP, Telegrams received, KH 33/10/13–27.

34. *HKT*, Nov. 21, 1907, p. 4; Nov. 23, p. 5; Nov. 26, p. 4; *SCMP*, Nov. 22, p. 7; Nov. 27, p. 7; *HTJP*, KH 33/10/15, p. 2; 10/16, p. 2; 10/18, p. 2; 10/21, p. 2; Wang Yün-sheng, *Liu-shih-nien-lai Chung-kuo yü Jih-pen* (Tientsin, 1932–33),

5:193–194; Kikuchi Takaharu, "Daini Tatsu Maru jiken no tai-Nichi boikotto," *Rekishigaku kenkyū*, no. 209, p. 4 (1957).

35. *HKT*, Nov. 22, 1907, p. 5; *HTJP*, KH 33/10/17, p. 2; 10/20, p. 2. On Shen, see Feng, *I-shih*, 3:142.

36. *SCMP*, Dec. 9, 1907, p. 7; Dec. 16, p. 7; *HKT*, Dec. 17, p. 4; Dec. 21, p. 4; Dec. 27, p. 4.

37. *HKT*, Dec. 11, 1907, p. 4; Dec. 24, p. 4.

38. *SCMP*, Dec. 14, 1907, p. 7; *HKT*, Dec. 19, p. 5; *NCH*, Dec. 27, p. 762; *KKWH*, 1.16: 596–597; WWP, Telegrams received, KH 33/10/13–27; *HTJP*, 33/10/20, p. 2.

39. *HKT*, Nov. 23, 1907, p. 5; *NCH*, Dec. 20, pp. 706–707; *SCMP*, Dec. 25, p. 7; WWP, Macao file, Chuan-tang, telegram from various Kwangsi groups, KH 33/11/13; *KKWH*, 1.16:597–598.

40. *KKWH*, 1.16:597–598; *TFTC*, 5.2: Chiao-t'ung, pp. 76–78 (KH 34/2); *HKT*, Dec. 17, 1907, p. 4; Dec. 21, p. 4; May 12, 1909, p. 4; *SCMP*, Dec. 25, 1907, p. 7; Jan. 14, 1908, p. 7; Feb. 14, p. 7; April 30, p. 4; July 16, p. 4.

41. *KKWH*, 1.16:596–597.

42. *HKT*, Nov. 21, 1907, p. 4; Nov. 23, p. 5; *SCMP*, Nov. 22, p. 7; Dec. 7, p. 7; Dec. 9, p. 7; *KKWH*, 1.16:597–598.

43. *NCH*, Dec. 20, 1907, p. 720; Dec. 27, p. 772.

44. *Tung-hua lu*, KH 33/11/20 and 21, pp. 5787–5789.

45. *KKWH*, 1.16:597–598.

46. *HTJP*, KH 33/10/21, p. 2; *NCH*, Jan. 10, 1908, pp. 59–60; Jan. 17, p. 158.

47. See WWP, West River file, Telegrams sent and received, KH 33/11–33/12.

48. *SCMP*, March 17, 1908, p. 7.

49. *HKT*, Jan. 28, 1908, p. 4; Jan. 29, p. 4; DS/NF, 190/16, Bergholz, Canton, Feb. 12; *TR*, 1907, Canton, p. 480; 1909, Canton, p. 579.

50. *NCH*, Feb. 7, 1908, p. 329.

51. On the diplomatic aspects of the *Tatsu Maru* case, see Wang Yün-sheng, 5:178–189; WWP, Tatsu Maru file; *TFTC*, 5.5: Wai-chiao, pp. 25–28 (KH 34/5). For a Japanese version, see *NCH*, Feb. 28, 1908, pp. 495–496; *SCMP*, March 10, p. 7. See also Akira Iriye, *Pacific Estrangement: Japanese and American Expansion, 1897–1911* (Cambridge, 1972), pp. 182–185.

52. *SCMP*, March 12, 1908, p. 7; March 13, p. 7; *NCH*, March 13, p. 649; March 27, p. 758; WWP, Tatsu Maru file, Ch'en Chi-chen (Ch'en Hui-p'u) et al. to WWP, KH 34/2/8, and Governor-General Chang to WWP, 2/13, enclosure.

53. *SCMP*, March 12, 1908, p. 7; *NCH*, April 3, p. 35; Wang Yün-sheng, 5:190, 193–194. On the developing boycott, see Kikuchi Takaharu; also Akira Iriye, "Public Opinion and Foreign Policy: The Case of Late Ch'ing China," in Feuerwerker et al., *Approaches to Modern Chinese History*, pp. 216–238.

54. FO 228/2541, Clipping from the *Shih-min pao*, KH 34/2/18; *SCMP*, March 23, 1908, p. 7; *NCH*, March 27, p. 758; *TFTC*, 5.3:Tsa-tsu, p. 10 (KH 34/3).

55. *SCMP*, April 2, 1908, p. 7; April 9, p. 7; April 11, p. 7; April 16, p. 7; April 29, p. 7; July 4, p. 4; *NCH*, April 10, p. 79; April 16, p. 142; May 16, p. 402; *TFTC*, 5.4: Tsa-tsu, p. 11 (KH 34/4).

56. WWP, Tatsu Maru file, Japanese ambassador to WWP, KH 34/3/8; *TFTC*, 5.6: Chiao-yü, p. 150 (KH 34/6); cf. *HKT*, Oct. 27, 1908, p. 5.

57. Cf. *NCH*, May 1, 1908, p. 284.

58. *NCH*, April 16, 1908, p. 142; *SCMP*, July 4, p. 4.

59. *NCH*, April 24, 1908, p. 218; DS/NF, 12705/3–4, Wilder, Hong Kong, April 16, 1908; 12705/8–9, Sharp, Hong Kong, May 1; 12705/10, Wilder, Hong Kong, May 8; *SCMP*, July 4, p. 4; Aug. 10, p. 7.

60. *NCH*, May 16, 1908, p. 402; June 27, p. 805; *SCMP*, July 4, p. 4; *TR*, 1908, Canton, pp. 520–521; see also *TR* for these ports for these years.

61. Wang Yün-sheng, 5:196; Hu Ying-han, p. 29.

62. Wang Yün-sheng, 5:192–193.

63. *SCMP*, Aug. 24, 1908, p. 7; Aug. 27, p. 7; *HKT*, Oct. 3, p. 4; Oct. 7, p. 4; Oct. 24, p. 5; DS/NF, 12705/16, Hull, Canton, Sept. 3, 1908; 12705/17–18, clipping from the Hong Kong *Daily Press*, Nov. 3; Wang Yün-sheng, 5:197–198; *TFTC*, 5.12: Chi-tsai, p. 141 (KH 34/12).

64. *SCMP*, Nov. 2, 1908, p. 7; *HKT*, Nov. 2, pp. 4–5; and subsequent issues of both papers; also FO 371/6238, Police report, Nov. 3.

65. *HKT*, Nov. 7, 1908, p. 4; Nov. 9, p. 5; FO 228/2541, item from the *An-ya pao*, Nov. 6.

66. WWP, Tatsu Maru file, Memorandum from Abe, KH 34/10/30; communication from Jordan to WWP, 11/2; WWP to Chang, KH 34/11/3; Wang Yün-sheng, 5:197–198; FO 228/2541, Fox to Lugard, Nov. 14, 1908.

67. *HKT*, Nov. 13, 1908, p. 4; FO 228/2541, Fox to Lugard, Nov. 14.

68. WWP, Tatsu Maru file, Chang to WWP, KH 34/11/8; *TFTC*, 5.12: Chi-tsai, p. 141 (34/12); *NCH*, Dec. 12, 1908, p. 644; *SCMP*, Dec. 15, p. 7; FO 371/6238; 228/2541; Hu Ying-han, pp. 8–9.

69. On Pratas case, see WWP, Pratas file; *TFTC*, 6.4: Chi-shih, pp. 60–69 (HT 1/3), and subsequent issues in the Chi-shih section; *SCMP*, March 16, 1909, p. 7; *HKT*, April 2, p. 4; April 15, p. 4.

70. *HKT*, May 11, 1909, p. 4.

71. *HKT*, Sept. 1, 1909, p. 4; Sept. 2, p. 4; Sept. 28, p. 4; Sept. 30, p. 5; Nov. 9, p. 4; Feb. 5, 1910, p. 4; *SCMP*, Sept. 3, 1909, p. 7; Oct. 2, p. 6; Oct. 13, p. 7; *NCH*, Oct. 23, p. 171. On the background to the controversy, see Des Forges, pp. 140–144.

72. *TFTC*, 6.3: Chi-shih, p. 20 (HT 1/#2); FO 371/236 and 228/2255; *HKT*, Dec. 2, 1908, p. 5; Dec. 3, p. 5; *SCMP*, Dec. 2, p. 7; Dec. 4, p. 4; Dec. 7, p. 7; Paul King, pp. 219–220.

73. *HKT*, Dec. 5, 1908, p. 5; Dec. 7, p. 4; *SCMP*, Dec. 9, p. 7; Dec. 10, p. 7; FO 371/236.

74. *SCMP*, Jan. 2, 1909, p. 7; Jan. 8, p. 7; *NCH*, Jan. 9, p. 93; *TFTC*, 6.3: Chi-shih, p. 22 (HT 1/#2); FO 371/236, no. 7103.

75. FO 228/2255, Fox to Jordan, Jan. 28, 1909.

76. FO 228/2255; 371/236, nos. 29900, 30079, 34056, 34725, 35086; *HKT*, June 19, 1909, p. 4; Aug. 7, p. 4; *NCH*, June 26, pp. 737–738; Aug. 21, p. 453; *TFTC*, 6.8: Chi-shih, p. 248 (HT 1/7); DS/NF, 2691/9–12, Bergholz, Canton, Aug. 23.

77. *TFTC*, 6.3: Chi-shih, pp. 20–22 (HT 1/#2); *SCMP*, March 10, 1909, p. 7;

June 19, p. 7; *NCH,* Aug. 21, p. 453; Dec. 11, p. 680; *HKT,* Aug. 24, p. 5; Aug. 25, p. 4.

78. *TFTC,* 6.4: Chi-shih, pp. 53–58 (HT 1/3).

79. WWP, Macao file, Chuan-tang, report from Acting Governor-General Hu to WWP, received KH 33/8/7; telegram from the Kwangtung–Kwangsi College of Languages, 10/19, and similar telegrams, 10/20–11/13.

80. WWP, Macao file, Chuan-tang, WWP to Chang, HT 1/1/6, and all preceding correspondence.

81. *TFTC,* 6.4: Chi-shih, pp. 54–55 (HT 1/3); WWP, Macao file, Canton newspaper clippings, *Yang-ch'eng jih-pao,* 1/2/18, 2/21; Hsiang-shan *HC,* 16:4.

82. Hsiang-shan *HC,* 16:4; WWP, Macao file, Shanghai newspaper clippings, *Shih-shih pao,* HT 1/#2/13; Canton newspaper clippings, "Pen-sheng chin-yao hsin-wen" (from *Yang-ch'eng jih-pao,* #2/12 and #2/15).

83. WWP, Macao file, Canton newspaper clippings, "Pen-sheng chin-yao hsin-wen" (from *Yang-ch'eng jih-pao,* HT 1/#2/12).

84. See *TFTC,* 6.4: Chi-shih, pp. 54–58 (HT 1/3); Hsiang-shan *HC,* 6:15b–19b; WWP, Macao file, Shanghai newspaper clippings, *Shih pao,* HT 1/#2/18.

85. For the "statement of opinion," see Hsiang-shan *HC,* 6:15b–19b.

86. WWP, Macao file, Hong Kong newspaper clippings, *HTJP,* HT 1/5/12; Chuan-tang, telegram from Ts'ui Ch'i-piao and Yang Jui-chieh to WWP, received 5/25; *HKT,* July 1, 1909, p. 4.

87. See the detailed correspondence between Commissioner Kao and the WWP, in WWP, Macao file, Chuan-tang, during the period of negotiation; also *TFTC,* 6.8: Chi-shih, pp. 242–244 (HT 1/7), and subsequent issues in the Chi-shih section.

88. WWP, Macao file, clipping from the Canton *Kuo-shih pao,* HT 1/7/3.

89. See, for example, WWP, Macao file, Chuan-tang, two reports by Kao to WWP, received HT 1/7/17 and 7/18, and the ministry's reply, sent on 7/18.

90. WWP, Macao file, Chuan-tang, Yüan to WWP, received HT 1/8/4; Kao to WWP, received HT 1/8/12 and 8/14; Hong Kong newspaper clippings, *Shang pao,* 8/19; *TFTC,* 6.11: Chi-shih, p. 376 (HT 1/10).

91. *TFTC,* 6.11: Chi-shih, p. 376 (HT 1/10); WWP, Macao file, Hong Kong newspaper clippings, *HTJP,* 1/9/6, 9/13, and 9/24; *Shang pao,* 9/9; *HKT,* Oct. 19, 1909, p. 4; Oct. 26, p. 4.

92. See WWP, Macao file, Chuan-tang, for the correspondence.

93. *TFTC,* 7.8: Chung-kuo ta-shih chi pu-i, pp. 65–66 (HT 2/8); see also 7.7: Chung-kuo ta-shih chi, pp. 90–92 (2/7).

94. See WWP, Macao file, Chuan-tang, correspondence from HT 3/5 to 3/#6.

95. *DR,* 1902–11, 2:170; *NCH,* June 27, 1908, p. 805; Feb. 20, 1909, p. 482; May 1, p. 284; Feb. 10, 1911, p. 306; *HKT,* Jan. 10, 1910, p. 4.

96. See Wang Yün-sheng, 5:197–198; see also FO 371/634, Report respecting the reform movement in Canton, Jan. 28, 1909.

97. See, for example, WWP, Telegrams received, KH 33/10/15, 19, 22, and 26.

98. *NCH,* Nov. 29, 1907, p. 558; *HTJP,* KH 33/10/27, p. 2; *HKT,* Nov. 24, 1909, p. 7; Feb. 18, 1910, p. 5.

99. *NCH,* June 13, 1908, p. 681; *SCMP,* Sept. 11, p. 7; Sept. 16, p. 7; *HKT,* June 5, 1909, p. 5; Dec. 23, p. 4.

100. *HKT*, Jan. 28, 1908, p. 4; *SCMP*, March 30, p. 7; April 15, p. 7; *HTJP*, HT 1/7/25, p. 2; 8/18, p. 2.

101. See Li Chien-nung, *Chung-kuo chin-pai-nien cheng-chih shih* (Taipei, 1962), 1: 265; Liu Kuei-wu, "Hsin-hai ko-ming ch'ien-hou ti li-hsien p'ai yü li-hsien yün-tung," *Li-shih chiao-hsüeh*, 1962, no. 8, p. 21; P'eng-yüan Chang, "The Constitutionalists," in Wright, ed., *China in Revolution*, p. 144.

102. *NCH*, Sept. 19, 1908, p. 744; *SCMP*, Sept. 22, p. 7; Sept. 24, p. 7; Sept. 26, p. 7; *HKT*, Oct. 7, 1910, p. 4.

103. *HKT*, Nov. 24, 1909, p. 7; Feb. 18, 1910, p. 3.

104. *TR*, 1909, Pakhoi, p. 656; WWP, Macao file, Newspaper clippings from the *Yang-ch'eng jih-pao*, HT 1/2/27 and 2/28.

105. *NCH*, May 20, 1908, p. 670; April 24, 1909, p. 187; *HKT*, Oct. 6, 1908, p. 4.

106. *DR*, 1902–11, 2:126–127; Ling Hung-hsün, pp. 399–400; *TFTC*, 6.10: Chi-shih, p. 325 (HT 1/9); 6.11: Chi-shih, p. 373 (1/10); DS/NF, 5315/448–450, Pontius, Swatow, June 25, 1909; 5315/466–467, Pontius, July 8; 5315/611, Pontius, Oct. 1.

107. FO 228/2255, enclosure in dispatch from Fox, Canton, May 25, 1909.

108. FO 228/2541.

7. Final Years of the Post-Boxer Decade, II: Constitutionalism

1. On the late Ch'ing constitutionalist movement, see Cameron, chap. 4; Fincher, "Chinese Self-Government Movement"; and Samuel Chu, chap. 4.

2. *HKT*, Oct. 22, 1907, p. 4; *SCMP*, Oct. 23, p. 7; *HTJP*, KH 33/10/2, p. 2; *TFTC*, 5.2: Nei-wu, p. 143 (34/2).

3. *HTJP*, KH 33/10/2, p. 2; 10/3, p. 3; 10/7, p. 2; 10/14, p. 2; *HKT*, Nov. 7, 1907, p. 4; Nov. 8, p. 5; Nov. 12, p. 4; *TFTC*, 5.2: Nei-wu, p. 143 (KH 34/2). On I Hsüeh-ch'ing, see Liu Po-chi, *Kuang-tung shu-yüan chih-tu* (Taipei, 1958), p. 277; on Yang Sheng, see Ch'ien Shih-fu, *Ch'ing-chi hsin-she chih-kuan nien-piao* (Peking, 1961), p. 88; on Lu Nai-chuang, see Shun-te *HC*, 8:19; on Teng Hua-hsi, see Shun-te *HC*, 8:34b; on Liang Ch'ing-kuei, see P'an-yü *HC*, 16:9.

4. *TFTC*, 5.3: Nei-wu, p. 212 (KH 34/3); 5.4: Nei-wu, p. 268 (34/4); *HKT*, Jan. 22, 1908, p. 4; *SCMP*, Jan. 23, p. 7.

5. *NCH*, Jan. 17, 1908, p. 125.

6. *SCMP*, March 30, 1908, p. 7; April 15, p. 7; *HKT*, Sept. 17, p. 5; *NCH*, Sept. 26, p. 768. See also Samuel Chu, p. 65; Fincher, "Chinese Self-Government Movement," p. 155.

7. Cameron, pp. 113–115.

8. DS/NF, 560/49, Bergholz, Canton, Feb. 4, 1909; *HKT*, Jan. 16, 1909, p. 4; Jan. 18, p. 5; *SCMP*, Jan. 29, p. 7; March 10, p. 7.

9. See Cameron, p. 121; P'eng-yüan Chang, pp. 146–147; Li Shou-k'ung, "Ko-sheng tzu-i chü lien-ho hui yü hsin-hai ko-ming," *Chung-kuo hsien-tai-shih ts'ung-k'an*, 3:327, n. 3 (1961).

10. *HTJP*, HT 1/4/22, p. 2; P'eng-yüan Chang, p. 150; *TFTC*, 6.7: Hsien-cheng

pien, pp. 351–353 (HT 1/6); Chung-li Chang, p. 164, table 32; see also Fincher, "Chinese Self-Government Movement," p. 115.

11. *TFTC*, 6.7: Hsien-cheng pien, pp. 351–353 (HT 1/6); also 6.5: Chi-tsai I, pp. 230–236 (1/4); FO 371/1142, Report by Mr. Campbell respecting the provincial assemblies of October 1909.

12. DS/DF, 893.00/351½, Bergholz, Canton, Dec. 20, 1909; *HTJP*, HT 1/6/1, p. 2; 6/5, p. 2; cf. P'eng-yüan Chang, p. 147. The turnout in Hunan and Hupeh was also quite low; see Esherick, "Reform, Revolution and Reaction," pp. 176–177.

13. See Yang-chiang *HC*, 27:34b–39; 28:3b, 5b; 37:17b.

14. *HTJP*, HT 1/6/7, p. 2.

15. *HTJP*, HT 1/6/8, p. 2.

16. DS/DF, 893.00/351½, Bergholz, Canton, Dec. 20, 1909; Li Shou-k'ung, p. 323; France, Archives des Affaires Etrangères, Correspondence de Chine, n.s., vol. 19, folio 23, dispatch from Canton, Sept. 6, 1909; *HTJP*, HT 1/7/17, p. 2; see also P'eng-yüan Chang, p. 148.

17. For a list of the assemblymen, see *TFTC*, 6.11: Ko-sheng tzu-i chü i-yüan hsing-ming lu (HT 1/11).

18. See the gazetteers for the following fifteen districts: Nan-hai, P'an-yü, Shun-te, Hsiang-shan, Tung-kuan, Ch'ing-yüan, K'ai-p'ing, Tseng-ch'eng, Yang-shan, Kao-yao, Ling-shan, Hsü-wen, En-p'ing, Yang-chiang, and Lo-ting. The dispatch is in *HTJP*, HT 1/7/24, p. 2.

19. P'eng-yüan Chang, pp. 149–151.

20. P'eng-yüan Chang, p. 151, table 3.3.

21. On I, see Liang Chia-pin, *Kuang-tung shih-san hang* (Shanghai, 1937), p. 325; on Ch'iu, see his chronological biography, "Ts'ang-hai hsien-sheng Ch'iu kung Feng-chia nien-p'u," and Harry J. Lamley, "The 1895 Taiwan Republic: A Significant Episode in Modern Chinese History," *Journal of Asian Studies*, 27:739–762 (1968); and on Ch'en, see Tseng-ch'eng *HC*, 16:17–18.

22. *HTJP*, HT 1/7/29, p. 2. In Hunan and Hupeh too, a number of leading gentry members declined to participate in the assembly; see Esherick, "Reform, Revolution and Reaction," pp. 176–177.

23. See *Wu-hsü pien-fa*, 4:405; on Chao, see *Shin-matsu jimmeiroku*, p. 634.

24. *HTJP*, HT 1/7/24, p. 2; Corr. de Chine, n.s., vol. 19, folio 140–143, extracts from a letter from Father Le Corre, Oct. 20, 1909, attached to a dispatch from Swatow, Nov. 8.

25. *HTJP*, HT 1/8/23, p. 2; Liang Chia-pin, p. 325.

26. Yang-shan *HC*, 4:15; *Gendai Shina jimmeikan* (Tokyo, 1916), under entry for Mo Jen-heng.

27. *Ch'en Ching-ts'un nien-p'u*, p. 12; Hsiang-shan *HC*, 9:9; Hsü-wen *HC*, 12:50b; K'ai-p'ing *HC*, 25:31b.

28. *Shin-matsu jimmeiroku*, p. 184; Peng-yüan Chang, p. 152, n. 28, says that two of the Kwangtung assemblymen "had studied either in Japan or in other foreign countries," but he does not identify them.

29. *TFTC*, 4.4: Chiao-yü, p. 127 (KH 33/4); 4.9: Chiao-yü, p. 227 (33/9).

30. Nan-hai *HC*, 10:15–15b; *Nung-kung-shang-pu t'ung-chi piao*, 1st and 2nd ser.,

section on chambers of commerce; *HTJP*, HT 1/7/24, p. 2; *TFTC*, 7.11: Chung-kuo ta-shih chi pu-i, p. 93 (HT 2/11).

31. See Chang Hui-ch'ang, "Li-hsien-p'ai jen ho Ssu-ch'uan tzu-i chü," *HIL*, 3:146–151; see also Esherick, "Reform, Reaction and Revolution," p. 118.

32. Brunnert and Hagelstrom, nos. 169, 171; Tsou, *Hui-ku lu*, p. 29.

33. For lists of the topics brought up before the Kwangtung assembly for debate and resolution at its first two regular sessions, see *TFTC*, 6.13: Chi-tsai I, pp. 495–496 (HT 1/12); DS/DF, 893.00/351½, Bergholz, Canton, Dec. 20, 1909; ---/501, Bergholz, Jan. 10, 1911; Corr. de Chine, n.s., vol. 20, folio 11–14, dispatch from Canton, Jan. 8, 1910.

34. WWP, Macao file, Chuan-tang, Kao Erh-ch'ien to WWP, HT 1/7/18; cf. Fincher, "Chinese Self-Government Movement," pp. 126–131.

35. On this point, see Bastid, chap. 3.

36. Corr. de Chine, n.s., vol. 20, folio 11–14, dispatch from Canton, Jan. 8, 1910.

37. See Li Shou-k'ung for a good account of the petition movement; see also P'eng-yüan Chang, pp. 160–168; and Des Forges, pp. 169–173.

38. *Ch'en Ching-ts'un nien-p'u*, p. 13.

39. *TFTC*, 6.13: Chi-tsai I, pp. 446–448 (HT 1/12).

40. *TFTC*, 7.3: Chi-tsai III, pp. 47–48 (HT 2/3); Corr. de Chine, n.s., vol. 20, folio 237, dispatch from Canton, May 9, 1910, and folio 260–1, dispatch from Canton, May 23; *HKT*, May 10, p. 4; May 17, p. 4.

41. *HKT*, Oct. 7, 1910, p. 4.

42. Li Shou-k'ung, p. 344.

43. *SCMP*, Oct. 6, 1910, p. 7; DS/DF, 893.00/469, Bergholz, Canton, Oct. 17; ---/501, Bergholz, Jan. 10, 1911.

44. *TFTC*, 6.11: Tsou-tu, pp. 97–103 (HT 1/10); 7.12: Kung-tu, pp. 37–38 (HT 2/12).

45. *TFTC*, 6.11: Tsou-tu, pp. 97–103 (HT 1/10); P'an-yü *HC*, 42:15b–16; Ch'ing-yüan *HC*, 3:46.

46. *HKT*, Nov. 12, 1910, p. 5; *TFTC*, 7.11: Chung-kuo ta-shih chi pu-i, pp. 90–91 (HT 2/11).

47. *HTJP*, KH 33/10/21, p. 2; *HKT*, Dec. 8, 1910, p. 5.

48. *SCMP*, March 17, 1909, p. 7; *NCH*, July 31, pp. 269–270; *HKT*, Sept. 21, p. 4; Nov. 10, p. 4; Corr. de Chine, n.s., vol. 20, folio 11–14, dispatch from Canton, Jan. 8, 1910.

49. *TFTC*, 6.11: Tsou-tu, pp. 97–103 (HT 1/10).

50. *TFTC*, 6.13: Chi-shih, pp. 483–484 (HT 1/12).

51. *TFTC*, 6.13: Chi-shih, pp. 483–485 (HT 1/12); *SCMP*, Dec. 20, 1909, p. 7; *HKT*, Dec. 21, p. 4.

52. *TFTC*, 7.4: Chi-tsai III, pp. 104–105 (HT 2/4); 7.7: Tsou-tu, pp. 79–83 (2/7). See also Winston Hsieh, "Triads, Salt Smugglers, and Local Uprisings," pp. 160–164.

53. *HKT*, June 4, 1910, p. 4; FO 228/1757, Canton intelligence report for the second quarter of 1910.

54. *TFTC*, 7.10: Chi-tsai I, p. 127 (HT 2/10); *Ta-Ch'ing li-ch'ao shih-lu* (Taipei, 1964), Hsüan-t'ung, 42:33b, HT 3/9/20.

55. *TFTC*, 7.11: Chung-kuo ta-shih chi pu-i, pp. 87–88 (HT 2/11); *SCMP*, Nov. 14, 1910, p. 5.

56. *SCMP*, Nov. 15, 1910, p. 7; *NCH*, Jan. 6, 1911, pp. 27–28.

57. *TFTC*, 7.11: Chung-kuo ta-shih chi pu-i, pp. 89–90 (HT 2/11); *SCMP*, Nov. 19, 1910, p. 7.

58. *TFTC*, 7.11: Chung-kuo ta-shih chi pu-i, pp. 90–91 (HT 2/11); cf. Tung-kuan *HC*, 36:13–15.

59. *TFTC*, 7.11: Chung-kuo ta-shih chi pu-i, pp. 91–94 (HT 2/11); *SCMP*, Nov. 23, 1910, p. 7.

60. *TFTC*, 7.11: Chung-kuo ta-shih chi pu-i, pp. 92–93 (HT 2/11); *HKT*, Dec. 6, 1910, p. 5; Dec. 7, p. 4.

61. *HKT*, Jan. 12, 1911, p. 5; *SCMP*, Jan. 16, p. 11.

62. *TFTC*, 8.2: Chung-hua ta-shih chi, p. 12 (HT 3/2); *HKT*, Jan. 24, 1911, p. 4; *SCMP*, Feb. 28, p. 7.

63. *NCH*, April 15, 1911, p. 166; *SCMP*, April 4, p. 3; photographs in *TFTC*, 8.2 (HT 3/2).

64. *SCMP*, May 16, 1911, p. 5; Aug. 29, p. 7; *NCH*, May 20, p. 484; June 17, p. 741.

65. DS/DF, 893.00/501, Bergholz, Canton, Jan. 10, 1911.

66. For the regulations, see *Foreign Relations of the United States*, 1909, pp. 130–144; cf. Hsiao I-shan, 4:1461–1465; Brunnert and Hagelstrom, nos. 524–526; Fincher, "Chinese Self-Government Movement," pp. 259–262.

67. Cf. Brunnert and Hagelstrom, no. 527; P'an-yü *HC*, 9:8b.

68. P'an-yü *HC*, 9:8b–9; *HKT*, May 10, 1910, p. 4; Ping-ti Ho, *Studies on the Population of China, 1368–1953* (Cambridge, 1959), pp. 73–79.

69. Brunnert and Hagelstrom, no. 525B; P'an-yü *HC*, 9:9; Ch'ing-yüan *HC*, 3:47.

70. Brunnert and Hagelstrom, no. 527A; Shun-te *HC*, 2:27; Yang-chiang *HC*, 18:51; Le-ch'ang *HC*, 19:16; En-p'ing *HC*, 9:13b; 14: 35b–36b; Shih-ch'eng *HC*, 4:34.

71. Brunnert and Hagelstrom, no. 525B; P'an-yü *HC*, 9:11b–14; Elvin, p. 54.

72. DS/DF, 893.101/2, Williams, Swatow, May 2, 1911; Yang-chiang *HC* 37:17b; Hsüan-t'ung Kao-yao *HC*, 8:12b; Nan-hai *HC*, 6:9.

73. On the Swatow council, see three reports by Consul Williams, DS/DF 893.101/1–3, Sept. 17, 1910, April 11 and May 2, 1911. On the Shanghai council, see Elvin.

74. *HTJP*, HT 1/4/28, p. 2.

75. See the analysis of the deliberative councils in Hupeh in Teraki Tokuko, "Shin-matsu Minkoku shonen no chihō jichi," *Ochanomizu shigaku*, 5:16 (1962).

76. P'an-yü *HC*, 9:10b–11b.

77. See *TFTC*, 6.5: Chi-shih, pp. 134–136 (HT 1/4); WWP, Macao file, Hong Kong newspaper clippings, *HTJP*, HT 1/9/8 and 9/24.

78. *NCH*, March 11, 1910, p. 542.

79. K'ai-p'ing *HC*, 2:3.

80. Shun-te *HC*, 6:1–6, as noted in Winston Hsieh, "Peasant-Bandits in Towns and Cities: The Phenomenon of People's Armies in Kwangtung, 1911–1924" (1969), p. 70;

see also Hsieh, "Triads, Salt Smugglers, and Local Uprisings," p. 162. For a contrary opinion about the costs of the reforms to the peasantry, see Des Forges, p. 56.

81. Chūzō Ichiko, "The Role of the Gentry: An Hypothesis," in Wright, ed., *China in Revolution,* pp. 302–303.

82. *NCH,* June 20, 1908, p. 734; March 17, 1911, p. 626.

83. See Kung Shu-to and Ch'en Kuei-ying, "Ts'ung Ch'ing Chün-chi-ch'u tang-an k'an hsin-hai ko-ming ch'ien ch'un-chung ti fan-k'ang tou-cheng," *Hsin-hai ko-ming wu-shih chou-nien chi-nien lun-wen chi* (Peking, 1962), 1:204–228; for a more extensive, corroborative account of this phenomenon, see Esherick, "Reform, Revolution and Reaction," chap. 5.

84. *TFTC,* 7.6: Chi-tsai I, p. 79 (HT 2/6), in *HHKM,* 3:368; *SCMP,* June 17, 1910, p. 7.

85. For the riot in Lo-ting, see *TFTC,* 7.7: Chi-tsai III, p. 194 (HT 2/7), in *HHKM,* 3:368–369. Hsin-an: see *TFTC,* 7.8: Chi-tsai III, pp. 225–226 (2/8); *SCMP,* July 25, 1910, p. 11; *NCH,* Aug. 12, p. 369. Ta-p'u: see *TFTC,* 7.8: Chi-tsai I, p. 104 (2/8), in *HHKM,* 3:369; 7.9: Chung-kuo ta-shih chi pu-i, p. 74 (2/9). Lei-chou: see *HKT,* mail supplement, Oct. 22, 1910, p. 366.

86. On the Lien-chou disturbances, see *TFTC,* 7.10: Chi-tsai I, pp. 140–141 (HT 2/10); 7.11: Chung-kuo ta-shih chi pu-i, p. 100 (2/11), in *HHKM,* 3: 370; 7.12: Chung-kuo ta-shih chi pu-i, pp. 108–109 (2/12), in *HHKM,* 3: 371; *SCMP,* Nov. 12, 1910, p. 7; Dec. 22, p. 5; J. S. Kunkle, "The Lienchow Riots," *Chinese Recorder,* 42:243–245 (1911); Presbyterian Board of Foreign Missions Papers, 51/50, R. M. Ross to Brown, Sept. 18, 1910; 51/51, Kunkle to Edwards, Sept. 24; 51/55, Kunkle to Brown, Oct. 11; 51/59, Kunkle to Brown, Nov. 12; Tso Shao-tso, "Lien-chou shih-chien jih-chi chai-lu," *Chin-tai-shih tzu-liao,* 1955, no. 4, pp. 70–84.

87. Kunkle, "The Lienchow Riots," pp. 243–244.

88. For the riot in Hsin-hui, see *SCMP,* April 17, 1911, p. 8; for the one in Ch'ing-yüan, see Ch'ing-yüan *HC,* 3:47; *SCMP,* April 19, 1911, p. 7; *NCH,* May 13, p. 415.

8. Final Years of the Post-Boxer Decade, III: Revolution

1. See, for example, Rankin, *Early Chinese Revolutionaries,* pp. 112–125, 190–201; see also Des Forges, pp. 110–114.

2. See K. S. Liew, chap. 6.

3. Cf. Rankin, *Early Chinese Revolutionaries,* pp. 190–201; Des Forges, pp. 127–128.

4. Cf. Gasster, pp. 98–99.

5. FO 371/411, Report by Vice-consul Myers after visit to Canton delta, Dec. 1907.

6. Feng, *Chung-hua,* 1:180–181; *I-shih,* 3:238; see also Jansen, pp. 127–128, 253 (n. 78).

7. Jansen, pp. 188–193.

8. Feng, *I-shih,* 3:242, 244.

9. Feng, *Chung-hua,* 1:182.

10. *HLHCC,* pp. 880, 1000–1001; Lin I-han, pp. 480–481; DS/DF, 893.918/---, Williams, Swatow, June 27, 1911. On Yeh Ch'u-ts'ang, see *HLHCC,* pp. 1000–1005.

11. *KKWH*, 1.2:539; T'an Li-yüan, p. 5; *HKT*, June 22, 1909, p. 2; Feng, *I-shih*, 3:243.

12. A Ying, *Wan-Ch'ing hsiao-shuo shih* (Peking, 1955), pp. 83, 135–138; Feng, *I-shih*, 2:46–51; cf. Lo Hsiang-lin, *Hong Kong and Western Cultures*, pp. 210–214.

13. Feng, *I-shih*, 2:243.

14. Feng, *I-shih*, 2:241–246; Ch'en Te-yün, p. 516; "Mo Chi-p'eng hsien-sheng shih-lüeh," *KKWH*, 1.14:536; Chao Lien-ch'eng, "T'ung-meng hui tsai Kang-Ao ti huo-tung ho Kuang-tung fu-nü-chieh ts'an-chia ko-ming ti hui-i," *HIL*, 2:305; see also Lu Tan-lin, *Ko-ming shih-t'an* (Chungking, 1945), pp. 257–258.

15. Feng, *I-shih*, 3:237–238, 242–243.

16. Feng, *I-shih*, 3:335.

17. *HLHCC*, pp. 445, 934; Wu Hsiang-hsiang, "Ku Ying-fen ch'i-jen ch'i-shih," p. 29.

18. Tsou, *Hui-ku lu*, p. 22.

19. Lin Tien-huang, "Ko-ming-tang-jen tsai Hui-chou," *KKWH*, 1.14:224–227; *HLHCC*, p. 189.

20. Kan Shan-chai, "Tzu-chin kuang-fu ch'ien-hou," *HIL*, 2:356.

21. P'eng Chung-ying, "Hua-chou kuang-fu ch'ien-hou shih-nien chien-wen lu," *HIL*, 2:402–403.

22. Tsou, *Hui-ku lu*, p. 22. On Ch'en Chiung-ming, see *Ch'en Ching-ts'un nien-p'u* and Boorman and Howard, 1:173–180. On Tsou Lu, see his *Hui-ku lu* and Boorman and Howard, 3:317–318. On Wu Han-ch'ih, see Feng, *I-shih*, 2:212–215, and *HLHCC*, pp. 319–324.

23. "Ts'ang-hai hsien-sheng Ch'iu kung Feng-chia nien-p'u," p. 406; Ch'iu Nien-t'ai, *Ling-hai wei-piao* (Taipei, 1962), p. 70; see also Tsou, *Hui-ku lu*, p. 30.

24. WWP, Macao file, clipping from *Yang-ch'eng jih-pao*, HT 1/10/20.

25. Tsou, *Hui-ku lu*, p. 29.

26. *HTJP*, HT 1/7/25, p. 2; 8/10, p. 2; Tsou, *Hui-ku lu*, p. 29.

27. WWP, Macao file, Shanghai newspaper clippings, *Shih-shih pao*, HT 1/#2/13.

28. *HTJP*, KH 33/10/20, p. 2.

29. *HLHCC*, p. 320.

30. There are two principal accounts of this abortive revolt. One is Feng, *I-shih*, 3:290–313; the other is Tsou, *Hui-ku lu*, pp. 23–26, and *Tang shih-kao*, pp. 772–774. Tsou's account is largely duplicated in *KKWH*, 1.13:497–504. See also the brief reference in *HKT*, Dec. 18, 1908, p. 5.

31. See Smythe, p. 62; Ta-ling Lee, p. 106.

32. Feng, *I-shih*, 3:296.

33. Feng, *I-shih*, 3:296.

34. Feng, *I-shih*, 1:201–202; on Ni Ying-tien, see *HLHCC*, pp. 109–112.

35. On Teng K'eng, see *HLHCC*, pp. 454–464; Boorman and Howard, 3:254–257. The latter are in error in identifying Teng as the "dean" of the Whampoa Military Primary School; he was only an "instructor" (*hsüeh-chang*). On *hsüeh-chang* as "instructor," see Brunnert and Hagelstrom, no. 709.

36. Mo Ch'ang-fan et al., pp. 85–87; Hsü Wei-yang, "Keng-hsü Kuang-tung hsin-chün chü-i chi," *KKWH*, 1.13:509–510; Feng, *I-shih*, 1:202, 209.

37. Feng, *I-shih*, 1:202, 209; 3:245.

38. Mo Ch'ang-fan et al., pp. 85–87; Feng, *I-shih*, 1:202–203.

39. Feng, *I-shih*, 1:203–204; 3:244–245; Hsü Wei-yang, "Keng-hsü chü-i chi," p. 510; *HLHCC*, p. 446; Tsou, *Hui-ku lu*, pp. 29–30. On Li Fu-lin, see Feng, *I-shih*, 2:238–240.

40. "Keng-hsü Kuang-chou hsin-chün chih i kung-chuang," *KKWH*, 1.13:528–530; Chün-tu Hsüeh, p. 76; T'an Jen-feng, p. 41; *HLHCC*, p. 566.

41. T'an Jen-feng, p. 41; Chang Lu-ts'un, "Hsin-chün ch'i-i ti hui-i," p. 283; *HLHCC*, p. 446; Hsü Wei-yang, "Keng-hsü chü-i chi," p. 510.

42. There are many accounts of the New Army mutiny, looking at it from various angles. Written depositions by captured rebels are found in "Keng-hsü Kuang-chou hsin-chün chih i kung-chuang." A contemporary newspaper account appears in *TFTC*, 7.2: Chung-kuo ta-shih chi, pp. 16–21 (HT 2/2). Governor-General Yüan's version is given in an undated memorial in *KKWH*, 1.13:550–554. Censor Ch'en Ch'ing-kuei's critique of Yüan's memorial, also undated, is in *KKWH*, 1.13:554–555. The results of the official investigation headed by former Governor-General Chang Jen-chün are summarized in a memorial, with a rescript dated HT 2/4/22, in *KKWH*, 1.13:555–559. Accounts from the revolutionaries' side include the following: Ch'en Ch'un-sheng, "Keng-hsü Kuang-chou hsin-chün chü-i chi," *HHKM*, 3:347–361; Hsü Wei-yang, "Keng-hsü chü-i chi," pp. 508–518; Mo Ch'ang-fan et al., pp. 88–92; Hu Han-min, "Tzu-chuan," pp. 403–406; Chang Lu-ts'un, "Hsin-chün ch'i-i ti hui-i," pp. 281–286; Feng, *I-shih*, 1:201–214; and Chün-tu Hsüeh, pp. 76–77. See also Hatano Yoshihiro, "Minkoku kakumei undō ni okeru shingun—Kanton shingun no hanran o chūshin to shite," *Nagoya daigaku bungakubu kenkyū ronshū*, 8:63–76 (1954).

43. *HKT*, Feb. 16, 1910, p. 5.

44. *KKWH*, 1.13:550–554; *TFTC*, 7.4: Chung-kuo ta-shih chi pu-i, pp. 10–11 (HT 2/4); see also "Keng-hsü Kuang-chou hsin-chün chih i kung-chuang."

45. *KKWH*, 1.13:558.

46. *KKWH*, 1.13:554–555.

47. *TFTC*, 7.2: Chung-kuo ta-shih chi, pp. 19–21 (HT 2/2); "Kuang-chou-shih yen-ko shih-lüeh," pp. 46–48, in *Kuang-chou-shih shih-cheng pao-kao hui-k'an* (Canton, 1924).

48. See Powell, pp. 268–271.

49. *HKT*, Feb. 24, 1910, p. 4; *TFTC*, 7.2: Chung-kuo ta-shih chi, p. 20 (HT 2/2).

50. *TFTC*, 7.2: Chung-kuo ta-shih chi, p. 21 (HT 2/2); 7.3: Chung-kuo ta-shih chi pu-i, pp. 1–4 (2/3); *HKT*, March 22, 1910, p. 4; "Kuang-chou-shih yen-ko shih-lüeh," p. 47; Yoshihiro Hatano, "The New Armies," in Wright, ed., *China in Revolution*, pp. 375–378.

51. See Rankin, *Early Chinese Revolutionaries*, p. 189, for a similar case in Chekiang.

52. *KKWH*, 1.13:555–559.

53. *KKWH*, 1.13:537.

54. *TFTC*, 7.5: Chung-kuo ta-shih chi, pp. 76–77 (HT 2/5).

55. Feng, *I-shih*, 3:246–248.

56. Li Hsi-wu, "Ch'ing-mo Chih-na an-sha-t'uan chi-shih," *Kuang-tung wen-wu t'e chi* (Canton, n.d.), pp. 18–19.

57. *KKWH*, 1.12:546; *HKT*, Nov. 4, 1910, p. 5; Feng, *I-shih*, 1:115.

58. Chün-tu Hsüeh, pp. 83–86; Tsou, *Kuang-chou ko-ming shih*, pp. 2–18.

59. Tsou, *Kuang-chou ko-ming shih,* pp. 19–20; the composition of the volunteer force can be inferred from the biographies of the eighty-six martyrs on pp. 86–93, 114–170.

60. Tsou, *Kuang-chou ko-ming shih,* pp. 24–28, 35–38; *Chung-kuo lao-kung yün-tung shih,* 1:53–54, 57–59; Feng, *I-shih,* 3:336; Chün-tu Hsüeh, pp. 86–87.

61. Tsou, *Kuang-chou ko-ming shih,* pp. 19–20, 28–32.

62. *HKT* Dec. 21, 1910, p. 5; Dec. 24, p. 4; *NCH,* Jan. 13, 1911, p. 83.

63. Tsou, *Kuang-chou ko-ming shih,* pp. 22–23; *Hui-ku lu,* pp. 35–36.

64. On the assassination of Fu-ch'i, see the three contemporary accounts in *KKWH,* 1.13:691–709, of which the best is that by "Ling-nan pan-weng," on pp. 697–704; Tsou, *Tang shih-kao,* pp. 798–800; *Chung-kuo lao-kung yün-tung shih,* 1:54–56; *SCMP,* April 10, 1911, p. 7; April 11, p. 7; April 12, p. 7; April 17, p. 8.

65. *HKT,* Feb. 25, 1911, p. 1.

66. Tsou, *Kuang-chou ko-ming shih,* pp. 38–39, 47.

67. *KKWH,* 1.12:540–546; Tsou, *Hui-ku lu,* pp. 36–39; *SCMP,* April 26, 1911, p. 7.

68. The literature on the Canton revolt in April 1911 is voluminous. The principal account is Tsou, *Kuang-chou ko-ming shih;* a good account in English is Chün-tu Hsüeh, chap. 6. Accounts by participants include the following: Huang Hsing, "Kuang-chou san-yüeh erh-shih-chiu ko-ming chih ch'ien-yin hou-kuo," in *HHKM,* 4:167–171; Hu Han-min, "Tzu-chuan," pp. 407–412; T'an Jen-feng, pp. 45–48; Yao Yü-p'ing, pp. 290–298; Liang Ching-ch'iu, "Kuang-chou san-yüeh erh-shih-chiu ko-ming chih ching-kuo," *KKWH,* 1.14:157–166; Wang Hsing-chung, "Hsin-hai san-yüeh nien-chiu Kuang-chou ko-ming chih ching-kuo," *KKWH,* 1.14:166–168; Mo Chi-p'eng, in Feng, *I-shih,* 1:222–229; Ma Chin-ch'un, "San-yüeh erh-shih-chiu-jih chih i yü Kuang-chou hsin-chün," *KKWH,* 1.14:204–217; Ho Chen, "Kuang-chou hsin-chün chih tung-t'ai," *KKWH,* 1.14:217–219; Ying Te-ming, "Huang-hua-kang ch'i-i ch'ien-hou tsa-i," *HIL,* 2:323–326; Hu Kuo-liang, "Hsin-hai Kuang-chou ch'i-i pieh-chi," *HHKM,* 4:263–274; and Tsou, *Hui-ku lu,* pp. 35–40. Other accounts include the following: Tsou, *Tang shih-kao,* pp. 801–838; Ch'en Ch'un-sheng, "Kuang-chou san-yüeh erh-shih-chiu fa-nan chüeh-ting chih ching-kuo," *KKWH,* 1.14:142–147; Liu K'uei-i, pp. 22–27; *Ch'en Ching-ts'un nien-p'u,* pp. 14–15; Hsü Wei-yang, "Huang-hua-kang Hua-hsien shih-pa lieh-shih hsün-nan chi," *KKWH,* 1.14:507–511; Chu Hao-huai, "Kuang-chou hsin-chün ch'i-i yü san-yüeh erh-shih-chiu-jih chih i," *KKWH,* 1.14:219–223; "Kuang-chou-shih yen-ko shih-lüeh," pp. 49–55. See also the 30-page memorandum on the revolt by Hamilton Butler, the vice consul, in DS/DF, 893.00/530.

69. On Lu Ling's uprising in Shun-te, see Tsou, *Kuang-chou ko-ming shih,* pp. 48–49; Teng Mu-han, "Hsin-hai san-yüeh erh-shih-chiu chih i Nan-Shun chan-chi," *KKWH,* 1.14:242–245; *HKT,* May 4, 1911, p. 1.

70. K. S. Liew, p. 94.

9. The Revolution in 1911

1. P'eng-yüan Chang, pp. 168–170; Samuel Chu, pp. 67–68; Li Shou-k'ung, pp. 345–347; Des Forges, pp. 173–176.

2. See, for example, *HKT,* mail supplement, Oct. 22, 1910, p. 366.

3. See *NCH*, Nov. 13, 1909, p. 364; July 1, 1910, p. 47; Aug. 12, p. 383; for text of Wu T'ing-fang's memorial, see *TFTC*, 7.8: Tsou-tu, pp. 98–100 (HT 2/8) and *HKT*, Aug. 9, 1910, p. 3; see also Shirley S. Garrett, *Social Reformers in Urban China: The Chinese Y.M.C.A., 1895–1926* (Cambridge, 1970), p. 73. For a contemporary view of the question, see Ching-chun Wang, "The Abolition of the Queue," *Atlantic Monthly*, 107:810–816 (1911). On Tsai-t'ao, see Ernest P. Young, "The Reformer as a Conspirator: Liang Ch'i-ch'ao and the 1911 Revolution," in Feuerwerker et al., *Approaches to Modern Chinese History*, p. 244.

4. *SCMP*, Nov. 1, 1910, p. 7; Nov. 8, p. 7; Dec. 5, p. 7; Dec. 15, p. 5; *HKT*, Nov. 12, p. 5; Dec. 5, p. 4; Dec. 27, p. 4; *NCH*, Dec. 2, p. 532; Jan. 6, 1911, p. 25; Woo Sing Lim, p. 98.

5. Cameron, pp. 178–179.

6. Peng-yüan Chang, pp. 170–172; Young, "Reformer as Conspirator," pp. 247–259.

7. Cameron, p. 128; Li Shou-k'ung, pp. 357–366.

8. Ch'üan Han-sheng, "T'ieh-lu kuo-yu wen-t'i yü hsin-hai ko-ming," *Chung-kuo hsien-tai-shih ts'ung-k'an*, 1:213–220 (1960).

9. *TFTC*, 8.5: Chung-kuo ta-shih chi, pp. 6–7 (HT 3/6); *SCMP*, June 8, 1911, p. 7; June 9, p. 7; *HKT*, June 9, p. 4; Sheng Hsüan-huai, *Yü-chai ts'un-k'ao* (Taipei, 1963), 77:29b–30b, Chang to Sheng, HT 3/5/11.

10. The compensation scheme is set forth in Ch'üan Han-sheng, pp. 225–226. For the railway controversy in Szechwan, see Ichiko Chūzō, "The Railway Protection Movement in Szechwan in 1911," *Memoirs of the Research Department of the Toyo Bunko*, 14:47–69 (1955); and Ch'üan Han-sheng, pp. 230–255.

11. Sheng Hsüan-huai, 79:26b, Chang to Sheng, HT 3/#6/23; 81:13b–14, 23b–24, Chang to Sheng, 7/12 and 7/15; *HKT*, Aug. 16, 1911, p. 5; Sept. 4, p. 5; *SCMP*, Aug. 17, p. 7. See also Ch'üan Han-sheng, p. 230; and Nozawa Yutaka, "Shingai kakumei no kaikyū kōsei: Shisen bōdō to shōshin kaikyū," *Rekishigaku kenkyū*, no. 150, p. 86 (1951).

12. Quoted in Ch'üan Han-sheng, p. 233; see also E-tu Zen Sun, *Chinese Railways*, chap. 4; Hatano Yoshihiro, "Shin-matsu ni okeru tetsudō kokuyū seisaku no haikei," *Nagoya daigaku ronshu*, 17:29–66 (1957).

13. *NCH*, Sept. 2, 1911, p. 582; *HKT*, Sept. 4, p. 5.

14. Sheng Hsüan-huai, 81:23b–24, Chang to Sheng, HT 3/7/15.

15. *NCH*, May 13, 1911, p. 415; *HKT*, Apr. 26, p. 3; *SCMP*, May 16, p. 5; May 17, p. 7.

16. See Chün-tu Hsüeh, pp. 99–107; K. S. Liew, pp. 91–103.

17. Feng, *I-shih*, 3:256; Chiang Yung-ching, p. 124.

18. DS/DF, 893.918/—, Williams, Swatow, June 27, 1911; ---/2, Williams, Sept. 15; Lin I-han, pp. 480, 481–482; *HLHCC*, pp. 1001, 1004.

19. Feng, *I-shih*, 2:321; 3:145; T'an Li-yüan, p. 5; *HTJP*, 3/8/11, p. 5; 8/19, p. 2; *SCMP*, June 30, 1911, p. 8; July 24, p. 8; Oct. 4, p. 8.

20. *SCMP*, Oct. 19, 1911, p. 6.

21. Chao Lien-ch'eng, pp. 307–312; *SCMP*, May 30, 1911, p. 7; Aug. 14, p. 8; Sept. 28, p. 7; *HKT*, July 27, 1911, p. 5; *NCH*, Sept. 2, pp. 572–573; "Revolutionary Propagation in Missionary Guise," *Chinese Recorder*, 42:549–550 (1911).

22. On the attempted assassination of Li Chun, see *Hung-hua-kang ssu lieh-shih chuan*, pp. 17–29 (Shanghai, 1927); Li Hsi-wu, pp. 19–20; Feng, *I-shih*, 4:213–216; *KKWH*, 1.13:636–647; *SCMP*, Aug. 16, 1911, p. 7.

23. *SCMP*, May 4, 1911, p. 7; May 17, p. 7.

24. See *NCH*, Feb. 17, 1911, p. 369; Feb. 24, p. 425; March 3, p. 489. On Lung Chi-kuang, see Boorman and Howard, 2:455–457.

25. On Chiang Tsun-kuei, see Rankin, *Early Chinese Revolutionaries*, p. 194; see also Young, "Reformer as Conspirator," p. 261, and *Shin-matsu jimmeiroku*, p. 703.

26. *HTJP*, HT 3/9/5, p. 2; *HHKM*, 7:256, telegram from Governor-General Chang to the Nei-ko, #6/21; *SCMP*, Aug. 22, 1911, p. 6; Sept. 2, p. 7.

27. *NCH*, May 27, 1911, p. 561.

28. *NCH*, Sept. 2, 1911, p. 581; *SCMP*, June 29, 1911, p. 2; Sept. 28, p. 7.

29. *HHKM*, 7:260.

30. DS/DF, 893.00/530, Memorandum by Hamilton Butler on the Canton revolt, May 24, 1911; *HKT*, May 18, p. 1; May 22, p. 3.

31. *HKT*, Aug. 4, 1911, p. 1; see also July 31, p. 5; *SCMP*, July 29, p. 7; Aug. 2, p. 7.

32. DS/DF, 893.00/553, Bergholz, Canton, Aug. 18, 1911; see also *SCMP*, Aug. 8, p. 8; *HKT*, Aug. 9, p. 5.

33. The riots occurred at Fo-shan: see *SCMP*, June 7, 1911, p. 7; June 9, p. 7; *HKT*, June 8, p. 4; *NCH*, June 24, p. 806; Sui-ch'i: see *HKT*, June 10, p. 1; Lung-men: see *HKT*, July 27, p. 5; Hsin-hui: see *HKT*, Aug. 1, p. 5; *NCH*, Aug. 5, p. 355; Sept. 2, p. 572; *TR*, 1911, Kongmoon, p. 726; Kao-chou: see *HKT*, Aug. 12, p. 5; *NCH*, Sept. 2, p. 582; Shih-lung: see *SCMP*, Sept. 8, p. 8; Sept. 16, p. 8; *HKT*, Sept. 7, p. 5.

34. *HHKM*, 7:256, telegram from Chang to the Nei-ko, HT 3/#6/21.

35. *SCMP*, May 10, 1911, p. 7; Ch'ing-yüan *HC*, 13:34–34b; *HTJP*, HT 3/8/23 and 8/25.

36. *HHKM*, 7:258–266, 268–270, memorials by Ch'en Ch'ing-kuei, Wen Su, Li Chia-chü and Mai Chih-yen; also *SCMP*, May 11, 1911, p. 7.

37. *HTJP*, HT 3/8/12. For the public mood in Hunan and Hupeh during these same months, see Esherick, "Reform, Revolution and Reaction," pp. 306–341.

38. Chiang Yung-ching, p. 124.

39. *HKT*, Oct. 18, 1911, p. 5; *SCMP*, Oct. 19, p. 6; Oct. 21, p. 8.

40. *SCMP*, Oct. 17, 1911, p. 8; Oct. 19, p. 7; Oct. 20, p. 7; Oct. 21, p. 7; Oct. 23, p. 7.

41. On Chang Ming-ch'i, see DS/DF, 893.00/470, Calhoun to State, Nov. 1, 1910; *NCH*, Dec. 30, p. 787; *HKT*, Jan. 3, 1911, p. 4.

42. See Ting Wen-chiang, p. 340; Young, "Reformer as Conspirator," pp. 259–265.

43. On Ch'en Ching-hua, see Lu Tan-lin, pp. 187–197; see also Feng, *I-shih*, 3:243; Teng Ching-ya, "Hsin-hai Kuang-tung tu-li ch'uan-hsin lu," *HIL*, 2:334; G. William Skinner, *Chinese Society in Thailand: An Analytical History* (Ithaca, 1957), pp. 156–158; *Saishin Shina kanshin roku*, p. 405; *HKT*, Nov. 17, 1911, p. 1; *HTJP*, HT 3/8/18.

44. "Kuang-tung tu-li chi," *Chin-tai-shih tzu-liao*, 1961, no. 1, p. 436; *SCMP*, Oct. 18, 1911, p. 7.

45. *HTJP*, HT 3/8/30.

46. *HKT,* Oct. 26, 1911, p. 5; *HTJP,* HT 3/9/4 and 9/5.

47. On the assassination of Feng-shan, see Tsou, *Tang shih-kao,* pp. 832–833; Li Hsi-wu, pp. 18, 20–21; Kuo Hsiao-ch'eng, "Kuang-tung kuang-fu chi," *HHKM,* 7:228; and two other accounts in *KKWH,* 1.13:712–716.

48. "Kuang-tung tu-li chi," pp. 435–437; see also *SCMP,* Oct. 28, 1911, p. 7; "Kuang-chou-shih yen-ko shih-lüeh," p. 56.

49. On Liang Ting-fen, see *Gendai Shina jimmeikan,* under his name.

50. DS/DF, 893.00/709, Bergholz, Canton, Oct. 27, 1911.

51. "Kuang-tung tu-li chi," pp. 437–438; see also *SCMP,* Oct. 30, 1911, p. 7; *HTJP,* HT 3/9/7, p. 2.

52. "Kuang-tung tu-li chi," pp. 437, 438; *SCMP,* Oct. 30, 1911, p. 7; *HTJP,* HT 3/9/9, p. 2.

53. *HTJP,* HT 3/9/11, p. 2, announcement by the Pao-chieh kung-hui; *SCMP,* Oct. 31, 1911, p. 7; T'an Li-yüan, p. 6.

54. *SCMP,* Oct. 26, 1911, p. 7; Oct. 30, pp. 6–7; Oct. 31, p. 7; FO 228/1797, Diary of events in Canton, entry of Oct. 30.

55. "Kuang-tung tu-li chi," pp. 438–439; *HTJP,* HT 3/9/10, p. 3.

56. "Kuang-tung tu-li chi," pp. 439–441; see also *HKT,* Oct. 31, 1911, p. 1. The "Kuang-tung tu-li chi" account identifies the moderator as T'an Li-yüan, but this seems to be a mistake. T'an Li-yüan was in Hong Kong with the delegation of newspapermen at the time. The moderator was probably T'an Min-san; see "Kuang-tung tu-li chi," p. 443, and Kuo Hsiao-ch'eng, p. 229. On T'an Min-san, see Feng Tzu-yu, *Chung-kuo ko-ming tsu-chih shih,* p. 74; *I-shih,* 3:237; *HLHCC,* p. 319.

57. On the Wen-lan Academy meeting and the celebrations afterwards, see "Kuang-tung tu-li chi," pp. 441–443; *HKT,* Oct. 31, 1911, p. 1.

58. See "Kuang-tung tu-li chi," pp. 443–444, 445–446, for the governor-general's proclamations.

59. *HTJP,* HT 3/9/13 and 9/14; *HKT,* Nov. 1, 1911; *SCMP,* Nov. 10, p. 8. See also the comments of Chiang K'ung-yin to Consul Bergholz in DS/DF, 893.00/779, Bergholz, Canton, Nov. 14.

60. "Kuang-tung tu-li chi," pp. 445–449; *HTJP,* HT 3/9/11, announcement by the Pao-chieh kung-hui; *SCMP,* Nov. 1, 1911, p. 1.

61. Feng, *I-shih,* 3:255; Cheng Pi-an, "Hsiang-shan ch'i-i hui-i," *HIL,* 2:340; *HKT,* Nov. 3, 1911, p. 4; *SCMP,* Nov. 9, p. 7. On these and other people's army uprisings, see Winston Hsieh, "Peasant-Bandits in Towns and Cities."

62. Cheng Pi-an, pp. 340–342; *TR,* 1911, Lappa, p. 711; *SCMP,* Nov. 9, 1911, p. 7; *HKT,* Nov. 10, p. 1.

63. Wang Hsing-chung, "Yüeh-sheng ti-ssu-chün ko-ming jih-chi," *KKWH,* 2.4:433–437.

64. On the siege of Hui-chou, see *Ch'en Ching-ts'un hsien-sheng nien-p'u,* pp. 16–17; Lin Hsi-heng, "Hsin-hai chiu-yüeh Hui-chou shou-i shih-lüeh," *KKWH,* 2.4:473–475; Ch'en Ching-lü, "Hui-chou kuang-fu chi," *Chin-tai-shih tzu-liao,* 1958, no. 2, pp. 50–52; Miao Chih-hsin, "Hui-chou kuang-fu chien-wen," *HIL,* 2:343–346; Wang Ying-lou, "Hui-chou-fu chung-hsüeh-sheng tsai hsin-hai ko-ming shih-ch'i ti huo-tung," *HIL,* 2:350–351; *HHKM,* 7:271–272, report of Ch'in Ping-shih, HT 3/10/16.

65. "Kuang-tung tu-li chi," pp. 449–450.

66. *HTJP*, HT 3/9/19, Ching-hua lu, p. 1; *KKWH*, 2.4:443. FO 228/1797, Diary, dates this meeting erroneously as Nov. 6.

67. For Li Chun's defection, see the following: Li's own account, "Kuang-fu Kuang-tung shih-mo chi," written in January 1912 and reprinted in *HHKM*, 7:245–246 and *KKWH*, 2.4:427–428; Hu Han-min's supporting account, "Nan-ching hsüan-pu fan-cheng shih ch'ing-hsing," written at about the same time and reprinted in *HHKM*, 7:247–249 and *KKWH*, 2.4:413–415; Li Po-ts'un's preface to a 1937 reprint of these two accounts, "Yüeh-yüan kuang-fu chi-shih," reprinted in *KKWH*, 2.4:440–441; Chiang Yung-ching, pp. 124–125; and Hu Han-min, "Tzu-chuan," pp. 414–416.

68. See Huang Ta-han, p. 475.

69. See Ma Hsiao-chin, "Kuang-chou kuang-fu yü Chou Chien-kung," *HHKM*, 7:251–255.

70. *SCMP*, Oct. 30, 1911, p. 7.

71. *HKT*, Nov. 8, 1911, p. 1; FO 228/1797, Diary, Nov. 6–8.

72. FO 228/1797, Diary, Nov. 8; see also Chang's memorial, *HKT*, Dec. 19, 1911, p. 1.

73. *KKWH*, 2.4:443; *HKT*, Nov. 9, 1911, p. 1; *SCMP*, Nov. 9, p. 7; *HTJP*, HT 3/9/20, p. 2; Kuo Hsiao-ch'eng, pp. 229–230.

74. See FO 228/1797, Diary, Nov. 8–9.

75. See "Kuang-tung tu-li chi," p. 452; *HTJP*, HT 3/9/20, pp. 2, 3.

76. Tsou, *Tang shih-kao*, pp. 902–903; Kuo Hsiao-ch'eng, p. 231; Teng Mu-han, "Hsin-hai Kuang-chou kuang-fu chi," *KKWH*, 2.4:429–430; "Kuang-tung tu-li chi," pp. 450–451.

77. Kuo Hsiao-ch'eng, pp. 231–232; "Kuang-tung tu-li chi," pp. 455–457.

78. Cf. Bergère, pp. 242–257.

79. There are four principal accounts of the revolution in the Swatow–Ch'ao-chou area: Sun Tan-yai, "Hsin-hai Ch'ao-chou ko-ming chi-lüeh," *KKWH*, 2.4:477–480; Lin I-han's "corrections" of Sun's account; Tsou, *Tang shih-kao*, pp. 903–904; and Chang Lu-ts'un, "Ch'ao-Shan kuang-fu hui-i," *HIL*, 2:358–362. Of these four authors, all but Sun are Hakkas. See also Edward Friedman, "Revolution or Just Another Bloody Cycle? Swatow and the 1911 Revolution," *Journal of Asian Studies*, 29:289–291 (1970).

80. Chang Lu-ts'un, "Ch'ao-Shan kuang-fu hui-i," pp. 358–359; Sun Tan-yai, p. 477.

81. Lin I-han, p. 483; Tsou, *Tang shih-kao*, p. 903; Corr. de Chine, dispatch from Swatow, Nov. 6, 1911.

82. Lin I-han, pp. 482–484; Chang Lu-ts'un, "Ch'ao-Shan kuang-fu hui-i," pp. 358–359; Corr. de Chine, dispatches from Swatow, Nov. 6 and 10, 1911; *NCH*, Nov. 25, p. 523.

83. Chang Lu-ts'un, "Ch'ao-Shan kuang-fu hui-i," pp. 359–361; Lin I-han, pp. 484–485; Sun Tan-yai, p. 478.

84. *NCH*, Dec. 16, 1911, p. 727; K'ai-p'ing *HC*, 22:1–1b; En-p'ing *HC*, 14:38; Ch'ih-hsi *HC*, 7:20b–21.

85. *HHKM*, 7:273–274; *SCMP*, Dec. 5, 1911, p. 7; *Chung-hua min-kuo Kao-yao hsien-chih ch'u-pien*, 1:1b; 22:2; Ch'ing-yüan *HC*, 3:48.

86. Lo-ting *HC,* 9:23; Ch'ih-hsi *HC,* 7:20b–21; *HHKM,* 7:242; *TR,* 1911, Pakhoi, p. 793; *SCMP,* Dec. 5, 1911, p. 7.

87. *NCH,* Dec. 23, 1911, p. 794.

10. Revolution and Counterrevolution

1. For a fuller, somewhat different analysis of the Kwangtung revolutionary regime, see Edward Friedman, "The Center Cannot Hold: The Failure of Parliamentary Democracy in China from the Chinese Revolution of 1911 to the World War in 1914," Ph.D. diss., Harvard University, 1968; for an account of the revolutionary government in Kiangsi, see Kupper, chaps. 4–5.

2. Kuo Hsiao-ch'eng, pp. 234–235; *HKT,* Nov. 20, 1911, p. 5; FO 228/1797, Diary of events in Canton, entries of Nov. 17 and 18.

3. On the political differences between Hu Han-min and Ch'en Chiung-ming, see Winston Hsieh, "The Ideas and Ideals of a Warlord: Ch'en Chiung-ming (1878–1933)," *Papers on China,* 16:208–209 (1962).

4. For lists of the officials at various times, see Chiang Yung-ching, pp. 126, 134–135; *SCMP,* July 28, 1913, p. 7. On Lo Wen-kan, see Boorman and Howard, 2:438–441; on Ch'ien Shu-fen, see *Shin-matsu jimmeiroku,* p. 728 (though the entry errs in identifying Ch'ien as a native of Chekiang). See *Shin-matsu jimmeiroku* also for Lo P'an-hui, Wang Ch'ung-yu, Kuan Ching-shen, and Ch'eng T'ien-tou. The others have previously been identified.

5. See Yang Hua-jih, *Chung Jung-kuang hsien-sheng chuan* (Hong Kong, 1967).

6. FO 228/1797, Diary, Dec. 1, 1911.

7. On Huang's departure from Canton, see FO 228/1797, Diary, Dec. 16, 1911.

8. On Chung Ting-chi, see Ma Chin-ch'un, p. 211; on Su Shen-ch'u, see Tsou, *Kuang-chou ko-ming shih,* p. 30; on Li E, see Feng, *I-shih,* 3:312–313; and on Chang Wo-ch'üan, see Feng, *I-shih,* 3:291. See also *Shin-matsu jimmeiroku,* pp. 435, 717, 748, and 785.

9. On the post-revolutionary scene in Swatow, see the following: Friedman, "Revolution or Just Another Bloody Cycle?" pp. 289–307; Chang Lu-ts'un, "Ch'ao-Shan kuang-fu hui-i," pp. 361–362; Sun Tan-yai, pp. 478–480; Lin I-han, pp. 486–489; *SCMP,* March 27, 1912, p. 3.

10. For a list of the people's armies in Canton, see Li Lang-ju and Lu Man, "Hsin-hai ko-ming shih-ch'i Kuang-tung min-chün kai-k'uang," *HIL,* 2:412–413; *HTJP,* Jan. 16, 1912, p. 2; Jan. 17, p. 2; Jan. 20, p. 2. See also FO 228/1797, Diary, Nov. 21 and Dec. 9, 1911; *SCMP,* Dec. 13, p. 8; and *HTJP,* Dec. 15, p. 2.

11. On disbandment of the people's armies, see FO 228/1797, Diary, Nov. 29, 1911; Feb. 9, 1912, and subsequent entries; *SCMP,* March 13, 1912, p. 3; March 15, p. 5; March 19, p. 7; Li Shui-hsien, "Ch'en Chiung-ming p'an-kuo shih," *Chung-kuo hsien-tai-shih ts'ung-k'an,* 2:425 (1960).

12. *SCMP,* March 19, 1912, p. 11.

13. FO 228/1797, Diary, Feb. 17, 1912.

14. Li Lang-ju and Lu Man, p. 414; *SCMP*, Dec. 18, 1912, p. 7. On Li Fu-lin's fortress on Ho-nan in the 1920's, see Harry A. Franck, *Roving Through Southern China* (New York, 1925), pp. 256–257.

15. Chang Lu-ts'un, "Ch'ao-Shan kuang-fu hui-i," p. 362; Sun Tan-yai, pp. 479–480; DS/DF, 893.00/1633, Williams, Swatow, March 27, 1913; *SCMP*, March 14, 1913, p. 6.

16. *SCMP*, May 9, 1912, p. 5; May 15, p. 5; May 18, p. 7; May 25, p. 7.

17. Feng, *I-shih*, 1:194; DS/DF, 893.00/795, George Anderson, Hong Kong, Nov. 16, 1911.

18. *SCMP*, Sept. 10, 1912, p. 7.

19. *SCMP*, April 8, 1912, p. 3; Aug. 8, p. 7; FO 228/1836, Canton intelligence reports for April to June and for July to September, 1912.

20. *SCMP*, Jan. 29, 1912, p. 5; Feb. 16, p. 11; April 16, p. 11.

21. *SCMP*, Sept. 10, 1912, p. 7; Sept. 14, p. 4; Oct. 9, p. 7; Nov. 14, p. 7; Nov. 16, p. 7; FO 228/1836, Canton intelligence report, July to Sept., 1912.

22. FO 228/1836, Canton intelligence report, July to Sept., 1912; *SCMP*, Feb. 18, 1913, p. 7.

23. FO 228/1836, Canton intelligence report, July to Sept., 1912.

24. Young, "Reformer as Conspirator," pp. 259–265; *SCMP*, Dec. 20, 1911, p. 8; Dec. 25, p. 8.

25. *SCMP*, Jan. 25, 1912, p. 8; Feng, *I-shih*, 2:9; 3:135.

26. FO 228/1836, Canton intelligence report, April to June, 1912, and Oct. 1912 to Jan. 1913; *SCMP*, May 24, 1912, p. 7; June 12, p. 7; July 2, p. 7; July 5, p. 3; July 9, p. 12; DS/DF, 893.00/1507, Buler, Canton, Oct. 31, 1912.

27. FO 228/1836, Jamieson to Jordan, Sept. 10, 1912; on Ch'en Ching-hua as police superintendent, see Lu Tan-lin, pp. 187–197.

28. *TR*, 1912, Swatow, pp. 661–662; *SCMP*, March 20, 1912, p. 3; March 23, p. 5; April 12, p. 5.

29. *SCMP*, Nov. 25, 1911, p. 7; FO 228/1797, Diary, Nov. 25.

30. FO 228/1797, Diary, Dec. 11, 1911; see also Dec. 2 and 4.

31. FO 228/1836, Jamieson to Jordan, Sept. 2, 1912.

32. David G. Marr, *Vietnamese Anticolonialism, 1885–1925* (Berkeley, 1971), pp. 215–221.

33. *HTJP*, Dec. 13, 1911, p. 2; *SCMP*, April 25, 1912, p. 11; May 17, p. 5.

34. *HKT*, Dec. 30, 1911, p. 1; *HTJP*, Feb. 7, 1912, p. 3; *SCMP*, April 29, p. 3.

35. *HTJP*, Dec. 18, 1911, p. 2; Feb. 28, 1913, p. 2; March 5, p. 2; *SCMP*, Dec. 20, 1911, p. 8; March 9, 1912, p. 11.

36. *HTJP*, Dec. 13, 1911, p. 2; Dec. 18; Jan. 18, 1912, p. 2; Jan. 29, p. 2; Jan. 31, p. 2; April 18, Ching-hua lu, p. 1; *SCMP*, Jan. 18, 1912, p. 5. On the Newspaper Society, see T'an Li-yüan, p. 9; *SCMP*, Dec. 20, 1911, p. 8; April 11, 1912, p. 3.

37. *HTJP*, Dec. 11, 1911, p. 2; Jan. 20, 1912, p. 6; FO 228/1869, Canton intelligence report, Oct. 1912 to Jan. 1913; *SCMP*, Feb. 24, 1912, p. 6.

38. George Yu, chap. 4; K. S. Liew, pp. 153–159; Miao Chih-hsin, p. 346; Huang Ta-han, p. 487; Min-kuo Kao-yao *HC*, 14:2, 4b–5; Lo-ting *HC*, 10:1b; Ch'ing-yüan *HC*, 13:41–41b; *SCMP*, Nov. 20, 1912, p. 7; Jan. 23, 1913, p. 7.

39. Feng, *I-shih*, 2:211; *SCMP*, July 19, 1912, p. 11; Boorman and Howard, 2:414; *Chung-kuo lao-kung yün-tung shih*, 1:85; Robert A. Scalapino and George T. Yu, *The Chinese Anarchist Movement* (Berkeley, 1961), p. 36.

40. *TR*, 1912, Canton; S. A. Polevoy, *Periodicheskaya Pechat v Kitae* (Vladivostok, 1913), pp. 161–162; *HTJP*, Jan. 18, 1912, p. 3; Feng, *I-shih*, 3:256; *DR*, 1902–11, 2:132.

41. See Chiang Yung-ching, pp. 125–128; Kuo Hsiao-ch'eng, pp. 232–238; "Kuang-tung tu-li chi," pp. 463–465.

42. For the regulations for the provisional assembly, see *HTJP*, Dec. 11, 1911, p. 2; Dec. 12, Ching-hua lu, p. 1; cf. Ch'ing-yüan *HC*, 10:35.

43. "Kuang-tung tu-li chi," pp. 466–468; *HTJP*, Dec. 9, 1911, p. 2.

44. *HTJP*, Dec. 20, 1911, Ching-hua lu, p. 1.

45. Lo-ting *HC*, 10:1, 5; Ch'ing-yüan *HC*, 10:35b, 39b–40; Boorman and Howard, 4:17–19; *SCMP*, Jan. 25, 1912, p. 11; *HTJP*, Dec. 18, 1912, p. 2.

46. See *Shin-matsu jimmeiroku*, pp. 191, 536, 730–731.

47. *SCMP*, April 17, 1912, p. 11; April 22, p. 5; June 11, p. 3; Chiang Yung-ching, p. 137.

48. DS/DF, 893.00/1490, Williams, Swatow, Oct. 17, 1912; ---/1544, Cheshire, Canton, Jan. 20, 1913; John Fincher, "Political Provincialism and the National Revolution," in Wright, ed., *China in Revolution*, pp. 209–211.

49. Friedman, "Revolution or Just Another Bloody Cycle?" pp. 303–305; DS/DF, 893.00/1490, Williams, Swatow, Oct. 17, 1912.

50. See *HTJP* for the committee assignments of 78 members at the Feb. 17, 1913, session.

51. Ch'ing-yüan *HC*, 10:35b; 13:40; DS/DF, 894c.032, Cheshire, Canton, Feb. 11, 1913; *KMWH*, 2:213.

52. *HTJP*, March 1, 1913, p. 2; DS/DF, 894c.032/1, Cheshire, Canton, March 6; 893.00/1632, Cheshire, March 15.

53. Ch'ing-yüan *HC*, 13:34b, 39b–40; Lo-ting *HC*, 10:1–1b; Le-ch'ang *HC*, 12:1–2; Min-kuo Kao-yao *HC*, 6:25, 26b; K'ai-p'ing *HC*, 22:2b; Ch'ih-hsi *HC*, 3:8b; *HTJP*, Jan. 22, 1912, p. 2; Feb. 6, p. 2; DS/DF, 893.00/1490, Williams, Swatow, Oct. 17, 1912.

54. Min-kuo Kao-yao *HC*, 1:2; 6:25, 26b–27; Lo-ting *HC*, 10:2; K'ai-p'ing *HC*, 22:4; cf. Brunnert and Hagelstrom, no. 526.

55. For the membership on these councils, see K'ai-p'ing *HC*, 22:2b; Min-kuo Kao-yao *HC*, 6:26b–27; Lo-ting *HC*, 10:2.

56. *HTJP*, Jan. 29, 1912, p. 2; Feb. 6, p. 2; May 2, 1913, p. 2.

57. Lo-ting *HC*, 10:1; Min-kuo Kao-yao *HC*, 6: appendix, p. 1b; K'ai-p'ing *HC*, 24:13b.

58. *SCMP*, Dec. 27, 1911, p. 8.

59. Lin I-han, p. 488; *HTJP*, March 26, 1913, p. 2.

60. FO 228/1797, Diary, Nov. 18, 1911; *SCMP*, Dec. 27, p. 8; Feb. 14, 1912, p. 6; *HTJP*, Feb. 26, 1913, p. 2; Li Shu-fan, pp. 48–49.

61. *SCMP*, Dec. 27, 1911, p. 8; Nov. 13, 1912, p. 11; Feb. 18, 1913, p. 7.

62. *SCMP*, Jan. 28, 1913, p. 6; Feb. 6, p. 6; Feb. 13, p. 7; cf. Feb. 17, p. 6; Feb.

18, p. 7. On the traditional system, see Lien-sheng Yang, "Schedules of Work and Rest in Imperial China," in his *Studies in Chinese Institutional History* (Cambridge, 1961), pp. 19–23.

63. See Li's autobiographical account, pp. 45–49.

64. *SCMP,* May 10, 1912, p. 3; March 8, 1913, p. 7; April 8, p. 7; June 10, p. 7.

65. *SCMP,* June 21, 1912, p. 7; June 25, p. 5.

66. *SCMP,* Dec. 28, 1911, p. 8; FO 228/1797, Diary, Nov. 22.

67. *SCMP,* Dec. 27, 1911, p. 8; Dec. 28, p. 8.

68. *SCMP,* Dec. 27, 1911, p. 8; FO 228/1797, Diary, Dec. 4.

69. George Yu, pp. 100–101; K. S. Liew, p. 177; *SCMP,* Sept. 23, 1912, p. 10; Oct. 18, p. 7; Nov. 14, p. 7. See also Witke, pp. 66–70.

70. *HTJP,* Jan. 12, 1912, p. 2; Feb. 5, p. 2; *SCMP,* July 1, p. 5.

71. *SCMP,* April 4, 1912, p. 3; Gamble, pp. 48–49, 60 (table 9).

72. Yang Hua-jih, pp. 33–36; *SCMP,* June 24, 1912, p. 6; July 15, p. 7.

73. Welch, p. 147, quoting Edward Bing-shuey Lee, *Modern Canton* (1936), p. 96; *SCMP,* Dec. 20, 1911, p. 8; Dec. 28, p. 8; June 15, 1912, p. 5; Jan. 22, 1913, p. 6; March 11, p. 6; Jean Rodes, *Scènes de la vie révolutionnaire en Chine, 1911–1914* (Paris, 1917), p. 139.

74. Latourette, p. 609, n. 259; cf. *History of the South China Mission,* pp. 127–128.

75. *SCMP,* June 24, 1913, p. 6.

76. *SCMP,* March 16, 1907, p. 7; July 15, 1909, p. 7; Jan. 31, 1913, p. 7; P'an-yü *HC,* 42:19; *Ta-Ch'ing li-ch'ao shih-lu,* Hsüan-t'ung, 43:36–37, HT 2/10/27; *HTJP,* Jan. 20, 1912, p. 2; FO 228/1797, Diary, Feb. 1, 1912; cf. Vogel, pp. 26–27.

77. FO 228/1836, Canton intelligence report, April to June, 1912; *SCMP,* Nov. 13, 1912, p. 11.

78. See Friedman, "The Center Cannot Hold," chap. 6.

79. *SCMP,* July 12, 1912, p. 5; Aug. 2, p. 5; Jan. 7, 1913, p. 10; "Kuang-tung tu-li chi," pp. 468–469.

80. *SCMP,* Nov. 13, 1912, p. 11; *TR,* 1913, Canton.

81. Quoted in George Yu, p. 85.

82. Chiang Yung-ching, pp. 138–139; *SCMP,* June 14, 1912, p. 7.

83. See *SCMP,* Feb. 26, 1913, p. 7; *HTJP,* March 21, p. 2; March 28, p. 2; March 31, p. 2; April 30, p. 3.

84. Cf. Bergère.

85. See, for example, "Kuang-tung tu-li chi," p. 463.

86. For these events from Yüan Shih-k'ai's perspective, see Ernest P. Young, "Politics in the Early Republic: Liang Ch'i-ch'ao and the Yüan Shih-k'ai Presidency," Ph.D. diss., Harvard University, 1964, chap. 4.

87. *SCMP,* Dec. 7, 1912, p. 5; Dec. 16, p. 7; Dec. 20, p. 7.

88. FO 228/1785, H. F. May, memorandum of a conversation with Liang Shih-i, March 1, 1913; *HTJP,* April 12, p. 2.

89. *SCMP,* Nov. 27, 1912, p. 7.

90. *SCMP,* March 26, 1913, p. 7; FO 228/1785, May to Harcourt, April 1, 1913. On Liang Shih-i, see Boorman and Howard, 2:354–357.

91. *HTJP,* March 14, 1913, p. 2; April 24, p. 2.

92. *HTJP,* May 2, 1913, p. 2; *SCMP,* May 7, p. 6; May 26, p. 7.

93. FO 228/1869, Canton intelligence report, Feb. to April 1913; SCMP, April 11, p. 6.

94. DS/DF, 893.00/1686, Cheshire, Canton, April 24, 1913; FO 228/1869, Jamieson to Jordan, April 26.

95. *SCMP,* July 21, 1913, p. 7; DS/DF, 893.00/1858, Cheshire, Canton, July 21.

96. DS/DF, 893.00/1858, Cheshire, Canton, July 21, 1913; ---/1859, Cheshire, July 22; Rankin, *Early Chinese Revolutionaries,* p. 213.

97. DS/DF, 893.00/1859, Cheshire, Canton, July 22, 1913; ---/1860, Cheshire, July 24; *SCMP,* July 30, p. 7.

98. *SCMP,* Aug. 2, 1913, p. 7; DS/DF, 893.00/1909, Cheshire, Canton, Aug. 4, 1913; ---/1883, Cheshire, Aug. 5; ---/1894, Cheshire, Aug. 6; *TR,* 1913, Canton.

99. DS/DF, 893.00/1898, Cheshire, Canton, Aug. 16, 1913; *TR,* 1913, Canton; FO 228/1869, Canton intelligence report, Sept. quarter, 1913.

100. DS/DF, 893.00/1715, Cheshire, Canton, May 17, 1913; FO 228/1785, May to Harcourt, May 10; 228/1869, Canton intelligence report, May to June 1913; *SCMP,* June 4, p. 7.

101. DS/DF, 893.00/2057, John K. Davis, Canton, Nov. 21, 1913; ---/2128, Cheshire, Canton, May 2, 1914; ---/2135, Cheshire, May 18.

102. Donald G. Gillin, *Warlord: Yen Hsi-shan in Shansi Province, 1911–1949* (Princeton, 1967), p. 19.

103. FO 228/1869, Canton intelligence report, Sept. quarter, 1913; Hu Han-min, "Tzu-chuan," p. 419.

104. FO 228/1869, Canton intelligence report, Sept. quarter, 1913; cf. DS/DF, 893.00/1961, Cheshire, Canton, Sept. 23.

105. DS/DF, 893.00/1964, Cheshire, Canton, Sept. 17, 1913; FO 228/1785, Claud Severn to Harcourt, Sept. 30; Rodes, *Scènes da la vie,* pp. 239–255: Lu Tan-lin, pp. 194–195.

106. FO 228/1869, List of principal officials in Canton, late 1913; Min-kuo Kao-yao *HC,* 6: appendix, p. 1b; Lo-ting *HC,* 10:1; K'ai-p'ing *HC,* 24:13b.

107. DS/DF, 893.00/1932, Nov. 27, 1913; K'ai-p'ing *HC,* 22:5, 6b; Min-kuo Kao-yao *HC,* 1:2b; 6:25; Le-ch'ang *HC,* 12:1.

108. DS/DF, 893.00/2057, Davis, Canton, Nov. 21, 1913; ---/2144, Myers, Swatow, June 12, 1914; Feng, *I-Shih,* 3:256; Boorman and Howard, 2:414.

109. FO 228/1869, Canton intelligence report, Sept. quarter, 1913.

110. Rodes, *Scènes de la vie,* pp. 223–224.

111. DS/DF, 893.00/2123, Myers, Swatow, April 20, 1914.

112. DS/DF, 894c.513, Cheshire, Canton, Oct. 26, 1914.

113. See Adams, pp. 376 ff.

114. DS/DF, 893.00/2057, Davis, Canton, Nov. 21, 1913; see also Friedman, "The Center Cannot Hold," chap. 6.

115. Marr, pp. 225–226.

Conclusion

1. See Wakeman, "The Secret Societies of Kwangtung," p. 46; Kuhn, pp. 186–188.

2. For some conflicting analyses of the effects of imperialism in China, see Chi-ming Hou; Schrecker, *Imperialism and Chinese Nationalism,* pp. 258–259; Wright, pp. 54–58; Andrew J. Nathan, "Imperialism's Effects on China," and Joseph Esherick, "Harvard on China: The Apologetics of Imperialism," *Bulletin of Concerned Asian Scholars,* 4.4:3–16 (1972).

3. Braisted, "The United States and the American China Development Company," p. 165.

4. Schrecker, *Imperialism and Chinese Nationalism,* pp. 169–170, 191, 199.

5. See *DR,* 1902–11, for the various Kwangtung ports.

6. Henry McAleavy, *Su Man-shu (1884–1918): A Sino-Japanese Genius* (London, 1960), pp. 8–9.

7. Schrecker, *Imperialism and Chinese Nationalism,* p. 208.

8. See also Wright, pp. 24–30.

9. Schrecker, *Imperialism and Chinese Nationalism,* pp. 149–152.

10. Karl W. Deutsch, "Social Mobilization and Political Development," *American Political Science Review,* 55:499 (1961).

11. Iriye, "Public Opinion and Foreign Policy," pp. 220–223.

12. See Paul A. Cohen, "Wang T'ao and Incipient Chinese Nationalism," *Journal of Asian Studies,* 26:559–574 (1967).

13. For a contrary opinion, see Chalmers A. Johnson, *Peasant Nationalism and Communist Power: The Emergence of Revolutionary China, 1937–1945* (Stanford, 1962), pp. 19–26.

14. See also Wright, pp. 32–44.

15. See Witke, chap. 2.

16. See also Wright, p. 3.

17. Rankin, *Early Chinese Revolutionaries,* pp. 187–188.

18. Noriko Tamada, "Sung Chiao-jen and the 1911 Revolution," *Papers on China,* 21:193–195 (1968); K. S. Liew, pp. 60–61, 65–67.

19. See Ichiko, "The Role of the Gentry," pp. 297–313; Jean Chesneaux, "Secret Societies in China's Historical Evolution," in his *Popular movements and Secret Societies,* pp. 10–11, and his review of the Wright volume in *Journal of Asian Studies,* 29:433 (1970).

20. Franz Michael, "Regionalism in Nineteenth-Century China," in Stanley Spector, *Li Hung-chang and the Huai Army: A Study in Nineteenth-Century Chinese Regionalism* (Seattle, 1964), pp. xxi–xliii.

21. See also Wright, pp. 58–60.

Bibliography

A Ying 阿英 (pseud., Ch'ien Hsing-ts'un 錢杏村). *Wan-Ch'ing hsiao-shuo shih* 晚清小説史 (A history of late Ch'ing novels). Peking: Tso-chia ch'u-pan she, 1955. Originally published in 1937.

Adams, Leonard P., II. "China: The Historical Setting of Asia's Profitable Plague." Appendix to Alfred W. McCoy, *The Politics of Heroin in Southeast Asia*. New York: Harper & Row, 1972. Pp. 365–383.

Ayers, William. *Chang Chih-tung and Educational Reform in China*. Cambridge: Harvard University Press, 1971.

Bastid, Marianne. *Aspects de la réforme de l'enseignment en Chine au début du 20ᵉ siècle, d'après des écrits de Zhang Jian*. Paris and The Hague: Mouton, 1971.

Bays, Daniel H. "The Nature of Provincial Political Authority in Late Ch'ing Times: Chang Chih-tung in Canton, 1884–1889," *Modern Asian Studies*, 4.4: 325–347 (October 1970).

Beale, Howard K. *Theodore Roosevelt and the Rise of America to World Power*. Baltimore: The Johns Hopkins Press, 1956.

Beresford, Lord Charles. *The Break-up of China, with an Account of its Present Commerce, Currency, Waterways, Armies, Railways, Politics and Future Prospects*. New York and London: Harper & Brothers, 1900.

Bergère, Marie-Claire. "The Role of the Bourgeoisie." In M. C. Wright, *China in Revolution*. Pp. 229–295.

Biggerstaff, Knight. *The Earliest Modern Government Schools in China*. Ithaca: Cornell University Press, 1961.

Bishop, G. T., C. S. Morton, and W. Sayers. *Hong Kong and the Treaty Ports:*

Postal History and Postal Markings. 2nd ed., rev. and enlarged by H. E. Lobdell and Adrien E. Hopkins. London: The Postal History Society, 1949.

Bonnique, Alfred. *La France à Kouang-Tchéou-Wan.* Paris: Editions Berger-Levrault, 1931.

Boorman, Howard L., and Richard C. Howard, eds. *Biographical Dictionary of Republican China.* New York: Columbia University Press, 1967–71. 4 vols.

Braisted, William Reynolds. "The United States and the American China Development Company," *Far Eastern Quarterly,* 11.2:147–165 (February 1952).

———— *The United States Navy in the Pacific, 1897–1909.* Austin: University of Texas Press, 1958.

Brinton, Crane. *The Anatomy of Revolution.* Rev. ed. New York: Vintage Books, 1952.

Britton, Roswell S. *The Chinese Periodical Press, 1800–1912.* Shanghai: Kelly & Walsh, Limited, 1933.

Brunnert, H. S., and V. V. Hagelstrom. *Present Day Political Organization of China.* Rev. N. Th. Kolessoff and trans. A. Beltchenko and E. E. Moran. 1912; Taipei reprint: Wen-hsing shu-chü, n.d.

Burgess, John Stewart. *The Guilds of Peking.* New York: Columbia University Press, 1928.

Cameron, Maribeth E. *The Reform Movement in China, 1898–1912.* Stanford: Stanford University Press, 1931.

Chan, Wellington Kam-kong. "Merchants, Mandarins and Modern Enterprise in Late Ch'ing China (1872–1911)." Ph.D. dissertation. Cambridge: Harvard University, 1972.

Chang Chih-tung 張之洞. *Chang Wen-hsiang kung ch'üan-chi* 張文襄公全集 (Complete works of Chang Chih-tung). Taipei reprint: Wen-hai ch'u-pan she, 1963. Originally published in 1928.

Chang, Chung-li. *The Chinese Gentry: Studies on their Role in Nineteenth-Century Chinese Society.* Seattle: University of Washington Press, 1955.

Chang, Hao. *Liang Ch'i-ch'ao and Intellectual Transition in China, 1890–1907.* Cambridge: Harvard University Press, 1971.

Chang Hui-ch'ang 張惠昌. "Li-hsien-p'ai jen ho Ssu-ch'uan tzu-i chü" 立宪派人和四川諮議局 (Constitutionalists and the Szechwan provincial assembly), *Hsin-hai ko-ming hui-i lu,* 3:145–173.

Chang Lu-ts'un 張醁村. "Keng-hsü hsin-chün ch'i-i ch'ien-hou ti hui-i" 庚戌新軍起義前后的回忆 (Recollections of events before and after the 1910 New Army revolt), *Hsin-hai ko-ming hui-i lu,* 2:281–286.

———— "Ch'ao-Shan kuang-fu hui-i" 潮汕光復回忆 (Recollections of the Revolution in Ch'ao-chou and Swatow), *Hsin-hai ko-ming hui-i lu,* 2:358–362.

Chang, P'eng-yüan. "The Constitutionalists." In M. C. Wright, *China in Revolution*. Pp. 143–183.

Chang Ts'un-wu 張存武. *Kuang-hsü sa-i-nien Chung-Mei kung-yüeh feng-ch'ao* 光緒卅一年中美工約風潮 (The controversy surrounding the Sino-American labor treaty in 1905). Taipei: Institute of Modern History, Academia Sinica, 1966.

Chang Wen-po 張文伯, ed. *Chih-lao hsien-hua* 稚老閒話 (Conversations with Wu Chih-hui). Taipei: Chung-yang wen-wu kung-ying she, 1952.

Chang Yu-jen 張友仁. "Keng-tzu Hui-chou San-chou-t'ien ch'i-i fang-wen lu" 庚子惠州三洲田起义訪問錄 (Interviews regarding the 1900 uprising at San-chou-t'ien, Hui-chou), *Hsin-hai ko-ming hui-i lu*, 2:263–280.

Chao Lien-ch'eng 赵連城. "T'ung-meng hui tsai Kang-Ao ti huo-tung ho Kuang-tung fu-nü-chieh ts'an-chia ko-ming ti hui-i" 同盟会在港澳的活动和广东妇女界参加革命的回忆 (Recollections of the activities of the Revolutionary Alliance in Hong Kong and Macao and of the participation of the women of Kwangtung in the revolution), *Hsin-hai ko-ming hui-i lu*, 2:302–322.

Chao Yung-liang 赵永良, Fu K'o-shun 傳克順, and Weng Tsu-tse 翁祖澤. "1897–1899-nien Chung-kuo jen-min ti fan-ti fan-feng-chien tou-cheng" 1897–1899年中国人民的反帝反封建斗爭 (The Chinese people's anti-imperialist anti-feudal struggles in 1897–1899), *Li-shih chiao-hsüeh* 历史教学 (History education), 1960, no. 9, pp. 7–14 (Tientsin, September 1, 1960).

Ch'en Ching-lü 陳景呂. "Hui-chou kuang-fu chi" 惠州光復記 (The revolution in Hui-chou), *Chin-tai-shih tzu-liao* 近代史資料 (Materials on modern history), 1958, no. 2, pp. 50–52.

Ch'en Ching-ts'un hsien-sheng nien-p'u 陳競存先生年譜 (Chronological biography of Ch'en Chiung-ming). Hong Kong, n.d.

Ch'en Ch'un-sheng 陳春生. "Ch'en Shao-pai hsien-sheng yü Hsiang-kang *Chung-kuo jih-pao* chi *Chung-kuo jih-pao* yü Chung-kuo ko-ming chih kuan-hsi" 陳少白先生与香港中國日报及中國日报与中国革命之关係(Ch'en Shao-pai and the *China Daily News* of Hong Kong and the relationship between the *China Daily News* and the Chinese revolution), *Chung-hua min-kuo k'ai-kuo wu-shih-nien wen-hsien*, 1.10:506–508.

——— "Keng-tzu Hui-chou ch'i-i chi" 庚子惠州起义記 (The 1900 Hui-chou uprising), *Hsin-hai ko-ming*, 1:235–244. Published originally in 1931.

——— "Jen-yin Hung Ch'üan-fu Kuang-chou chü-i chi" 壬寅洪全福广州举义記 (The 1903 Hung Ch'üan-fu uprising in Canton), *Hsin-hai ko-ming*, 1:315–321. Published originally in 1931.

——— "Ting-wei Huang-kang ch'i-i chi" 丁未黃岡起义記 (The 1907 Huang-kang uprising), *Chung-hua min-kuo k'ai-kuo wu-shih-nien wen-hsien*, 1.13:64–72.

————"Kuang Ching-ch'uan Ch'en Shou-t'ien so shu Ch'in Fang Chen-nan-kuan Ho-k'ou chu-i ch'i-i hsiang-ch'ing" 邝敬川陳寿田所述欽防鎮南关河口諸役起义詳情 (Accounts by Kuang Ching-ch'uan and Ch'en Shou-t'ien of the uprisings at Ch'in-chou, Fang-ch'eng, Chen-nan-kuan and Ho-k'ou), *Chung-hua min-kuo k'ai-kuo wu-shih-nien wen-hsien*, 1.13:130–136.

————"Ting-wei Fang-ch'eng ch'i-i chi" 丁未防城起義記 (The 1907 Fang-ch'eng uprising), *Chung-hua min-kuo k'ai-kuo wu-shih-nien wen-hsien*, 1.13: 126–130.

————"Keng-hsü Kuang-chou hsin-chün chü-i chi" 庚戌广州新軍举义記 (The 1910 Canton New Army uprising), *Hsin-hai ko-ming*, 3:347–361. Published originally in 1932.

————"Kuang-chou san-yüeh erh-shih-chiu fa-nan chüeh-ting chih ching-kuo" 广州三月二十九發难決定之経过 (The decision to revolt on April 27, 1911, in Canton), *Chung-hua min-kuo k'ai-kuo wu-shih-nien wen-hsien*, 1.14: 142–147.

Ch'en Hsü-lu 陳旭麓 and Lao Shao-hua 劳紹华. "Ch'ing-mo ti hsin-chün yü hsin-hai ko-ming" 清末的新軍与辛亥革命 (The New Armies at the end of the Ch'ing and the 1911 Revolution), *Hsin-hai ko-ming wu-shih chou-nien chi-nien lun-wen chi* 辛亥革命五十週年紀念論文集 (Essays in commemoration of the fiftieth anniversary of the 1911 Revolution). Peking: Chung-hua shu-chü 1962.

Ch'en Shao-pai 陳少白. "Hsing-Chung hui ko-ming shih-yao" 兴中会革命史要 (An outline of the revolutionary history of the Society to Restore China's Prosperity), *Hsin-hai ko-ming*, 1:21–84.

Chen Ta. *Emigrant Communities in South China: A Study of Overseas Migration and Its Influence on Standards of Living and Social Change*, English version ed. Bruno Lasker. New York: Secretariat, Institute of Pacific Relations, 1940.

Ch'en Te-yün 陳德芸, comp. "Ch'en Shao-pai hsien-sheng nien-p'u" 陳少白先生年譜 (Chronological biography of Ch'en Shao-pai), *Chung-hua min-kuo k'ai-kuo wu-shih-nien wen-hsien*, 1.10:510–520. Published originally in 1936.

Cheng Pi-an 郑彼岸. "Hsiang-shan ch'i-i hui-i" 香山起义回忆 (Recollections of the Hsiang-shan uprising), *Hsin-hai ko-ming hui-i lu*, 2:338–342.

Cheng, Shelley Hsien. "The T'ung-meng-hui: Its Organization, Leadership and Finances, 1905–1912." Ph.D. dissertation. Seattle: University of Washington, 1962. University Microfilms 62–6625.

Cheng, Ying-wan. *Postal Communication in China and its Modernization, 1860–1896*. Cambridge: East Asian Research Center, Harvard University, 1970.

Chesneaux, Jean, with the collaboration of Marianne Rachline. *Les Sociétés sécrètes en Chine (XIXᵉ et XXᵉ siècles)*. Paris: Collections Archives, 1965.

————Review of M. C. Wright, *China in Revolution. Journal of Asian Studies*, 29.2:432–433 (February 1970).

————"Secret Societies in China's Historical Evolution." In his *Popular Movements and Secret Societies in China, 1840–1950*. Stanford: Stanford University Press, 1972. Pp. 1–21.

Chiang Yung-ching 蔣永敬, comp. "Hu Han-min hsien-sheng nien-p'u kao" 胡汉民先生年譜稿 (A draft chronological biography of Hu Han-min), *Chung-kuo hsien-tai-shih ts'ung-k'an* 中国现代史丛刊, 3:79–320 (1961).

Chiao-yü tsa-chih 教育杂誌 (Education magazine). Shanghai. Monthly, 1909–1911.

Chiao-yü t'ung-chi t'u-piao 教育統計图表 (Statistical charts and tables on education). Comp. Department of General Affairs of the Ministry of Education. Peking, n.d. 3 series, for 1907 to 1909. Pagination by provinces.

Ch'ien Shih-fu 錢實甫, comp. *Ch'ing-chi hsin-she chih-kuan nien-piao* 清季新設职官年表 (Chronological table of the newly created official posts in the Ch'ing period). Peking: Chung-hua shu-chü, 1961.

Ch'ih-hsi hsien-chih 赤溪県志 (Ch'ih-hsi gazetteer). 1920.

Chin Tsu-hsün 金祖勳. "1905-nien Kuang-tung fan-Mei yün-tung ti p'ien-tuan hui-i" 1905年广东反美运动的片斷回忆 (Reminiscences of the 1905 anti-American movement in Kwangtung), *Chin-tai-shih tzu-liao*, 1958, no. 5, pp. 52–55.

China, Imperial Maritime Customs. *Decennial Reports on the Trade, Navigation, Industries, etc., of the Ports Open to Foreign Commerce in China and Corea, and on the Condition and Development of the Treaty Port Provinces*. Shanghai. First issue, 1882–91, in 1 volume (1903); 2nd issue, 1892–1901, in 2 volumes (1904, 1906); 3rd issue, 1902–11, in 3 volumes (1913).

————Imperial Maritime Customs. *Returns of Trade and Trade Reports*. Shanghai. Annual, 1896–1913. Especially Part II, "Port Statistics and Reports."

————Wai-wu pu 外務部 (Ministry of Foreign Affairs) archives. On deposit at the Institute of Modern History, Academia Sinica, Taipei, Taiwan.

The China Mission Hand-book. Shanghai: American Presbyterian Mission Press, 1896.

"The Chinese Reform Movement of the 1890's: A Symposium," *Journal of Asian Studies*, 29.1:7–53 (November 1969).

Ch'ing-yüan hsien-chih 清远県志 (Ch'ing-yüan gazetteer). 1937.

Ch'iu Nien-t'ai 丘念台. *Ling-hai wei-piao* 岭海微熯 (Soft breezes over mountain and sea). Taipei: Chung-hua jih-pao she, 1962.

The Christian Occupation of China: A General Survey of the Numerical Strength and Geographical Distribution of the Christian Forces in China. Shanghai: China Continuation Committee, 1922.

Chu Hao-huai 朱浩怀. "Kuang-chou hsin-chün ch'i-i yü san-yüeh erh-shih-chiu-jih chih i" 广州新軍起义与三月二十九日之役 (The Canton New Army uprising and the April 27th revolt), *Chung-hua min-kuo k'ai-kuo wu-shih-nien wen-hsien*, 1.14:219–223.

Chu, Samuel C. *Reformer in Modern China: Chang Chien, 1853–1926.* New York: Columbia University Press, 1965.

Chuang Chi-fa 莊吉發. "Keng-tzu Hui-chou ko-ming yün-tung shih-mo" 庚子惠州革命运动始末 (The revolutionary movement in Hui-chou in 1900), *Ta-lu tsa-chih* 大陆杂誌 (Continent Magazine), 41.4: 124–131 (August 30, 1970).

Chung-hua min-kuo k'ai-kuo wu-shih-nien wen-hsien 中华民国开国五十年文獻 (Documents on the fiftieth anniversary of the founding of Republic of China). Taipei, 1962–65. 1st ser., 15 vols.; 2nd ser., 5 vols.

Chung-hua min-kuo Kao-yao hsien-chih ch'u-pien 中华民国高要县志初編 (First draft of the Kao-yao gazetteer for the Republican period). 1947. Available at the library of the Ministry of the Interior, Taipei, Taiwan.

Chung-kuo lao-kung yün-tung shih 中国劳工运动史 (A history of the Chinese labor movement). Compiled under the general editorship of Ma Chao-chün 馬超俊. Taipei: Chung-kuo lao-kung fu-li ch'u-pan she, 1959. 5 vols.

Ch'ü, T'ung-tsu. *Local Government in China under the Ch'ing.* Cambridge: Harvard University Press, 1962.

———— *Law and Society in Traditional China.* Paris and La Haye: Mouton & Co., 1965.

Ch'üan Han-sheng 全汉昇. "T'ieh-lu kuo-yu wen-t'i yü hsin-hai ko-ming" 鉄路国有问题与辛亥革命 (The railroad nationalization question and the 1911 Revolution), *Chung-kuo hsien-tai-shih ts'ung-k'an,* 1:209–271 (1960).

Cohen, Paul A. "Wang T'ao and Incipient Chinese Nationalism," *Journal of Asian Studies,* 26.4:559–574 (August 1967).

Cohen, Warren I. *America's Response to China: An Interpretative History of Sino-American Relations.* New York: John Wiley & Sons, Inc., 1971.

Coolidge, Mary Roberts. *Chinese Immigration.* New York: Henry Holt and Company, 1909.

Corbett, Charles Hodge. *Lingnan University: A Short History Based Primarily on the Records of the University's American Trustees.* New York: Trustees of Lingnan University, 1963.

Cressey, George Babcock. *China's Geographic Foundations: A Survey of the Land and Its People.* New York and London: McGraw-Hill Book Company, Inc., 1934.

Davies, James C. "Toward a Theory of Revolution," *American Sociological Review,* 27.1:5–19 (February 1962).

Dennys, N. B. *The Treaty Ports of China and Japan.* London: Trübner and Co. and Hong Kong: A. Shortrede and Co., 1867.

Des Forges, Roger V. *Hsi-liang and the Chinese National Revolution.* New Haven: Yale University Press, 1973.

Deutsch, Karl W. "Social Mobilization and Political Development," *American Political Science Review,* 55.3:493–514 (September 1961).

Dutt, Vidya Prakash. "The First Week of the Revolution: The Wuchang Uprising." In M. C. Wright, *China in Revolution*. Pp. 383–416.

Eastman, Lloyd. "The Kwangtung Anti-foreign Disturbances during the Sino-French War," *Papers on China*, 13:1–31 (1959). Harvard University, East Asian Research Center.

——— "Political Reformism in China before the Sino-Japanese War," *Journal of Asian Studies*, 27.4:695–710 (August 1968).

Eckstein, Harry. "On the Etiology of Internal Wars," *History and Theory*, 4.2: 133–163 (1965).

Elvin, Mark. "The Gentry Democracy in Chinese Shanghai, 1905–14." In Jack Gray, ed., *Modern China's Search for a Political Form*. London: Oxford University Press, 1969.

En-p'ing hsien-chih 恩平県志 (En-p'ing gazetteer). En-p'ing: Kuang-hua shu-chü, 1934.

Endacott, G. B. *A History of Hong Kong*. London and Hong Kong: Oxford University Press, 1964.

Esherick, Joseph. "Harvard on China: The Apologetics of Imperialism," *Bulletin of Concerned Asian Scholars*, 4.4:9–16 (December 1972).

——— "Reform, Revolution and Reaction: The 1911 Revolution in Hunan and Hupeh." Ph.D. dissertation. Berkeley: University of California, 1971.

Evans, Nancy. "The Banner-School Background of the Canton T'ung-wen kuan," *Papers on China*, 22A:89–103 (May 1969). Harvard University, East Asian Research Center.

Fang Chao-ying 房兆楹, comp. *Ch'ing-mo Min-ch'u yang-hsüeh hsüeh-sheng t'i-ming lu ch'u-chi* 清末民初洋学学生題名錄初輯 (A preliminary compilation of lists of names of students studying abroad at the end of the Ch'ing and the beginning of the Republic). Taipei: Institute of Modern History, Academia Sinica, 1962.

Feng Tzu-yu 馮自由. *Ko-ming i-shih* 革命逸史 (Anecdotal history of the revolution). Taipei: Shang-wu yin-shu kuan, 1953 and 1965. 5 vols. Originally published in 1945–47.

——— *Chung-kuo ko-ming yün-tung erh-shih-liu-nien tsu-chih shih* 中国革命运动二十六年組织史 (A history of the organizations in the twenty-six years of the Chinese revolutionary movement). Shanghai: Shang-wu yin-shu kuan, 1948.

——— *Chung-hua min-kuo k'ai-kuo ch'ien ko-ming shih* 中华民国开国前革命史 (A history of the Chinese revolution before the founding of the Republic). Taipei: Shih-chieh shu-chü, 1954.

——— "Ch'en Shu-jen shih-lüeh" 陳树人史略 (Biography of Ch'en Shu-jen), *Kuo-shih-kuan kuan-k'an* 国史館舘刊 (Journal of the National Historical Institute), 1.4:101–103 (Nanking; November 1948).

Feuerwerker, Albert. *China's Early Industrialization: Sheng Hsüan-huai (1844–*

1916) and Mandarin Enterprise. Cambridge: Harvard University Press, 1958.

——— *The Chinese Economy, ca. 1870–1911.* Ann Arbor: Center for Chinese Studies, University of Michigan, 1969.

Fielde, Adele M. *Pagoda Shadows: Studies from Life in China.* Boston: W. G. Corthell, 1884.

Fincher, John Howard. "Political Provincialism and the National Revolution." In M. C. Wright, *China in Revolution.* Pp. 185–226.

——— "The Chinese Self-Government Movement, 1900–1912." Ph.D. dissertation. Seattle: University of Washington, 1969. University Microfilms 69-18,287.

Folsom, Kenneth E. *Friends, Guests, and Colleagues: The Mu-fu System in the Late Ch'ing Period.* Berkeley: University of California Press, 1968.

Foreign Relations of the United States. Washington: Government Printing Office. For 1905 and 1909.

Forrest, R. A. D. "The Southern Dialects of Chinese." Appendix to Victor Purcell, *The Chinese in Southeast Asia*, 2nd ed. London: Oxford University Press, 1965. Pp. 569–571.

France, Archives des Affaires Etrangères, Correspondence de Chine.

Franck, Harry A. *Roving through Southern China.* New York and London: The Century Co., 1925.

Franke, Wolfgang. *The Reform and Abolition of the Traditional Chinese Examination System.* Cambridge: East Asian Research Center, Harvard University, 1963.

Freedman, Maurice. *Lineage Organization in Southeastern China.* London: The Athlone Press, University of London, 1958.

Friedman, Edward. "The Center Cannot Hold: The Failure of Parliamentary Democracy in China from the Chinese Revolution of 1911 to the World War in 1914." Ph.D. dissertation. Cambridge: Harvard University, 1968.

——— "Revolution of Just Another Bloody Cycle? Swatow and the 1911 Revolution," *Journal of Asian Studies*, 29.2:289–307 (February 1970).

Gamble, Sidney D. *Ting Hsien: A North China Rural Community.* 1954; Stanford: Stanford University Press, 1968.

Garrett, Shirley S. *Social Reformers in Urban China: The Chinese Y.M.C.A., 1895–1926.* Cambridge: Harvard University Press, 1970.

Gasster, Michael. *Chinese Intellectuals and the Revolution of 1911: The Birth of Modern Chinese Radicalism.* Seattle: University of Washington Press, 1969.

Gendai Shina jimmeikan 現代支那人名鑑 (Biographical dictionary of contemporary China). Tokyo, 1916.

Giles, Herbert A. *From Swatow to Canton: Overland.* London: Trübner & Co. and Shanghai: Kelly & Walsh, 1877.

Gillin, Donald G. *Warlord: Yen Hsi-shan in Shansi Province, 1911–1949.*

Princeton: Princeton University Press, 1967.

Gray, John Henry. *Walks in the City of Canton*. Hong Kong: de Souza & Co., 1875.

Great Britain, Foreign Office archives. London: Public Record Office, 1905–1911. Two sets of materials were consulted: FO 228, Embassy and Consular Archives, China; and FO 371, Foreign Office correspondence.

———Naval Intelligence Division, *China Proper*. 1944–45. 3 vols.

———War Office archives, 33/509, "Field Notes on China. 1.–The Army," 1910. On deposit at the Public Record Office, London.

Groves, R. G. "Militia, Market and Lineage: Chinese Resistance to the Occupation of Hong Kong's New Territories in 1899," *Journal of the Hong Kong Branch of the Royal Asiatic Society*, 9: 31–64 (1969).

Hao, Yen-p'ing. "Cheng Kuan-ying: The Comprador as Reformer," *Journal of Asian Studies*, 29.1:15–22 (November 1969).

——— *The Comprador in Nineteenth Century China: Bridge between East and West*. Cambridge: Harvard University Press, 1970.

Hatano Yoshihiro 波多野善大. "Minkoku kakumei undō ni okeru shingun—Kanton shingun no hanran o chūshin to shite" 民国革命运动における新軍―廣東新軍の叛亂を中心として(The new armies in the republican revolutionary movement, especially with respect to the mutiny of the Kwangtung New Army), *Nagoya daigaku ronshū* 名古屋大学論集 (Journal of Nagoya University), 8:63–76 (1954).

———"Shin-matsu ni okeru tetsudō kokuyū seisaku no haikei" 清末における鐵道国有政策の背景 (Background to the railroad nationalization policy at the end of the Ch'ing), *Nagoya daigaku ronshū*, 17:29–66 (March 1957).

———"The New Armies." In M. C. Wright, *China in Revolution*. Pp. 365–382.

Hedtke, Charles Herman. "Reluctant Revolutionaries: Szechwan and the Ch'ing Collapse, 1898–1911." Ph.D. dissertation. Berkeley: University of California, 1968. University Microfilms 69–3609.

Henry, B. C. *Ling-Nam or Interior Views of Southern China, including Explorations in the Hitherto Untraversed Island of Hainan*. London: S. W. Partridge and Co., 1886.

History of the South China Mission of the American Presbyterian Church, 1845–1920. Shanghai, 1927.

Ho Chen 何振. "Kuang-chou hsin-chün chih tung-t'ai" 广州新军之动态 (Activities of the Canton New Army), *Chung-hua min-kuo k'ai-kuo wu-shih-nien wen-hsien*, 1.14:217–219.

Ho Ke-en. "The Tanka or Boat People of South China." In F. S. Drake, ed., *Symposium on Historical, Archeological and Linguistic Studies on Southern China, South-East Asia and the Hong Kong Region*. Hong Kong: Hong Kong University Press, 1967.

Ho Ping-ti 何炳棣. *Studies on the Population of China, 1368–1953*. Cambridge:

Harvard University Press, 1959.

———— *The Ladder of Success in Imperial China: Aspects of Social Mobility, 1368–1911.* New York: Columbia University Press, 1962.

———— *Chung-kuo hui-kuan shih-lun* 中国会舘史論 (A historical survey of *Landsmannschaften* in China). Taipei: T'ai-wan hsüeh-sheng shu-chü, 1966.

Hong Kong Telegraph, daily (except Sunday) with weekly mail supplement, January 1900–December 1905, October 16, 1907–January 31, 1908, September 1908–December 1911. Seen at the Supreme Court library, Hong Kong, and the Library of Congress, Washington.

Hou, Chi-ming. *Foreign Investment and Economic Development in China, 1840–1937.* Cambridge: Harvard University Press, 1965.

Hsiang-shan hsien-chih hsü-pien 香山県志续編 (Continuation of the Hsiang-shan gazetteer). 1920.

Hsiao I-shan 蕭一山. *Ch'ing-tai t'ung-shih* 清代通史 (A comprehensive history of the Ch'ing period). Taipei: Shang-wu yin-shu kuan, 1962–63. 5 vols.

Hsiao, Kung-chuan. *Rural China: Imperial Control in the Nineteenth Century.* Seattle: University of Washington Press, 1960.

Hsieh, Winston. "The Ideas and Ideals of a Warlord: Ch'en Chiung-ming, 1878–1933," *Papers on China,* 16:198–252 (1962). Harvard University, East Asian Research Center.

———— "Peasant-Bandits in Towns and Cities: The Phenomenon of People's Armies in Kwangtung, 1911–1924." Paper prepared for the conference on Urban Society and Political Development in Modern China, St. Croix, Virgin Islands, Dec. 28, 1968, to Jan. 3, 1969.

———— "Triads, Salt Smugglers and Local Uprisings: Observations on the Social and Economic Background of the Waichow Revolution of 1911." In Jean Chesneaux, ed., *Popular Movements and Secret Societies in China, 1840–1950.* Stanford: Stanford University Press, 1972.

Hsin-hai ko-ming 辛亥革命 (The 1911 Revolution). Ed. Chinese Historical Association. Shanghai: Jen-min ch'u-pan she, 1957. 8 vols.

Hsin-hai ko-ming hui-i lu 辛亥革命回忆錄 (Reminiscences of the 1911 Revolution). Peking: Chung-hua shu-chü, 1961–63. 5 vols.

Hsü Wei-yang 徐維揚. "Keng-hsü Kuang-tung hsin-chün chü-i chi" 庚戌广东新軍举义記 (The 1910 Kwangtung New Army uprising), ed. Teng Mu-han 邓慕韩, *Chung-hua min-kuo k'ai-kuo wu-shih-nien wen-hsien,* 1.13:508–518.

———— "Huang-hua-kang Hua-hsien shih-pa lieh-shih hsün-nan chi" 黄花崗花県十八烈士殉难記 (The martyrdom of the eighteen heros from Hua-hsien at Huang-hua-kang), *Chung-hua min-kuo k'ai-kuo wu-shih-nien wen-hsien,* 1.14:507–511.

Hsü-wen hsien-chih 徐闻県志 (Hsü-wen gazetteer). Lei-chou: Lei-yang yin-shu kuan, 1936.

Hsüan-t'ung Kao-yao hsien-chih 宣統高要県志 (Kao-yao gazetteer for the Hsüan-t'ung period). 1936.

Hsüeh, Chün-tu. *Huang Hsing and the Chinese Revolution*. Stanford: Stanford University Press, 1961.

Hu Han-min 胡汉民. "Tzu-chuan" 自傳 (Autobiography), *Ko-ming wen-hsien*, 3:373–442.

——— "Nan-ching hsüan-pu fan-cheng shih ch'ing-hsing" 南京宣佈反正時情形 (A declaration from Nanking concerning the circumstances of the revolution), *Hsin-hai ko-ming*, 7:247–249.

Hu Kuo-liang 胡国樑. "Hsin-hai Kuang-chou ch'i-i pieh-chi" 辛亥广州起义別記 (A side account of the 1911 Canton revolt), *Hsin-hai ko-ming*, 4:263–274.

Hu Ying-han 胡应汉. *Wu Hsien-tzu hsien-sheng chuan-chi* 吳宪子先生傳記 (Biography of Wu Hsien-tzu). Hong Kong, 1953.

Hua-tzu jih-pao (Wah Tsz Yat Po) 华字日报 (The Chinese Mail). Hong Kong, daily except Sunday, KH 33/10/1–29, HT 1/4/1–8/30, October 1911–May 1913. Its daily supplement: *Ching-hua lu* 精华錄. Seen at the Fung Ping Shan Chinese Library, University of Hong Kong.

Huang Chen-wu 黃珍吾. *Hua-ch'iao yü Chung-kuo ko-ming* 华侨与中国革命 (The overseas Chinese and the Chinese revolution). Taipei: Kuo-fang yen-chiu yüan, 1963.

Huang Fu-luan 黃福鑾. *Hua-ch'iao yü Chung-kuo ko-ming* 华侨与中国革命 (The overseas Chinese and the Chinese revolution). Hong Kong: Ya-chou ch'u-pan she, 1954.

Huang Hsing 黄兴. "Kuang-chou san-yüeh erh-shih-chiu ko-ming chih ch'ien-yin hou-kuo" 广州三月二十九革命之前因後果 (The causes and effects of the April 27th revolution at Canton), *Hsin-hai ko-ming*, 4:167–171. Speech delivered at Nanking, February 1912.

Huang, Philip C. *Liang Ch'i-ch'ao and Modern Chinese Liberalism*. Seattle: University of Washington Press, 1972.

Huang Ta-han 黃大汉, comp. "Hsing-Chung hui ko t'ung-chih ko-ming kung-tso shih-lüeh" 興中会各同志革命工作史略 (The revolutionary activities of the various comrades of the Society to Restore China's Prosperity), *Chung-hua min-kuo k'ai-kuo wu-shih-nien wen-hsien*, 1.9:458–489. Apparently first published in 1929.

Hung-hua-kang ssu lieh-shih chuan 紅花岡四烈士傳 (Biographies of the four martyrs at Hung-hua-kang). Shanghai: Min-chih shu-chü, 1927.

Ichiko Chūzō. "The Railway Protection Movement in Szechwan in 1911," *Memoirs of the Research Department of the Toyo Bunko*, 14:47–69 (1955).

——— "The Role of the Gentry: An Hypothesis." In M. C. Wright, *China in Revolution*. Pp. 297–317.

Iriye Akira 入江昭. "Chūgoku ni okeru Nihon Bukkyō fukyō mondai" 中国に

おける日本佛教布教问题 (Japanese Buddhist missionary activities in China), *Kokusai seiji* 国际政治 (International politics), no. 28, pp. 87–100 (April 1964).

———"Public Opinion and Foreign Policy: The Case of Late Ch'ing China." In Albert Feuerwerker et al., *Approaches to Modern Chinese History*. Berkeley: University of California Press, 1967. Pp. 216–238.

———*Pacific Estrangement: Japanese and American Expansion, 1897–1911.* Cambridge: Harvard University Press, 1972.

Israel, John. *Student Nationalism in China, 1927–1937.* Stanford: Stanford University Press, 1966.

James, D. Clayton. *The Years of MacArthur.* Vol. 1. Boston: Houghton Mifflin Company, 1970.

Jansen, Marius B. *The Japanese and Sun Yat-sen.* Cambridge: Harvard University Press, 1954.

Jen-hua hsien-chih 仁化県志 (Jen-hua gazetteer). 1931.

Jen Yu-wen (Chien Yu-wen). "The Youth of Dr. Sun Yat-sen." In Jen Yu-wen and Lindsay Ride. *Sun Yat-sen: Two Commemorative Essays.* Hong Kong: Centre of Asian Studies, University of Hong Kong, 1970. Pp. 1–22.

Johnson, Chalmers A. *Peasant Nationalism and Communist Power: The Emergence of Revolutionary China, 1937–1945.* Stanford: Stanford University Press, 1962.

———*Revolutionary Change.* Boston: Little, Brown and Company, 1966.

Johnson, William R. "Revolution and Reconstruction in Kweichow." Paper presented at the 1965 Wentworth, New Hampshire, conference on the 1911 Revolution.

———"Revolution and Reconstruction in Yunnan: A Sketch." Paper presented at the 1965 Wentworth, New Hampshire, conference on the 1911 Revolution.

K'ai-p'ing hsien-chih 开平県志 (K'ai-p'ing gazetteer). 1933.

Kan-en hsien-chih 感恩県志 (Kan-en gazetteer). Hoihow: Hai-nan shu-chü, 1931.

Kan Shan-chai 甘善齋. "Tzu-chin kuang-fu ch'ien-hou" 紫金光復前后 (Tzu-chin district before and after the revolution), *Hsin-hai ko-ming hui-i lu*, 2:352–357.

"Keng-hsü Kuang-chou hsin-chün chih i kung-chuang" 庚戌广州新軍之役供狀 (Depositions concerning the 1910 Canton New Army mutiny), *Chung-hua min-kuo k'ai-kuo wu-shih-nien wen-hsien*, 1.13:520–530.

Kent, Percy Horace. *Railway Enterprise in China: An Account of Its Origin and Development.* London: Edward Arnold, 1908.

Kerr, John G. "The Native Benevolent Institutions of Canton," *China Review*, 2.2:88–95 (September–October 1873) and 3.2:108–114 (September–October 1874).

————A Guide to the City and Suburbs of Canton. Hong Kong: Kelly & Walsh, Ltd., 1904.

Kikuchi Takaharu 菊池貴晴. "Daini Tatsu Maru jiken no tai-Nichi boikotto" 第二辰丸事件の対日ボイコット (The *Tatsu Maru II* anti-Japanese boycott), *Rekishigaku kenkyū* 歴史学研究 (Historical research), no. 209, pp. 1–13 (July 1957).

King, Frank H. H. *Money and Monetary Policy in China, 1845–1895*. Cambridge: Harvard University Press, 1965.

————and Prescott Clarke. *A Research Guide to China-Coast Newspapers, 1822–1911*. Cambridge: East Asian Research Center, Harvard University, 1965.

King, Paul. *In the Chinese Customs Service: A Personal Record of Forty-Seven Years*. London: T. Fisher Unwin Ltd., 1924.

Ko Kung-chen 戈公振. *Chung-kuo pao-hsüeh shih* 中国报学史 (A history of Chinese journalism). Peking: San-lien shu-tien, 1955. Originally published in 1927.

Ko-ming hsien-lieh hsien-chin chuan 革命先烈先進傳 (Biographies of revolutionary martyrs and heros). Taipei: Chung-yang wen-wu kung-ying she, 1965.

Ko-ming wen-hsien 革命文献 (Documents on the revolution). Ed. Lo Chia-lun 罗家倫. Taipei: Party History Committee of the Central Committee of the Chinese Nationalist Party. Vols. 1–3. 1958 reprint. Continuous pagination.

"Kuang-chou-shih yen-ko shih-lüeh" 广州市沿革史略 (An outline history of Canton city). Supplement to *Kuang-chou-shih shih-cheng pao-kao hui-k'an* 广州市市政报告彙刊 (A collection of Canton municipal government reports). Canton, 1924.

"Kuang-tung tu-li chi" 广东独立記 (A record of the declaration of independence in Kwangtung). Comp. Ta-Han jih-hsin jen 大汉热心人 (The Great Han Enthusiast), *Chin-tai-shih tzu-liao*, 1961, no. 1, pp. 435–471. A scrapbook of news clippings.

Kuhn, Philip A. *Rebellion and Its Enemies in Late Imperial China: Militarization and Social Structure, 1796–1864*. Cambridge: Harvard University Press, 1970.

Kung Shu-to 龔书鐸 and Ch'en Kuei-ying 陳桂英, "Ts'ung Ch'ing Chün-chi-ch'u tang-an k'an hsin-hai ko-ming ch'ien ch'un-chung ti fan-k'ang tou-cheng" 从清軍机处档案看辛亥革命前群众的反抗斗争 (The resistance struggles of the masses before the 1911 Revolution as seen from the archives of the Ch'ing Grand Council), *Hsin-hai ko-ming wu-shih chou-nien chi-nien lun-wen chi* 辛亥革命五十週年紀念論文集 (Essays in commemoration of the fiftieth anniversary of the 1911 Revolution). Peking: Chung-hua shu-chü, 1962. Pp. 204–228.

Kunckle, J. S. "The Lienchow Riots," *Chinese Recorder*, 42.4:243–245 (April 1911).

Kuo Hsiao-ch'eng 郭孝成. "Kuang-tung kuang-fu chi" 广东光復記 (The revolution in Kwangtung), *Hsin-hai ko-ming*, 7:227–245. A selection from his *Chung-kuo ko-ming chi-shih pen-mo* 中国革命紀事本末 (A complete account of the Chinese revolution). Originally published in 1912.

Kupper, Samuel Yale. "Revolution in China: Kiangsi Province, 1905–1913." Ph.D. dissertation. Ann Arbor: University of Michigan, 1973. University Microfilms 73–24, 611.

LaFargue, Thomas E. *China's First Hundred*. Pullman: State College of Washington, 1942.

Lamley, Harry J. "The 1895 Taiwan Republic: A Significant Episode in Modern Chinese History," *Journal of Asian Studies*, 27.4:739–762 (August 1968).

Latourette, Kenneth Scott. *A History of Christian Missions in China*. New York: The MacMillan Company, 1932.

Launay, Adrien. *Histoire des missions de Chine: Mission du Kouang-tong, monographies des districts par les missionnaires*. Paris: P. Tequi, 1917.

Le-ch'ang hsien-chih 乐昌県志 (Le-ch'ang gazetteer). 1931.

Lee, Ta-ling. *Foundations of the Chinese Revolution, 1905–1912 (An Historical Record of the T'ung-meng Hui)*. New York: St. John's University Press, 1970.

Lethbridge, Henry James. "The Evolution of a Chinese Voluntary Association in Hong Kong: The Po Leung Kuk," *Journal of Oriental Studies*, 10.1:33–50 (January 1972).

Levenson, Joseph R. *Liang Ch'i-ch'ao and the Mind of Modern China*. Cambridge: Harvard University Press, 1959.

Levi, Werner. *Modern China's Foreign Policy*. Minneapolis: University of Minnesota Press, 1953.

Levy, Howard S. *Chinese Footbinding: The History of a Curious Erotic Custom*. New York: Walton Rawls, 1966.

Lewis, Charlton M. "Foreign Encroachment, Reform and Revolution, 1900–1907: The Response of the Hunan Gentry." Paper presented at the 1965 Wentworth, New Hampshire, conference on the 1911 Revolution.

———— "The Hunanese Elite and the Reform Movement, 1895–1898," *Journal of Asian Studies*, 29.1:35–42 (November 1969).

Li Chien-nung 李劍农. *Chung-kuo chin pai-nien cheng-chih shih* 中国近百年政治史 (A political history of China during the last century). Taipei: Shang-wu yin-shu kuan, 1962. 2 vols.

Li Chun 李準. "Kuang-fu Kuang-tung shih-mo chi" 光復广东始末記 (A complete account of the revolution in Kwangtung), *Hsin-hai ko-ming*, 7:245–246. Dated January 11, 1912.

Li En-han 李恩涵. *Wan-Ch'ing ti shou-hui k'uang-ch'üan yün-tung* 晚清的收回矿权运动 (The movement to recover mining rights in the late Ch'ing). Taipei:

Institute of Modern History, Academia Sinica, 1963.

——— "China's Response to Foreign Investment in her Mining Industry (1902–1911)," *Journal of Asian Studies*, 28.1:55–76 (November 1968).

Li Hsi-wu 李熙武. "Ch'ing-mo Chih-na an-sha-t'uan chi-shih" 清末支那暗殺團紀实 (The Chinese Assassination Corps at the end of the Ch'ing), *Kuang-tung wen-wu t'e-chi* 广东文物特輯 (A special edition of *Kuang-tung wen-wu*). Canton, n.d. Pp. 17–23.

Li Lang-ju 李朗如 and Lu Man 陆满. "Hsin-hai ko-ming shih-ch'i Kuang-tung min-chün kai-k'uang" 辛亥革命時期广东民軍概況 (The people's armies in Kwangtung at the time of the 1911 Revolution), *Hsin-hai ko-ming hui-i lu*, 2:410–416.

Li Po-ts'un 李柏存. "Yüeh-yüan kuang-fu chi-shih" 粤垣光復紀实 (A true account of the revolution in Canton), *Chung-hua min-kuo k'ai-kuo wu-shih-nien wen-hsien*, 2.4:440–441. Dated June 1937.

Li Shao-ling 李少陵. *Ou Chü-chia hsien-sheng chuan* 歐榘甲先生傳 (A biography of Ou Chü-chia). Taipei, 1960.

Li Shou-k'ung 李守孔. "Ko-sheng tzu-i chü lien-ho hui yü hsin-hai ko-ming" 各省諮议局联合会与辛亥革命 (The federation of provincial assemblies and the 1911 Revolution), *Chung-kuo hsien-tai-shih ts'ung-k'an*, 3:321–373 (1961).

Li Shu-fan (Li Shu-fen). *Hong Kong Surgeon*. London: Victor Gollancz Ltd., 1964.

Li Shui-hsien 李睡仙. "Ch'en Chiung-ming p'an-kuo shih" 陈烔明叛国史 (A history of Ch'en Chiung-ming's rebellion against the nation), *Chung-kuo hsien-tai-shih ts'ung-k'an*, 2:423–496 (1960) and 3:403–438 (1961). Originally published in 1922.

Liang Chia-pin 梁嘉彬. *Kuang-tung shih-san hang* 广东十三行 (The thirteen guilds at Canton). Shanghai: Shang-wu yin-shu kuan, 1937.

Liang Ching-ch'iu 梁鏡球. "Kuang-chou san-yüeh erh-shih-chiu ko-ming chih ching-kuo" 广州三月二十九革命之経过 (Experiences of the April 27 revolt in Canton), *Chung-hua min-kuo k'ai-kuo wu-shih-nien wen-hsien*, 1.14:157–166.

Liang Jen-ts'ai. *Economic Geography of Kwangtung*, JPRS/DC-389 (1958). A translation of *Kuang-tung ching-chi ti-li*. Peking, 1956.

Liao P'ing-tzu 廖平子. "Shih Chien-ju an shih-i" 史堅如案拾遺 (Notes on the Shih Chien-ju case), *Hsin-hai ko-ming*, 1:249–250.

——— "Hung Ch'üan-fu ch'i-i shih-mo" 洪全福起义始末 (A complete account of the Hung Ch'üan-fu uprising), *Chung-hua min-kuo k'ai-kuo wu-shih-nien wen-hsien*, 1.9:667–670.

Liew, K. S. *Struggle for Democracy: Sung Chiao-jen and the 1911 Chinese Revolution*. Berkeley: University of California Press, 1971.

Lin Hsi-heng 林希衡. "Hsin-hai chiu-yüeh Hui-chou shou-i shih-lüeh" 辛亥九

月惠州首义事略 (The November 1911 initial uprising at Hui-chou), *Chung-hua min-kuo k'ai-kuo wu-shih-nien wen-hsien*, 2.4:473–475.

Lin I-han 林一厂. "'Hsin-hai Ch'ao-chou ko-ming chi-lüeh' ting-cheng shu" 「辛亥潮州革命紀略」訂正书 (Correction of Sun Tan-yai's "Record of the 1911 Revolution in Ch'ao-chou"), *Chung-hua min-kuo k'ai-kuo wu-shih-nien wen-hsien*, 2.4:480–490.

Lin Tien-huang 林典煌. "Ko-ming-tang-jen tsai Hui-chou" 革命党人在惠州 (The revolutionaries at Hui-chou), *Chung-hua min-kuo k'ai-kuo wu-shih-nien wen-hsien*, 1.14:223–242.

Lin Yu-tang. *A History of the Press and Public Opinion in China*. 1936; New York reprint: Greenwood Press, 1968.

Ling Hung-hsün 淩鴻勛. *Chung-kuo t'ieh-lu chih* 中国鉄路志 (Railroads in China). Taipei: Ch'ang-liu pan-yüeh-k'an she, 1954.

Lingnan University archives. On deposit at the Chinese-Japanese Library of the Harvard-Yenching Institute, Harvard University.

Ling-shan hsien-chih 灵山县志 (Ling-shan gazetteer). Canton: Hsin Chung-hua yin-wu chü, 1914.

Liu Kuei-wu 刘桂五. "Hsin-hai ko-ming ch'ien-hou ti li-hsien-p'ai yü li-hsien yün-tung" 辛亥革命前后的立宪派与立宪运动 (The constitutionalist party and the constitutionalist movement before and after the 1911 Revolution), *Li-shih chiao-hsüeh* 历史教学 (History education), 1962, no. 8, pp. 19–28 (August 1962).

Liu K'uei-i 刘揆一. *Huang Hsing chuan-chi* 黃兴傳記 (Biography of Huang Hsing). Taipei: Pa-mi-erh shu-tien, 1953. Originally published in 1929.

Liu, Kwang-Ching. "Nineteenth-Century China: The Disintegration of the Old Order and the Impact of the West." In Ping-ti Ho and Tang Tsou, eds., *China in Crisis*. Chicago: University of Chicago Press, 1968. Vol. 1, bk. 1, pp. 93–178.

Liu Po-chi 刘伯驥. *Kuang-tung shu-yüan chih-tu* 广东書院制度 (The organization of academies in Kwangtung). Taipei: Chung-hua ts'ung-shu wei-yüan hui, 1958. Original edition dated 1938.

Lo Hsiang-lin 罗香林. *K'o-chia yen-chiu tao-lun* 客家研究導論 (An introduction to the study of the Hakkas). Hsin-ning, 1933.

———*Hong Kong and Western Cultures*. Tokyo: The Centre for East Asian Cultural Studies and Honolulu: East-West Center Press, 1963.

Lo, Jung-pang, ed. and trans. *K'ang Yu-wei: A Biography and a Symposium*. Tucson: The University of Arizona Press, 1967.

Lo Shou-chang 罗綬章. "Ch'in-hsien San-na fan-k'ang t'ang-chüan tou-cheng yü Ch'in Fang chih i" 欽県三那反抗糖損斗爭与欽防之役 (The resistance to the sugar tax in the San-na villages, Ch'in-hsien, and the Ch'in-chou and Fang-ch'eng uprisings), *Hsin-hai ko-ming hui-i lu*, 2:392–395.

Lo-ting chih 罗定志 (Lo-ting gazetteer). Canton: Ta-Chung kung-yeh she, 1935.

Lo, Wan. "Communal Strife in Mid-Nineteenth-Century Kwangtung: The Establishment of Ch'ih-ch'i," *Papers on China*, 19:85–119 (1965). Harvard University, East Asian Research Center.

Lu Tan-lin 陆丹林. *Ko-ming shih-t'an* 革命史譚 (Talks on the history of the revolution). Chungking: Tu-li ch'u-pan she, 1945.

Lung-men hsien-chih 龙门県志 (Lung-men gazetteer). Taipei reprint: Ch'eng-wen ch'u-pan she, 1967. Originally published in 1936.

Lü Shih-ch'iang 吕实强. *Chung-kuo kuan-shen fan-chiao ti yüan-yin (1860–1874)* 中国官紳反教的原因 (1860–1874). (The origins of the opposition to Christianity among the Chinese officials and gentry, 1860–1874). Taipei: Institute of Modern History, Academia Sinica, 1966.

Ma Chin-ch'un 馬錦春. "San-yüeh erh-shih-chiu-jih chih i yü Kuang-chou hsin-chün" 三月二十九日之役与广州新军 (The April 27th uprising and the Canton New Army), *Chung-hua min-kuo k'ai-kuo wu-shih-nien wen-hsien*, 1.14:204–217.

Ma Hsiao-chin 馬小进. "Kuang-chou kuang-fu yü Chou Chien-kung 广州光復与周劍公 (Chou Chien-kung and the revolution in Canton), *Hsin-hai ko-ming*, 7:250–255. Originally published in 1936.

McAleavy, Henry. *Su Man-shu (1884–1918): A Sino-Japanese Genius*. London: The China Society, 1960.

MacGillivray, D., ed. *A Century of Protestant Missions in China (1807–1907)*. Shanghai, 1907.

MacKinnon, Stephen R. "The Peiyang Army, Yüan Shih-k'ai, and the Origins of Modern Chinese Warlordism," *Journal of Asian Studies*, 32.3:405–423 (May 1973).

Marr, David G. *Vietnamese Anticolonialism, 1885–1925*. Berkeley: University of California Press, 1971.

Meisner, Maurice. *Li Ta-chao and the Origins of Chinese Marxism*. Cambridge: Harvard University Press, 1967.

Miao Chih-hsin 苗致信. "Hui-chou kuang-fu chien-wen" 惠州光復見闻 (Experiences of the revolution in Hui-chou), *Hsin-hai ko-ming hui-i lu*, 2:343–347.

Michael, Franz. "Regionalism in Nineteenth-Century China." Introduction to Stanley Spector, *Li Hung-chang and the Huai Army: A Study in Nineteenth-Century Regionalism*. Seattle: University of Washington Press, 1964. Pp. xxi-xliii.

Miyazaki Torazō 宮崎寅藏. "Hui-chou chih ko-ming" 惠州之革命 (The Hui-chou revolution), *Chung-hua min-kuo k'ai-kuo wu-shih-nien wen-hsien*, 1.9:564–568. A Chinese translation of a portion of his *Sanjūsannen no yume* 三十三年の夢 (Thirty-three years' dream).

Mo Ch'ang-fan 莫昌藩, Chung Te-i 钟德貽, and Lo Tsung-t'ang 罗宗堂. "I-chiu-i-ling-nien Kuang-tung hsin-chün ko-ming chi-shih" 一九一〇年

广东新軍革命紀实 (The 1910 Kwangtung New Army revolt), *Chin-tai-shih tzu-liao*, 1955, no. 4, pp. 85–93.

"Mo Chi-p'eng hsien-sheng shih-lüeh" 莫紀彭先生事略 (Biography of Mo Chi-p'eng), *Chung-hua min-kuo k'ai-kuo wu-shih-nien wen-hsien*, 1.14:536–538.

Morgan, W. P. *Triad Societies in Hong Kong*. Hong Kong: Government Press, 1960.

Morse, Hosea Ballou. *The Gilds of China, with an Account of the Gild Merchant or Co-hong of Canton*. 1909; Taipei reprint: Ch'eng-wen Publishing Company, 1960.

——— *The International Relations of the Chinese Empire*. 1910–18; Taipei reprint: Book World Co., n.d. 3 vols.

Munholland, J. Kim. "The French Connection That Failed: France and Sun Yat-sen, 1900–1908," *Journal of Asian Studies*, 32.1:77–95 (November 1972).

Nan-hai hsien-chih 南海県志 (Nan-hai gazetteer). 1910.

Nan Shina sōran 南支那綜覽 (A comprehensive view of South China). Compiled by the Foreign Affairs Bureau of the Office of the Taiwan Governor-General. Taihoku: Nampō shiryōkan, 1943.

Nan-yang hsiung-ti yen-ts'ao kung-ssu shih-liao 南洋兄弟烟草公司史料 (Materials on the history of the Nanyang Brothers' Tobacco Company). Shanghai: Jen-min ch'u-pan she, 1958.

Nathan, Andrew J. "Imperialism's Effects on China," *Bulletin of Concerned Asian Scholars*, 4.4:3–8 (December 1972).

The National Sun Yat-sen University: A Short History. 2nd English ed. J. D. Bush. Canton, 1937.

North China Herald (Shanghai), weekly, 1895–1899, July 1904–March 1912.

Novikov, Boris. "The Anti-Manchu Propaganda of the Triads, ca. 1800–1860." In Jean Chesneaux, ed., *Popular Movements and Secret Societies in China, 1840–1950*. Stanford: Stanford University Press, 1972. Pp. 49–63.

Nozawa Yutaka 野澤豊. "Shingai kakumei no kaikyū kōsei: Shisen bōdō to shōshin kaikyū" 辛亥革命の階級構成：四川暴动の商紳階級 (The class structure of the 1911 Revolution: The merchant-gentry class in the Szechwan rebellion), *Rekishigaku kenkyū*, no. 150, pp. 84–91 (March 1951).

Nung-kung-shang-pu t'ung-chi piao 农工商部統計表 (Statistical tables of the Ministry of Agriculture, Industry and Commerce). Peking, 1908–09. 2 series.

Ou Chü-chia 歐榘甲. "Hsin Kuang-tung" 新广东 (New Kwangtung). In Chang Nan 張枬 and Wang Jen-chih 王忍之, eds., *Hsin-hai ko-ming ch'ien shih-nien chien shih-lun hsüan-chi* 辛亥革命前十年間時論选集 (Selected articles on current affairs written during the ten years preceding the 1911 Revolution). Hong Kong: San-lien shu-tien, 1962. Vol. 1, bk. 1, pp. 269–311.

P'an-yü hsien hsü-chih 番禺県续志 (Continuation of the P'an-yü gazetteer). 1931.

P'eng Chung-ying 彭中英. "Hua-chou kuang-fu ch'ien-hou shih-nien chien-wen lu" 化州光復前后十年見聞錄 (Experiences of the ten years surrounding the revolution in Hua-chou), *Hsin-hai ko-ming hui-i lu*, 2:396–404.

Playfair, G. M. H., *The Cities and Towns of China: A Geographical Dictionary*. 2nd ed. 1910; Taipei reprint: Ch'eng-wen Publishing Company, 1967.

Polevoy, S. A. *Periodicheskaya Pechat v Kitae*. Vladivostok, 1913.

Powell, Ralph L. *The Rise of Chinese Military Power, 1895–1912*. Princeton: Princeton University Press, 1955.

Presbyterian Board of Foreign Missions Papers, for the China field. Microfilm copy on deposit at the United Presbyterian Mission Library, 475 Riverside Drive, New York.

Rankin, Mary Backus. "The Manchurian Crisis and Radical Student Nationalism, 1903," *Ch'ing-shih wen-t'i*, 2.1:87–106 (October 1969).

——— *Early Chinese Revolutionaries: Radical Intellectuals in Shanghai and Chekiang, 1902–1911*. Cambridge: Harvard University Press, 1971.

Rawlinson, John L. *China's Struggle for Naval Development, 1839–1895*. Cambridge: Harvard University Press, 1967.

"Revolutionary Propagation in Missionary Guise," *Chinese Recorder*, 42:549–550 (September 1911).

Rhoads, Edward J. M. "Nationalism and Xenophobia in Kwangtung (1905–1906): The Canton Anti-American Boycott and the Lienchow Anti-Missionary Uprising," *Papers on China*, 16:154–197 (1962). Harvard University, East Asian Research Center.

Ride, Lindsay. "The Early Medical Education of Sun Yat-sen." In Jen Yu-wen and Lindsay Ride. *Sun Yat-sen: Two Commemorative Essays*. Hong Kong: Centre of Asian Studies, University of Hong Kong, 1970. Pp. 23–31.

W. W. Rockhill papers. On deposit at the Houghton Library, Harvard University.

Rodes, Jean. *Le Céleste empire avant la révolution*. Paris: Librairie Félix Alcan, 1914.

——— *Scènes de la vie révolutionnaire en Chine (1911–1914)*. Paris: Plon-Nourrit et Cie, 1917.

Saishin Shina kanshin roku 最新支那官紳錄 (The latest directory of Chinese officials and gentry). Comp. Peking Shina Kenkyū-kai. Tokyo, 1918.

Scalapino, Robert A. "Prelude to Marxism: The Chinese Student Movement in Japan, 1900–1910." In Albert Feuerwerker et al., *Approaches to Modern Chinese History*. Berkeley: University of California Press, 1967. Pp. 190–215.

——— and Harold Schiffrin "Early Socialist Currents in the Chinese Revolutionary Movement: Sun Yat-sen versus Liang Ch'i-ch'ao," *Journal of Asian Studies*, 18.3:321–342 (May 1959).

————and George T. Yu. *The Chinese Anarchist Movement*. Berkeley: Center for Chinese Studies, Institute of International Studies, University of California, 1961.

Schiffrin, Harold Z. "Sun Yat-sen's Early Land Policy: The Origin and Meaning of 'Equalization of Land Rights,'" *Journal of Asian Studies*, 16.4: 549–564 (August 1957).

————*Sun Yat-sen and the Origins of the Chinese Revolution*. Berkeley: University of California Press, 1968.

Schrecker, John E. "The Pao-kuo Hui: A Reform Society of 1898," *Papers on China*, 14:50–69 (1960). Harvard University, East Asian Research Center.

————*Imperialism and Chinese Nationalism: Germany in Shantung*. Cambridge: Harvard University Press, 1971.

Schwartz, Benjamin. *In Search of Wealth and Power: Yen Fu and the West*. Cambridge: Harvard University Press, 1964.

Shabad, Theodore. *China's Changing Map: National and Regional Development, 1949–71*. New York and Washington: Praeger Publishers, 1972. Revised edition of a work first published in 1956.

Sheng Hsüan-huai 盛宣怀. *Yü-chai ts'un-k'ao* 愚齋存稿 (Collected papers of Sheng Hsüan-huai). Taipei reprint: Wen-hai ch'u-pan she, 1963. Originally published about 1930.

Shih-ch'eng hsien-chih 石城県志 (Shih-ch'eng gazetteer). An-p'u: Hua-an yin-wu shu-chü, 1931.

Shin-matsu Minsho Chūgoku kanshin jimmeiroku 清末民初中国官紳人名錄 (A directory of Chinese officials and gentry at the end of the Ch'ing and the beginning of the Republic). Peking: Chūgoku kenkyūkai, 1918.

Shina shobetsu zenshi 支那省別全誌 (A complete gazetteer of China's provinces). Comp. Tōa Dōbun-kai. Tokyo, 1917. Vol. 1, for Kwangtung.

Shun-te hsien hsü-chih 順德県续志 (Continuation of the Shun-te gazetteer). 1929.

Silvestre, J. "La France à Kouang-Tchéou-Ouen," *Annales des Sciences Politiques*, 17.4:473–493 (Paris, July 15, 1902).

Skinner, G. William. *Chinese Society in Thailand: An Analytical History*. Ithaca: Cornell University Press, 1957.

————"Marketing and Social Structure in Rural China, Part II," *Journal of Asian Studies*, 24.2:195–228 (February 1965).

Smythe, E. Joan. "The Tzu-li Hui: Some Chinese and Their Rebellion," *Papers on China*, 12:51–68 (1958). Harvard University, East Asian Research Center.

South China Morning Post (Hong Kong), daily except Sunday, January 1906– August 1913. Seen at the Supreme Court library, Hong Kong, and the Library of Congress, Washington.

Van der Sprenkel, Sybille. *Legal Institutions in Manchu China: A Sociological Analysis*. London: The Athlone Press, University of London, 1962.

Stone, Lawrence. "Theories of Revolution," *World Politics*, 18.2:159–176 (January 1966).

Sun, E-tu Zen. "The Chinese Constitutional Missions of 1905–1906," *Journal of Modern History*, 24.3:251–268 (September 1952).

——*Chinese Railways and British Interests, 1898–1911*. New York: King's Crown Press, 1954.

Sun Tan-yai 孙丹崖. "Hsin-hai Ch'ao-chou ko-ming chi-lüeh" 辛亥潮州革命紀略 (Record of the 1911 Revolution in Ch'ao-chou), *Chung-hua min-kuo k'ai-kuo wu-shih-nien wen-hsien*, 2.4:477–480.

Ta-Ch'ing li-ch'ao shih-lu 大清历朝实錄 (Veritable record of the successive reigns of the Ch'ing dynasty). Taipei reprint: Hua-wen shu-chü, 1964. For the Hsüan-t'ung reign.

Tamada, Noriko. "Sung Chiao-jen and the 1911 Revolution," *Papers on China*, 21:184–229 (1968). Harvard University, East Asian Research Center.

T'an Cho-yüan 譚卓垣. "Kuang-chou ting-ch'i k'an-wu ti tiao-ch'a" 广州定期刊物的調查 (Periodicals published in Canton, 1827–1934), *Ling-nan hsüeh-pao* 岭南学报 (Lingnan University journal), 4.3:1–92 (August 1935).

T'an Jen-feng 譚人鳳. "Shih-sou p'ai-tz'u hsü-lu" 石叟牌詞叙錄 (Reminiscences), *Chin-tai-shih tzu-liao*, 1956, no. 3, pp. 26–76.

T'an Li-yüan 譚荔垣. "Ssu-shih-ch'i-nien lai pao-yeh shih kai-lüeh" 四十七年來报业史概略 (A sketch history of the press in the last forty-seven years). In *Hua-tzu jih-pao ch'i-shih-i chou-nien chi-nien k'an* 华字日报七十一週年紀念刊 (A commemorative volume on the 71st anniversary of the *Hua-tzu jih-pao*). Hong Kong, 1934.

Teng Ching-ya 邓警亞. "Hsin-hai Kuang-tung tu-li ch'uan-hsin lu" 辛亥广东獨立傳信錄 (An account of the Kwangtung independence in 1911), *Hsin-hai ko-ming hui-i lu*, 2:334–337.

Teng Mu-han 邓慕韓. "Kuo-fu i-wei Kuang-chou chü-i shih-mo chi" 国父乙未广州拳义始末記 (An account of Sun Yat-sen's 1895 uprising in Canton), *Kuang-tung wen-wu* 广东文物 (Kwangtung arts), pp. 1–5.

——"Shu ting-wei Fang-ch'eng ko-ming chün-shih" 书丁未防城革命军事 (On the military operations of the 1907 revolt at Fang-ch'eng), *Hsin-hai ko-ming*, 2:546–549.

——"Ting-wei Shan-wei chü-i shih-mo chi" 丁未汕尾拳义始末記 (The 1907 Shan-wei uprising), *Chung-hua min-kuo k'ai-kuo wu-shih-nien wen-hsien*, 1.13:349–352.

——"Hsin-hai san-yüeh erh-shih-chiu chih i Nan-Shun chan-chi" 辛亥三月二十九之役南順戰記 (The fighting in Nan-hai and Shun-te during the April 27 revolt), *Chung-hua min-kuo k'ai-kuo wu-shih-nien wen-hsien*, 1.14:242–245.

——"Hsin-hai Kuang-chou kuang-fu chi" 辛亥广州光復記 (The 1911 Revolution in Canton), *Chung-hua min-kuo k'ai-kuo wu-shih-nien wen-hsien*, 2.4:428–430.

Teng, Ssu-yü. *The Taiping Rebellion and the Western Powers: A Comprehensive Survey*. Oxford: The Clarendon Press, 1971.

Teraki Tokuko 寺木德子. "Shin-matsu Minkoku shonen no chihō jichi" 清末民国初年の地方自治 (Local self-government at the end of the Ch'ing and in the first years of the Republic), *Ochanomizu shigaku* お茶の水史学 (Ochanomizu studies in history), 5:14–30 (1962).

Thomson, J. *The Straits of Malacca, Indo-China and China: Ten Years' Travels, Adventures and Residence Abroad*. London: Sampson Low, Marston, Low, & Searle, 1875.

T'ien T'ung 田桐. "T'ung-meng hui ch'eng-li chi" 同盟会成立記 (The formation of the Revolutionary Alliance), *Ko-ming wen-hsien*, 2:142–144.

Tilly, Charles. "The Analysis of a Counter-Revolution," *History and Theory*, 3.1:30–58 (1963).

"Ting-wei Ch'ao-chou Huang-kang erh i pieh-chi" 丁未潮州黄岡二役別記(An informal account of the two uprisings at Ch'ao-chou and Huang-kang in 1907), *Chung-hua min-kuo k'ai-kuo wu-shih-nien wen-hsien*, 1.13:72–80.

Ting Wen-chiang 丁文江, comp. *Liang Jen-kung hsien-sheng nien-p'u ch'ang-pien ch'u-kao* 梁任公先生年譜長編初稿 (First draft of a chronological biography of Liang Ch'i-ch'ao). Taipei: Shih-chieh shu-chü, 1962. 2 vols.

Ting Yu 丁又. "1905-nien Kuang-tung fan-Mei yün-tung" 1905年广东反美运动 (The 1905 anti-American movement in Kwangtung), *Chin-tai-shih tzu-liao*, 1958, no. 5, pp. 8–52.

Townsend, James R. *Political Participation in Communist China*. Berkeley: University of California Press, 1969.

"Ts'ang-hai hsien-sheng Ch'iu kung Feng-chia nien-p'u" 倉海先生丘公逢甲年譜 (Chronological biography of Ch'iu Feng-chia), *Ling-yün-hai jih-lou shih-ch'ao* 岭云海日樓詩鈔 (The poems of Ch'iu Feng-chia), 3 vols. Taipei: Bank of Taiwan, 1960. Pp. 387–410. Compiled in 1934.

Tse Tsan Tai (Hsieh Tsan-t'ai). *The Chinese Republic: Secret History of the Revolution*. Hong Kong: South China Morning Post, Limited, 1924.

Ts'en Ch'un-hsüan 岑春煊. *Lo-chai man-pi* 乐斋漫笔 (Rambling notes from the Lo Studio). Taipei: Wen-hsing shu-tien, 1962. Originally published in 1943. This edition also includes a biography of Ts'en by Wu Hsiang-hsiang 吳相湘.

Tseng-ch'eng hsien-chih 增城県志 (Tseng-ch'eng gazetteer). 1921.

Tso Shao-tso 左紹佐, "Lien-chou shih-chien jih-chi chai-lu" 連州事件日記摘錄 (Extracts from his diary about the Lien-chou incident), *Chin-tai-shih tzu-liao*, 1955, no. 4, pp. 70–84.

Tsou Lu 鄒魯. *Kuang-chou san-yüeh erh-shih-chiu ko-ming shih* 广州三月二十九革命史 (A history of the April 27th Canton revolt). Taipei: Pa-mi-erh

shu-tien, 1953. Revised and enlarged edition of a work published originally in 1926.

———*Chung-kuo Kuo-min tang shih-kao* 中国国民党史稿 (A draft history of the
Chinese Nationalist Party). Taipei: Shang-wu yin-shu kuan, 1965. Originally published in 1929.

———*Hui-ku lu* 回顧錄 (Memoirs). Nanking and Taipei: Tu-li ch'u-pan she,
1947 and 1951. 2 vols.

Ts'ui T'ung-yüeh 崔通約, "Wo chih ko-ming ching-kuo" 我之革命経过 (My
revolutionary experiences), *Chung-hua min-kuo k'ai-kuo wu-shih-nien wen-
hsien*, 1.9:629–638. First published in 1935.

Tung-fang tsa-chih 東方杂誌 (Eastern miscellany). Shanghai. Monthly, 1904–
1912.

Tung-hua lu 东华錄 (Tung-hua records). Taipei reprint: Ta-tung shu-chü, 1968.
For the Kuang-hsü reign, 10 vols.

Tung-kuan hsien-chih 东莞県志 (Tung-kuan gazetteer). 1921.

United States, General Records of the Department of State, Record Group 59.
Washington: National Archives. Three sets of material were consulted:
(1) Dispatches from U.S. Consuls from Canton, 1901–06. Microcopy
no. 101; (2) The Numerical File of the Department of State, 1906–10 (not
microfilmed); and (3) Records of the Department of State relating to
Internal Affairs of China, 1910–29, file no. 893. Microcopy no. 329.

Varg, Paul A. *Open Door Diplomat: The Life of W. W. Rockhill*. Urbana:
University of Illinois Press, 1952.

———*Missionaries, Chinese, and Diplomats: The American Protestant Missionary
Movement in China, 1890–1952*. Princeton: Princeton University Press,
1958.

Vogel, Ezra F. *Canton under Communism: Programs and Politics in a Provincial
Capital, 1949–1968*. Cambridge: Harvard University Press, 1969.

Wakeman, Frederic, Jr. *Strangers at the Gate: Social Disorder in South China,
1839–1861*. Berkeley: University of California Press, 1966.

———"The Secret Societies of Kwangtung, 1800–1856." In Jean Chesneaux,
ed., *Popular Movements and Secret Societies in China, 1840–1950*. Stanford:
Stanford University Press, 1972. Pp. 29–47.

Wang Erh-min 王爾敏. *Ch'ing-chi ping-kung-yeh ti hsing-ch'i* 清季兵工业的兴起
(The beginnings of military industry in the Ch'ing period). Taipei:
Institute of Modern History, Academia Sinica, 1963.

Wang Hsing-chung 王兴中. "Hsin-hai san-yüeh nien-chiu Kuang-chou ko-
ming chih ching-kuo" 辛亥三月廿九广州革命之経过 (Experiences of the
April 27th, 1911, Canton revolt), *Chung-hua min-kuo k'ai-kuo wu-shih-nien
wen-hsien*, 1.14:166–168.

———"Yüeh-sheng ti-ssu-chün ko-ming jih-chi" 粤省第四军革命日記 (The
revolutionary diary of the Kwangtung Fourth Army), with notes by

Chou Hui-chün 周惠均, *Chung-hua min-kuo k'ai-kuo wu-shih-nien wen-hsien*, 2.4:433–440.

Wang Hsing-jui 王兴瑞. "Ch'ing-chi Fu-jen wen-she yü ko-ming yün-tung ti kuan-hsi" 清季辅仁文社与革命运动的关系 (The relationship between the Fu-jen Literary Society and the revolutionary movement), *Shih-hsüeh tsa-chih* 史学杂誌 (History magazine), 1.1:35–45 (Chungking, December 1945).

Wang, Y. C. "Free Enterprise in China: The Case of a Cigarette Concern, 1905–1953," *Pacific Historical Review*, 29.4:395–414 (November 1960).

———*Chinese Intellectuals and the West, 1872–1949*. Chapel Hill: University of North Carolina Press, 1966.

Wang Ying-lou 王映樓. "Hui-chou-fu chung-hsüeh-sheng tsai hsin-hai ko-ming shih-ch'i ti huo-tung" 惠州府中学生在辛亥革命時期的活动 (Activities of the Hui-chou prefectural middle school students at the time of the 1911 Revolution), *Hsin-hai ko-ming hui-i lu*, 2:348–351.

Wang Yün-sheng 王芸生. *Liu-shih-nien lai Chung-kuo yü Jih-pen* 六十年來中国与日本 (China and Japan during the last sixty years). Tientsin: Ta-kung pao she, 1932–33. 6 vols.

Watt, John. "Leadership Criteria in Late Imperial China," *Ch'ing-shih wen-t'i*, 2.3:17–39 (July 1970).

Welch, Holmes. *The Buddhist Revival in China*. Cambridge: Harvard University Press, 1968.

Wen Kung-chih 文公直, "Hsin-hai ko-ming yün-tung-chung chih hsin-chün" 辛亥革命运动中之新军 (The new armies in the 1911 revolutionary movement), *Hsin-hai ko-ming*, 3:323–346.

Wiens, Herold J. *China's March to the Tropics*. Hamden, Conn.: The Shoe String Press, 1954.

Willoughby, Westel W. *Foreign Rights and Interests in China*. Baltimore: The Johns Hopkins Press, 1920.

Witke, Roxane Heater. "Transformation of Attitudes towards Women during the May Fourth Period of Modern China." Ph.D. dissertation. Berkeley: University of California, 1970. University Microfilms 71–868.

Woo Sing Lim (Wu Hsing-lien 吴醒濂). *The Prominent Chinese in Hong Kong*. Hong Kong: The Five Continents Book Co., 1937. Title in Chinese: *Hsiang-kang hua-jen ming-jen shih-lüeh* 香港华人名人史略.

Wright, Arnold, and H.A. Cartwright, eds. *Twentieth Century Impressions of Hong Kong, Shanghai, and other Treaty Ports of China: Their History, Commerce, Industries, and Resources*. London: Lloyd's Greater Britain Publishing Company, Ltd., 1908.

Wright, Mary Clabaugh, ed. *China in Revolution: The First Phase, 1900–1913*. New Haven: Yale University Press, 1968.

———"Introduction: The Rising Tide of Change." In *China in Revolution*, pp. 1–63.

Wu Hsiang-hsiang 呉相湘, "Chu Chih-hsin chih hsing ho-i" 朱執信知行合一 (Chu Chih-hsin's unity of knowledge and action), *Chuan-chi wen-hsüeh* 傳記 文学 (Biographical literature), 6.6:30–33 (June 1965).

——— "Ku Ying-fen ch'i-jen ch'i-shih" 古应芬其人其事 (The life and works of Ku Ying-fen), *Chuan-chi wen-hsüeh*, 9.2:29–30 (August 1966).

Wu-hsü pien-fa 戊戌变法 (The reform movement of 1898). Ed. Chinese Historical Association. Shanghai: Jen-min ch'u-pan she, 1957. 4 vols.

Wu Jui 呉甦. "Ta-Ming shun-t'ien kuo: Hsing-Chung hui ti wai-i chang" 大明順天国：兴中会的外一章 (The Great Ming Heavenly Kingdom: A side-light on the Society to Restore China's Prosperity), *Ch'ang-liu* 暢流 (Smooth current), 32.4:11–13 (Taipei, October 1, 1965).

Yang, C. K. *A Chinese Village in Early Communist Transition*. Cambridge: The M.I.T. Press, 1959.

Yang-chiang chih 陽江志 (Yang-chiang gazetteer). 1925.

Yang Hua-jih 楊华日. *Chung Jung-kuang hsien-sheng chuan* 钟荣光先生傳 (A biography of Chung Jung-kuang). Hong Kong: Ling-nan ta-hsüeh t'ung-hsüeh hui, 1967.

Yang, Lien-sheng. "Schedules of Work and Rest in Imperial China." In his *Studies in Chinese Institutional History*. Cambridge: Harvard University Press, 1961. Pp. 18–42.

Yang-shan hsien-chih 陽山県志 (Yang-shan gazetteer). 1939.

Yao Yü-p'ing 姚雨平. "Chui-i keng-hsü hsin-chün ch'i-i ho hsin-hai san-yüeh erh-shih-chiu-jih chih i" 追忆庚戌新军起义和辛亥三月二十九日之役 (In commemoration of the 1910 New Army uprising and the April 27 revolt), *Hsin-hai ko-ming hui-i lu*, 2:287–298.

Ying Te-ming 应德明. "Huang-hua-kang ch'i-i ch'ien-hou tsa-i" 黄花崗起义前 后杂忆 (Assorted recollections of the events before and after the Huang-hua-kang uprising), *Hsin-hai ko-ming hui-i lu*, 2:323–326.

Young, Ernest P. "The Reformer as a Conspirator: Liang Ch'i-ch'ao and the 1911 Revolution." In Albert Feuerwerker et al., *Approaches to Modern Chinese History*. Berkeley: University of California Press, 1967. Pp. 239–267.

——— "Politics in the Early Republic: Liang Ch'i-ch'ao and the Yüan Shih-k'ai Presidency." Ph.D. dissertation. Cambridge: Harvard University, 1964.

Yu, George T. *Party Politics in Republican China: The Kuomintang, 1912–1924*. Berkeley: University of California Press, 1966.

Glossary

Ai-yü (charitable hall) 爱育善堂
An-jung (company) 安荣公司
An-ya jih-pao 安雅日报

Cha-tan tui 炸彈隊
Chan-chiang (Hsi-ying) 湛江（西營）
Chan T'ien-yu 詹天佑
Chang Chu-chün 張竹君
Chang Jen-chün 張人駿
Chang Ku-shan 張谷山
Chang Ming-ch'i 張鳴岐
Chang Pi-shih 張弼士
Chang Ping-lin 張炳麟
Chang Po-ch'iao (Shu-nan) 張伯喬（樹枏）
Chang Wo-ch'üan 張我权
Chang Yü-nan 張煜南
ch'ang-pei chün 長備军
Ch'ang-sha-lan 長沙蘭
Chao-ch'ing 肇慶
Chao Sheng 赵声
Chao Tsung-t'an 赵宗壇
Ch'ao-chou (Ch'ao-an) 潮州（潮安）
Ch'ao-yang 潮陽
chen (division) 鎮
chen (town) 鎮

Chen-chi chü 偵緝局
Chen-nan-kuan 鎮南关
Ch'en Chao-t'ang 陈兆棠
Ch'en Chien-ch'ih 陳鑑持
Ch'en Ching-hua 陳景華
Ch'en Ching-yüeh 陳敬岳
Ch'en Ch'ing-kuei 陳慶桂
Ch'en Chiung-ming 陳烱明
Ch'en Hui-p'u 陳惠普
Ch'en Hung-e 陳宏尊
Ch'en Hung-sheng 陳宏生
Ch'en Keng-fu 陳耿夫
Ch'en Lo-sheng 陳羅生
Ch'en Nien-tien 陳念典
Ch'en Pao-ch'en 陳宝琛
Ch'en Po-t'ao 陳伯陶
Ch'en Shu-jen 陳樹人
Ch'en Te-chü 陳德駒
Ch'en Yung-po 陳湧波
Cheng-hai 澄海
Cheng Kuan-i (Kuan-kung) 鄭貫一（貫公）
Cheng Kuan-ying 鄭官應
Cheng Shih-liang 鄭士良
ch'eng (city) 城

Ch'eng T'ien-tou 程天斗
Chi-ch'i yen-chiu kung-hui 機器研究公會
chi-p'u shan-p'iao 基鋪山票
Ch'i-nü-hu 七女湖
Ch'i-shih-erh hang 七十二行
Ch'i-shih-erh hang shang-pao 七十二行商報
Chia-ying (Mei-hsien) 嘉應（梅縣）
Chiang K'ung-yin 江孔殷
Chiang-pien hsüeh-t'ang 將弁學堂
Chiang Tsun-kuei 蔣尊簋
Chiang-ts'un 江村
Chiang-wu t'ang 講武堂
Ch'iang-hsüeh hui 強學會
Chiao-chung (normal school) 教忠師範學堂
chiao-yü hui 教育會
Chiao-yü tsung-hui 教育總會
Chieh-yen hui 戒煙會
Chien Chao-nan 簡照南
Chien Yü-chieh 簡玉階
Ch'ien-shan 前山
Ch'ien Shu-fen 錢樹芬
Chih-hsin pao 知新報
chih-li chou 直隸州
chih-li t'ing 直隸廳
Chih-na an-sha t'uan 支那暗殺團
Ch'ih-hsi 赤溪
Ch'ih shih-tzu hui 赤十字會
Chin Chang 金章
Chin-pu tang 進步党
chin-shih 進士
chin-tu hui 禁賭會
Ch'in-chou 欽州
ching-wei chün 警衛軍
Ch'ing-hsiang shan-hou tsung kung-so 清鄉善後總公所
Ch'ing-i pao 清議報
Ch'ing-yüan 清遠
Chiu shan-t'ang 九善堂
Ch'iu Chin 秋瑾
Ch'iu Feng-chia 丘逢甲
chou (department) 州
Chou Chao-ling 周兆齡
Chou Fu 周馥
Chu Chih-hsin (Ta-fu) 朱執信（大符）

Chu Shao-mu 朱少穆
ch'u-chi shih-fan hsüeh-t'ang 初級師範學堂
chuan-men hsüeh-t'ang 專門學堂
ch'uan-hsüeh so 勸學所
Chung-hsi jih-pao 中西日報
chung hsüeh-t'ang 中學堂
Chung-hua hsin pao 中華新報
Chung-hua jih-pao 中華日報
Chung-hua kung-ch'eng-ssu hui 中華工程司會
Chung Jung-kuang 鍾榮光
Chung-kuo jih-pao 中國日報
Chung-kuo ko-ming t'ung-meng hui 中國革命同盟會
Chung-kuo pao-kuan chü-chin hui 中國報館俱進會
Chung Ting-chi 鍾鼎基
Chung-wai hsin-pao 中外新報
Chung-yüan pao 中原報
Ch'ung-yang (festival) 重陽節
chü-jen 舉人
Chü-yüeh hui 拒約會
Chü-yüeh pao 拒約報
Ch'üan-kuo nung-wu lien-ho hui 全國農務聯合會
Chün-t'uan hsieh-hui 軍團協會
Ch'ün pao 群報

En-ming 恩銘
En-p'ing 恩平

Fa-cheng hsüeh-t'ang 法政學堂
Fan Hung-ch'ou 范洪疇
fan-t'an 番攤
Fang-ch'eng 防城
Fang-yen hsüeh-t'ang 方言學堂
Feng Hsia-wei 馮夏威
Feng Hua-ch'uan 馮華川
Feng I-ch'i 馮伊僑
Feng-shan 鳳山
Fo-shan (Fatshan) 佛山
Fu-cheng t'ung-meng hui 扶正同盟會
Fu-ch'i 孚琦
Fu-jen wen-she 輔仁文社

Hai-feng 海豐

Hainan (island) 海南島

Hakka (K'o-chia) 客家

Han (river) 韓江

hang (guild) 行

Hao-shan 鶴山

Ho Chien-shih 何劍士

Ho Chien-wu 何劍吾

Ho Hsiang-ning 何香凝

Ho I 何毅

Ho Kai (Ho Ch'i) 何啓

Ho-k'ou 河口

Ho-nan (suburb of Canton) 河南

Ho Pin 何斌

Ho-po-ssu 河泊司

Ho-p'u 合浦

Ho Sui-t'ien 何穗田

Ho T'ien-chiung 何天烱

Ho T'ien-han 何天翰

Ho Tung 何東

Hoihow (Hai-k'ou) 海口

Hoklo (Fu-lao) 福佬

Hōsei daigaku 法政大学

hou-tun 後盾

Hsia Ch'ung-min 夏重民

hsiang (rural area) 鄉

Hsiang-chou 香洲

Hsiang-shan (Chung-shan) 香山（中山）

hsiang-tung 鄉董

Hsiao Chih-chen 蕭之楨

hsiao hsüeh-t'ang 小學堂

Hsiao-lan 小欖

Hsiao Yung-hua 蕭永華

Hsieh Chi-yüan 謝己原

Hsieh Chih-wo 謝贊我

Hsieh I-ch'iao 謝逸橋

Hsieh Liang-mu (Yen-yü) 謝良牧（延譽）

Hsieh T'ao 謝陶

Hsieh Tsan-t'ai (Tse Tsan Tai) 謝讚泰

Hsieh Yen-chih 謝延祉

Hsieh Yen-hui 謝延惠

Hsieh Yen-mei 謝延美

Hsieh Ying-po 謝英伯

hsien (district) 縣

Hsien-cheng ch'ou-pei hui 宪政籌備會

Hsien-cheng kung-hui 宪政公會

hsien-sheng 先生

Hsien-shih kung-ssu 先施公司

Hsin-an (Pao-an) 新安（宝安）

Hsin Chung-hua pao 新中華報

Hsin-chün 新軍

Hsin-hui 新會

Hsin-min ts'ung-pao 新民叢報

Hsin-ning (T'ai-shan) 新宁（台山）

Hsin she 心社

hsin-wen chih 新聞紙

Hsing-Chung hui 興中會

Hsing-ning 興宁

Hsiung Ch'eng-chi 熊成基

Hsiung Fei ch'i-i 熊飛起義

Hsü Ch'in 徐勤

Hsü Hsüeh-ch'iu 許雪秋

hsü-pei chün 续備軍

Hsü Tsung-han 徐宗漢

Hsü-wen 徐聞

Hsü Ying-hung 許應鴻

Hsü Ying-k'uei 許應騤

Hsüan-t'ung 宣統

hsüeh-ch'ao 學潮

Hsüeh-hai t'ang 學海堂

hsüeh-hui 學會

hsüeh-kung 學宮

hsüeh-t'ang 學堂

Hsüeh-wu ch'u 學務處

hsüeh-wu kung-so 學務公所

Hsün-ching tsung-chü 巡警總局

Hsün-fang tui 巡防隊

Hsün-huan jih-pao 循環日報

Hu Han-min (Yeh-hung) 胡漢民（衍鴻）

Hu I-sheng (I) 胡毅生（毅）

Hu Jui-feng 胡瑞峰

Hu-kuang 湖廣

Hu-men 虎門

Hu Ming-p'an 胡銘槃

Hua-chou 化州

Hua-hsien 花縣

Hua-lin (temple) 華林寺

Hua-shang kung-chü 華商公局

Hua-tzu jih-pao 華字日報

Huan-hai sheng-ch'en lu 宦海升沉錄

Huang Chih-ch'ang 黃之裳

Huang Chin-fu 黃金福

Huang Ching-t'ang 黃景棠
Huang Hsi-ch'üan 黃錫銓
Huang Hsüan-chou 黃軒冑
Huang-kang 黃岡
Huang-sha (Wongsha) 黃沙
Huang Sheng 黃勝
Huang Shih-chung 黃世仲
Huang Shih-lung 黃士龍
Huang Ying-ch'i 黃潁奇
Huang Yung-shang 黃永商
hui (association) 會
Hui-chou (Waichow) 惠州
hui-kuan 會舘
Hui-lai 惠來
Hui-ming hsüeh-she 晦鳴學舍
hui-tang 會党
hun-ch'eng hsieh 混成協
Hung Ch'üan-fu 洪全福
Hung Hsiu-ch'üan yen-i 洪秀全演議

I Hsüeh-ch'ing 易學清
I-hsüeh kung-chin hui 医學共進會
i-shih hui 議事會

Jao Ching-hua (Ch'i-kung) 饒景華（齊公）
Jao-p'ing 饒平
Jen-ch'üan pao 人權報
Jen-hua 仁化

K'ai-p'ing 開平
Kakchio (Chiao-shih) 角石
Kan-en 感恩
Kan Hui-ju 甘暉如
K'an-chieh wei-ch'ih hui 勘界維持會
Kang-i 剛毅
Kao Chien-fu (Lun) 高劍父（崙）
Kao-chou (Mao-ming) 高州（茂名）
Kao Erh-ch'ien 高而謙
Kao Ping-chen 高秉貞
kao-teng hsiao hsüeh-t'ang 高等小學堂
kao-teng hsüeh-t'ang 高等學堂
Kao-teng kung-yeh hsüeh-t'ang 高等工業學堂
Kao-yao 高要
Kayano Chōchi 萱野長知
Kiungchow (Ch'iung-chou) 瓊州

Ko Ch'ien 葛謙
Ko-lao hui 哥老會
Ko-ming chün-shih hsüeh-hsiao 革命軍事學校
Ko-sheng chiao-yü tsung-hui lien-ho hui 各省教育總會聯合會
Ko-sheng tzu-i chü lien-ho hui 各省諮議局聯合會
K'o pao 可報
Kōbun gakuin 弘文學院
Kongmoon (Chiang-men) 江门
Kōun Maru 幸運丸
Ku Ying-fen 古應芬
kuan-chih 官治
Kuan Ching-shen 関景燊
kuan-li 官立
Kuan-yin-shan 觀音山
Kuang-chi (hospital) 廣濟医院
Kuang Ch'i-chao 鄺其照
Kuang Ching-ch'uan 鄺敬川
Kuang-chou 廣州
Kuang-fu hui 光復會
Kuang-hsü 光緒
Kuang pao 廣報
Kuang-tung jih-pao 廣東日報
Kuang-tung tu-li hsieh-hui 廣東獨立協會
Kuang-ya shu-yüan 廣雅書院
Kuei-shan (Hui-yang) 歸善（惠陽）
Kung-chuang (river) 公莊水
Kung-ho tang 共和党
Kung-i 公益
kung-li 公立
kung-sheng 貢生
kuo-ch'ih 國恥
Kuo-ch'ih chi-nien hui 國恥紀念會
Kuo-ch'üan hui 國權會
Kuo-ch'üan wan-chiu hui 國權挽救會
Kuo-hui 國會
Kuo-hui t'ung-chih hui 國會同志會
Kuo Jen-chang 郭人漳
Kuo Kung-chieh 郭公接
Kuo-min jih-pao 國民日報
Kuo-min tang 國民党
Kuo-min t'uan-t'i hui 國民團体會
Kuo-shih pao 國事報
Kwangchowwan 廣州湾

lang-chung 郎中
Lao Wei-meng 勞緯孟
Le-ch'ang 樂昌
Le-ts'ung 樂從
Lei-chou (Luichow) 雷州
Li (tribal people) 黎
Li Chi-t'ang 李紀堂
Li Chieh-ssu 李戒斯
Li Chih-sheng 李植生
Li Chiu 李就
Li E 黎尊
Li Fu-lin 李福林
Li Hai-yün 李海雲
Li Han-chang 李瀚章
Li I-heng 李以衡
Li K'ai-shen 李開侁
Li Kuan-hua 李冠華
Li Kuo-lien 黎國廉
Li Lieh-chün 李烈鈞
Li P'ei-chi 李沛基
Li P'ei-shih 黎佩詩
Li Shu-fen 李樹芬
Li Tzu-ch'ung 李自重
Li Wen-ch'i 李文啓
Li Wen-fu 李文甫
Li Ying-sheng 李應生
Li Yung-ssu 黎勇錫
Li Yü-t'ang 李煜堂
Liang Ch'eng 梁誠
Liang Chin-ao (Kuan-san) 梁金鰲 (冠三)
Liang Ch'ing-kuei 梁慶桂
Liang-Kuang yu-ch'uan hui-she 兩廣郵船
　　會社
Liang Kuo-hsüan 梁國璿
Liang Mu-kuang 梁慕光
Liang Shih-i 梁士詒
Liang Ting-fen 梁鼎芬
Liang T'ing-k'ai 梁庭楷
Liang Tun-yen 梁敦彥
Liao Chung-k'ai 廖仲愷
Liao P'ing-tzu 廖平子
Lien-chou (in west Kwangtung) 廉州
Lien-chou (in north Kwangtung) 連州
Lien-hua shan 蓮花山
Lin Chi-chen 林激真
Lin Chih-mien 林直勉

Lin Kuan-tz'u 林冠慈
Lin Yü 林堉
Ling-hai jih-pao 嶺海日報
Ling-hsüeh pao 嶺學報
Ling-nan jih-pao 嶺南日報
Ling-shan 靈山
Ling-tung jih-pao 嶺東日報
Liu Hsüeh-hsün 劉學詢
Liu Kung-kuan 劉公冠
Liu Ssu-fu 劉思復
Liu Wei-t'ao (Ch'ün-li) 劉維燾 (群立)
Liu Yao-yüan 劉曜垣
Liu Yüeh-hang 劉樾杭
Lo Huan-hsiung 羅桓熊
Lo Kuan-shih 羅關石
Lo Kuang-t'ing 羅光廷
Lo P'an-hui 羅泮輝
Lo Shao-ao 羅少翱
Lo-ting 羅定
Lo Wen-kan 羅文幹
Lu-chün 陸軍
Lu-chün su-ch'eng hsüeh-t'ang 陸軍速成
　　學堂
Lu Hao-tung 陸皓東
Lu Hsin 盧信
Lu Lan-ch'ing 陸蘭清
Lu Ling 陸領
Lu Nai-chuang 盧乃潼
Lu O-sheng (Yüeh-sheng) 盧諤生 (岳生)
Lu Po-lang 盧博郎
Lung Chi-kuang 龍濟光
Lung-chou 龍州
Lung-men 龍門
Lü-ying 綠營

Ma-ning 馬宁
Ma Ta-ch'en 馬達臣
Mei (river) 梅江
min-cheng chang 民政長
Min-chih tang 民治党
Min-chu cheng-tang 民主政党
min-chün 民軍
Min pao 民報
min-tang 民党
Ming-lun (hall) 明倫堂
Mo Jen-heng 莫任衡

Mo Tsao-ch'üan 莫藻泉

Na-ssu 那思
Nan-hai 南海
Nan-ling 南嶺
Nan-wu (school) 南武學堂
Nan Yüeh pao 南越報
Ni Ying-tien 倪映典
Nien shih-chi pao 廿世紀報
Nippon Yūsen Kaisha 日本郵船會社
Nishizawa 西潭
nung-hui 農會
Nung-wu tsung-hui 農務總會

Ou Tsan-sen 區贊森

p'ai (platoon) 排
Pakhoi (Pei-hai) 北海
P'an Hsin-ming 潘信明
P'an Ta-wei 潘達微
P'an-yü 番禺
Pao-chieh kung-hui 報界公會
Pao-huang hui 保皇會
Pao-kuo hui 保國會
Pao-lu hui 保路會
Pao-Ya p'iao 保亞票
Pao-yeh kung-she 報業公社
piao (regiment) 標
P'ing-Liu-Li (uprising) 萍瀏醴
P'ing-min pao 平民報
P'ing-t'an 平潭
Po Leung Kuk (Pao-liang chü) 保良局
Po-lo 博羅
Pu-ch'an-tsu hui 不纏足會
P'u-ning 普宁
p'u-p'iao 鋪票
Punti (Pen-ti) 本地

Rikugun shikan gakkō 陸軍士官學校

Samshui (San-shui) 三水
San-chiang 三江
San-chou-t'ien 三洲田
Sha-k'ou 沙口
Shameen (Sha-mien) 沙面

shan-p'iao 山票
shan-t'ang 善堂
Shan-wei 汕尾
shang-hui 商會
Shang pao 商報
shang-wu chü 商務局
Shang-wu tsung-hui 商務總會
Shang-yang-wei 上楊圍
Shao-chou (Shao-kuan, Ch'ü-chiang)
　韶州（韶关，曲江）
Shao-nien pao 少年報
She-hui tang 社會党
Shen Hsiao-tse 沈孝則
shen-p'an t'ing 審判庁
Shen Ping-jen 沈秉仁
shen-shih 紳士
Shen-tsun (Shumchun) 深圳
Sheng-t'ang 聖堂
sheng-yüan 生員
Shih-ch'eng 石城
Shih-ch'i 石岐
Shih-chieh kung-i pao 世界公益報
Shih Chien-ju 史堅如
Shih Chin-ch'üan 石錦泉
Shih-fan hsüeh-t'ang 師範學堂
Shih-hsüeh kuan 實學舘
Shih-min hsüeh-t'ang 時敏學堂
Shih Nien-tsu 史念祖
Shih-shih hua-pao 時事畫報
Shih-wu hsüeh-t'ang 時務學堂
Shih-wu pao 時務報
shu-yüan 書院
Shui-lu shih hsüeh-t'ang 水陸師學堂
Shun-te 順德
Ssu-i 四邑
Su Leng-feng 蘇棱颯
Su Man-shu 蘇曼殊
Su Ping-shu 蘇秉樞
Su Shen-ch'u 蘇愼初
Sui-ching ch'u 綏靖處
sui-ying hsüeh-t'ang 隨營學堂
Sun Mei 孫眉
Sun Tan-yai 孫丹崖
Sung Chiao-jen 宋教仁
Sung I-mei 宋以梅
Sung Ting-yüan 宋鼎元

Swatow (Shan-t'ou) 汕頭

Ta Hang-ch'in 大橫琴
ta hsüeh-t'ang 大學堂
ta lao-yeh 大老爺
Ta-liang 大良
Ta-ma-p'ien 大馬扁
Ta-Ming shun-t'ien kuo 大明順天國
ta-p'ien 大騙
Ta-p'u 大埔
Ta-t'ung hsüeh-hsiao 大同學校
Tan-shui 淡水
T'an Chung-lin 譚鍾麟
T'an Fu 譚馥
T'an Min-san 譚民三
T'an Yen-k'ai 譚庭闓
T'ang Ts'ai-ch'ang 唐才常
Tanka (Tan-chia) 蛋家
taotai 道台
T'ao Ch'eng-chang 陶成章
T'ao Mo 陶模
Tatsu Maru 辰丸
Te-shou 德寿
Teng Hua-hsi 鄧華熙
Teng K'eng 鄧鏗
Teng Tzu-yü 鄧子瑜
Teng Yin-nan 鄧蔭南
ti-fang tzu-chih 地方自治
Ti-fang tzu-chih ch'ou-pan ch'u 地方自治籌辦處
Ti-fang tzu-chih yen-chiu she 地方自治研究社
ti-fang tzu-chih yen-chiu so 地方自治研究所
Tien-pao hui 電報會
T'ien-min pao 天民報
T'ien t'ao 天討
Ting Hsien 定縣
Ting Jen-chang 丁仁長
Tou-shan 斗山
Tsai-feng 載灃
Tsai-t'ao 載涛
ts'ai-p'iao 彩票
ts'an-shih hui 參事會
Tseng-ch'eng 增城
Tseng-ch'i 增祺

Tso Tsung-fan 左宗蕃
Ts'un-ku hsüeh-t'ang 存古學堂
Tsung shang-hui pao 總商會報
Tu Ch'ing-ch'ih 杜清池
Tu Kung-shih (Chih-chang) 杜貢石（之杖）
tu-tu 都督
T'u-hua pao 圖畫報
t'uan (local defense association) 團
tui (company) 隊
Tui-mien-shan 對面山
Tung-fang jih-pao 東方日報
Tung-hsi hsin-wen 東西新聞
Tung-hsing 東興
Tung-hua i-yüan 東華医院
Tung-sha tao 東沙島
tung-shih hui 董事會
T'ung-chih 同治
T'ung-wen (school) 同文學堂
T'ung-wen kuan 同文館
Tzu-cheng yüan 資政院
tzu-chih 自治
Tzu-chih t'uan 自治團
Tzu-chin 紫金
tzu-i chü 諮議局
tzu-li 自立

Wan-tzu 彎子
Wan-mu ts'ao-t'ang 萬木草堂
Wan-nien-feng 萬年豐
Wan-shou kung 萬寿宮
Wang Ching-wei (Chao-ming) 江精衛（兆銘）
Wang Ch'ung-yu 王寵佑
Wang Fu 王斧
Wang Ho-shun 王和順
Wang Ping-en 王秉恩
Wang Po-ch'ün 王伯群
Wang Shih-hsin 王師信
Wang T'ao 王韜
Wei-ch'ih t'u-huo hui 維持士貨會
wei-hsing 闈姓
Wei-i-ch'ü pao 唯一趣報
Wei Yuk (Wei Yü) 韋玉
Wen-lan (academy) 文瀾書院
Wen Sheng-ts'ai 溫生才

Wen Su 溫肅
Whampoa (Huang-p'u) 黃埔
Wu Chieh-ming 吳介銘
Wu Fei 吳霏
Wu Han-ch'ih 伍漢持
Wu Hsiang-ta 吳祥達
Wu Hsien-tzu 伍宪子
Wu-pei hsüeh-t'ang 武備學堂
Wu Tao-jung 吳道鎔
Wu T'ing-fang 伍廷芳
Wu Tsung-yü 吳宗禹
Wu Tzu-shou 吳子寿
Wu Yüan-chang 伍元長

Yang-ch'eng jih-pao 羊城日報
Yang-chiang 陽江
Yang-ch'un 陽春
Yang Ch'ü-yün 揚衢雲
Yang-shan 陽山
Yang Sheng 揚晟
Yang Ying-lin 揚應麟
Yang Yung-t'ai 楊永泰
Yao (tribal people) 猺

Yeh Ch'u-ts'ang 葉楚傖
Yeh Hsia-sheng 葉夏声
Yen An-lan 晏安瀾
Yen-fa yen-chiu hui 鹽法研究會
yen-shuo hui 演說會
Yen-t'ang 燕塘
ying (battalion) 營
Ying-te 英德
Yu-chi shih-fan hsüeh-t'ang 優級師範學堂
yung (braves) 勇
Yü Chi-ch'eng 余既成
Yü-hsien (girls' school) 育賢女學
Yü-pei li-hsien kung-hui 預備立宪公會
Yüan Shu-hsün 袁树勛
Yüeh Fei pao kuo-ch'ou 岳飛報國仇
Yüeh hai-kuan chien-tu 粤海关監督
Yüeh-hua (academy) 越華書院
Yüeh pao 粤報
Yüeh-shang tzu-chih hui 粤商自治會
Yüeh-shang wei-ch'ih kung-an hui 粤商維持公安會
Yün-wu shan 雲霧山

Index

Agricultural associations, 126, 128
Ai-yü Charitable Hall, 25
American China Development Company, 59, 63, 268
Anti-American boycott, 83-91, 138
Anti-opium societies, 95-96, 124, 166. *See also* Opium suppression
Army of the Green Standard, 57-58
Assemblies, city and town, 171-175; in Swatow, 173-174
Assemblies, district, 171, 249-250, 264
Assemblies, provincial: in Ch'ing, 98, 153-170, 220-221, 228; and revolutionary movement, 186; in Republic, 246-249, 264
Assembly, National, 98, 155, 163, 164
Association of Comrades for a Parliament, 163
Associations, popular: ban on, 24-26, 36, 134, 264; proliferation of, 33, 127-128, 245-246, 271; intra- and interprovincial federations of, 128, 163. *See also* individual associations
Associations for the study of self-government, 147, 154, 169, 170, 174, 175, 208, 247

Bandit gangs: recruited for revolutionary attempts, 40-41, 115-116, 119, 191, 198, 202; involved in 1911 Revolution, 225, 232. *See also* People's armies
Bannermen, 19, 57, 156, 221-223, 242
Bergholz, Leo, 90, 171
Boat people. *See* Tanka
Boundary Delimitation Auxiliary Society, 144-147, 151, 187
Boxer Rebellion, 37, 42; allied intervention against, 29
Boycott: of French ships (1884), 28; anti-American (1905), 83-91, 138; *Tatsu Maru* (1908), 135-141; of Butterfield & Swire (1908), 141-143
Braves, 57
Brinton, Crane, 2-4
Britain: territorial holdings, 14, 15, 31; railroad concessions, 31-32, 94; military presence, 60, 220; military intervention, 17, 130, 135, 243; postal system, 60; attitude toward opium suppression, 95, 96, 125; relations with revolutionary regime, 243-244
Buddhism: supported by Japanese missionaries, 61; under attack, 76-77, 255
Bureau for commercial affairs, 35, 58

Cabinet, 155, 164, 206-207
Calender, reform of, 252-253
Canton Christian College, 18

HARVARD EAST ASIAN SERIES